The New Day Recalled

Lives of Girls and Women in English Canada, 1919–1939

The New Day Recalled

Lives of Girls and Women in English Canada, 1919–1939

Veronica Strong-Boag

Copp Clark Pitman Ltd.
A Longman Company
Toronto

"Depression Suite, Part iii," reprinted by permission of Dorothy Livesay.

ISBN: 0-7730-4741-7

Editing: Barbara Tessman
Design: Susan Coull
Cover Design: Brant Cowie/Artplus Limited
Typesetting: Compeer Typographic Services Limited
Printing and Binding: Alger Press Limited

Canadian Cataloguing in Publication Data

Strong-Boag, Veronica Jane, 1947–
  The new day recalled

Includes bibliographical references and index.
ISBN 0-7730-4741-7 (bound) ISBN 0-140-10838-6 (pbk.)

1. Women — Canada — Social conditions. 2. Girls — Canada — Social conditions. I. Title.

HQ1453.S87 1987   305.4'0971   C87-094736-2

Copp Clark Pitman Ltd.
2775 Matheson Blvd. East
Mississauga, Ontario

Associated companies:
  Longman Group Ltd., London
  Longman Inc., New York
  Longman Cheshire Pty., Melbourne
  Longman Paul Pty., Auckland

Printed and bound in Canada.

TABLE OF CONTENTS

ABBREVIATIONS

CAS	Children's Aid Society
CCF	Co-operative Commonwealth Federation
CGIT	Canadian Girls in Training
CP	Communist Party
Glenbow	Glenbow-Alberta Institute
IODE	Imperial Order of the Daughters of the Empire
NCWC	National Council of Women of Canada
PAA	Public Archives of Alberta
PABC	Public Archives of British Columbia
PAC	Public Archives of Canada
PAM	Public Archives of Manitoba
PAO	Public Archives of Ontario
SAB	Saskatchewan Archives Board
SCM	Student Christian Movement
TPLBR	Toronto Public Library Baldwin Room
UCAVC	United Church Archives Victoria College
UFA	United Farmers of Alberta
UFO	United Farmers of Ontario
UFWA	United Farm Women of Alberta
UFWO	United Farm Women of Ontario
VCA	Vancouver City Archives
VGGH	Vancouver Girl Guides Headquarters
WCTU	Woman's Christian Temperance Union
WJC	Women's Joint Committee
YWCA	Young Women's Christian Association

ACKNOWLEDGEMENTS

Rethinking the past is never easy. Without the inspiration and support of the modern feminist movement this book could not have been written. Feminism demands the fair appreciation of women that historians have too often resisted. I have been fortunate enough to share in a collective re-evaluation of Canada's and, indeed, North America's and Europe's human heritage. Beginning in graduate school, I benefitted from the comraderie and excitement of feminist investigations. At the University of Toronto Jill K. Conway and Natalie Zemon Davis persuaded me that women's history could be simultaneously rigorous and political. Since then I have treasured a community of feminist scholars without which the study of women and men would be immeasurably poorer. Colleagues and students in history at Trent, Concordia, and Simon Fraser universities have also encouraged my enthusiasm for the study of women. Today, participation in Simon Fraser's Women's Studies Program continues to sharpen my consciousness of the connection between past and present struggles for equality. While welcome for women in academe is far from universal, I am acutely conscious of how much we owe the pioneers who first challenged the misogyny of essentially patriarchal institutions.

During the course of this project I have also accumulated more particular debts. The Social Science Research Council of Canada provided support in the form of a Research Time Stipend and a Sabbatical Leave Fellowship and Simon Fraser University contributed funds for research assistance and manuscript preparation. This book has been published with the help of a grant from the Social Science Federation of Canada, using funds provided by the Social Science and Humanities Research Council of Canada. More especially I should like to thank Kathyrn McPherson, Elaine Bernard, Elizabeth Lees, Kandice Kerr, Daryl Madill, Karen van Dieren, and Diane Rogers for their research assistance, Frances Wasserlein for her preparation of the index, and Barbara Tessman of Copp Clark Pitman for her early encouragement and later editorial skills. Good friends also set aside their own work to read a penultimate version of the entire manuscript. The talents of Greg Kealey, Linda Kealey, Angus McLaren, Arlene Tigar McLaren, Joy Parr, Ruth Roach Pierson, and Mary Lynn Stewart have made this a better book. I would also like to thank my mother, Daphne Bridges Strong-Boag, for her unfailing faith, and my sons, Christopher and Dominic Ross, for all they have taught me about motherhood, some of which appears in chapter 5. Finally, I owe more than I can say to Douglas Ross whose good humour, fair mindedness, and intellectual enthusiasm help me harbour hopes for a better world. For reasons he will understand, I am dedicating *The New Day Recalled* to our niece Miranda whose courage had been unforgettable.

INTRODUCTION

The writing of *The New Day Recalled: Lives of Girls and Women in English Canada, 1919–1939* began with a question: what happened to Canadian women after the vote was won? The suffrage campaigns have always loomed large in any acknowledgement of women in modern history, but the aftermath of enfranchisement has frequently been taken for granted.[1] For the most part, observers have tended to hold one of two contradictory opinions—either that the success of the woman suffrage movement has been demonstrated by the achievement of formal political equality and some specific pieces of legislation, or its failure by the absence of large numbers of female office-holders or clearly distinctive female voting patterns.[2] In any case, conclusions as to what happened and even as to what was important about women's experience in Canada in the post-suffrage period have too often been reached without sufficient research or analysis. Recently, this neglect has begun to change with major studies of female political behaviour, labour force participation, and even domestic life.[3] An overview of the post-suffrage decades that attempts to integrate the various elements of women's lives into a discussion of the whole has not, until now, been done. *The New Day Recalled* attempts to fill that gap in the historical record.

Many people who lived during the post-suffrage decades would have been astonished at the lack of subsequent attention paid to the women of this period. In the years that followed the conferral of the federal franchise during World War I, Canadians believed themselves to be on the brink of a "New Era" or a "New Day"[4] about which they had great expectations and perhaps equal amounts of hope and fear. A good deal of uncertainty focussed on women's role and the relationship between the sexes in this "brave new world." The time had arrived, it seemed, for testing the dire forecasts of social breakdown and a world turned topsy-turvy set out by anti-feminists like Goldwin Smith, Andrew MacPhail, Henri Bourassa, and Stephen Leacock[5] and the bold predictions of social justice and a fair deal for all espoused by feminists such as Emily Howard Stowe, Flora Macdonald Denison, Emily Ferguson Murphy, and Nellie Mooney McClung.[6] Social critics of very different persuasions believed that they were watching the emergence of a community that was distinctly different from that which had gone before. Conservatives and progressives alike were intensely interested in the outcome for women and men of the social transformation they feared or hoped would occur after the formal political equality of the "New Day" had been won.

In many ways, the 1920s and the 1930s demonstrated the folly of attempting to see into the future. While girls had a better chance for education, more women took paid work, more unhappy wives sued for divorce, mothers had fewer babies, and female voters took part in elections, predictions of major, even revolutionary, change from feminists and anti-feminists turned out to be far wide of the mark. To a large extent there was no great discontinuity with the past. Instead, these decades carried on the steady transformation of a community long grounded in the demands of pioneering, a colonial attachment to the British Empire, the small scale, artisanal workplace, domestic manufacture, relative ethnic and racial homogeneity, high fertility and high mortality, and the near restriction of women to the private sphere. In the process, the nature of modern Canadian society came into clearer focus. More than ever before, citizens had to acquaint themselves with the personal consequences of living in a nation where modernity often appeared to mean increased urbanization, the weakening of local cultures, greater racial and ethnic diversity, the growth of white-collar bureaucratic and blue-collar service employment, the emergence of a domestic economy based on credit and consumption rather than thrift and production, and the inauguration of new public roles for women. Not all Canadians shared in such developments, but few avoided them entirely; old and new ways of thought and practice frequently dwelt, albeit uneasily, together. The result perplexed conservatives and progressives alike.

In the first decade after World War I, women had the opportunity to discover just what all the talk of new directions, whether in child care, education, employment, domestic technology, or politics, meant for them in particular. As the years passed, few women lived precisely the way their mothers had, but equally few found themselves able or willing to experiment with the sexual autonomy and material abundance embodied in the contemporary image of the flapper. The Great Depression of the 1930s only confirmed what Canadians in the main already appreciated: changes in human behaviour were hard won, deeply resisted, and not always what they seemed. By 1939 no thoughtful Canadian woman or man could be entirely satisfied with the way their community had responded to the possibilities seemingly offered after World War I.[7] For better or worse, the exigencies of a second international conflict appeared to signal a chance to reconstruct the present and forge a new future. Whether this meant a fresh opportunity for feminism would be another story, one that Ruth Roach Pierson has helped to tell in her provocative study *"They're Still Women After All": The Second World War and Canadian Womanhood.*[8] Until 1939, however, growing up and growing old ultimately meant less for most women than conservatives had threatened and feminists had aspired to during the suffrage campaigns.

In Canada in these decades a variety of differences rooted in history and material circumstance distinguished women from one another. The objective and subjective realities of capitalism, in which society was divided into classes that had greater or lesser control of the means of production, was especially powerful and shaped many aspects of human awareness and behaviour. While the fact of gender has always limited women's access to capital and power, women's particularly intense engagement in family life and their restricted access to the public sphere encouraged class loyalties shared with male relatives. The benefits of allegiance to home and hearth could be considerable in both material and psychological terms. By identifying with the reality conferred by their family's place in Canada's socioeconomic hierarchy, women helped ensure their own ability to function on a daily basis within a pre-existing patriarchal system whose assumptions and discipline touched every social relationship. As the chilly reception given feminists and the prevalence of domestic violence suggested, critics or detractors were never easily tolerated.

Nevertheless, for all its power to affect beliefs and circumstances, class stratification did not supersede sex stratification. The routine assignment of women to the classes of their husbands and fathers by contemporaries and social scientists has reflected women's subordination within patriarchal society and the fact of their primary identification by sex.[9] Yet, since no model of social stratification exists that takes into account both the relationship of women and men within the family and the results of the unequal ownership of the means of production, there is no easy alternative to identifying wives and husbands as members of the same class. Thus, while class designation may sometimes be useful, it remains a fundamentally imperfect method of indicating a woman's relationship to a capitalist male hierarchy. Accordingly, in this volume, the terms "working class" and "middle class" should be regarded as a guide to the status and power of women's families rather than as a reliable measure of women's ability to command resources or to share in full the values of male capitalist society.

Obscured as it might be from time to time by the exigencies of class, gender was finally at the core of the way people in the 1920s and the 1930s, as now, understood and treated themselves and each other. As a collectivity, female Canadians in these years, were "defined and delimited, not so much by any lesser capacity for work or determination or thought, but by patriarchal custom and male authority. . . . Men's sisters, however privileged relative to other women, encountered more confined horizons than their brothers."[10] The ubiquitous nature of this sexual hierarchy is one of the fundamental assumptions of this study. From birth onward, Canadian women daily worked through the consequences of a gender identity that informed every part of their experience. Girl babies found the world harboured distinct expectations of them and their brothers. Female students took different subjects, played different games, and graduated in different numbers at every educational level. Women workers entered a segregated labour market with lower pay and fewer opportunities. Mothers assumed the heaviest domestic burden. Old women might be more appreciated by their relatives, but they were also likely to be poorer than men of the same age. In Canada between 1919 and 1939 such distinctions remained very much the order of the day.

Useful as political events are in capturing contemporaries' own sense of periodization—wars and elections were after all as visible to them as they are to us—they were not, for the vast majority of people, the stuff of everyday life. In the interwar period, women in many ways responded practically to a personal timetable that was shaped by other forces. To a large degree, women, in a manner that was similar to but also fundamentally different from comparably situated males, responded to a series of overlapping experiences from birth to death: socialization, paid work, courtship and marriage, domestic labour, childbirth and child rearing, and aging. Although individual stories varied, sometimes dramatically, women's lives generally unfolded in the stages that form the basis of the modified life course approach to the study of women that has been adopted here.

The New Day Recalled does not, as is often customary with the life course approach, follow a select age cohort of women through critical stages in their life histories.[11] Rather, the attempt here is to capture the essence of what it meant to be female in Canada in the 1920s and 1930s by focussing on crucial periods and activities in women's lives. Although individuals can move through time and space in ways that are particular and sometimes eccentric, and the division of lives by stages and concerns inevitably detracts from the simultaneousness of human actions, Canadian women as a whole experienced childhood, the labour force, courtship and marriage, housekeeping and child care, and aging in ways that remained similar enough to be collectively characterized in the following six chapters.

Chapter 1 assesses the period of childhood, adolescence, and early adulthood, those formative years that centred on two institutions, the family and the school, and preceded the onset of paid work or marriage. Chapter 2 takes up the subject of waged employment that, more than ever before, became a normal part of female experience and remained an area where systematic discrimination in remuneration and opportunity was the order of the day. Chapter 3 considers the meaning for women of heterosexual courtship and marriage and surveys the alternatives explored by an extraordinary generation of talented "spinsters." Chapter 4 gets down to the practical business of living—household management, shopping, and housework—all of which came under the influence of a dawning revolution in domestic credit and personal consumption. Chapter 5 turns to childbirth and child rearing, that part of family life that women were most likely to prize but where their authority was increasingly challenged by a host of professionals in medicine, social work, and education. Chapter 6 appraises the prospects for women after age forty. It points to their psychological vulnerability in an increasingly youth-centred popular culture, their economic marginality at the end of lives whose labours were almost always seen as meriting less recompense than men's, and their potential power in club and political affairs, once age had freed them from many urgent family responsibilities. The Conclusion then reviews the meaning of these two decades for Canadian women. In summary, during a period bounded by two international conflagrations and in the face of a world that was very far from giving them an equal chance but that also never entirely denied them the prospect of individual fulfilment, most women retained the courage to cope and the determination to make the most of whatever life offered.

Ambitious as the above itinerary may seem, I am all too aware that it remains painfully incomplete. Most notably, this study does not include French Canada. Women's experience there needs the separate assessment that feminist historians such as those in the Clio Collective in *L' Histoire des femmes au Québec depuis quatre siècles*[12] are now so ably providing. These chapters also tell less than I would have liked about the experience of the poor, Native peoples, the working class, non-English-speaking racial and ethnic groups, and women who lived outside of major urban centres and, more particularly, in the North. The disadvantages these women faced in life are reflected in the near absence of a sufficient documentary record upon which the historian can draw. I hope nonetheless that, where possible, I have given the voices of women normally outside the public spotlight the wider hearing they so generally lacked in the 1920s and 1930s.

Finally, some readers may argue that the more systematic inclusion of references to boys and men would have helped to illuminate my assessment of female experience. Certainly comparative treatment of the sexes is often invaluable and at certain points I have alluded or made direct reference to male experience. I have, however, deliberately chosen not to do so in detail. In part this choice is purely practical. Comparable treatment of boys and men requires more and different research and analysis. It is not a small task and I have left it to others. Still more importantly, however, *The New Day Recalled* is not an examination of how both sexes experienced different periods and activities in their lives. It is first and foremost a study of girls and women. Boys and men have had their turn, many of them. Although the "New Day" of the post-suffrage decades rarely brought the justice advocated by feminists, in this volume women get to tell their side of the Canadian story.

NOTES

1. On the historiography of Canadian women see Margaret W. Andrews, "Review Article: Attitudes in Canadian Women's History 1945-1975," *Journal of Canadian Studies* (Summer 1977): 69-78; Veronica Strong-Boag, "Raising Clio's Consciousness: Women's History and Archives in Canada," *Archivaria* (Summer 1978): 70-82; Eliane Silverman, "Writing Canadian Women's History 1970-1982: An Historiographical Analysis," *Canadian Historical Review* (Dec. 1982): 513-33; and Beth Light and Veronica Strong-Boag, "Introduction," *True Daughters of the North. Canadian Women's History: An Annotated Bibliography* (Toronto: OISE Press, 1980).

2. Appendix A to Catherine L. Cleverdon's pioneering study, *The Woman Suffrage Movement in Canada*, introduced by Ramsay Cook (Toronto: University of Toronto Press, 1950, 1974) shows how both points of view originated with suffragists themselves.

3. See for instance, the articles by Margaret Conrad, Marjorie Griffin Cohen, Marilyn Barber, Marta Danylewycz, Susan Walsh, and Gail Cuthbert Brandt in *The Neglected Majority: Essays in Canadian Women's History,* vol. 2, edited by Alison Prentice and Susan Mann Trofimenkoff (Toronto: McClelland and Stewart, 1985).

4. See, for example, J.O. Miller, ed., *The New Era in Canada* (Toronto: J.M. Dent and Sons Ltd., 1917), especially the chapter, "Women and the Nation" by Marjory MacMurchy, and Ellen M. Knox, *The Girl of the New Day* (Toronto: McClelland and Stewart, 1919). See also Robert Craig Brown and Ramsay Cook, *Canada 1896-1921* (Toronto: McClelland and Stewart, 1974), especially chap. 15, "O Brave New World . . . ," and chap. 16, ". . . That Has Such People In't."

5. See Goldwin Smith, *Essays on the Questions of the Day, Political and Social* (New York: Macmillan, 1893); Andrew MacPhail, *Essays in Fallacy* (New York: Longmans, Green and Co., 1910); Susan Mann Trofimenkoff, "Henri Bourassa and 'the Woman Question'," *Journal of Canadian Studies* (Nov. 1975): 3-11; and Stephen Leacock, *Essays and Literary Studies* (New York: John Lane, 1916).

6. See Wayne Roberts, "Six New Women: A Guide to the Mental Map of Women Reformers in Toronto," *Atlantis* (Fall 1977): 145-64; Nellie McClung, *In Times Like These*, introduction by Veronica Strong-Boag (Toronto: University of Toronto Press, 1972); Byrne Hope Sanders, *Emily Murphy, Crusader* (Toronto: Macmillan, 1945); and Strong-Boag, "'Ever a Crusader': Nellie McClung, First-Wave Feminist" in *Rethinking Canada: The Promise of Women's History*, edited by Veronica Strong-Boag and Anita Clair Fellman (Toronto: Copp Clark Pitman, 1986).

7. For a bleak overview of these years see John H. Thompson with Allen Seager, *Canada 1922-1939. Decades of Discord* (Toronto: McClelland and Stewart, 1985).

8. (Toronto: McClelland and Stewart, 1986).

9. For an invaluable examination of this tendency by social scientists see Margrit Eichler, *The Double Standard. A Feminist Critique of Feminist Social Science* (New York: St. Martin's Press, 1980), 100-15.

10. Strong-Boag and Clair Fellman, "Introduction," *Rethinking Canada*, 2.

11. For a useful introduction to the life course approach see Ellen M. Gee, "The Life Course of Canadian Women: An Historical and Demographic Analysis," *Social Indicators Research* (1986): 263-83.

12. (Montreal: Quinze, 1982).

CHAPTER 1
GROWING UP FEMALE

Two images of girls dominate the interwar years. The first to appear, in the 1920s, was the flapper. Women's wartime efforts as suffragists, "far-merettes," munitions workers, army nurses, and volunteers, and feminists' long assault on male privilege in the home, the paid workplace, and public life had, it seemed, borne fruit in liberated youth. Brimming with the promise of adolescence, teenagers, like those in the Canadian Girls in Training (CGIT) in their white midis, or "Girls of the New Day,"[1] as one observer characterized the flapper generation, symbolized that sense of new beginnings for women with which the postwar decade began. The second image, emerging from the 1930s, retreated from the sexual brinkmanship typified by the flapper to return to the innocence of young childhood. This was the girl as "moppet." The Dionne quintuplets, the British princesses Elizabeth and Margaret Rose, and, especially, Shirley Temple were its most visible expression. Their pictures decorated magazines and newsstands and gripped imaginations and hearts from coast to coast in the depression decade. While the flapper with her short hair and short skirts was an essentially confrontational figure, poised to contest the conventions of workplace and bedroom, the curly-headed moppet, simultaneously conventionally feminine, touchingly dependent, and often implicitly flirtatious, appeared more calculated to appeal for protection and support, as indeed Ontario's first quints received from Premier Mitch Hepburn's government in 1934. The shift in public attention from flapper to moppet accompanied a retreat from the optimism of the early 1920s, from the essentially liberal faith that women could manage gender politics to the advantage of themselves and their daughters. To be sure, adventurous young women survived the Great Depression and continuing anti-feminism, but tough times robbed them of any certainty that the world would welcome new initiatives from their sex.

The reality behind these two images was complex. Girls had to deal with a world that appeared to offer new experiences but simultaneously retained strong resistance to any significant change in sex roles. In addition, many had to confront the special problems of class and race in an economy that, even in supposedly boom times, kept large numbers in poverty and without power. Yet, whatever the particularities of their situation, whether perhaps as the child of an agricultural labourer or as the offspring of Canada's Native peoples, girls all across the country were distinguished in vital ways from boys. This chapter examines the years from infancy to young adulthood when the outlook of and the options for Canadian women were critically moulded. Individuals and institutions of every sort, from the mother to the police magistrate, from the family to the school, regarded and treated girls differently from boys. With few exceptions, female Canadians were engaged from birth in a series of relationships that finally subordinated them and their interests to male prerogatives. As we shall see, girls and women were not always unconscious of this inequality. In their youthful encounters with a world that was only too likely to value their needs and accomplishments less than those of their brothers, they stored up an experience of self-assertion that remained a powerful component of female culture.

To deal with the challenges facing them, the nation's daughters needed every ounce of the learning, courage, and tolerance that anxious champions such as Agnes Macphail desired for their inheritance.[2] Canada's first female MP went right to the heart of the dilemma facing her sex in observing one of her parliamentary colleagues with his nine-year-old daughter:

> He was getting the funnies for her to read. I said: "Where does she come in the family; the youngest?" He said: "No, the older; I have only two children, a boy and a girl, the boy is the best." I was startled, and this in May 1939. But, controlling my countenance as well as I could . . . I said: "I am very fond of little girls; they are my favourites." I wanted to save that child from a scar she will carry all her life. But the father wouldn't have it. He said to his daughter: "You think the boy is best; don't you?" And she sullenly answered: "Yes." That story illustrates perfectly why women haven't more confidence. I have heard mothers do similar things many a time. It is unforgivable.[3]

And as Macphail found time and time again, the patriarchy that found expression in the preference for sons over daughters was not easily circumvented.

Fortunately, in their reception of children, as in many other matters, Canadians were not unanimous. Many little girls found a hearty welcome. A woman from British Columbia remembered the flood of delight and determination produced by the birth of a daughter. She swore then and there that this "little woman" was not going to suffer as a result of her sex.[4] A strong sense of injustice produced by growing up "in a household where boys were kings and girls scullery maids" moved one Jewish woman married to a marginal shopkeeper to treat her daughters "with a fierce protective joy."[5] When war loomed nearer in the 1930s, the birth of a daughter might be especially desired. A critic of international events summed up her feelings this way: "I wanted a girl badly. I don't want to raise any more cannon fodder."[6]

Such attitudes shaped the consciousness and the experience of little girls across the Dominion. For the lucky there was continued encouragement. Feminist Helen Gregory MacGill, for instance, helped inspire two daughters to pursue graduate degrees in unconventional fields, sociology and aeronautical engineering, in the 1930s.[7] The Jewish mother who repudiated her own family's favouritism to sons prepared Fredelle Bruser to go on for a Ph.D. in English. Close relationships between mothers and daughters, and between several generations of women, as in the MacGill household, laid the foundations for a network of female associations in which girls from their earliest moments would move.[8] Sisters or female relatives of a similar age, as with the novelist Mazo de la Roche and her cousin Caroline or the artist Emily Carr and her sisters, also formed life-long attachments whose intimacy matched or surpassed heterosexual ties.[9] These relationships formed the bedrock of many women's experiences, preparing them to move easily into subsequent female friendships. The resulting female culture may not have offered the prestige of female-male coupling, but it persisted as a vital component of many women's lives and challenged the heterosexual biases that the popular culture of the day celebrated.

Succoured as they might be by a preference for girls and strong female relationships, babies were also marked fundamentally by their particular experience of class, race, culture, and region. Although they did not encounter these factors in precisely the same way as adults, they could not escape their consequences. In many ways, childhood was integrated into adult worlds right from its beginning. An expectant mother's health helped determine the weight and viability of her offspring.[10] Her choice of, or perhaps sole recourse to, midwife, nurse, or doctor, and home, clinic, or hospital, similarly linked infants to a specific set of expectations and possibilities. Babies born in private wards in up-to-date city hospitals with obstetricians in attendance encountered life in a way very different from those delivered in Halifax's black neighbourhood by a Victorian Order Nurse or those helped into the world by fathers on Labrador's north coast.[11]

Although life expectancy remained tied to economic resources, enhanced public health campaigns did help reduce the number of deaths among Canada's young children. Between 1921 and 1939, neonatal mortality fell from 43 to 31 per one thousand live births, and deaths of infants under one year fell from 102 to 61 per thousand.[12] The institution of widespread vaccination and immunization programs meant that children of all classes were less likely to fall victim to smallpox and diptheria.[13] Other commonplace innovations such as "tonsils and adenoids parties," in which doctors found surgical solutions to the problems of chronic illness, were of more questionable benefit. Public health education also enlisted youngsters themselves in nation-wide campaigns. In the elementary schools the Junior Red Cross spread the gospel of good hygiene through the medium of plays such as "The Conversion" on the need for pasteurized milk,[14]

"David and the Good Health Elves" on the prevention of TB,[15] and "An Argument in the Kitchen" on the virtues of milk.[16] As one Mother Goose "health rhyme" sung in classrooms across the country put it:

> I'm little Bo Peep, I need lots of sleep
> I go to bed bright and early.
> Windows wide are my great pride
> For I'm a Fresh Air girlie.[17]

What such admonitions lacked in elegance they undoubtedly made up in the verve with which they were recited. Together with toothbrush drill, handkerchief presentation, and nail inspection, they encouraged pupils to accept higher standards of personal hygiene. For girls this message was hammered home again in domestic science classes. Such instruction not only improved child health, it accorded especially well with patterns of socialization that emphasized that little girls should be neater and cleaner than their brothers.

Such directives notwithstanding, certain groups remained especially vulnerable to illness and physical disability in general. Even in better times, poverty robbed numerous youngsters of good health and security. Such was the case with the Native peoples who confronted challenges that only the hardiest offspring survived.[18] The 1928–29 New Brunswick investigation into child welfare revealed conditions in homes and in poor law institutions throughout the province that would not have been out of place a century or so earlier in Charles Dickens' London.[19] In an impoverished Toronto household a few years later, a little girl stricken with infantile paralysis remained, not untypically for the condition, strapped to her bed all day; every morning revealed fresh bedbug bites.[20] In contrast, additions to the families of the well-to-do, celebrated in the pages of *Saturday Night* and local society columns across the country, did not have to worry about the poor nutrition and unsanitary accommodation that stunted so many young bodies and minds.

Even little girls brought up to attend elite institutions such as Edgehill School for Girls in Windsor, Nova Scotia, or Queen Margaret's School in Duncan, B.C.,[21] did not, however, entirely escape one persisting scourge of childhood. The sexual abuse of children, particularly girls, by male family members and strangers was not limited to any single social or economic group. While some assaults eventually came to trial, most victims had no recourse against the more powerful adults who governed their lives. Such was the case with a thirteen-year-old just before World War II. Many years later she remembered an attempted rape by her forty-six-year-old uncle: "I had no one to talk to and I did not understand. My parents had deceased. He threatened to throw me on the streets."[22] The appearance of very young prostitutes in Canadian cities was only the most visible expression of a more general problem of sexual abuse that afflicted as many as one in two girls.[23]

Although sexual mistreatment of children drew only intermittent attention at best, and its real extent was never acknowledged, the broader and related question of the socialization of girls sparked constant discussion among progressive and conservative commentators alike. Progressives, like one writer published by the B.C. Board of Health, argued for similar treatment of the sexes:

> Remember from the first that boys must be trained to be fathers as well as girls to be mothers. Is it the man who loves and understands children, or the man who does not, that makes the best husband and father and the happiest home? If it is good for your little girl to love babies and help you by minding them, it is good for your little boy, and if it is good for your little boy to play games, climb and run about to make him grow strong and healthy, it is good too for your little girl. God knows she will need all her bodily health and strength and courage if she is to make a worthy mother for the next generation![24]

Some parents, whether they read such advice or not, acted in keeping with the sentiment underlying it. There were daughters who remembered being raised in the 1920s "with the attitude that we had to be independent."[25]

While progressive parenting seemed far from rare, feminist critics surveyed the period with general dismay. A contributor to the *Canadian Forum*, the leading social democratic journal in the Dominion, bleakly concluded that girls were still being "brought up to marry."[26] Another critic put it slightly differently:

> Girls usually do a number of things around the house, but it is not such a common thing for boys to undertake responsibility within the home. This is only because they have never been shown that it is as much their duty as their sisters' to help to run the home.[27]

Such complaints point to the widespread resistance to any transformation in sex roles. As far as most Canadians were concerned, the bottom line remained: adult females bore final responsibility for family life and on its success rested the ultimate fate of western civilization.[28] Any style of parenting that questioned this fundamental allocation of duties was at best suspect and, often, fiercely opposed.

Despite the fact that mothers clearly had somewhat different feelings about giving birth to girls or boys, the fact that babies came in both sexes was rarely, if ever, explicitly acknowledged in the child care manuals of the day. The dominant pronoun was always masculine, and a young infant was viewed more or less as a *tabula rasa*.[29] Babies were to be shaped by the regular affirmation of good habits in everything from bowel movements to emotions. Subject from their earliest days to strict, clock-regulated regimes in eating, sleeping, and elimination, offspring would be secure enough to be independent and simultaneously habituated to accept the disciplined rhythms of home and workplace. The quints, Yvonne, Annette, Cécile, Emilie, and Marie, the most famous examples of the application of such theories, inspired many imitations, but the artificial situation in which they lived—a hospital separated from parents and other siblings with nurses or early childhood education teachers in attendance—could fortunately not be easily duplicated. Babies, including the "Famous Five," coming with a range of needs and personalities, did not always take easily to up-to-date instruction, even when parents were eager and knowledgeable practitioners of the new behaviouralist psychology.[30] In fact, mothers of every description continued to bring to the task of child rearing a set of assumptions and skills learned from relatives, neighbours, trial and error, and just plain common sense. Raised too, as most mothers and fathers were, to expect different things of daughters and sons, they were hard put not to teach, if only by example, preferred behaviours specific to each sex. Early childhood might resemble that blank slate that many psychologists in these years postulated—and this is very debatable—but what is certain is that most parents assumed without question that girls required somewhat different treatment from boys, in everything from dress to discipline.

In particular, since girls' destiny was generally conceded to be in marriage, their training was often directed more or less explicitly to this end. From the time they could turn to a mirror or another person for confirmation, girls were encouraged to ape the preoccupation with appearance that was believed to characterize the normal adult of their sex. Like Shirley Temple, who inspired a line of dolls fervently desired by little girls in the 1930s, female youngsters might aspire to spunkiness but above all they were to be cute and affectionate. No more than their mothers could they entirely ignore the barrage of advertising directed at female Canadians of all ages that insisted that "You are in a Beauty Contest every day of Your Life"[31] Male admiration was the ultimate goal. Boys and men were routinely portrayed as preferring beauty to brains in their girlfriends and wives, or at least preferring the latter quality to be relatively invisible, thus constituting no threat to their public authority.[32] One adviser in the Junior Red Cross magazine cited modern psychology in explaining that "The boys, and later the men, like the girls and the women who make them feel they are heroes. That is the simple secret of feminine popularity."[33]

More important still, little girls were expected to be mothers in the making. "Little Mother" classes joined homemaking badges in Guides and lectures in CGIT to prompt members to accept special responsibility for and find particular reward in the care of those younger than themselves. Dolls, homemade or store-bought, confirmed the same message. In homes where mothers bore heavy obligations for bearing and rearing children, not to mention housework and paid labour, daughters were also expected to help out regularly. No wonder that the sight of girls wheeling carriages and carrying children not much smaller than themselves was commonplace across the Dominion.[34] The loss of parents, especially mothers, also readily led to daughters like Anna Borisevich, aged eleven, taking on heavy responsibilities for younger siblings.[35] Not all girls enjoyed baby-minding; some regretted the time lost to play or school. For others, however, the social approval they earned as "little mothers" and the affection they might win from those in their care were powerful inducements to nurture. The lesson of such early experiences was difficult to ignore. Even should they be able to reject a maternal role for themselves, girls would be hard put to escape the realization that normalcy for their sex was inextricably linked with mothering, whether biological or social.

Although the forms they took varied tremendously, marriage and children were routinely presented to girls in all walks of life as the fulfilment of every true woman's ambitions. Even exposure for the more fortunate to an ostensibly wider range of career choices could not make much headway against the ubiquitous influence of youthful socialization. One 1938 survey of 167 young women graduating from McGill, Queen's, and Toronto universities, for instance, revealed that 149 preferred marriage to a career and that the vast majority did not intend to keep their jobs after marriage.[36] Anticipating motherhood, 113 respondents desired three or four children and twenty wanted five or more.[37] Girls reached such conclusions despite occasional public recognition that a wedding ring brought no guarantee of security against want and desertion, and children no certainty of love and respect.[38] That breath of harsh reality had trouble penetrating a popular mythology that relentlessly directed girls to wedding vows, childbearing, and child rearing.

The 1920s and 1930s also saw little girls, and children in general, being especially targeted, as were their mothers, by increasingly powerful advertisers. Toys that in the past had been largely restricted to special occasions such as Christmas and birthdays were now available throughout the year, at least for the fortunate. Similarly, where ten- to twelve-year-olds previously were expected to have outgrown playthings, they were now permitted such distractions a few years longer.[39] This expanded market was also reflected in year-round mass advertising campaigns that more than ever before turned to premiums—toys, candy, cards—directed at children.[40] Of course, youngsters did not benefit equally from this potential largesse. Most children relied on a few well-worn favourites and had far fewer possessions than merchandisers would have liked. But if they could not always provoke sales, they could stimulate, as never before, desire for new products.[41] One salesgirl remembered an Eaton's Christmas with Shirley Temple dolls priced at $9 to $16, "a lot more than some families got in a month of relief." She watched

> the faces of those little girls, from about four or five right up to about eleven. Some used to come at opening time and just stand there looking at those pink-cheeked, golden-haired lovely Shirley Temples. Little faces, they needed food. You could see a lot who needed a pint of milk a day a thousand times more than they needed a Shirley doll. They'd stare for hours. We tried to shush them away but it didn't do any good. They'd go once around toyland and be back. This, mind you, went on day after day, day after day, until some of the girls thought they would go crazy. One girl had a crying fit just over that, those hundreds of poor kids who would never own a Shirley Temple in a hundred years. They were lucky if they had breakfast that morning, or soup and bread that night.[42]

Shirley Temple dolls were only one of a barrage of new items available to the favoured child in these decades. Shifting fashions in toys were matched by changes in what constituted an up-to-date wardrobe. Here, at least, was the appearance of liberation from old tenets that confined the female form. Most obviously, like women's wear, skirts became shorter and clothes generally somewhat more casual and sporty. In the 1920s pyjamas arrived as alternatives to the traditional nighties.[43] Bare legs, tanned by sun or commercial lotions, succeeded stockings, at least for the summer.[44] Greater physical freedom was also linked to major changes in undergarments. Where previously, respectable young women would be trained early to the restraints of back-laced and, by the beginning of the twentieth century, increasingly front-laced corsets, the 1920s and 1930s saw a major revolution in consumer preference. While the traditional corset industry financed a campaign of disparagement,[45] corselettes and bras and girdles won over their traditional customers. Fears that opposition might extend even to girdles led stores to open up junior sections, to introduce corselettes for twelve to fourteen year olds and to shift to the term "foundation garment" instead of corset, lest an old-fashioned term deter the young buyer.[46] Girls' desire to move freely and to participate in sports was countered by claims that "natural curves were being further enlarged by active games" and that proper girdles held organs in place even for those who were thin and that they would help "keep the figure from getting larger."[47] The strength of resistance to old styles, including some young women buying men's clothing for themselves and complaining that there was no athletic women's underwear available in Canada,[48] was extremely powerful. By the end of the 1920s, bras and girdles had won over all but the most old-fashioned. When combined with silk, cotton, or rayon, new latex with its "two-way stretch" made lighter garments all the more popular.[49] Over the long term, up-to-date manufacturers also benefitted. Old corsets had been relatively durable while new model undergarments came in many styles and had to be replaced more regularly, all adding to profits.[50] In part too, as the undergarment controversy demonstrated, the advantage of simpler clothing for children in these decades was countered by the same stress on slenderness, rather than healthiness, that afflicted fashions for adult women. No more than their mothers, could girls easily mould themselves to fit the figure of the day or escape the message that any other body shape ultimately brought into question both their femininity and their ability to compete for boyfriends and husbands.

Girls growing up in these decades easily became part of a mass consumer culture that depended on thousands of purchases replacing the homemade and the rarely bought items that had been the norm in years past. Some families consciously resisted the dictates of fashion—religious objectors such as those in the Doukhobor and Mennonite communities being perhaps the most obvious dissenters—but poverty was the more common cause of failure to participate. One B.C. woman remembered, for example, that "we were encouraged not to wear shoes in the summer. . . . The girls were encouraged to wear boys' boots because they wear longer."[51] In such cases a choice between various types of preferred underwear or anything else was obviously irrelevant. For those who could afford to ape fashion, new styles of clothing did offer physical freedom that was absent in long skirts and corsets. They did not, however, ignore the erotic appeal of the female body. Only the focus changed: in the 1920s from the waist and the bottom to the legs and the arms, and in the 1930s to the breasts and hips.[52] Little girls could hardly ignore such visible instruction as to the source of female attractiveness.

Clothing styles told wearers and observers alike an important story about gender differences, but more explicit sexual information was harder to come by. Objections that such knowledge hardened and coarsened "a girl's moral tone" and nipped "in the bud those tender shoots of purity which are a girl's best attributes"[53] remained commonplace after the First World War and never disappeared during these years. To be sure, there was also popular acknowledgement of the need for more education in this area.[54] Some parents became more conscious of the necessity of telling their daughters the "facts of life."[55] Reflecting the lack of consensus about how much advice was appropriate, however, the CGIT, like many organizations dealing with girls, moved cautiously. Under the guise of "Health" or "Family Life" programming, it broached the whole question of female sexuality very carefully.[56] Reticence was not easily overcome. One doctor's daughter was far from untypical in remembering that pregnancies were never mentioned to children or in "polite conversation." At age eleven her mother told her

> that once a month there would be "bleeding" and that I had to wear a napkin while it lasted. I don't think she mentioned what purpose it served, but just said that it was the lot of all women, and we had to accept it. During the "period," she said, we had to be very careful not to catch a cold, and we couldn't take a bath or wash our hair. . . . I was left with the feeling that the whole thing was terribly unjust to females, and with the misconception that the "blood" came from the nipples.[57]

The tendency to greater explicitness in advertising "feminine hygiene" products in these years, as with ads for Kotex and Modess sanitary napkins,[58] and the douches and gels that even the family standby *Eaton's Catalogue* offered,[59] must have countered some ignorance, but many girls remained woefully ill-informed, as later unwanted pregnancies revealed.[60]

While ideally mothers were supposed to communicate both the "facts of life" and the standards for successful femininity to their daughters, children early came into contact with institutions, other than the family, where information could be sought and shared. In these encounters girls tested themselves and their families. Information and skills could stand the challenge or be found wanting. While the great majority of children remained within their parents' homes until they were old enough to attend elementary school, a few could always be found in creches, day nurseries, and orphanages. All of these institutions were the special preserve of the poor. In Halifax, for instance, local charwomen's daughters and sons, from the age of three months on, passed their days in the nursery of the Jost Mission. Here they found the toys, healthy food, and sanitary conditions that their own homes frequently lacked. Little girls also received the domestic lessons that were their special prerogative. For many needy applicants to the mission, the benefits of care outweighed the liabilities of enforced religious instruction and social patronage.[61] In Vancouver, the City Creche performed a function similar to that of the Jost Mission for female day workers. When their mothers had work, babies and preschoolers stayed at the creche from 8 a.m. to 6 p.m. Poverty made them welcome even a creche's monotonous menu: typically a dinner of soup, pudding, and potatoes at 11 a.m. and a supper of porridge, bread, butter, jam, and milk at 3:30 p.m.[62] Imperfect as such institutional options were, they were frequently superior to the more haphazard arrangements that poor mothers might otherwise have had to make.[63] In any case, they gave children new opportunities to add to their store of knowledge and to understand the highly stratified adult world they would eventually enter.

Preschoolers whose parents were more well-to-do normally stayed home. A small minority, however, were beginning to explore other options in these years. Child study centres funded by the Rockefeller Foundation at the universities of McGill and Toronto welcomed trend-setting middle-class youngsters into group settings that promised a further head start on the business of life.[64] In such centres, the domination of behavioural psychology demanded a regularity and simplicity of schedule and nutrition that children in the poor institutions would have recognized. In contrast, however, McGill's and Toronto's privileged situation meant a much more favourable staff-student ratio, immeasurably greater individual attention, and significantly better food and equipment. Their pupils experienced the same advantages in schooling that they knew at home.

In contrast to the situation at the child study centres, inadequate staffing and accommodation was endemic to child care institutions for Canada's poor. Refuges such as New Westminster's Providence Orphanage, Burnaby's United Church Home for Girls, and Vancouver's Salvation Army Maternity Hospital Rescue and Children's Home crowded occupants together in facilities that, whatever the good will of their custodians, could not provide adequate supervision.[65] Despite recognition of their shortcomings for psychological and physical development throughout these decades, orphanages continued to house children whose parents were unable or unwilling to care for them. In 1927, for instance, 180 children came under the care of the Vancouver Children's Aid Society but only nine were placed in paid boarding homes. An unknown but small number of children were sheltered for free by individual families, but the great majority remained in CAS accommodation. For those dubbed defective or delinquent, as with inmates of the Maritime Home for Girls at Truro, Nova Scotia, or the Girls' Cottage Industrial School at Sweetsburg, Quebec, conditions were equally far from ideal. Bereft of what benefits intimate family life could offer, institutionalized children were handicapped from the outset.

Not surprisingly, fostering out became more and more popular, although never universal, as a solution to the dilemmas of institutional care. In many instances, youngsters were readily handed out to whomever would take them. Young girls, like Anne of Green Gables in an earlier period, might very well find themselves expected to perform a multitude of chores in exchange for room and board. Not all such children were Canadians. These years still saw pauper children from Great Britain brought in as home-helpers by emigration societies.[66] The perennial shortage of good foster homes led to attempts by the emerging social work profession and philan-thropic women to keep natural families together through state allowances and expert supervision. The modern transformation from institutions to fostering to family case work was well underway during these years, but children remained vulnerable to the stinginess with which public and pri-vate authorities undertook their responsibilities.[67] Anne Shirley had many successors in finding herself passed casually from hand to hand, although there is little reason to believe that most orphans finally found a Marilla and Mathew Cuthbert to shelter them. The fate of an illegitimate Vancouver girl who, at age nine, was left behind to shift for herself when foster par-ents and another child, whom she had believed to be her natural family, moved away, was at least as common.[68]

When they could, most families resisted the permanent loss of their chil-dren. Mutual affection was important, and the presence of even very young family members had long been essential to the domestic economy of many Canadians. Such had always been the case with Athabaskan peoples. One Native woman born in 1930 remembered her mother teaching her to sew moccasins when she was eight: "Mom made me start over again if I made a mistake. I watched her tan skin—cut hair, flesh, wash, hang. Dry it and smoke it with rotten wood. Soak in rain water for two or three days, then start to tan."[69] Useful contributions were not unique to those living in the bush or to families in any one culture. Girls of many different backgrounds were regularly kept at home as housekeepers and child-minders. A family's need for such assistance varied with a number of factors. The season, the number, age, and sex of siblings, the health and temperament of the mother, and the prosperity of the family all made a difference. At critical times, such as at the birth of a baby or during threshing, even little girls could be called on to lend a hand. An ill or overworked mother meant that duties might begin early, as with Lauretta, born in 1916, who was "busy in the kitchen when she was six years old."[70] In such situations, daughters could well pride themselves on their own accomplishments and their par-ents' trust. Costs were paid as well. One daughter remembered foregoing a much desired high school education as she was the "only girl and Mother . . . [was] rather sickly."[71] In good times and bad, chances for schooling remained firmly tied to the rhythms of the family economy.

Schools themselves could be a mixed blessing. While some girls found intense friendships on the playground and sought-after learning in the classroom, others found themselves uncomfortably singled out by virtue of their appearance, accents, or ability. Whether they were participant, observer, or intruder, children regularly divided according to sex, age, and social group. Different entrances, play areas, and games affirmed the importance of these distinctions. Girls skipped, played hopscotch and tag, and swung, leaving boys for the most part to rowdier contests. On occasion though, especially when numbers were small, both sexes might engage in spirited games of softball or Red Rover.[72] Chants, songs, and rhymes were also a vital part of this playground culture.[73] Class routines offered further opportunities to discover the world beyond the family. For pupils like the future historian Hilda Neatby in Saskatchewan, education promised release from farm labour and opened up the possibility of a career.[74] Other students, like one resident of small town Ontario, remembered:

> I liked all my teachers, and I guess I liked school, though I don't remember being stimulated by it. I worked fairly hard and usually headed my class, but I think I learned only enough to pass exams. I went to school because everyone else went to school.[75]

The less well off had still greater cause for disinclination. A Toronto girl whose family fell on hard times in the 1930s "dreaded hearing that school bell and walking into the hall and into the class" for fear that a classmate would recognize her second-hand clothes.[76]

Such anxieties and aspirations were part of the lives of both boys and girls, but the latter had to contend as well, especially once they entered high school, with resistance to equality in education. Anti-feminists in both decades, but especially in the decade of the 1930s with its reinvigorated fears about the survival of western civilization, the nuclear family, and traditional sex roles, challenged the merits of co-education. A typical critic identified so-called god-given differences between the sexes: "a boy is a boy" and will grow up to be "restless, adventurous, creative, active, a maker, while a girl, under normal conditions, grows calm, home-loving, receptive, passive, a user."[77] Here in a nutshell was the language and thinking that, whether rooted in newer scientific mythology or older misogynist traditions, assigned Canadian girls to a different, and finally subordinate, role in the home and the paid workplace. Denied the option by female nature itself, so it was suggested, of independence, initiative, and ambition, girls were routed, subtly perhaps but nonetheless forcefully, into homes and public employments where their abilities would not directly compete with those of men and, not so incidentally, would prove immediately beneficial to male relatives and bosses. Housewives and secretaries helped nuture male creativity, authority, and independence. In the process their own talents could well be lost sight of.

What seemed equally clear was that many women in these decades believed that men preferred them less educated.[78] As a female observer put it:

When it comes to leaping off the deep end, beauty has it over brains yesterday, today and forever. Of course, I know the old saw . . . about the beautiful but dumb woman wearing down the resistance and taking the edge off a finely tempered disposition in time, but by that time, there isn't anything to do about it— he's been caught hook, line, and sinker. Meanwhile the brainy prospect isn't a prospect. She is still sitting in somebody's office making pot hooks for a living and maligning fate because she hasn't a pretty face to bewitch it for her. . . . Give me a cute nose and I won't need to know how to spell. Correct spelling will bring me in $25 a week, perhaps, but a cute nose will give me a meal ticket to punch for the rest of my life. . . . An ounce of complexion is worth a pound of grey matter.[79]

External beauty was seen as the real secret of female popularity and success.

The prevalence of such views undermined whatever academic talents girls might lay claim to. It also aided and abetted the incursion of home economics or domestic science into school classrooms. This subject had been entering public schools since the end of the nineteenth century,[80] and in the 1920s and 1930s it continued to find new recruits in school systems that could afford the additional expense. In its North American origins, the domestic science movement had raised important questions about just how homes and families could best take advantages of improvements in production, transportation, and services, and simultaneously offer mothers and wives a marked degree of independence, authority, and convenience. Co-operative solutions in everything from cooking to washing and child care, for instance, envisioned a highly sociable future in which women's domestic labour would be valued and alleviated.[81] That co-operative vision faded before corporate capitalism's preference for homemakers who were isolated in single-family residences and who made a host of individual purchases. By the 1920s, domestic science, as institutionalized in Canada's elementary and secondary schools, showed little sign of its radical heritage. Students were groomed to accept the privatization of the household and the strict division of labour between the female homemaker and the male breadwinner.

Yet, for all its evolving conservatism, domestic science remained a poor cousin to more explicitly "masculine" components of the curriculum. In 1922, for example, the province of British Columbia paid only 50 percent of home economics equipment costs while it assumed all the expenses of manual training for boys.[82] Educating girls, even in their "proper" accomplishments, was to be done, as much as possible, on the cheap. Despite such reservations and the onslaught of the Great Depression, which caused towns like Trail, Fernie, Armstrong, and Port Moody to discontinue domestic science classes for a time, the number of B.C. schools offering such classes increased steadily, from 51 domestic science centres in 1919, to 86 in 1929, to 120 in 1939. By 1930, approximately 75 percent of the province's school girls took "home ec," and they would have found much the same opportunity in many other regions of the country. [83]

The exact results of formal instruction are difficult to measure but, taken to their logical conclusion, they meant the homogenizing of domestic culture from one coast to another. As Barbara Riley has observed in her discussion of the situation in B.C. schools:

> In place of family customs in diet, menus, and methods, the girls were introduced to new foods and recipes whose selection was on scientific grounds and whose preparation was taught according to standardized procedures. Finally, many girls may have first been introduced to new consumer goods . . . and new patterns of consumption through domestic science classes.[84]

In the great majority of cases, girls' new information and skills could not contend with the immediate economic and social reality of family life where domestic arrangements in everything from stoves to meals were difficult to update. Over time, however, many girls would seek to apply in their own homes at least some of "the standardized methods, the authoritative cookbooks, and the new technological devices first introduced in the classroom."[85] In this way, budding homemakers helped bring their families into the domestic revolution of modern consumer society.

For students of non-British origins, household science classrooms provided yet one more exposure to the forces of Canadianization. Here they learned that the domestic standards, recipes, and procedures that engaged their mothers were no longer to be preferred. If cookbooks and teachers were any guide, for instance, "real" Canadians ate roast beef and potatoes not spaghetti and tomato sauce. Newcomers were left to cope with what such instruction meant for mothers proud of their traditional skills and daughters encouraged to remake themselves and their "foreign" families into a more acceptable image. Domestic progress in its Canadian form could well be a mixed blessing. Whatever its limitations, instruction in household science raised few unsettling questions about girls or their behaviour in the minds of most observers. As one enthusiast observed, in the somewhat different context of employment security, "As a training for living, Household Science is the safest risk in the list of girls' vocations."[86]

Almost equally safe in terms of its relevance for subsequent employment in these years and almost as good a guarantor of femininity were commercial classes. The private sector had been the first to respond to a massive expansion in clerical occupations that relied on relatively well-educated young women of respectable appearance. Business colleges such as Pitman's and Shaw's were well-established by the turn of the century. Public school educators were much slower in meeting the needs of a changing economy, but by 1920 pupils in many towns and cities could take courses in narrowly defined and practically oriented subjects such as typing, shorthand, stenography, and bookkeeping. Applicants for such instruction were overwhelmingly female. In 1923 Toronto's Central High School of Commerce reported 69 percent female enrolment and three years later 74 percent. In Vancouver the Cecil Rhodes High School of Commerce claimed 72.7 percent in 1919 and, ten years later, 74 percent.[87] Such figures reflect the fact that, as Nancy Jackson and Jane Gaskell have argued, "The clientele and raison d'être for commercial programs were increasingly restricted to women and to the limited prospects in the business world that were associated with women's employment."[88] Labour market segmentation on the basis of sex, so that there were in fact two distinct labour markets, meant that young women of very different origins might well be jointly groomed to become secretaries, salesclerks, and banktellers.[89] Background and years of schooling were not finally as important as the structural limitations on women's opportunities. The inauguration in the 1920s of a department of secretarial science at the University of Western Ontario, for instance, implicitly recognized the existence of a dual labour market in which sex was the determining factor.[90] By the 1920s, commercial courses at every level attracted both working- and middle-class girls who found that their presence did not raise unsettling questions about competition with boys and, if they were fortunate, promised stable and respectable occupations before marriage.

Secondary education was girls' surest route to white-collar jobs. The interwar decades, with their elimination in many jurisdictions of tuition, their tighter enforcement of child labour laws, and their increase in school-leaving ages to sixteen in provinces such as Ontario, saw working-class youngsters enter high schools and collegiates in unprecedented numbers. These influences especially benefitted girls.[91] Tuition fees, for example, were a special deterrent for girls when their education was widely viewed as less important than that of their brothers. Abolishment of fees allowed for a continuing female majority in secondary educational institutions. In B.C., for example, girls made up 57.3 percent of high school pupils in 1920, 55.1 percent in 1930, and 54.0 percent in 1940.[92] The situation was much the same elsewhere. The school attendance of the fifteen-to nineteen-year-old age group is shown in table 1. The social and economic advantages of a high school diploma helped counter long-existing prejudices against the education of girls in these years. Toronto's Harbord Collegiate Institute, for example, enrolled increasing numbers of Jewish girls who previously would have been relegated to a formal education far inferior to that of boys of their own age.[93]

TABLE 1

PERCENTAGE OF EACH SEX AGED 15 TO 19 AT SCHOOL

	1921	1931	1941
Girls	27	36	37
Boys	22	32	35

Source: Jane Gaskell, "Education and Job Opportunities for Women: Patterns of Enrolment and Economic Returns" in *Women and the Canadian Labour Force*, edited by Naomi Hersom and Dorothy Smith (Ottawa: SSHRCC, 1982), 261.

Not only were teenage girls more likely than boys to be in school, they were more likely to do well and to graduate.[94] Their schooling was further distinguished by different enrolment patterns. Domestic science and commercial classes joined languages and literature in welcoming large numbers of girls; math, sciences, and shop work did not. To an important degree, such segregation meant that high school education was in fact not co-educational for much of the day. Girls and boys learned different skills and information in separate settings. The result, as Jane Gaskell has pointed out, segmented "the labour force by sex on entry to the labour market and on entry to post-secondary education."[95] When they graduated from high school, middle-class girls who traditionally had spent their teenage years in the classroom found themselves competing for many of the same kinds of jobs with working-class girls who were likely to be the first generation in their families to complete high school.

For all the disadvantages they faced in entering the labour market, high school graduates were relatively fortunate. Girls with physical and mental handicaps had far fewer opportunities. Although they were more likely than ever before to find a place in public schools, they were also more likely than their luckier sisters to drop out or fail to register, either to remain at home or to begin a desperate search for employment. The Protestant School Board of Montreal had begun work with academically handicapped pupils as early as 1913 but only in the late 1920s were "opportunity classes" formally established. Even then, the marriage of one teacher in 1934, and hence her automatic dismissal, meant the closure of one such class. By 1938, there were eleven "opportunity classes" in nine Montreal schools. There students spent three-fifths of their time on academic work and the rest on handwork.[96] Also introduced sporadically across the country wherever jurisdictions were willing to take on the additional expense were habit and guidance clinics for troubled students. In Montreal, a Habit Clinic for Children, established in 1923, assembled two psychologists, a psychiatrist, and a social worker two mornings a week to deal with fifteen to twenty-five children referred by schools, parents, courts, and social agencies.[97] In Vancouver, a Provincial Child Guidance Clinic, established in the 1930s, endeavoured, through IQ testing, home investigations, parental education, and, sometimes, removal from the home, to transform the actually or potentially incorrigible into obedient citizens.[98]

All too frequently, reflecting the belief in women's particular responsibility for children and in the emerging Freudian-influenced psychology of the day, concern focussed on individual causes of behavioural problems, especially the shortcomings of mothers. In Vancouver cases included an eight-year-old girl in 1938 whose extreme stubbornness was linked to the impatience and bad temper of her mother and a teenager whose troubles were blamed on "an irregularity in the personal life of her mother."[99] Whatever outpatient care could be found at the hands of the new generation of psychologists, psychiatrists, and psychiatric social workers was always limited to the very few who could afford such treatment. It was much more likely that girls encountering difficulty in adhering to acceptable patterns of behaviour would find themselves in institutions such as the Mercer Reformatory for Girls in Toronto or the Industrial Home for Girls in Vancouver. Between 1914 and 1937 the latter institution received from all over B.C. 600 admissions ranging in age from seven to twenty years, although the great majority were between fourteen and seventeen.[100] Most inmates were incarcerated for incorrigibility and immorality, but there were also those like eight-year-old Florence. Officially charged with theft, she had in fact been committed more to extract her from an unsuitable home situation than anything else.[101] Not surprisingly, such tragic cases were recruited overwhelmingly from the ranks of the poor. The training in domestic labour that they received in the Dominion's industrial homes and reformatories practically guaranteed that they would return to the same condition.

A very different situation awaited those that could afford the private schools that flourished in these years. In Rosary Hall in Toronto, for example, parents paid $6 to $8 a week in the 1920s to ensure that daughters received the benefits of a good Catholic education and the enjoyment of a pool, library, pianos, and extensive grounds.[102] Schools with such privileges helped to produce a separate upper-class culture and to instil in their well-to-do pupils a sense of the appropriateness of the existing social order. It was all too easy for young women trained in such an environment to ignore the plight of others whose entire family income would not have equalled tuition costs at a prestigious private school. Only a few individuals, like Dorothy Livesay, who attended the select Glen Mawr school in Ontario's capital, were able to make that imaginative leap.[103] For many, a sojourn at a private school merely helped guarantee and publicize their fortunate position in Canada's class hierarchy.

Equally privileged were the small numbers of young women entering university. Women made significant gains in enrolment during the 1920s although they failed by far to catch up with male registration. The 1930s hurt them more than their brothers, especially when one considers how enlistment in the armed forces reduced the number of male students in 1939–40. The repercussions of the dramatic decrease in women's graduate registration would be felt well into the second half of the century in terms of leadership in employment. Equally problematic was the concentration of women in relatively few areas of study. In 1920, 81.62 percent of Canadian co-eds were found in arts and science compared to 48.84 percent of males. The great majority of the remainder of women turned up in such traditional fields as education, nursing, and household science. Twenty years later, 70.09 percent of female undergraduates took arts as compared to 46.46 percent of males, with the remainder of women distributed no more widely than before as teachers, social workers, and the like. In addition, there was a critical decline in the percentage of women enrolled in male-dominated fields between 1920 and 1940. In medicine, their numbers fell from 2.14 percent of undergraduates to 1.97 percent; in law from .40

to .23 percent, and in religion and theology from 1.06 to .44 percent.[104] Explanations for this decline are not yet entirely clear, but it owed something to the absence in these years of an articulate feminist movement that had nurtured the pioneers who had breached male monopolies in the nineteenth century. Lacking both this critical support and the inspiration of an older maternalist ideology that offered women a special role in many professions, women were more ill-equipped than before to challenge the restrictions of their socialization and the hostility of misogynist male preserves.[105] Smaller numbers of female students at every level of postsecondary education reflected the greater unwillingness of parents to invest in the education of daughters and the assumption by both that higher education was less suitable or necessary for girls. Just as in the high schools, patterns of female enrolment reflected the segregated nature of the job market many would enter after graduation. An arts education prepared young women for the career opportunities that existed for their sex, notably as teachers, social workers, librarians, clerical workers, saleswomen, and wives.

TABLE 2

FULL-TIME UNIVERSITY ENROLMENT, BY SEX, SELECTED YEARS, FOR CANADA

Year	Female		Male		Women as a percentage of all students	
	undergrad.	graduate	undergrad.	graduate	undergrad.	graduate
1920	3 716	108	19 075	315	16.3	25.5
1925	5 272	221	19 580	625	21.2	26.1
1930	7 428	352	24 148	998	23.5	26.1
1935	7 494	388	26 028	1 198	22.4	24.5
1940	8 107	326	26 710	1 243	23.3	20.8

Source: Series W340–438, *Historical Statistics of Canada.*

TABLE 3

PERCENTAGE CHANGES IN UNDERGRADUATE AND GRADUATE ENROLMENT, BY SEX, SELECTED YEARS, FOR CANADA

Year	Female		Male	
	undergraduate	graduate	undergraduate	graduate
1920–25	+ 41.8	+ 104.63	+ 2.65	+ 98.41
1925–30	+ 40.9	+ 59.28	+ 23.33	+ 59.68
1930–35	+ .89	+ 10.23	+ 7.79	+ 20.04
1935–40	+ 8.18	− 15.98	+ 2.62	+ 3.76

Source: Calculated from Series W340–438, *Historical Statistics of Canada.*

The distribution of female enrolment attracted the attention of contemporaries who foresaw overcrowding in female-dominated employments, but women were not necessarily dissatisfied with their lot.[106] A survey of 167 graduates of McGill, Queen's, and Toronto universities, for instance, discovered general approval of an education that fitted them for the segregated labour market. When these women were asked for their job preferences, secretarial work headed the list, teaching took second place, and journalism came in third.[107] Some young women admitted attending university solely because other options in employment, presumably including marriage, looked unattractive.[108] The opportunities that might lure even non-academically inclined co-eds to the halls of scholarship were summed up by one father well satisfied with his daughter's presence in a degree program in household science: "They say you know that when a girl finishes that course, she gets her M.R.S."[109] To an important degree, higher education in general for middle-class girls was acceptable because it did not fundamentally threaten the primacy of the family headed by the male breadwinner. As co-eds' supporters regularly argued,

> homes are all the happier because . . . there is a wife and mother who, in the successful practice of a profession, learned self-control and human nature and how to apply every bit of her powers to her daily problems and who knows that if death should break her marriage she can maintain the independence of herself and her children.[110]

Even when the majority of female students harboured relatively modest ambitions, misogyny continued to flourish on campus. At Dalhousie University in the 1930s, for example, President Carleton Stanley conscientiously favoured young men, funding two scholarships in honours mathematics and classics solely for their benefit.[111] Nor was he alone in this favouritism. A host of awards from the Rhodes on down were formally and informally restricted to males. Prejudice appeared elsewhere as well. In 1935 the head of the University of Alberta's Woman-Haters' Club was elected president of the students' union,[112] and in both decades girls were exposed to instructors like Stephen Leacock in political economy at McGill whose anti-feminism was flaunted in a host of articles.[113] The outcome of such pervasive anti-woman feeling at universities is impossible to measure, but it contributed to undermining intellectual confidence and self-esteem among co-eds just as it no doubt bolstered male egos.

Accustomed as they were to casual anti-feminism, female students managed to find their own pleasures in university life. Here, as in the high schools, a flourishing youth culture emerged. This was often far from sedate. At Hamilton's McMaster, newcomers participated, one supposes more or less willingly, in rites planned for their benefit:

> To the roll-call each freshette replied with the name of that animal which she thought she most resembled, after which her personal appearance was improved by the addition of onion earrings. The

various animals were then called upon to perform characteristic
stunts, and all joined in an exciting game of leap-frog. Probably
the most exciting of all the contests was that of picking up beans
with one's nose to which a generous coating of glue had been
previously applied. The question was raised, "Why take swimming lessons at the 'Y' when they can be so successfully administered with the aid of a piano stool?" which was followed by
enlightening illustration of the same. Dire punishments were
meted out to those guilty of ignoring previous orders of the
Sophettes.[114]

Such highjinks contributed to the special campus culture that women were
beginning to share with men. More than ever before, the term co-ed did
not have to be synonymous with the serious-minded. Unlike the committed pioneers of the 1880s and 1890s, this was a successor generation who
could afford to take participation, at least in arts, largely for granted.

Like many men, women came to care intensely about campus life, par-
ticipating in a wide range of athletic, cultural, religious, political, and
scholarly activities. Yet their involvement remained distinctive. In many
ways the university contained two worlds differentiated by gender. Intercourse of any kind was firmly discouraged by the separation, for the most
part, of the two sexes into different programs, an isolation confirmed further by a division of social space within the university. To a large degree,
young women and men found separate places to sleep, eat, study, and
play. In Toronto, for example, the Students' Administrative Council had
two sections, like the washrooms, male and female. Similarly, Hart House,
the major athletic building on the Varsity campus, was restricted to men,
except for dances when even this bastion of male prerogative could hardly
forbid "ladies." At the University of British Columbia, separate English
classes for co-eds were the order of the day until 1941. Junior faculty
taught the women while male professors set the exams and organized the
courses that they personally taught to young men.[115] At the University of
Toronto, the long-time chairman of the history department, George M.
Wrong, made prevailing prejudices quite clear in his assertion that "What
I want is a scholar and a gentleman, and if he knows any history, so much
the better."[116] The restriction of membership in the department's prestigious History Club to young men confirmed the lack of welcome for their
sisters. No wonder there were few female historians in the country, and
none at all at Toronto, for many years. To be sure, young women found
countless ways of getting around restrictions, frequently finding ample
opportunity to meet the young men of their choice. Dances, teas, and
public lectures mingled the sexes for many purposes and provided the
highlight of countless lives.

As always, there were outstanding individuals who questioned prevailing
views. Those with religious faith often joined the Student Christian Movement (SCM), which espoused a practical Christianity and called into question the inequities of a class society and, more occasionally, sex

prejudice.[117] Other radical students repudiated religion altogether. Such was the case with Dorothy Livesay and her friend "Jim" or Jennie Watts at the University of Toronto, both of whom engaged in fierce debates over birth control, free love, Marxism, atheism, and the future of the family. These two rebels later took up the struggle against the right in the 1930s with Watts going to fight Franco in Spain and Livesay joining the Canadian League Against War and Fascism.[118] Some young women also remained resolutely "career-minded." In her very early teens, for example, Agnes Macphail had done

> a lot of thinking on the subject; men, women, and marriage. I saw that men did a job in the world outside their home and women did not. At fourteen I turned it around in my mind this way; a woman has children, the boys do things and the girls marry and have other children, of which the boys do things and the girls marry and have other children, of which the boys do a job in the world of affairs and the girls do not, but in turn have other children in which family the boys do—, and I asked myself: "Does this thing never end in a woman being a person and making a contribution, in addition to, or in place of having children?"[119]

Brave hopes never disappeared, but the trend of the two decades was against them. Initial research suggests, for instance, that university graduates of the 1920s were substantially more likely to find jobs than co-eds who completed degrees in the 1930s and 1940s. These more limited horizons were in keeping with a significant decrease in the rate of women's entry into university; indeed, in some institutions, such as Dalhousie, there was an absolute reduction in their numbers. Professional careers fell by the wayside for many, confirming the collapse of women's hopes for education that had flourished in the 1920s.[120]

Fortunately, intellectual challenges were not restricted to formal schooling. The poet Adele Wiseman has left an evocative testament to the power of the printed word in inspiring young people to test the boundaries of their society. A voracious appetite for reading helped this Jewish youngster come to terms with her particular situation in North Winnipeg during the 1930s. Her salvation was shared by readers of every sort. As she explained,

> Books were a route into life and reality and simultaneously an escape from life and reality, from the searing quality of every moment of the raw-nerved child's immediate encounters with existence. Books carved a path through the life into which I was locked, showed possible ways through the jungle of experience to the yearned-for civilization of the happy endings. . . . I belonged where I read, if nowhere else. . . .[121]

Immersion in everything from comic books to classics occupied endless hours for children who discovered their delights. Girls, like other disadvantaged groups—Jews, blacks, workers—rarely, however, found their reality reflected in what they perused. As Wiseman recollected,

> The girls and women I read about in books were usually quite other than what I knew myself and the girls and women I knew to be. But I saw children trying to become the simpering goody girls they read about in books. And didn't I myself practice trying to keep a stiff upper lip, which was the way to be, while simultaneously getting my sensitive lower lip to quiver tremulously which was also the way to be.[122]

Yet for many pages, in their enthralment with literature's pleasures, Adele and her sister "book-molesters" largely managed to ignore the misogyny they encountered. They were not alone in this escape from reality. The burgeoning sales of magazines like *Chatelaine*, with their hefty doses of fiction, spoke volumes for the importance of reading as women's chief leisure and distraction.

Whereas reading was normally a solitary activity, many young women turned to more sociable pastimes. These decades saw the prospering of clubs founded by middle-class women, sometimes at the instigation of potential girl recruits, to channel the energy and character of adolescents into responsible womanhood. In particular, the Canadian Girl Guides, the Canadian Girls in Training, and the Junior Red Cross enrolled thousands in programs from the mundane to the exciting and the innovative. Such experiences became commonplace for many youngsters and were important contributors to the evolution of a nation-wide youth culture.

The Guides had been imported from Great Britain just before World War I. Their imperial connections made them especially likely to be sponsored by the Anglican Church, the Salvation Army, the Imperial Order of the Daughters of the Empire, and the Fellowship of the Maple Leaf. The introduction of "Lone Guides" meant that even those far removed from settled communities could participate.[123] Other special groups were served with the introduction of Rangers for older girls, Extension Guiding for the handicapped, and Auxiliary Companies for girls in penitentiaries and prevention and rescue homes. In general, the Guide movement was to engage respectable preteen and teen girls. Leaders in particular were to be above reproach. No supervising Guider, for example, could be recruited from an Auxiliary Company.[124] Attractive camp programs, a strong spirit of international fellowship, a somewhat secular nature, opportunities for good friendship, and, no doubt, the patronage of the British royal princesses kept the movement expanding throughout the interwar years. Badges earned for "Character and Intelligence" (e.g., artist, booklover, homemaker, interpreter, rifle-shot), "Handicrafts, Professions" (e.g., child nurse, carpenter, domestic service, gardener, poultry farmer), "Physical Development and Strength" (e.g., athlete, cyclist, health, pioneer, skater), and "Service for Others" (e.g., fire brigade, pathfinder, sick nurse) were worn with pride and enthusiasm.[125]

Not everyone approved of Guides. By 1920 the YWCA, for instance, had withdrawn from Guides and Brownies in repudiation of their British and non-sectarian orientation.[126] Uniformed Guides, like Scouts, were also vulnerable to charges of militarism.[127] Leaders repeatedly challenged such characterizations: one speaker to B.C.'s South Cowichan Guides insisted that there was "no surer way to secure the world peace . . . than that which the guide movement took as its watchword 'Be Prepared'."[128] Defenders also endorsed Guiding as "practical Christianity."[129] The first *Canadian Policy, Organization, and Rules* manual did not appear until 1945. Prior to that date, Guiders made do with British books with addenda for Canadian leaders.

The maintenance of its imperial connections helped recruit Guides among those of British origin, but another organization believed its own "made-in-Canada" origins to be a source of special appeal. The Canadian Girls in Training was founded in 1917 as an explicitly Canadian and Christian response to the needs of adolescent girls and, incidentally, to the appeal of Guiding, which was distrusted as too competitive, authoritarian, secular, and British.[130] Heavily influenced by "progressive education" with its liberal, child-centred philosophy,[131] the CGIT spoke for a broad-minded, internationalist Christianity in its emphasis on modern biblical criticism. The life of Jesus was believed to offer up-to-date lessons in dealing with the problems of the world. The benefits of Canadian citizenship and the importance of enfranchised women assuming a significant role in national development were also central to CGIT philosophy in a way that recalled suffragists' emphasis on the particular moral responsibility of women. Such qualities often made the early organization appear in direct line of succession to the maternal feminism of an earlier generation. Whatever the attractions of its reform-minded agenda, the CGIT's extensive summer camp, craft, and social programs were critical in keeping membership high throughout the worst years of the Depression. In 1933–34, for instance, there were nearly 40 000 girls enrolled in the CGIT in 1 100 communities.[132] Determined as it was to differ from Guiding, the CGIT shared a similar concern to produce an independent and responsible adult who as a mother would serve her family and as a citizen her nation. Strong women leaders in both organizations, many with university degrees and some employment experience, personified what the "Girl of the New Day" might achieve.

In some ways, Guiding and the CGIT represented only a more formal opportunity to participate in a long-existing female culture and cultivate female friendships. Occasionally this tendency sparked some homophobia, as with an article in the *Canadian Guider* by a University of Toronto psychologist who characterized crushes on leaders by young girls as unnatural.[133] For all such negative assessments, intense relationships among girls and women remained an important part of organizational life, fostering co-operation and encouraging leadership. No wonder many graduates of the CGIT, for example, went on to become community leaders, helping to bridge the gap between the first and the second feminist movements with their activities on behalf of peace and consumer protection. In the meantime, both Guides and the CGIT provided girls, mostly of the middle class, with many hours of enjoyment and some experience of the wider world beyond their families. Working-class girls occasionally enrolled, but their time was more fully taken up with contributing to family survival through domestic and paid labour. From time to time, radical organizations such as the Women's Labour Leagues tried to establish working-class children's groups in competition with the Guides and the CGIT, but these floundered, no rivals for the urgent economic pressures on the young people they hoped to reach or the comparatively resource-rich, middle-class initiatives.[134]

After World War I, the Junior Red Cross enlisted teachers, the majority of whom were female, to inculcate in both girls and boys in elementary and, occasionally, high school classrooms across the Dominion the principles of better hygiene and nutrition, good citizenship, and international co-operation. By 1930 there were 236 394 members in the Junior Red Cross, and numbers remained high throughout the decade.[135] Girls shared many aspects of the program with their brothers, but no more than in the organizations devoted to their sex did they escape reminders of their special responsibility for parenting and housework. Lessons in home nursing and care of babies were matters of course. And yet, as with Guides and CGIT, there was a simultaneous emphasis on the new responsibilities of modern citizenship. While that message did not always escape racism and ethnocentrism,[136] it regularly affirmed a "world-mindedness" that was espoused by all three organizations.[137] Such philosophy could only help to make listeners more tolerant and peace-loving. In as much as girls were especially susceptible to such appeals, it also helped differentiate them from their brothers who might be involved in cadet training and competitive rather than co-operative activities.

Not all competitive activity was limited to males. In the 1920s and 1930s, athletics, for instance, developed a special appeal for girls. Liberated from the heavy dresses that had so impeded movement in the past, young women took an unprecedented place in a diverse range of sports. There were individual champions. Toronto resident Gladys Robinsen, in regular practice since she was ten, won a speed skating title in Lake Placid in 1921.[138] Eighteen-year-old Lela Brooks, a skater by five or six years of age, set six world records in speed skating in 1926. In the 1932 Olympics, Jean Wilson, who started on ice at fifteen, won the 500 metre women's speed skating event and was only deprived of a gold medal because this was still an unofficial or demonstration sport.[139] Track and field also produced its stars. Bobbie Rosenfeld, "wearing her brother's 'Y' teeshirt and swim trunks and her father's socks, set Canadian records in the broad jump, the discus and on the track" at the 1928 Amsterdam Olympics.[140] In the same games Ethel Smith took a gold in the 4 x 100 metre relay and a bronze in the 100 metres. Ethel Catherwood, nicknamed "The Saskatoon Lily," brought home a gold medal in the high jump in the same year. Hilda Strike, who won two silver medals in the 100 metres and the 4 x 100 metre relay in the 1932 Olympics, repeated the same feats in the 1934 British Empire

Games. Swimming found a champion in Phyllis Dewar, who captured three gold medals at the 1934 British Empire Games and another in the 1938 Games. In golf it was Ada Mackenzie, like Rosenfeld an all-round athlete, who began her winning ways as a teenager and went on to victories throughout the 1920 and 1930s. Such successes came despite a notable absence of facilities, trainers, and, often, encouragement for girls and women. Also significant was the fact that many of these sports "heroines" appear to have come from the working class. Bobbie Rosenfeld worked in a chocolate factory. Ethel Smith left school at fourteen for a job in an embroidery concern. Phyllis Dewar married a CPR conductor. Although more research is needed before we will know for sure, working-class women may have been less intimidated by stereotypical assumptions of what was suitable for their sex and therefore uniquely placed to take advantage of some of the sports opportunities opening up in the 1920s.

Team sports, as the relay wins in the 1928 Olympics suggest, also found recruits in these decades. In 1921, for instance, the University of Manitoba participated in the first interprovincial girls' basketball games against the Universities of Alberta and Saskatchewan.[141] The most famous team was the Edmonton Grads. These basketball players, originally all graduates of Edmonton's McDougall Commercial High School, won steadily from their first game in 1915 to their last in 1940. This included the first Canadian women's championship in 1922 when they beat the London Shamrocks, and a host of other victories against the state champions of Illinois, Missouri, Kansas, Washington, Oklahoma, Iowa, Michigan, Minnesota, Texas, Arkansas, and Ohio. They also went undefeated in games played, unofficially, at the Olympics in 1928, 1932, and 1936. While no other team ever matched this record, their success attracted players in schools all across the Dominion.[142] Softball was another team sport to attract female enthusiasts, although it failed to match basketball's wide appeal.

Not all observers of such developments were positive. One quaint theory held that female athletes produced mainly girl babies or puny boys.[143] More common was the assertion that women's nerves paid the toll of intense physical activity.[144] There was also general agreement that men did not like the look of athletic women. As one opponent put it, "The men want the gals to stay beautiful, graceful, and sightly, not tie their bodies in scrawny, sinewy knots."[145] These chauvinistic views found support from authorities like Dr. A.S. Lamb, of McGill's department of physical education, who opposed women's participation in strenuous sports.[146] Such arguments and experts helped keep numerous events, such as women's speed skating, out of the Olympics for many years.

Outspoken female athletes like Bobbie Rosenfeld challenged critics,[147] but still more important in offsetting the stereotypes was the widespread publicity given to women's sports. For the first time, individuals like Rosenfeld, who also edited a newspaper column in the 1930s, became household names. Support from businesses such as Silverwood Dairies in Toronto, which sponsored a basketball club in 1924–25, suggests the generally positive public perception of female athletics. More important still, women became their own promoters. Toronto had its Lakeside Ladies' Athletic Club, which sponsored basketball and softball. Ada Mackenzie founded the same city's Ladies' Golf and Tennis Club. Myrtle Cook, a gold medalist as a member of Canada's "Matchless Six" running team in the Amsterdam Olympics, became an eager supporter of Canadian women four years later in 1932 in Los Angeles.[148] Women athletes decried not only sexual discrimination in sports. Eva Dawes, who won the bronze medal for the high jump at the 1932 Olympics, bluntly repudiated its Berlin sequel for its racism and anti-Semitism: "I'll hang up my spikes rather than take part in an amateur world meet where discrimination is keeping many fine sportsmen from taking part."[149] Such opinions were every bit a match for the idealistic internationalism expressed by the Guides, CGIT, and Red Cross, but the chief impact of female athletes was rarely directly political. It may be, as Nellie McClung argued, that they did "much to widen the conception of beauty. Durability and strength have entered the picture."[150] Finally, the blossoming of women's athletics also permitted girls and women the opportunity, previously limited largely to males, to test their physical mettle, bask in the support of a crowd, and forge the friendships of the playing field. Such opportunites were welcomed by many girls and young women, even if they could not in these years finally lay the myth of the delicate female to rest.

Girls in urban centres during the 1920s and 1930s encountered a wider range of formal activities than ever before. If their labour was not crucial to family survival, their free hours could easily be taken up with clubs and sports. Adults in general preferred the troubling years of adolescence to be occupied and constrained in highly regulated situations. Notwithstanding the suspicions of their elders, girls, particularly those whose families could spare neither the time nor the energy for supervision, flocked to movies, dances, and, occasionally, automobiles, where their behaviour was not so tightly checked. The celluloid world of Mary Pickford, Lillian Gish, Joan Crawford, Katharine Hepburn, Clark Gable, Douglas Fairbanks, and Rudolph Valentino captured girls everywhere who could afford the 5¢ price of admission. In dance halls, big and little bands played the music of the blackbottom and other modern dance crazes that made parents shake their heads. The arrival of radio also meant that it was not always necessary to leave home for entertainment. Young children, for instance, learned early on to tune in to their favourite shows such as the "Sleepy Town Express" on radio CFCY in Charlottetown. Traditional music and dancing also got a boost. Don Messer and the Islanders, initially Don Messer and his New Brunswick Lumberjacks, for instance, got their start in these years.[151] Nor were people shy about making their own music. Agnes Macphail was typical in her enthusiasm for dancing. In her rural community of Grey County, Ontario, "a couple of sleigh-loads of young people, two fiddlers, and a caller" could make up "a party that went on till all hours of the night."[152] Parents had no more reason than usual to worry about such familiar pursuits, but the advent of the automobile—registrations jumped from 196 367 in 1919, to 1 061 500 in 1930, dropped during the worst years of the Great Depression and recovered to reach 1 191 914 in 1939[153]—just like the bicycle in the 1890s fanned consternation among those who feared new opportunities for licence. Critics wondered publicly "What Shall We Do With 'Our' Flapper?"[154] and prescribed stiff doses of hard work, simple living, and early marriage. Yet young people always found their defenders, especially in the 1930s when there seemed to be some agreement that "flaming youth" had "cooled off."[155]

Girls in the decade of the Great Depression certainly had ample cause to question the optimism that countenanced experimentation in the 1920s. A very few continued to chance radical solutions, but many more hungered for security and reassurance in traditional social and economic relationships. To some extent at least, Shirley Temple's audiences shared their heroine's essential trust that pluck, helped along by a pretty face, would save the day. And they discovered, when they entered the world of paid work, that they could need all the hope they could muster.

NOTES

1. Ellen Knox, *The Girl of the New Day* (Toronto: McClelland and Stewart, 1919).

2. Agnes Macphail, M.P., "Citizenship," *Canadian Mentor* (Feb.-March 1931): 48.

3. PAC, Agnes Macphail Papers, v. 10, folder, "Speeches, Women Role in Society," "How Far Can Women Help Solve National Problems," CBC, May 21, 1939 (typescript), 5–6. See also the disappointment of a grandmother at the birth of a girl in "Letters of a Countrywoman," *Canadian Countryman* (April 15, 1922).

4. SFUA, taped interview with Ruth Bullock by Sara Diamond, 1979.

5. Fredelle Bruser Maynard, *Raisins and Almonds* (Toronto: Doubleday, 1972), 181–82.

6. SAB, Violet McNaughton Papers, v. 16, folder 37, Mrs. C. Langerok to McNaughton, Dec. 2, 1936.

7. See Elsie MacGill, *My Mother the Judge* (Toronto: Ryerson Press, 1955).

8. For a provocative assessment of the significance of the mother-daughter bond see Nancy Chodorow, *The Reproduction of Mothering: Psychoanalysis and the Sociology of Gender* (Berkeley: University of California Press, 1978).

9. For a fascinating revelation of these relationships see Mazo de la Roche, *Ringing the Changes. An Autobiography* (Toronto: Macmillan, 1957) and Emily Carr, *The Book of Small* (Toronto: Clarke, Irwin, 1966) and *Growing Pains* (Toronto: Clarke, Irwin, 1971). On the family and female friendships see Margaret Conrad, "'Sundays Always Make Me Think of Home': Time and Place in Canadian Women's History" in *Rethinking Canada: The Promise of Women's History*, edited by Veronica Strong-Boag and Anita Clair Fellman (Toronto: Copp Clark Pitman, 1986).

10. On the relationship between class, maternal health, and birth weight see W. Peter Ward and Patricia C. Ward, "Infant Birth Weight and Nutrition in Industrializing Montreal," *American Historical Review* (Feb. 1984): 324–45.

11. See Veronica Strong-Boag and K. McPherson, "'The Confinement of Women: Childbirth and Hospitalization in Vancouver 1919–1939," *BC Studies* (Summer 1986): 142–74 for a discussion of treatment of expectant women within hospitals; K. McPherson, "Nurses and Nursing in Early Twentieth-Century Halifax" (M.A. thesis, Dalhousie University, 1982), especially chap. 4 for an assessment of the VON in Nova Scotia's capital, and Elizabeth Goudie, *Woman of Labrador* (Toronto: Peter Martin Associates, 1973) for an autobiographical account of such home births.

12. Series B51–58, *Historical Statistics of Canada*, 2nd ed., edited by F.H. Leacy (Ottawa: Statistics Canada, 1983).

13. See Norah Lewis, "Advising the Parents: Child Rearing in British Columbia During the Inter-War Years" (Ph.D thesis, University of British Columbia, 1980), chap. 6.

14. *The Junior* (May 1922): 10–11. The outstanding pediatrician of the day, Dr. Alan Brown of the Hospital for Sick Children in Toronto, one of the inventors of Pablum, did not believe that anyone needed tonsils. He was once asked "'At what age do you take tonsils out?'" to which he replied "'Not before the umbilical cord is cut.'" Quoted in Pierre Berton, *The Dionne Years* (Toronto: McClelland and Stewart, 1978), 146.

15. *The Junior* (March 1923): 13–15.

16. *The Junior* (March 1926): 8–11.

17. "Mother Goose in Health Land," *The Junior* (March 1930): 21.

18. See, for instance, the close relationship between poverty and child distress reported in *Indian Conditions: A Survey* (Ottawa: Indian and Northern Affairs, 1980), passim.

19. New Brunswick Child Welfare Survey, *Report* (1929).

20. Marjorie Bell, "Are We Exaggerating? Experiences of Visiting Homemakers," *Social Welfare* (June-Sept. 1937): 39.

21. For a description of such schools see Thomas A. McMaster, "A Study of Private Schools in Canada" (M.Ed. thesis., University of Manitoba, 1940).

22. Quoted in the Report of the Committee on Sexual Offences Against Children and Youths, *Sexual Offences Against Children* (Ottawa: Queen's Printer, 1984), I: 192.

23. *Sexual Offences Against Children* made this estimate based on a National Population Survey of 2 008 Canadians. It also concluded that "On the basis of offences reported by adults of all ages, it appears that there has not been a sharp increase in recent years in the incidence of sexual offences" (p. 193). On the kinds of offences reported see chap. 13, ibid. Terry Chapman, in "Women, Sex and Marriage in Western Canada 1890–1920," *Alberta History* (Autumn 1985): 1–12, examines this problem for a slightly earlier period and again the evidence suggests a relatively widespread phenomenon. On youth prostitution see Rebecca Coulter, "The Working Young of Edmonton, 1921–1931" in *Childhood and Family in Canadian History*, edited by Joy Parr (Toronto: McClelland and Stewart, 1982), 143–44.

24. Mrs. House, "God Saw That It Was Good," *Some Thoughts for Wives and Mothers and Some Teaching to be given to Children by Parents who find it difficult to put their own Thoughts into Words* (B.C. Board of Health, 1936).

25. SFUA, taped interview with Ruth Bullock by Sara Diamond, 1979.

26. Gwethalyn Graham, "Women, Are They Human?" *Canadian Forum* (Dec. 1936): 22.

27. "New Fashioned Chores," *Grain Growers' Guide* (March 21, 1923): 24.

28. See, for example, Garrett Elliott, "What I Wish for My Daughter," *Chatelaine* (May 1934): 14, 48–49. On the same phenomenon in French Canada see Susan Mann Trofimenkoff, *The Dream of Nation* (Toronto: Gage, 1984), passim.

29. See Alton Goldbloom, *The Care of the Child* (Toronto: Longmans, Green and Co., 1928) and Alan Brown and Frederick Tisdall, *Common Procedures in the Practice of Paediatrics. Being a Detailed Description of Diagnostic, Therapeutic and Dietetic Methods Employed at the Hospital for Sick Children, Toronto* (Toronto: McClelland and Stewart, 1926).

30. See Veronica Strong-Boag, "Intruders in the Nursery: Childcare Professionals Reshape the Years One to Five, 1920–1940" in *Childhood and Family in Canadian History*, and Berton, *The Dionne Years*.

31. The title of a full-page ad for Calay Soap, *Chatelaine* (Jan. 1932): 53.

32. See, for example, Mona E. Clark, "Are Brains a Handicap to a Woman?" *Canadian Magazine* (Feb. 1928): 27.

33. Margaret I. Laurence, "Romance of the Difficult," *The Junior* (Feb. 1932): 20.

34. See Jean Barman, "Working Kids" in *Working Lives. Vancouver 1886–1986*, edited by the Working Lives Collective (Vancouver: New Star Books, 1985).

35. Helen Potrebenko, *No Streets of Gold: A Social History of Ukrainians in Alberta* (Vancouver: New Star Books, 1977), 227–29.

36. Alice H. Parsons, "Careers or Marriage?" *Canadian Home Journal* (June 1938), 63.

37. Ibid., 64.

38. See "Where Are You Going My Pretty Maid?" *Chatelaine* (Feb. 1936): 12–13.

39. See "Toy Trade Comes Into Its Own," *Dry Goods Review* (June 1920): 106.

40. See "Experiment Showed Premiums Having Strongest Pull with Children," *Marketing* (June 5, 1937): 4; "Children Can Exert Great Influence on Food Purchases for the Home," ibid. (April 22, 1939); and "Appeal to Collector in Every Child Sure Way to Hold Juvenile Market," ibid. (Aug. 12, 1939): 2.

41. On the massive increase in advertising pressure in these years see Stuart Ewen, *Captains of Consciousness* (New York: McGraw-Hill, 1976).

42. "Does Shirley Temple Know?" in *Ten Lost Years*, edited by Barry Broadfoot (Toronto: Doubleday, 1973).

43. See "Demand for Pyjamas Steadily Growing," *Marketing* (Jan. 1922): 144 and "Practical Underthings Being Shown," ibid. (Aug. 1922): 66–67.

44. See "Spread of Bare Leg Fancy Would Have Far Reaching Effect," *Dry Goods Review* (Jan. 1929): 14, 52. See also the opposition of the hosiery industry in "More and More . . . It's Less and Less," ibid. (Aug. 1929): 15–16.

45. See "Campaign to be Waged Against Corsetless Fad," ibid. (Oct. 1921): 105. Some Canadian manufacturers claimed to have learned from the failure of the campaign in the U.S., concluding "There is no use trying to force women's opinion. The abandoning of heavy material and boning for elastic marks a change in women's attitude of mind just as much as the wearing of knickers has done." "Severe Types Unlikely to Return," ibid. (Jan. 1923): 98. They did, however, engage in active publicity campaigns to ward off the threat of the girdleless young girl. See "Teach Girls They Must Wear Corsets," ibid. (Sept. 1923): 81.

46. See "Junior Section Lays Good Foundation," ibid. (May 1926): 50; "'Foundation Garment' Replacing 'Corset' as Descriptive Name," ibid. (Oct. 1926): 62; and "A Corset Corner for the Younger Set," ibid. (Nov. 1927): 41.

47. "The Whys and Hows of Modern Corsetry," ibid. (Sept. 1926): 54; "Thin Women Need Corsets More than Stout Women," ibid. (July 1926): 67; and "Modern Corsets Are Scientific and Healthful," ibid. (Jan. 1927): 64.

48. "Athletic Underwear for Women," ibid. (April 1922): 76–77.

49. "Experiments with Two-Way Stretch," ibid. (June 1932): 40, 42.

50. See "Women Wear a New Type of Corsetry," ibid. (April 1928): 48 and "Ultra-Feminine Fashions Mark Prosperity for Corset Departments," ibid. (March 25, 1938): 16.

51. SFUA, taped interview with Ruth Bullock by Sara Diamond, 1979.

52. For an introduction to the fashions of these decades see Jane Dorner, *Fashion in the Twenties & Thirties* (London: Ian Allan, 1973).

53. Beatrice M. Shaw, "The Age of Uninnocence," *Saturday Night* (May 24, 1919): 31.

54. See Isabel Dingman, "Your 'Teen Age' Daughter," *Chatelaine* (Oct. 1934): 19, 63.

55. See, for example, "Teaching Children," *Free Press Prairie Farmer* (Oct. 19, 1932): 4.

56. Margaret Prang, "'The Girl God Would Have Me Be': The Canadian Girls in Training," *Canadian Historical Review* (June 1985): 168–69.

57. TPL "Growing Up in a Small Ontario Town," *We Came to Thornhill*, Interview with Helen Elizabeth Coleman, pp. 31–32, New Horizons Project. See also Mary MacFarlane, "Recollections of A Wrinkled Radical," *Canadian Woman Studies* (Winter 1986): 98–99.

58. See, for example, "All Doctors Agree on Kotex," *Chatelaine* (March 1928): 65 and "Women are Turning to Modess . . . for Softness," ibid. (July 1930): 43. *Eaton's Catalogue* also offered a brandless sanitary towel and belt, see (Summer/Spring 1924): 285

59. See Johnson and Johnson's Ortho-Gynol for feminine hygiene in *Eaton's Catalogue* (Fall/Winter 1934–35): 222 and Wampole's Antiseptic Vaginal Cones in ibid. (Fall/Winter 1933–34): 204.

60. We can only guess at the number of these. The number of abortions, for example, is an uncertain guide at best. See Angus McLaren and Arlene Tigar McLaren, "Discoveries and Dissimulations: The Impact of Abortion Deaths on Maternal Mortality in British Columbia," *BC Studies* (Winter 1984–85): 3–26. See also the confirmation in a 1922 survey by the Canadian Social Hygiene Council that "Sex education was conspicuous by its absence." Ontario Provincial Archives, Pamphlet 1922, no. 55, Mildred Kensit, *Results of Survey of Venereal Disease Patients in Hospital Clinics in the City of Toronto During the Months of July and August* (1922), 9.

61. See Christina Simmons, "'Helping the Poorer Sisters': The Women of the Jost Mission, Halifax, 1905–1945" in *Rethinking Canada*.

62. Mrs. Nelson, "The City Creche," *Western Woman's Weekly* (Dec. 25, 1920): 10–11.

63. See Simmons, "'Helping the Poorer Sisters," 16. On the whole issue of the problems associated with private arrangements see Laura Climenko Johnson, *Taking Care* (Report of the Project Child Care Survey of Caregivers in Metropolitan Toronto, April 1978).

64. See Strong-Boag, "Intruders in the Nursery" on these schools. McGill's folded with the onset of the Great Depression while Toronto's exists today.

65. See PAC, Canadian Council on Social Development Papers, v. 43, folder 208, "Report of the B.C. Child Welfare Survey on the Children's Aid Society of Vancouver" [1927], typescript mimeograph.

66. On the difficult situation facing many immigrant children see Joy Parr, *Labouring Children* (Montreal: McGill-Queen's University Press, 1980).

67. On these developments see Patricia T. Rooke and R.L. Schnell, *Discarding the Asylum. From Child Rescue to the Welfare State in English Canada (1800–1950)* (New York: University Press of America, 1983), chap. 8.

68. Jean Archibald Hood, "Some Behaviour Problems and Their Treatment"(M.A. thesis, University of British Columbia, 1937), Case 15, pp. 27–28.

69. Quoted in Julie Cruickshank, *Athabaskan Women: Lives and Legends*, Canadian Ethnology Service Paper No. 57, National Museum of Man, Mercury Series (Ottawa: Queen's Printer, 1979), 9–10.

70. Barbara Riley, "Six Saucepans to One: Domestic Science vs. the Home in British Columbia 1900–1930" in *Not Just Pin Money: Selected Essays on the History of Women's Work in British Columbia*, edited by Barbara Latham and Roberta Pazdro (Victoria: Camosun College, 1984), 161.

71. "Food Carried In," *Free Press Prairie Farmer* (Oct. 16, 1935): 4. See also the editorial "The Daughter Who Stays Home," *Grain Growers' Guide* (Jan. 10, 1923): 43; "The Girl Who Stays Home," ibid., 12, 20; and Jean Barman, "Working Kids" in *Working Lives*, 121.

72. For an instructive discussion of child play see Neil Sutherland, "'Everyone Seemed Happy in Those Days': the Culture of Childhood in Vancouver Between the 1920s and the 1960s" (Working Paper of the Canadian Childhood History Project, March 1986).

73. On children's songs see Edith Fowke, *Ring Around the Moon* (Toronto: McClelland and Stewart, 1977) and *Sally Go Round the Sun* (Toronto: McClelland and Stewart, 1969).

74. See Michael Hayden, ed., *So Much to Do, So Little Time: The Writings of Hilda Neatby* (Vancouver: University of British Columbia Press, 1983).

75. TPLBR, Coleman, "Growing Up in a Small Ontario Town," 24.

76. "Lucille, That's My Dress" in *Ten Lost Years*.

77. A.M. Pratt, "Co-education? No!" *Maclean's* (Oct. 15, 1934): 16. See also G.E. Kingsford, "The System is Bad," *Saturday Night* (Oct. 27, 1934): 5; Willis J. Ballinger, "Does Education Help Women?" *Maclean's* (Nov. 1, 1932): 28; J.A. Lindsay, "Sex in Education," *Dalhousie Review* (July 1930): 147.

78. See, for example, the argument put forth in "Co-education," *McMaster University Monthly* (Feb. 1929): 202.

79. Nan Robins, "I Would Rather Have Beauty Than Brains," *Chatelaine* (Feb. 1931): 3.

80. See Robert Stamp, "Teaching Girls Their 'God Given Place in Life': The Introduction of Home Economics in the Schools," *Atlantis* (Spring 1977): 18–34 and Marta Danylewycz, Nadia Fahmy-Eid and Nicole Thivierge, "L'Enseignement ménager et les 'Home Economics' au Québec et en Ontario au début du 20e siècle: une analyse comparée" in *An Imperfect Past: Education and Society in Canadian History*, edited by J. Donald Wilson (Vancouver: Centre for the Study of Curriculum and Instruction University of British Columbia, 1984).

81. See Dolores Hayden, *The Grand Domestic Revolution: A History of Feminist Designs for American Homes, Neighborhoods, and Cities* (Cambridge, Mass.: The MIT Press, 1981).

82. British Columbia. *Public School Report* (1922), 52.

83. See ibid. (1919–40).

84. Riley, "Six Saucepans to One," 161.

85. Ibid., 176.

86. Ethel Chapman, "Household Science—The Oldest Profession for Women," *Maclean's* (Oct. 1919): 105.

87. Nancy S. Jackson and Jane S. Gaskell, "White Collar Vocationalism: The Rise of Commercial Education in Canada" (unpublished paper, 1986), 18.

88. Ibid., 19.

89. On the existence of a dual labour market see David M. Gordon, *Theories of Poverty and Underemployment: Orthodox, Radical, and Dual Labor Market Perspectives* (Lexington, Mass.: D.C. Heath, 1972); Richard C. Edwards, Michael Reich, and David M. Gordon, eds., *Labor Market Segmentation* (Lexington, Mass.: D.C. Heath, 1975); Marcia Freedman, *Labor Markets: Segments and Shelters* (Montclair, N.J.: Allanheld, Osmun, 1976); and Graham Lowe, "Women, Work and the Office: the Feminization of Clerical Occupations in Canada, 1901–1931" in *Rethinking Canada*.

90. On the Department of Secretarial Science see Margaret Pennell, "Interesting Canadian Women," *Canadian Magazine* (Aug. 1927): 29–33.

91. See Robert M. Stamp, "Canadian High Schools in the 1920s and 1930s: The Social Challenge to the Academic Tradition," Canadian Historical Association *Historical Papers* (1978), 79.

92. Jane Gaskell, "Education and Job Opportunities for Women: Patterns of Enrolment and Economic Returns" in *Women and the Canadian Labour Force*, edited by Naomi Hersom and Dorothy E. Smith (Ottawa: SSHRCC, 1982), 295.

93. See Lynne Marks, "Kale Meydelach or Shulamith Girls: Cultural Change and Continuity Among Jewish Parents and Daughters—A Case Study of Toronto Harbord Collegiate Institute in the 1920s," *Canadian Woman Studies* (Fall 1986): 85–89.

94. Gaskell, "Education and Job Opportunities for Women," 261.

95. Ibid., 267.

96. See Norman A. Williams, "Opportunity Classes in the Protestant Schools, Montreal," *School Progress* (Dec. 1938): 7–8.

97. G.S. Mundie, B.A., M.D., "Child Guidance Clinics," *Canadian Medical Association Journal* (June 1924): 508–11.

98. See Hood, "Some Behaviour Problems and Their Treatment,"

99. Ibid., Case 12, p. 23 and Case 14, pp. 26–27.

100. Indiana Matters, "Sinners or Sinned Against?: Historical Aspects of Female Juvenile Delinquency in British Columbia" in *Not Just Pin Money*, 269.

101. Ibid., 270.

102. "Rosary Hall, Toronto," *The Canadian League* (May 1923), 10.

103. Dorothy Livesay, *Right Hand Left Hand* (Erin, Ont.: Press Porcepic Ltd., 1977), 20 and passim.

104. Series W439–455, *Historical Statistics of Canada*.

105. On feminism and the maternalist ideology see Veronica Strong-Boag, "'Ever a Crusader': Nellie McClung, First-Wave Feminist" in *Rethinking Canada*, 181.

106. See Elsinore Macpherson, "Careers of Canadian University Women" (M.A. thesis, University of Toronto, 1920), 108.

107. A. Harriet Parsons, "Careers or Marriage?" *Canadian Home Journal* (June 1938): 63.

108. See A. Harriet Parsons, "Varsity or Work?" *Canadian Home Journal* (Aug. 1936): 10–11, 32–33.

109. Quoted in Anne Elizabeth Wilson, "Schools for the Home-Maker - #3," *Maclean's* (Nov. 15, 1927), 63.

110. Ursilla N. MacDonnell, "After University—What?" *Chatelaine* (June 1931): 14.

111. Paul Axelrod, "Moulding the Middle Class: Student Life at Dalhousie University in the 1930s," *Acadiensis* (Autumn 1985), 97.

112. "Woman Hater," *Free Press Prairie Farmer* (April 17, 1935): 6.

113. See Stephen Leacock, "The Woman Question" in *The Social Criticism of Stephen Leacock*, edited and introduced by Alan Bowker (Toronto: University of Toronto Press, 1973). See also the individuals mentioned in Axelrod, "Moulding the Middle Class" and the situation at the University of British Columbia for a slightly earlier period in Lee Stewart, "Women on Campus in British Columbia: Strategies for Survival, Years of War and Peace 1906–1920" in *Not Just Pin Money*.

114. "Women's Department," *McMaster University Monthly* (Oct. 1922), 28.

115. See Lee Jean Stewart, "The Experience of Women at the University of British Columbia, 1906–56" (M.A. thesis, University of British Columbia, 1986), 136–37, 156–57, note 43.

116. Revealingly, this quote was reproduced without editorial comment in a campaign to increase subscriptions to the largest professional history journal in the country in 1987. See the poster "The Canadian Historical Review" put out by the University of Toronto Press, 1987.

117. On the significance of the SCM for some young people see Stephen Endicott, *James G.: Rebel Out of China* (Toronto: University of Toronto Press, 1980).

118. Livesay, *Right Hand Left Hand*, passim.

119. Quoted in Margaret Street and Doris French, *Ask No Quarter: A Biography of Agnes Macphail* (Toronto: Doubleday, 1959), 30.

120. See Axelrod, "Moulding the Middle Class," 93 for a sensitive discussion of these limited opportunities.

121. Adele Wiseman, "Memoirs of a Book-Molesting Childhood," *Canadian Forum* (April 1986): 21–22. See also Mary MacFarlane, "Recollections of a Wrinkled Radical."

122. Wiseman, ibid., 24–25.

123. See the extraordinary efforts on behalf of Guides made by Monica Storrs as a missionary for the Fellowship, in W.L. Morton, ed., with the help of Vera Fast, *God's Galloping Girl: The Peace River Diaries of Monica Storrs, 1929–1931* (Vancouver: U.B.C. Press, 1979). See also IODE, *The Golden Jubilee: 1900–1950* (Toronto: IODE, 1950), 35–36 for a brief mention of the association with Guides and Brownies that lasted until 1946.

124. See Auxiliary Guides, *Policy, Rules and Orders* (1934), no. 11.

125. See *Rules, Policy and Orders* (1934): 42.

126. See Diana Pederson, "'Keeping Our Good Girls Good': The Young Women's Christian Association, 1870–1920" (M.A. thesis, Carleton University, 1981), 108. See also her "'Keeping Our Good Girls Good': The YWCA and the 'Girl Problem,' 1870–1930," *Canadian Woman Studies* (Winter 1986): 20–24.

127. For an assessment that is in general agreement with the critics see Bonnie MacQueen, "Domesticity and Discipline: The Girl Guides in British Columbia 1910–1943" in *Not Just Pin Money*.

128. Vancouver Girl Guides' Headquarters, clipping from the *Victoria Times* (March? 1926).

129. See VGGH, clipping "The Girl Guide Movement in Relation to Citizenship," Vancouver *Sun* (Nov. 6, 1925).

130. Prang, "'The Girl God Would Have Me Be'," 159.

131. Ibid., 163–64.

132. Ibid., 161.

133. Professor J.D. Ketchum, "Some Emotional Problems," *Canadian Guider* (Jan. 1937): 3.

134. See Rebecca Coulter, "The Working Young of Edmonton, 1921–1931," 158–59.

135. "Ten Years of Junior Red Cross," *The Junior* (Jan. 1935): 20–21.

136. See, for instance, Margaret Isabel Laurence, "The Time of Suffering," *The Junior* (April 1932): 19 with its portrayal of the Japanese as backward and pagan and Europeans as the vanguard of world civilization.

137. See, for instance, Louise Franklin Bache, "Christmas in Many Lands," *The Junior* (Dec. 1923): 6.

138. Gladys Robinsen, "How I Trained for Speed Skating—and Won Title," *Maclean's* (April 1, 1921): 62.

139. See David McDonald and Lauren Drewery, *For the Record: Canada's Greatest Women Athletes* (Toronto: Mes Associates, 1981).

140. Ibid., 10.

141. See "One of the Beginners," "Western Women Begin Athletics," *Western Home Monthly* (Sept. 1931): 26–27.

142. See Helen Lenskyj, "We Want to Play . . . We'll Play," *Canadian Woman Studies* (Spring 1983): 16, for an introduction to one Ontario team.

143. "Should Feminine Athletes be Restrained," *Saturday Night* (May 28, 1921): 36.

144. See Andy Lytle, "Girls Shouldn't Do It," *Chatelaine* (May 1933): 12.

145. Elmer W. Ferguson, "I Don't Like Amazon Athletes," *Maclean's* (Aug. 1, 1938): 9.

146. Ibid., 32.

147. Bobbie Rosenfeld, ". . . Girls Are in Sports for Good," *Chatelaine* (June 1933): 6–7, 29.

148. McDonald and Drewery, *For the Record*, 35–37.

149. "Eva Dawes on U.S.S.R.," *B.C. Workers' News* (Nov. 1, 1935): 2.

150. N. L. McClung, " 'I'll Never Tell My Age Again!!' " *Maclean's* (March 15, 1926): 15.

151. See "Marianne Morrow," *The Birth of Radio in Canada: Signing On* (Toronto: Doubleday, 1982), 44.

152. Stewart and French, *Ask No Quarter*, 39.

153. From Series T147–194, *Historical Statistics of Canada*.

154. A.N. Plumptre, "What Shall We Do With Our Flapper?" *Maclean's* (June 1, 1922): 64.

155. Mrs. Rip Van Winkle, "Flaming Youth Cools Off," *Chatelaine* (Aug. 1935): 16, 58–59. See also Judge J. McKinley, "Why Slander Youth?" ibid. (Nov. 1935): 10–11, 75.

CHAPTER 2
WORKING FOR PAY

For girls growing up in the interwar years, maturity was increasingly associated with paid work. Like their brothers, women came to expect to spend at least some of their adult life in the labour force. In unprecedented numbers they would come into direct contact with economic, social, and political forces external to but always having an impact on the family. Whereas the authority of male heads of households rested to a significant degree on their greater ability to operate autonomously outside the home, more and more women could now hope to match at least a part of that experience. In large measure, however, the issues of just how independent women were to be and how greater freedom was to be understood in the context of women's unique relationship with the family remained unsettled.

While the great majority of working-class girls had always helped with the domestic work in their own households, some in addition had long been accustomed to finding jobs outside the home as servants, seamstresses, and factory hands.[1] Traditionally too, most of these workers left waged labour when they married or when babies began to arrive. The demands of an impoverished domestic economy and a succession of pregnancies necessitated a heavy input of labour in the home. Women's responsibility for housework and child care, coupled with the reality of female wage rates, which were regularly only forty to sixty percent of those paid for comparable male labour, meant that women who wanted to add to the family income were most likely to take on tasks, such as sewing, baby-minding, and taking in boarders, that could be performed at home and that did not require hiring domestic substitutes. Rarely, if ever, were such money-making activities acknowledged in the census.[2] Only the very poor re-entered waged labour as mature women.

Since many families, such as a majority of those with adult males in hourly work in Montreal in the 1920s,[3] required two wage earners to survive, their standard of living was closely related to their stage in the life cycle. This commonplace situation was summed up vividly by one Calgary public health nurse in 1928:

> Over a period of twelve years it has been interesting to watch the development of some of these little homes. First we find them in small quarters daintily but inexpensively furnished showing their

> early ambitions for a comfortable home, then the little family
> comes along probably more frequently than they have antici-
> pated and with other reverses their early ambitions are tempo-
> rarily set aside in their zeal to keep their children healthy and
> happy, their little home becomes shabby and for a few years they
> struggle along, then the bigger ones commence to earn a little
> and once again they build up a home on a more substantial basis.
> Eventually they reach the time when they can indulge in a luxury,
> it is again interesting to watch the trend of their first extrava-
> gance, very often it is a trip back home but more frequently it is
> a musical instrument of some sort. . . .[4]

As this sympathetic observer noted, families with children who were too young for paid work and who needed some degree of care were especially likely to be in difficult circumstances. Those with no offspring or with older children able to contribute to the domestic economy were much better placed. In the years between school and marriage, working-class girls could make vital contributions to their parents' budgets through their labour as domestic servants, factory workers, sales clerks, and clerical employees. Segregated in relatively few blue- and white-collar employment ghettos, such wage earners often found their incomes too low to permit independent residence, a fact of life that helped to ensure that they, much more than their better-paid brothers, stuck close to home. There they could be both valued and exploited.

A newer phenomenon, although it originated in the nineteenth century, was the entry of middle-class girls into the paid labour market. Employed in large numbers first as teachers, nurses, and clerical help, they clustered in relatively few occupations and left their jobs upon marriage. The great majority would not enter paid employment again. Their situation, espe-cially with the expansion of the white-collar sector in the 1920s and the reports of female firsts in fields from accounting to gold-mining, initially looked promising enough. That optimism, however, would be hard put to withstand the attack upon women's right to "good" employments in the 1930s. Middle-class women who stayed in paid employment normally found themselves "dead-ended," even in the female professions. Like their working-class sisters, these women often maintained especially close ties with other family members, fulfilling the additional emotional and domes-tic duties that society was accustomed to ask first of its daughters, even when they worked outside the home, and only secondly of its sons.

The tendency of women to find employment in their youth and then to return to the domestic economy after some ten years or so is evident in table 1, which shows the breakdown of labour force participation rates by age. Higher school-leaving ages and the introduction of old age pensions, beginning in 1928 in British Columbia, helped reduce the number of very young and very old workers (although it should be remembered that work by these two groups was especially likely to go unreported in the census). Women commonly entered paid employments in their teens or twenties, with those aged between twenty and thirty-four years showing a significant increase in participation from 1921 to 1941. By World War II, a period of waged work was a familiar stage in the life cycle, occupying many young women of all classes in the years between the classroom and marriage.

TABLE 1
FEMALE LABOUR FORCE PARTICIPATION RATES, BY AGE

	10–13	14–19	20–24	25–34	35–64	65+	Total
1921	.3%	29.6%	39.8%	19.5%	12.0%	6.6%	17.7%
1931	.2%	26.5%	47.4%	24.4%	13.2%	6.2%	19.4%
1941	—	26.8%	46.9%	27.9%	15.2%	5.8%	22.9%

Source: Series D107–122, *Historical Statistics of Canada*, 2nd ed., edited by F.H. Leacy (Ottawa: Statistics Canada, 1983).

Women also made up an increasing proportion of an expanding total labour force during these decades—15.45 percent, or 490 150 workers, in 1921; 16.96 percent, or 665 859, in 1931; 19.85 percent, or 832 840, in 1941.[5] Even these figures tend to underestimate the extent of female employment. In the first place, the censuses of 1921 and 1931 occurred during depressions; many more women would have been found at work in 1927 or 1935, for example. In 1941, recovery was still incomplete from the downturn of 1937. When the war economy jumped into full-gear in 1941–42, female wage earners increased sharply in number.[6] Just as important as the timing of the census was its persistent failure to include certain categories of workers. Part-timers, whether hired regularly or seasonally, commonly escaped census-takers, as did women who worked in family businesses and on farms, as storekeepers, clerks, and labourers, in anticipation not only of room and board but of a share in the common profits of the enterprise.[7] Despite the problem of underenumeration, the clear rise in women's participation in the labour force, together with their age profile and their concentration in a limited number of occupations, reveal the evolution of a mature capitalist economy in which secondary industry and more particularly the tertiary service sector, both public and private, employed and depended on the availability of a large pool of relatively cheap female labour.[8] More so than ever before, the waged labour economy in Canada in the 1920s and 1930s cannot be understood without reference to women. Girls in general had come to expect some period of employment and employers had come to anticipate their availability.

After World War I there was considerable optimism about women's economic opportunities. The first major vocational texts devoted to young women sketched out promising futures. One author predicted that "the increasing opportunities of girls, both in home-making and paid employment, are likely to become a contributing factor in the humanizing of every form of industry." Benefits were more than merely altruistic, for "work well done" was portrayed as "a door-way to whatever good things [women] most desire."[9] Another job counsellor was also sanguine, although she was troubled enough by opposition to equality in the workplace to advise young Canadians to strengthen their resolve by modelling themselves on the "women who went before you, who toiled, hemmed in by the ever-lasting trees, who wearied in the loneliness by day, and shuddered at the howling of the wolves by night."[10]

Feminists remained acutely conscious of the importance of new economic opportunities in the 1920s and 1930s. They identified the limitations on and undervaluing of female labour as central to women's oppression by men[11] and pinned their hopes on a future in which "all woman's work must be paid for at a rate based on the quality and quantity of the work done, not on her sex."[12] They were to be disappointed. In the face of recurring widespread male unemployment and persisting misogynous critics, women were hard put, especially during the Great Depression, to advance the cause that feminists understood as central to their second-class status.

No assessment of female experience in the workplace could be complete without a review of the opposition to economic equality. While this strengthened appreciably during the 1930s to become something of a public debate, and undoubtedly won more support at this time, it surfaced regularly in the immediate post-World War I decade as well. Women's unequal treatment was common knowledge. One article in *Maclean's*, for instance, reflected soberly on the discrimination facing professional women:

> It is not, or at any rate, it is not mainly because a man can endure prolonged stress and the strain of which woman is incapable. In any profession a puny man has an enormous advantage over the strong and vigorous woman. The prime cause of her failure is the fact that she is obviously a woman. If she could disguise her sex and put on the outward semblance of a man she could double her success.[13]

In a letter to Irene Parlby, a former Alberta MLA, Violet McNaughton, women's editor of the *Western Producer*, discussed the unwillingness to advance women:

> The Canadian Women's Press Club feels quite strongly on this. . . . This is particularly true, I understand, of teachers' positions. . . . I'm told there is a rule . . . that promotion to the vice-principalship is based on seniority, but it is a rule that is not observed. A lady who for several years was a member of the school board in one of our cities [in Saskatchewan] told me of instances in which women who were obviously and logically in line for these positions were passed over for comparatively unknown men.
> I haven't any data on the business world except that one well-known business woman told me that promotion to the higher-paid positions seldom included women, even though they were obviously eligible, and we all know the bank rules regarding women.[14]

Neither competence nor seniority were, it seemed, to be guarantees of equality.

Anti-feminists, women and men alike, recited a litany of female sins in justifying discrimination. Working women were accused of lacking appropriate qualities—leadership, tolerance, seriousness, etc.—of undermining male dedication and opportunity—by everything from flirtation to low wages—and of needing only "pin money."[15] Abuse, often masquerading as humour, remained a staple of the popular and even the academic press. Much of the attack, especially in the 1930s, centred on married women. Although all female professionals were suspect, teachers emerged as a special object of calumny.[16]

Feminists were far from silent in the face of such assaults. They defended women's right to work and challenged the attack on female autonomy. Central to their defence was the argument of expediency: women worked because of economic need. Judge Helen Gregory MacGill, a prominent exponent of women's causes, was typical in pointing out that wage-earning women supported not only themselves but, in many instances, others as well and that their income helped keep entire families off relief.[17] A defence was also made on principle. Just as in the suffrage campaigns, feminists asserted "natural rights."[18] Put most simply, this insisted that "the issue to be faced is whether or not women shall be entitled, as individuals, to work for the sake of work itself."[19] Feminists employed both the expediency and natural rights justifications, although the former had practical appeal that few realists could resist.

Indeed, women's champions often got right down to brass tacks. The trade unionist and Vancouver alderman Helena Gutteridge, for instance, opposed the barring of married women from city employment with the sharp reminder:

> Let's let all this sentimental bosh go by and get down to facts. . . .
> Nobody ever objected to women scrubbing floors or bending
> over a washboard. This business of placing women on a pedestal
> is one of the oldest yarns I've heard. Men only object to women
> working when they start earning money. . . . Madame Curie
> would never have discovered radium if women had been barred
> from work. . . . As for the amount of work which would be pro-
> vided if married women retired from the labour market, why it
> wouldn't amount to the snap of a finger. It's a very plausible red
> herring in this question.[20]

In the country's newspapers, women far from the public spotlight and sympathetic to the opinions of Gutteridge and other feminists also joined in this debate. One representative writer to the *Free Press Prairie Farmer* attacked a male contributor who had pilloried female teachers. She pointed out that most men had scrupulously avoided this profession before the Depression: salaries were too low. Now they were trying to put women out of their traditional jobs. She urged female teachers not to budge:

> And I say girls, if ever you have a chance to get out and earn
> money do so and not sit at home and let a man take your place.
> Because if you get married you can be independent and not have
> to ask your man for every cent you would like to spend on a
> good magazine or home paper.[21]

Such grass-roots supporters regularly bolstered the campaigns, not to mention the morale, of feminist champions.

The most famous exchange in this public argument occurred in 1933 between Mederic Martin, former mayor of Montreal, and Agnes Macphail, MP, in *Chatelaine*, the major women's magazine of these decades. Martin blamed women for male unemployment and recommended legislating them out of work, asking,

> Wouldn't national life be happier, saner, safer if a great many of
> these men [the unemployed] could be given work now being
> done by women, even if it meant that these women would have
> to sacrifice their financial independence? go home to be sup-
> ported by father, husband, or brother as they were in the old
> pre-feministic days?[22]

The feisty former teacher from Grey County responded in the next issue.[23] Taking her antediluvian opponent from fiction to reality in a few deft phrases, she noted that homes and families were very far from being the potential havens he envisioned. Much of women's traditional work had left the home with industrialization and now provided paid work for men. In taking waged employment, women were doing what they could to ensure the survival of themselves and their families. For male unemployment, the agrarian radical faulted not women but the economic system itself.

Despite these protests and surveys, such as one conducted in 1928 among three hundred married stenographers and secretaries in Toronto that showed a substantial majority at work because of need,[24] women regularly encountered restrictions in employment. Governments were some of the worst offenders. Those in power in Manitoba, for example, argued that most married women did "not need to work" and would not hire them in the 1930s.[25] This policy of the prairie province had influential precedents and allies in administrations at all levels across the Dominion. Pressed by MPs such as J. Eugene Tetreault who thundered ". . . in times of depression we certainly should give preference to the married man who has a wife and family to support,"[26] the federal government rigorously pursued discrimination in the civil service in the 1920s and 1930s.[27]

A preference for men combined with overall belt tightening to produce tragic results, as in the case of one laid-off stenographer who appealed to Prime Minister Bennett in 1931:

> I was in the Department of Public Works, Secretary's Branch,
> from June 21st, 1930 to March 20, 1931. Since then I have not
> been able to secure work anywhere, although I have tried very
> hard. . . .

> I am a widow with three children to support, and as they are
> very young and all going to school it strikes me very hard. The
> eldest is 11 years and the youngest 7 years.
> I am up against it now, the merchants have closed my accounts
> because I was unable to pay them last month, that means I will
> starve as I charged my groceries.[28]

The ruthlessness with which women were hounded from employments
and scapegoated for men's loss of jobs suggests how much many Canadians, both female and male,[29] had invested in ideas about family, home,
and women's place. For such individuals, as Alice Kessler-Harris has suggested with respect to the United States in the same years, waged work
was not a human right but "a gender-based privilege."[30] Yet, if feminist
hopes for major advances on the economic front were stymied, the Great
Depression, with all the efforts it saw to drive out female labour, finally
proved that women could not be herded home again. Despite fears about
their presence, they were in the workforce to stay.[31] Not only did women's
obvious need for paid work rally sympathizers, but the structure of the
labour market itself was such that there was a wide range of employments
that everyone agreed they ought not to be hounded from, that men in fact
would not do.

Whatever their individual hopes and prospects for security in marriage,
women survived, and even prospered, through flexibility and initiative in
seeking cash incomes. This was nothing new. Initial investigations by
mothers' pensions commissions suggested that single parents, for instance,
had long showed remarkable ingenuity in keeping families together.[32] As
recipients of the state assistance that became available in the 1920s and
1930s, sole-support mothers still found themselves compelled to piece
together a minimum budget. Poverty posed a special threat to groups
barred in law or practice from whatever largesse public charity had to offer.
They learned not to look beyond their own resources. A Chinese widow,
Anna Ma, left with nine young children in Toronto in the 1930s, rented
out rooms, grew vegetables, and worked for the Presbyterian Church. In
desperate avoidance of a request for relief that might jeopardize their right
to stay in Canada, the family "ate fish heads for a long time."[33]

Even when husbands were present and industrious, wives' economic
contributions frequently remained essential. Such was the case with many
family businesses. Toronto's Macedonian women, for instance, typically
assisted storekeeper, barber, shoeshine parlour operator, and restauranteur
husbands with essential day-to-day tasks.[34] Female labours could mean survival, as was the case with a Nova Scotia fishing and farming couple in the
1930s. Refused bank credit, the demoralized husband was contemplating
disaster when his wife, largely without his help, mobilized the children to
offer Sunday fish dinners. Thanks to their efforts, the family prospered. As
one child later concluded, "I've heard this kind of story about the Thirties
over and over, how the women took over. It must have made the men
feel lowly, but the women took over."[35]

Women could be extremely sensitive to the threat to male morale. In both the 1920s and 1930s, advertisements for the Auto-Knitter, a machine whose purchase permitted the homemaker to contribute to family finances through piecework while remaining relatively invisible as a wage earner, directly addressed this anxiety. In one typical full-page ad, a young couple was depicted as having a hard time making ends meet but the husband's pride would not allow his wife to "work." That plucky woman solved his and her dilemma, and paid their bills, by making socks to sell to the Auto-Knitter Hosiery Company in West Toronto.[36] Although it is impossible to know for certain how widespread such home industries were, they were common enough to receive regular press attention. Whether it was with money from socks, or eggs, or cheese,[37] or indeed more formal employment, a resourceful woman could make the difference between comfort and penury for her family.[38]

Initiative began early. Working-class daughters regularly entered paid employment at fourteen. During a decade of waged work before marriage, girls often took it for granted that they would make a significant contribution to family income.[39] One 1920 study of 356 school drop-outs in Toronto revealed that 37.4 percent left because of economic necessity. Two-thirds of these were assessed as

> cases where a critical point had been reached in the development of the family and the eldest child at school had to help out. The size of the family, irregularity of work for the breadwinner, the decease or ill-health of one parent, the presence of a delicate or crippled child, were the main factors.[40]

An English-born fifteen-year-old hired by a candy factory at $9.00 a week became a wage earner because it was "customary in her family" to leave school early.[41] The daughter's pay envelope was handed over, unopened, to her mother who divided the proceeds between the girl and the family exchequer.[42] Although there were exceptions, this contribution appears widespread, especially among younger workers. As one Jewish immigrant from Poland explained, "I was under the impression that when you live at home and get along with your family and work, what you earn you bring home and then you get what you need and the rest is for the family need."[43]

When children entered the stage when they might become producers rather than merely consumers of resources, families could benefit significantly. Socialized to a greater sensitivity to domestic relationships, and despite the fact that their brothers regularly earned more, girls of all classes were especially susceptible to the economic claims of family.[44] They might very well continue to contribute to their parents' support long after they married or expected to marry.[45] As the old saying went, "A son is yours until he weds; a daughter is yours forever."

For all the incentives to leave work upon marriage, not all married women wished to or could leave paid employment. General economic uncertainty, low male wages, and hopes for a better life in general always drove some to search out a second income. A monograph on housing prepared for the 1931 census pointed to the importance of such "supplementary wage-earners in the earnings structure" of "normal" families, that is those with male breadwinners. Their contribution was essential if decent housing was to be obtained.[46] Irene Berezowski, who immigrated to Edmonton from the Ukraine in 1930, for instance, knew full well that her marriage three years later did not bring any release from twelve-hour days of paid domestic labour for a family of twelve.[47] Yet not all jobs were held purely out of grim necessity. Social workers were amazed to find that "for some women, 'going out to work' has an attraction; it is a diversion as it were from the drab existence in their own lives." One client put it this way, "she had worked since she was fifteen and she just could not remain home."[48] Such enthusiasm infected women of all classes. Professionals such as Dorothy Livesay became "depressed" when forced to give up employments that brought income and contact with the community.[49] Even for radicals such as Livesay and the CCF pioneer Grace Woodsworth MacInnis,[50] it was difficult to know how to combine marriage and a family with life in the paid labour force.

Women, wives among them, sometimes clung to jobs with incredible tenacity, using a variety of strategies to counter the social disapproval engendered by their paid labour. Two arguments were especially prevalent. One insisted on the supposedly "feminine" nature of the employment. Teaching, nursing, and domestic service, for instance, were jobs that Canadians were willing to acknowledge as particularly women's preserve. The second argument was more idiosyncratic, depending on the supposed ability of singular individuals to maintain feminine attributes despite contact with so-called masculine employments. The latter was the case with a married newspaper columnist. A sympathizer explained that,

> As a rule, women are not employed on the advertising staff of a newspaper. The work is too strenuous, too nerve-racking. . . . Yet in spite of a multiplicity of business contacts, one could not find a more completely feminine type of woman than Mary Baker. "I'm afraid I'm quite incurably domestic," is how she describes herself. . . . Mrs. Baker manages to keep serene and retain the womanly characteristics of the most stay-at-home daughter of Eve. Were you to meet her, not knowing of her vocation, her gentle, even shy air, quiet low voice and calm expression would probably make you exclaim, "Now, there's a real home woman."[51]

As this example indicates, women seeking to retain non-traditional employments found considerable incentive to display styles and behaviours appropriate to their sex. Such acquiescence, for the most part probably unconscious, made life easier for them while simultaneously helping to camouflage the contradictions of a labour market that was segmented first on the basis of sex and only later on the basis of inclination and talent. Whatever the particular public rationale espoused by individual married women in the workforce, the reality suggests that many valued their independence and resisted, in every way they could, efforts to oust them from employment. Necessity and inclination helped create a situation in which contemporaries had increasingly to question the old assumption that women had always to be regarded as short-term employees.[52]

Demonstrate, as some might, their attachment to the paid labour force, married women did not in return easily lay down any domestic responsibilities. Husbands did not readily change their ways. Even when unemployed, they might "loaf" at home waiting for their wives to return from work to "do it all."[53] Daughters soon learned that paid work did not free them, as it largely did their brothers, from domestic tasks. They knew before they married that opportunities for rest, reflection, and leisure came only after household duties were performed. Once wedded, work outside the home, for whatever reason, meant that they held down two full-time jobs. Such a double shift demanded the uppermost in stamina and application. Sympathizers recognized that "Only a Super-Woman Can Juggle Both a Family and a Career."[54] To some extent, to be sure, the more well-to-do could buy themselves out of this predicament with servants and modern technology, but the vast majority had no such options. It was this reality, just as much as misogynous opposition, that encouraged married women to leave the paid work force as soon as it was financially feasible. Even so, their numbers increased from 7.19 percent of the female labour force in 1921, to 10.03 percent in 1931, and to 10.26 percent in 1941.

Once the decision to seek employment had been made, women, like their male counterparts, turned first to familiar and, frequently, family resources. For many this meant jobs at home. The "putting out" system of subcontracting enrolled large numbers of home workers. Housebound girls and women laboured at piecework rates, especially in the clothing industry, able to add to cash incomes while still carrying out domestic duties.[55] News of openings in local homes, restaurants, shops, or factories also spread through family networks, and applicants might well be sponsored by friends and relatives.[56] The sense of familiarity was reinforced when industries such as textiles and baking, for example, regularly hired several family members.[57] Even when it was necessary to leave home to locate employment, as happened with two clerical workers from small-town Ontario who moved to Montreal in the 1930s, relatives might well reside together or keep in constant touch.[58] Such contacts were important in making the transition between home and paid workplace less intimidating.

In the 1920s, vocational advice from schools, magazines, and private and public employment bureaus increasingly augmented older informal networks. In 1918, the Employment Service of Canada opened up "a national network of labour exchanges" to succeed the sporadic efforts previously made only by Quebec and Ontario.[59] The arrival of the agrarian Progressives in Ottawa in 1921, with their resistance to programs that might enhance the urban labour market and thus make farm labour still more difficult to recruit, eventually helped doom this federal initiative, but women were not in any case well served. Government bureaus did little more than direct them to domestic service, an unpalatable option to most female job-seekers. Not uncommonly, like young unemployed factory workers in Hamilton in the 1920s, they "registered for housework" but intended "to return to their trades when an opportunity arose."[60] Girls and women in search of duties more congenial than domestic labour applied regularly to commercial agencies run by typewriter companies such as Underwood's and searched out individual employers. In both the 1920s and 1930s, however, as high school commercial programs, normal schools, and hospital training schools prepared large number of graduates, there were likely to be more applicants than jobs. The results could be disastrous. In the 1930s, one Edmonton "five and dime" made this discovery in advertising for salesgirls. Hundreds of applicants joined "a line going down the block and around it." The outcome was a riot for, as it happened, only three vacancies.[61]

The chronic problem of oversupply that afflicted female job-seekers in both decades was a direct response to their ghettoization in relatively few employments, so that there were in reality two separate labour markets distinguished by sex. This dual or segmented labour market meant that there was in effect little competition between men and women for the same jobs. Certain employments were labelled by virtue of their "skill and educational requirements, working conditions, and salary levels" as appropriate or inappropriate for each sex.[62] In helping to sex-type occupations, employers were able to keep wages low and truncate mobility for a substantial part of their work force. In the process, new management positions and better salaries were made possible for male principals, hospital superintendents, sales managers, office supervisors, and factory foremen. Entry into the male labour market, whether as managers within female ghettos or as workers of any type within male-dominated industries, was nowhere a possibility for the vast majority of female job-seekers.[63]

While men were widely dispersed over a broad range of industrial groups, women were heavily concentrated in far fewer, with 70.9 percent of women in only six of the twenty-five categories covered by the census — textiles and clothing, retail and wholesale trade, education, health and welfare services, food and lodging, and personal and recreational services — in 1921, 73.20 percent in 1931, and 71.98 percent in 1941.

Women's ghettoization during these years becomes still more evident in examining their distribution by occupational group. Most women were employed as factory hands and small shop assemblers, clerks and salespeople, teachers and nurses, servants and waitresses, and typists and secretaries. The Great Depression retarded the long-term decline in personal service, especially domestic service, slowed the growth of the professional and clerical sectors, and slightly accentuated the long drop in the number in manufacturing and mechanical occupations. Finally, however, it had

TABLE 2

FEMALE WORK FORCE BY INDUSTRIAL CATEGORY, AND PERCENTAGE OF WORK FORCE,
1921 TO 1941

Category	1921 No.	1921 %	1931 No.	1931 %	1941 No.	1941 %
Total	490 150	15.5	665 859	16.9	832 840	19.9
Agriculture	17 912	1.7	24 255	2.2	19 146	1.8
Forestry	7	.02	243	.5	479	.5
Fishing & trapping	395	1.2	508	1.1	369	.7
Coal mining	64	.2	73	.2	78	.3
Other mining	139	.7	282	.7	506	.8
Food, beverage, & tobacco manufacturing	11 343	18.5	17 693	17.1	21 133	19.4
Leather & rubber products	7 027	23.7	9 842	25.2	13 840	29.9
Textiles & clothing	58 332	59.2	61 737	51.1	83 004	52.1
Wood products, paper, & publishing	10 242	7.9	14 607	9.6	18 489	10.3
Metal products, machinery & transport equipment	6 251	4.5	11 311	5.9	30 558	8.9
Chemical, petroleum, & non-metallic mineral products	2 930	10.8	4 342	10.1	8 851	14.6
Other & unspecified manufacturing	9 754	21.5	2 895	18.2	6 022	26.5
Electricity & gas	619	5.9	1 752	7.8	1 955	8.5
Construction	578	.3	1 576	.6	1 489	.01
Railway transport	5 303	3.9	5 025	3.6	3 931	3.1
Other transport	15 831	13.8	17 628	12.9	15 824	11.4
Retail & wholesale trade	61 335	18.7	85 394	20.1	112 104	22.6
Finance, insurance, & real estate	15 218	24.8	24 965	27.0	28 369	31.6
Education	57 031	73.2	71 291	70.7	75 074	67.7
Health & welfare services	47 720	67.7	52 864	66.6	63 814	69.5
Food & lodging	22 884	39.4	48 766	45.6	62 008	51.5
Personal & recreational services	100 213	70.5	167 365	70.7	203 440	77.2
Other services	6 578	10.5	22 210	25.8	29 429	32.2
Government	12 583	12.9	15 514	13.3	28 002	20.1
Industry unspecified	19 850	14.7	3 721	2.2	4 926	10.7

Source: Series D8–85, *Historical Statistics of Canada*, 2nd ed., edited by F.H. Leacy (Ottawa: Statistics Canada, 1983).

TABLE 3
DISTRIBUTION OF THE FEMALE LABOUR FORCE BY OCCUPATIONAL GROUP, 1921-41

	1921		1931		1941	
	No.*	%	No.*	%	No.*	%
All Occupations	489	100.0	665	100.0	832	100.0
Agriculture	17	3.7	24	3.6	18	2.3
Manufacturing	89	18.3	101	15.2	148	17.8
Transportation	14	3.0	17	2.7	16	2.0
Trade/Finance	47	9.8	56	8.5	74	8.9
Professional	92	19.0	118	17.6	127	15.3
Personal service	132	27.1	227	34.3	288	34.7
Clerical	90	18.5	117	17.5	154	18.6

* Thousands of workers.
Source: John H. Thompson with Allen Seager, *Canada 1922–1939: Decades of Discord* (Toronto: McClelland and Stewart, 1985), table XIb.

limited impact on patterns that were becoming obvious in the first twenty years of the twentieth century. The majority of women continued to work in a range of occupations that was distinctly different from men's.

First ghettoized by gender, female workers' choices were further restricted by the effects of class. For the daughters of many working-class Canadians, jobs meant personal service and blue-collar occupations. If they were among the growing numbers of poorer folk who were fortunate enough to possess a high school diploma, their prospects were more likely in these decades to include clerical and sales employments as well. These "pink-collar" occupations also attracted middle-class applicants who lacked professional qualifications but whose dress, demeanour, and language had for some time made them suitable secretaries, bank stenographers, and salesclerks. Girls and women possessing the resources and the ability to take extended periods of professional training tended to find jobs in "female" professions such as nursing, teaching, social work, home economics, and library science. Only the most intrepid and well-armed penetrated such male monopolies as medicine, law, engineering, and theology.

In addition, individual occupational groups developed their own hierarchies, different levels of which might recruit from somewhat different classes. Private secretaries and stenographers headed the clerical field, calling on specialized skills and offering higher prestige and salaries. In nursing, the division between private, institutional, and public health practitioners often meant much in terms of training, working conditions, wages, and aspirations. Teaching too was internally stratified by the fact that recruits from very different socio-economic origins could enter the profession from high schools, normal schools, or universities. The less qualified were more likely to teach lower grades and in smaller schools, although the increased penetration of this profession by males in these decades meant that its upper rungs were effectively closed to female applicants of any class.

Personal service, containing as it did domestic servants, was the oldest and the largest of female occupational groups. It was also among the most assiduously avoided and the lowest in status.[64] World War I continued a long-standing trend away from domestic service by the native-born.[65] After the armistice in 1918, contemporaries believed that new skills together with "the possession of fairly substantial bank accounts as a result of war work, [and] the great increase in the number of marriages subsequent to the return of the troops" added to "the disinclination to turn to an occupation whose social standing is erroneously rated below that of factory work."[66] Distaste, however, gave way before necessity. The growth in the personal service sector in the 1920s and 1930s reflected the straitened condition of the economy in much of the interwar period.[67] As domestics, waitresses, laundresses, and hairdressers, women encountered traditionally small work units, low productivity, non-standardized conditions, and unregulated authority. Since such occupations stressed health and stamina, workers by and large had little need for formal schooling. Not only did such jobs attract the poorly educated, they also enlisted both the youngest and oldest of paid workers—those presumably whose skills or power might be least and whose need and vulnerability greatest.[68] A heavy immigrant makeup helped lower these occupations' prestige within the working woman's world. By 1931, for example, 64.44 percent of all gainfully-employed Central European women and 70.43 percent of Eastern European women toiled as domestics.

Between 1921 and 1931, the number of general servants or maids-of-all-work jumped from 78 118 to 134 043. Much of this gain was due to the especially severe economic crisis of 1931, although 1921 was also depressed. Only when unemployment was widespread or need otherwise desperate did workers turn to personal service. For those with limited resources it offered the promise of housing and feeding children. The Employment Bureau of Toronto, for instance, noticed that women regularly sought "positions where they can take a child . . . [even] two or sometimes three children."[69] When affordable accommodation was scarce, even the chance that one might either bunk "with the children or [have] a makeshift place to sleep"[70] was better than the alternative on the street. The persistence of domestic openings, however unsatisfactory, meant that such service operated as the unemployment insurance of the poor. Few with alternatives stayed on. The reaction of twelve White Russian refugees placed as domestics in Ottawa would have been unremarkable but that five were "aristocrats." Ontario's Employment Service had to report that "within two months only two remained in domestic service."[71] Notably, none of the "ladies" stayed; all fled to Toronto and a department store.

When they could not escape domestic service, women tried to obtain either day work or employment other than in a private home. In particular, the great majority resisted "living-in" with all the control and supervision this entailed. For all the ingenuity of governments in promoting domestic service (an effort they made for no other industry to the same degree),[72] women voiced familiar grievances. Relatively unchanged from the nineteenth century were "the long hours and the lack of freedom." Servants remained "the only class of labour who continue to work, not from seven to seven but often from seven to nine or ten o'clock with only every other Sunday afternoon off."[73] Long hours were aggravated by lack of privacy, poor accommodation, and low status—in a word, dependence. The situation was worsened by the special threat of sexual harassment. As one woman who worked as a domestic in the 1930s remembered, you were very lucky if "you didn't have the men in the family after you as well."[74] Vulnerability to sexual exploitation, along with loneliness and low pay, made domestic service too often a recruiting ground for prostitution.[75]

Recurring efforts by well-intentioned, if sometimes self-serving, reformers to modernize the occupation through emphasis on professional conduct and sound training, as with "The Nine-Point Plan" proposed by the Economic Relations Committee of the YWCA in 1934, always floundered.[76] Still more radical proposals such as those for a forty-eight hour week and a minimum wage coming from the Houseworkers' Union of Toronto, an organization affiliated with the labour movement in the 1930s, encountered fierce opposition from middle-class householders.[77] The popular evaluation of housework as women's work, therefore meriting low pay and prestige, shipwrecked every scheme, ensuring that even the Great Depression could not permanently reverse the long decline in the percentage of women employed as servants.

Restaurant dining proliferated along with Canadian cities in these years. By the 1920s women were commonly finding employment as waitresses, cooks, and kitchen help in this highly competitive field, especially in smaller establishments. On occasion, lower-wage women displaced male waiters.[78] Like domestic service, hours were long and pace uneven with precise conditions fluctuating unpredictably from one business to another.[79] Meals, often eaten on the run, were generally provided by the establishment and gratuities were essential to survival. The variability of this tip income added immeasurably to the instability of the employment. Conditions were also extremely difficult to monitor as Minimum Wage Boards across the country found in both the 1920s and 1930s. The abuse of wage and hour regulations by Regina's Elite, Depot, and Zenith cafes in the 1920s were typical.[80] The Depot Cafe, for instance, worked four women "from 8 a.m. to 8 p.m. with 2 hours off during the afternoon for a seven day week. . . . Three of them receive[d] $50 per month with board and one received $40 with board. The minimum wage for a 56 hour week" was "$53 per month with board."[81] Waitresses could also be sexually vulnerable as one unemployed graduate of Edmonton Commercial College discovered. This nineteen-year-old found that "getting screwed" by a "most objectionable little creep," who happened to be the owner, was "part of the job."[82] In league with another former employee she soon found a way to make the boss pay for his pleasure but, as she reflected years later, "I never said anything, that's how badly my family needed the money. It kept us alive. My poor mother, she would have died."[83] Nevertheless, while waitresses were often at the mercy of supervisors, skills could be quickly acquired and jobs, even in the worst years, were frequently available. They also had, as servants rarely did, contact with a world of equals as well as bosses.[84] Alliances, such as that between the two Edmonton girls above, offered at least some prospect of alleviating otherwise intolerable conditions.

Women did not predominate in manufacturing as they did in personal service. Nonetheless, it too remained a major employer in certain centres. In Toronto, for example, 29.6 percent and 23.8 percent of the female labour force worked in this sector in 1921 and 1931 respectively. In Winnipeg in the same years the figures were 14.2 percent and 10.4 percent. There were also single-industry mill towns, like Paris, Ontario, whose major employer, Penman's hosiery and knit goods, drew overwhelmingly on female recruits, offering little else to women and little at all to men.[85] Low-wage, highly competitive industries such as clothing, but also textiles, shoes, and food processing, had hired relatively large numbers of women and girls for many years, but higher wage, capital intensive, often monopolistic firms engaged in the production of such commodities as automobiles, electrical machinery, farm equipment, and liquor, had little, if any, room for them. This ghettoization occurred despite women's experience in munitions during the First World War. With the armistice, some skilled women workers were "attracted by the work on farm implements at the Massey-Harris firm,"[86] but hope for decent money and secure positions in heavy industry soon fell victim to economic collapse, persisting discrimination, and the needs of returning veterans. Women who had taken "men's jobs" for the war found themselves assessed as having "lost some . . . charm in doing work that helped to win the war and releasing men for more important jobs. . . . [The women were] spoiled . . . in doing it."[87]

The dual labour market meant not only the exclusion of women from entire areas of production but often their segregation into distinct operations within individual industries. In clothing, for instance, women were generally barred from the most skilled and well-paid work, earning as was common in most industrial categories some forty to sixty percent of a male wage. Even when it was difficult to appreciate the difference of expertise or effort involved, as in pocketmaking (male) and buttonhole sewing (female) in the ready-made clothing industry, one could still be sure of substantial wage differences.[88] What Gail Cuthbert Brandt has demonstrated with regard to the Quebec cotton industry was characteristic of the manufacturing sector in general: the "gender identification of specific jobs could vary" over time, but "a gender hierarchy" giving the "highest ranking production positions in terms of status, authority, and monetary rewards" to men remained constant.[89]

Not surprisingly, female apprenticeship, when it existed, was short. Neither bosses nor unions nor governments were willing to invest much in a labour force that they perpetually identified as short-term and limited in ability. Furthermore, bosses did not just designate women as short-term labour; they designated as women's jobs those without possibilities of advancement, without benefits, and with no incentive to stay. The result ensured that the secondary labour market staffed by women would operate at the lowest possible cost to the employer.

Since so little was invested in their training, women were especially vulnerable to layoffs. Once out of work, however, their low wages, plus the feeling that hiring men "implied a more permanent commitment," gave women certain advantages in finding jobs, especially when bad times occurred simultaneously with deskilling in industries.[90] This happened in 1921 in Vancouver when new cigar-making machinery permitted employers to switch from more expensive men to cheaper women and children.[91] Ironically enough, the introduction of women's minimum wage laws sometimes failed to protect female employees. In Quebec's cotton mills, for instance, employers replaced women with men and boys whose wages were unregulated. The implications of technological innovation for the gender identification of the labour force were nowhere cast in stone. While the combination of French-Canadian Catholic conservative values and technological change in Quebec's cotton goods industry reduced women's job options in these years, Ontario's knit goods industry had no difficulty accepting both new technology and a heavily female work force.

Wherever it occurred, the installation of more up-to-date equipment was also accompanied by a general speed-up. Typically, Edmonton's Great West Garment Company installed "special two needle machines" in 1929 and was able both to cut staff and maintain production levels.[92] Closely related to speed-up in manufacturing were piecework and bonuses. Neither policy was unheard of earlier, but they appear to have been taken up with a vengeance in the 1920s and 1930s as a way of reducing costs of production in highly competitive industries.[93] Piecework, characteristic of subcontracting in home industries, often followed women into the factory. Paid by unit of production rather than by time, quicker workers earned the most. Rates, however, were regularly moved downward so that it took more effort to earn the same amount. Bonuses were closely associated with the piecework system. They were used to bring up wages that were so dismal they could not meet even the low requirements of the Minimum Wage Boards. A thrifty employer could keep piece rates at a level that, even if he gave bonuses to all employees, was cheaper than bringing rates up to where fast workers could earn far above the minimum. Bonuses also carried the especially insidious connotation that women did not really merit even a minimum wage; they had to be subsidized by a "generous" employer.[94] Cut-throat tactics were not limited to fly-by-night or smaller firms. Even the Eatons, with their much publicized on-the-job "philanthropy," did not hesitate to take advantage of clothing trades workers. One long-time employee of the merchandising giant contrasted her situation in the 1930s with what she had first encountered in 1916:

> Well, things were not so easy for us. We could not make our dresses and things quite so comfortably. We were not looked after quite so well; we didn't have the same help, and around 1929, 1930 and 1931 the wages were cut and cut and cut . . . and then, of course, they began to use the speeding up system. . . . I cannot say when the stop watch began exactly; I think that began in 1933. But . . . we were badgered and harassed and worried.[95]

Stress was especially acute since those who could not still make the minimum wage of $12.50 a week at the lower rates were liable to be let go.

In contrast, some manufacturing workers met a relatively firm demand for their labour throughout both decades. In the 1920s, the Penman's Company of Paris, Ontario, for example, was regularly unable to meet its needs except by bringing in new recruits from elsewhere in Canada and the hosiery districts of England. Protected by high tariffs, the knitted goods industry was also shielded from the worst impact of the Great Depression. The wages of women who worked, from an early age and often throughout marriage, in the mills remained a dependable mainstay of family income. Not surprisingly, Paris was known as a "good place for women."[96]

Women's relatively strong bargaining position in the Paris mills—mothers could work flexible hours and foremen were especially cautious about exerting their authority—was not, however, the norm. Elsewhere, where employers could find ready substitutes for recalcitrant employees, industrial wage earners more often than not found themselves facing abysmal conditions. Factory environments were a case in point. The construction of modern premises and the remodelling of older establishments had improved safety, ventilation, and sanitation somewhat since the abuses uncovered by the 1889 Report of the Royal Commission on the Relations of Labour and Capital, but numerous dangers went uncorrected. The 1938 Report of the Royal Commission on the Textile Industry, a notorious employer of large numbers of women and children, condemned the heat, humidity, gases, and dust that left in their wake chronic coughs and worse.[97] Safer conditions sprang from unrelated developments. Two popular fashions, bobbed hair and short skirts, freed workers in certain industries from being scalped or pulled into machinery.[98] In some factories, the introduction of individual motors with their elimination of overhead belting also helped do away with a cause of earlier accidents. Despite the possibility of improvement, workers had to be vigilant. As government investigators regularly discovered, employers often objected to "modern safety equipment being placed on their machines, fearing it will retard production."[99] Accidents remained a normal feature of working life.

Industrial hygiene was similarly lamentable. The 1920 Nova Scotian commission investigating women's working conditions branded firms with a typical indictment:

> The toilets in a great many factories should be condemned. It would appear in many cases, as if the management thought it a waste of room to give up to toilets a greater space than four or five feet square, even for the use of a large number of employees. Frequently they were found to be dirty, ill ventilated, indifferently lighted, and . . . toilets for women, instead of being entirely separate, were found to be entered directly from the factory and separated from the men's toilet by only a thin wooden partition.[100]

The survival of such conditions well into the 1930s made a laughingstock of government regulations respecting sanitary facilities.

Yet, for all the failings of factories, they remained preferable to the home labour that continued to be so much a feature of clothing manufacture in particular.[101] Throughout these decades, provincial inspectors observed that increasing amounts of work were escaping supervision by being sub-contracted either to small middlemen or to the individual homeworker. Not all operations abandoned the factory. A subcontracting workman could employ others to help him in the plant, but they never appeared on the factory payroll nor received the official minimum wage. The majority of subcontracting was, however, removed from the factory into more unsatisfactory premises. A "family group of foreign origin who baste and hem around the kitchen stove"[102] might recall pre-industrial patterns, but exploitation was right up-to-date. Although sheltered from critical eyes of strange foremen, workers also lost whatever limited protection the law or a union might offer. Sweatshops survived because they were "an ideal arrangement of course from the employers' viewpoint as it is much cheaper labour and at the same time saved him factory space and the purchase of extra sewing machines."[103]

The shortcomings of domestic service and manufacturing made job-seekers all the readier to explore options in the expanding white-collar sector. Between 1921 and 1941, women's proportion of all clerical and sales workers rose from 32.8 percent to 40.5 percent and their numbers from 127 863 to 210 012.[104] These employees were a mix of working-class girls newly armed with high school diplomas and their middle-class sisters whose families were long familiar with white-collar occupations. Where previously post-elementary education had prepared young middle-class males for employment as clerks, a first step on the ladder to eventual managerial responsibility, twentieth-century commercial life had changed dramatically. The white-collar labour force was increasingly feminized, drawn from a broader sector of society, and no longer normally on a career path of advancement into senior administration.[105] The emergence of large offices and powerful retailers created a new pool of repetitive, subordinate employments into which women were directed.

Female applicants may have commanded lower salaries but, as Bell Telephone discovered in its shift to women operators in the nineteenth century, their manners and demeanour were especially suited to dealing with clients.[106] Well-spoken and polite, they helped Canadian governments and companies put their best foot forward. As the following recommendation indicates, girls were left in little doubt about their role in the sexual politics of the office:

> Don't expect all the men to fall in love with you—but don't forget that a man's a man in business as well as out of it—and appearance and graciousness count. If you possess that wonderful thing called Personality, take it with you into the office. The average man in business is quite susceptible to a well-groomed, refined appearance.[107]

Faced with such instructions, it was difficult for girls to avoid the conclusion that the office was yet one more arena in which courtship, and thus eventually marriage, women's ultimate vocation, might be pursued.

Male management reaped special rewards from this role differentiation. In charting their way to modern employments, women readily transferred domestic skills to the new work situation. As one critic noted, if they weren't wives "in their own homes, looking after their husbands' buttons and meals, they practically are in downtown offices, looking after the details of men's business affairs."[108] The highly personal nature of many relationships between bosses and white-collar workers helped make such employments especially palatable to women normally socialized to place especially high value on human contact. And yet there were dangers as well. One postwar counsellor admitted that philandering bosses could be a problem. Her only advice was tact and polite disapproval, followed by resignation from the employment. In effect, she admitted women's powerlessness in the face of sexual harassment.[109] Pretty faces and courteous manners were double-edged assets.

Disturbing signs of the limitations of white-collar employments had appeared well before the armistice. A 1914 survey of four Winnipeg department stores reported, depending on the time of the year, between 2 432 and 3 200 female employees, yet not one female department head. In most cases assistant buyer was the most senior position open to women. One of these stores explicitly prohibited female managers.[110] Five years later, there was little improvement. The journalist Marjory MacMurchy had to advise high school students that, although it was occasionally possible to move to the headship of a department "and in somewhat rare cases to become a buyer," prospects for promotion were almost non-existent.[111]

To be sure, there were exceptions to the rule, and these were sometimes hailed as harbingers of better things. The first female president of a store chain, in surveying postwar Canadian merchandising, foretold great things for women. Noting that some 90 percent of shopping was done by women, she concluded that women would "prove to be the best buyers and executive heads in the long run." Practical experience and, in some instances, college degrees, Mrs. Emma Almy was confident, would permit other women to match her accomplishments.[112] Yet, while individual success stories never disappeared in these decades, men continued to dominate commerce's upper rungs. The example of the pioneering Mrs. Almy was not nearly as prophetic as the discrimination encountered by bond saleswomen during the Victory Loan Campaigns of World War I. Barred from early participation in the issue's most profitable stages, they were called in at the last moment to canvas telephone girls, who, as the female brokers knew full well, did not offer the potential of much profit. The men had already tapped the most profitable share of the bond market.[113]

Opportunities for industry and ambition were little, if any, better in the smaller notion stores where, "though there are from four to five times as many women and girls as men and boys, . . . the position of management is seldom open to women."[114] Chances for promotion were best in areas clearly marked as fields of female expertise such as millinery and notions. Here, almost alone, female managers could be found. Other sectors of the retail trade were much the same. Self-service grocery chains such as Loblaws of Toronto and Carroll's of Hamilton discriminated as a matter of course as did drug store chains like G. Tamblyn Company and Louis K. Liggett of Toronto. Retailers of every description justified failure to give female staffers greater responsibility by referring to their alleged lack of "independence of thought."[115] The prevailing unwillingness to recognize or reward female ability led to women in trade occupations receiving, on average, forty-four percent of male salaries in 1921 and forty percent in 1931.[116] Meagre rewards and hard work soon caused the observant to dismiss long-term prospects in merchandising. One former salesclerk voiced not uncommon sentiments, even if she put them perhaps rather excessively, "Girls used to marry fellows they didn't even care for, to be free of Eaton's."[117]

Clerical employments, with their long history of respectability and opportunities for promotion, held many of the same attractions as sales. However, there were more applicants than openings for such positions. In 1920, for instance, the Toronto office of the Employment Service lamented that "the sign of the armistice had its effects upon the clerical . . . situation. The closing of many offices left a great number of stenographers and clerks without positions."[118] Oversupply continued into the 1930s as private and public schools competed in turning out graduates. The problem of too many workers chasing too few jobs was all the more permanent a phenomenon because women were relegated to the lowest ranks of business and government. Although journalist Marjory MacMurchy advised that "the girl who is a college grad is not too well equipped to be a stenographer,"[119] even superior qualifications did not guarantee promotion. The inauguration of a degree course in secretarial science at the

University of Western Ontario in the mid-1920s illustrated how even the college-educated were expected to limit their horizons.[120]

The federal government harboured typical reservations about its female clericals. While they had enlisted in its ranks by the 1870s, World War I brought a great influx of women into the "inside" service in Ottawa. There were well-publicized examples of promotion into administrative positions: Edna L. Inglis, who had joined the civil service in 1903 and was highly dedicated to her career with the federal government, foresaw in 1921 "a great future for women" in its service.[121] Such hopes were quickly shattered. The rapid expansion in the number of female clerks sparked alarm lest they disrupt male recruitment to the higher levels of the service. Traditional stereotypes were brandished to justify restrictions on women's "unseemly" progress.[122] Ottawa went so far as to institutionalize discrimination in allowing the Civil Service Commission to set job competitions on the basis of sex in 1918. Male veterans did not have to worry that women would take "their" jobs.[123] Ottawa's policy of equal pay for equal work, in place since the inauguration of a federal civil service, was meaningless because women were never offered equal opportunities. In 1921, equality was still further undercut by stringent regulations on the hiring of married women. They could keep posts only if a real need for their particular services could be proven, a rather dubious proposition in any recession. "Lucky" working wives were rehired as new and temporary appointees, sacrificing all former seniority and receiving the minimum wage rate in their classification. The number of women in federal and provincial employment in Ottawa dropped 13.2 percent from 4 296 in 1921 to 3 729 in 1931. It is unlikely that this decline was due solely to severe economic conditions since the number of male civil servants climbed from 6 080 in 1921 to 6 466 ten years later, a gain of 6.5 percent.

Even when they could find openings, typists and clerks increasingly encountered regimes that bore a marked resemblance to those in industrial establishments. Office workers too experienced speed-up, unpaid overtime, long hours, and fines.[124] Typists in larger firms sat "chained to [their] . . . desk[s] in a stuffy office, taking down endless letters which inevitably begin, 'In answer to yours of the first instant. . . ,' " only to emerge at the endof the day "too tired to do anything except crawl home, have some supper, and go to bed."[125] The radical poet, Dorothy Livesay, put it this way:

> I sit and hammer melodies
> Upon the keys; the snappy tunes
> Go pounding down the room; O quick
> My girl! Yessir, and click click click,
>
> She's at it harder still, the fear
> Like rigid tentacles, like arms
> Gripping her back; a wave of heat
> Must be fought down, the lips drawn in

And faster faster, Sir, we have
Your letter of the fifteenth instant
How do you like my harmonies
Better than jazz dear Sir, click click.

Better than jazz and kisses are
The pounding minutes, nickels, dimes
The dancing whirling hours, the fear
The keys, quick, quick, the fear! [126]

Jazz-age white-collar jobs might be cleaner, less dangerous, and somewhat better paid than their blue-collar predecessors, but they turned out to be no harbingers of equality or justice in the work place.

In the nineteenth century, feminist hopes for a more egalitarian future had rested in large measure with women's entrance into professions. In Canada, as elsewhere in North America and Europe, women quickly came to dominate teaching and nursing, with home economics, library science, and social work emerging slowly as alternative female professions. Teachers and nurses were the majority and the archetypical female professionals. In their concentration in the lower strata of increasingly hierarchical educational and health systems, their dependence on the public purse, and their difficulty in enforcing professional standards, they were extremely vulnerable to low wages, poor working conditions, and male supervision. In the 1920s and 1930s, women saw an occasional first but, in general, they could not break men's long monopoly in medicine, law, politics, theology, and the military nor find a place in newer scientific professions such as engineering, forestry, architecture, and veterinary medicine. Nor was it always easy to maintain even the status quo. Married women teachers came under considerable pressure to give up their positions. Hospital-trained nurses were hard pressed to defend their jobs against competitors. The special qualifications of social work professionals were ignored by cost-cutting public officials.

Female teachers had been in the majority since the mid-nineteenth century,[127] and education continued to be highly recommended as a career for girls. For many young women who wished respectable employment and enjoyed children, teaching offered a prized opportunity for some independence and challenge. Since schools varied tremendously in the qualifications they required and could afford, parents and candidates might invest anything from a little to a lot in preparations for a teaching post. As a result, the profession included members with everything from a few years of secondary education to postgraduate degrees. Differences in training helped account for variations in salary, status, and position among women but more remarkable was the fact that similarly qualified men inevitably found themselves more senior and well-paid. In 1927, for example, the average salary of female teachers with a first class certificate in Prince Edward Island was $648 compared to the male wage of $793. In Nova Scotia, women with class A certificates got $816 and men received $1 357.

In New Brunswick, a first class certificate earned women an average of $944 and men $1 259. Precise differences varied but they existed in every province.[128] Such favouritism to male professionals helped make teaching a stepping stone for many women to matrimony or other professions.

Aspiring teachers graduated in such numbers during these decades that it was not uncommon for some to scour the country for employment. In the mid-1920s, one eighteen-year-old, with a second class certificate from Nova Scotia, discovered that Ontario offered no opportunities for the inexperienced and travelled by colonist coach to an Alberta school that had thirteen children enrolled. There the good behaviour of her pupils helped compensate for other discomforts. As she remembered that first winter, "For days we never removed our galoshes, coats or sweaters and I always wore my mitts to write on the board."[129] Material conditions tended to be better in favoured positions in urban centres, but school boards everywhere were reluctant or unable to raise sufficient funds to make teaching anything but a profession requiring considerable physical and mental stamina.

Dedication was especially tested during the Great Depression. One Saskatchewan girl recalled her rural school with its books "in tatters." She and her class eagerly consulted *Eaton's Catalogue* as a text for reading and spelling.[130] Another resourceful young woman turned her hand to feeding hungry students:

> We had a big black stove at the back of the room that the boys kept clean and lit every morning and I got one of those big blue enamel pans . . . and every morning about 10:30 I'd start porridge. Crushed oats, raisins, prunes which you could buy for practically nothing, grated cheese which was cheap and onions I could get by just asking for them. Everything would go into the pot with the water and one big tin of condensed milk and there would be this tiny, black-haired teacher standing back at the stove about 11:30 every morning instead of being at the front of the room and stirring with a spoon I'd whittled from a poplar stick and calling out the lessons. "All right, Grade Fives, turn to page 26 and do two pages because I've got some questions to ask you." That sort of thing. It worked.
>
> The kids had their own bowls and spoons and they'd clean up the pan and I even got those who had brought lunches to share with the others, a communal sort of thing, and everything went well.[131]

Dealing with impoverished pupils was no novelty, but the 1930s found teachers, often victims themselves of reduced salaries and worsened conditions, all the more often on the front line against social misery.

For all its shortcomings, teaching had no trouble in finding recruits. Despite warnings, such as those by lecturers in social work, public health, journalism, and business to Queen's female undergraduates in 1926, to turn to less competitive fields,[132] women clung to this traditional career. What counsellors failed to note was that, so long as women were particularly socialized to see their futures as involving children and were restricted to a few sex-labelled employments, the problem of over-crowding was bound to remain. Finally, neither opposition to their presence nor a host of rivals succeeded in driving women from a profession that many needed to survive and many loved.

Women's position in nursing was less a subject of debate in these years, in part because the female-male hierarchy was more highly institutionalized. It was largely taken for granted that women's special qualities of nurturance, patience, and obedience were well exercised in nursing under the supervision of a male medical profession. Even so, as the institution in the 1920s of a two-week course for training attendants or practical nurses by the Montreal YWCA indicated,[133] graduate nurses (those trained and certified in hospitals) had regularly to defend their claim to professional status. Faced with chronic unemployment among private duty nurses in particular, organizations like the Association of Registered Nurses of Quebec recognized full well the threat posed by initiatives like the Y's "subsidiary nurse workers."[134] Yet nursing professionals' determination to win support for a monopoly position comparable to that of doctors ran head on into the desire to reduce health care costs to a minimum, the need of relatively untrained women for respectable employment, and widespread assumptions that any competent woman could assist the ill.[135] The need of the untrained for employment was the predicament, for instance, of two applicants to the program of the Montreal Y. Wrote one, "I have been thinking seriously of late of training for to be a nurse [and] for some reason I cannot take a General Hospital three year course as I mean I cannot afford it."[136] Another voiced somewhat different concerns: "I am fifty years of age and very healthy, I taught school for five years and have been married a number of years. There is a great demand these days for nurses but so many people are not able to pay the fee that the regular nurses ask."[137] The competition of such applicants in the private duty field was especially worrying to graduate nurses. For such nurses, alternative employments in public health care were not only relatively limited but generally required additional training. Moreover, hospitals that might have provided positions preferred the cheap labour of their own nursing students.

Distinctions among private duty, public health, and hospital nurses were fundamental in shaping women's experience of the profession.[138] Private nurses, long the majority of graduates but steadily declining in numbers in these decades, had the advantage in good times of being their own bosses, of picking and choosing among employments. They were also especially vulnerable to instability of demand. Public health nurses, such as those in the Victorian Order of Nurses, were likely to have both more training and more security of employment. The creation in the 1920s of special programs in public health nursing at the Universities of Toronto and British Columbia confirmed the professional pre-eminence of this group. In hospitals, graduates had long been hard pressed to compete with trainees. Nevertheless, as more specialized equipment such as X-ray machines and procedures such as blood transfusions increasingly entered public institutions, as the costs of housing students rose, and as licensing bodies such as the American Hospitals' Association demanded higher standards of nursing staff, the number of graduate nurses employed in institutions such as Vancouver General Hospital increased.[139]

Despite the chronic problem of oversupply between the wars, the shifting character of nursing brought significant improvements in conditions and salaries. The 1932 *Survey of Nursing Education in Canada* portrayed an occupation that had come a long way since the nineteenth century in raising standards of training and employment. Much remained to be done, but outstanding leaders such as Ethel Johns of the Winnipeg Children's Hospital, Vancouver General, and the University of British Columbia,[140] Eunice Dyke, first superintendent of Public Health Nursing in Toronto's Department of Public Health,[141] and Charlotte Hannington, chief superintendent of the Victorian Order of Nurses,[142] gave nursing extraordinary leadership in these years. Their heroic example was a powerful inspiration to many young women. It helped recruits cope with long hours, heavy work, and poor pay. Indeed, in the deadly days before the introduction of sulfa drugs in the late 1930s, illness and even death were the special companions of nurses. Practitioners were particularly susceptible to contagious diseases of all types, notably tuberculosis, diptheria, and typhoid, and many student nurses left their programs dangerously weakened in health. On the front line of the battle against illness, nursing was perhaps the most physically demanding of the female professions.

Education and health care engaged the largest number of female professionals but home economics, library science, and social work had also emerged as "suitable" employments.[143] University programs were producing graduates in the latter three areas by the 1920s and in each case the overwhelming predominance of students was female. Social work, responding to the expansion of public and private social services, was the largest of these new women's professions. Trained caseworkers, led by pioneers such as Charlotte Whitton, director of the Canadian Council on Child Welfare from 1920 to 1941,[144] replaced married women volunteers who had long staffed the nation's charitable and social service institutions.

In a way remarkably similar to nurses in the nineteenth century, the first generation of social workers defined "a professional field for themselves, linked closely to women's traditional nurturing identity."[145] This was not the only similarity. By the 1920s, many in social work's female majority understood that gender was more important than training or experience in guaranteeing good jobs and salaries. As delegates to a social work conference in Ottawa were reminded, "equal pay for equal work is a principle which is recognized but not practised."[146] Despite the fact that "women constituted over two-thirds of all social welfare workers in Canada before 1941 and over 84 percent of the professionally-trained membership,"[147] men were overwhelmingly preferred for senior offices. The fact that marriage pretty much required an end to paid professional work, as was the case for Dorothy Livesay, also kept a large pool of experienced women from moving into executive positions. Nor was women's claim to professional expertise secure. Cost-conscious administrations were just as likely to believe that family casework could be done quite well by "nice motherly volunteers" or even done away with altogether. The firing of forty female social workers employed by Ottawa's Public Welfare Board in 1936 and their replacement by eleven male detectives demonstrated the vulnerability of the female professions.[148] When it came to paying for expertise, whether it be in education, medicine, or social work, communities were still susceptible to the belief that men could do a better job and that, if women were necessary, their professional training was not. To some degree, the problem of credibility affected all the female professions in these years.

And yet individual women's credibility was no greater in professions in which they were a minority. Although female doctors, police officers, accountants, veterinarians, ministers, psychologists, coroners, lawyers, engineers, forest rangers, film directors, university instructors, dentists, publishers, pilots, and undertakers were frequently mentioned in the periodical literature of the 1920s, and never entirely disappeared even in the 1930s, they were never more than a meagre, if resourceful, handful.[149] Some particular combination of good fortune and talent equipped a few women to withstand a broad range of disincentives, from quotas in medical schools to a film projectors' union for men only in the case of a "directress." Survivors like Lydia Gruchy, who in 1936 became the first woman ordained by the United Church,[150] gave hope to some ambitious little girls. But an intrepid few could not demolish patriarchal structures that flourished—albeit with somewhat greater covertness—even after initial feminist assaults. Defenders of male privilege could pretend that it was not so much lack of opportunity as lack of character and ability that explained women's inferior position in the world outside the home. Women like the Toronto sculptor Merle, originally Muriel, Foster, whose new androgynous name had, she well recognized, its "advantage in business,"[151] developed numerous ways of coping with resistance, but it is hard not to wonder how much more they could have achieved if they had not had to dissipate energy in justifying their existence.

One last category of female workers defied every attempt at enumeration. Unlike all the occupations above, prostitution was recommended by no one, except, of course, pimps. Women such as the teenage "Miss X," who in loneliness and poverty took to turning tricks in Edmonton in 1929,[152] were the target of numerous campaigns but little real assistance. Reports on Canadian women deported from the United States in 1939 illustrate the desperate situation of prostitutes. Gertrude, born in 1908, was first jailed at 17. Hilda, born in 1915, bore "scars on both sides of [her] lower right forearm; [she had] several front teeth missing, [and the] balance of front teeth blackened." Vera, born in 1913, had been suffering from syphilis for at least five years. Elizabeth, born in 1918, had been under the supervision of the Toronto Children's Aid Society since age ten. Jeannette, born in 1916, had as a child been committed to a reformatory by her mother.[153] Such women paid in hard coin for whatever good times and easy money came their way. Eventually, some would vanish from the public record and make the transition to respectable homemaker. As the experience of one Winnipeg widow with three children who was forced to prostitute herself to a relief investigator in the 1930s suggests,[154] the line separating "decent working folk" from their "fallen sisters" was only too easy to cross, for shorter or longer periods, when times were bad.

Employments of every kind had their shortcomings, but it was unemployment that women feared most. With themselves and others to feed, few working women could afford to go without wages for any length of time. And yet seasonal layoffs characterized many blue- and white-collar employments. As one 1916 Ontario commission on unemployment observed, strategies were developed to cope with just such eventualities:

> There is a certain amount of interchange between women's seasonal employments. The woman factory operator often becomes a waitress in a summer hotel, and women teachers are sometimes engaged in picking fruit in the summer.[155]

Such initiatives worked best for single women and, even then, they presumed a generally prosperous economy. Just as frequently, women were hard put to find alternatives, especially ones with decent conditions and pay. In the days before unemployment insurance, the Great Depression only worsened an already chronic problem. No wonder, as YWCA workers in charge of city residences understood, girls lived in "constant terror" of being without employment.[156]

Yet, because the female unemployed appeared to pose no threat to public order, at least not in the sense of directly threatening capitalism, their predicament was largely ignored by governments. As women's defender, Agnes Macphail, put it in Parliament in 1936:

> Often in listening to the debates in this chamber I have thought that we have a pretty masculine society, and at no time am I so impressed with that condition as when we are dealing with unemployment. A great deal has been said and written in times past about the "weaker sex." If men are not capable of taking care of themselves during periods of stress and unemployment, does parliament think women are more capable of taking care of themselves? If they are not, what provisions has the government made, or what provision does it propose to make for single, unemployed women?[157]

The answer, as the agrarian feminist knew, was little indeed. Relief from local governments was inadequate and sometimes absent altogether, and isolated federal initiatives like the Dominion-Provincial Youth Training Program introduced in 1937 directed women relentlessly and finally fruitlessly to domestic service.[158] The state's response to female need was not to provide opportunities for independence, but to affirm women's dependence and subordination within the political and the domestic economies.

There is plenty of evidence that women understood and even resented their vulnerability in the waged labour market. For some, more desperate, more politically sophisticated, or just luckier, the solution was organization. Even domestic workers, lacking all the advantages of the traditional artisanal crafts that had permitted men to co-operate against employers, made regular, if short-lived, attempts to organize in both the 1920s and the 1930s.[159] White-collar workers and professionals formed mutual aid societies, such as the Commercial Girls' Club of Winnipeg, founded in 1931,[160] the Saskatoon Women Teachers' Association, formed in 1918,[161] and the Ontario Federation of Women Teachers' Associations, also established in 1918,[162] that, despite their often heated resistance to identification with unions, signalled an emerging self-consciousness of women's position in the labour force. It was, however, among blue-collar women that collective action was most common. The records of the federal Department of Labour and its publication, the *Labour Gazette*, are filled with instances of collaboration among waitresses, laundry workers, telephone operators, bookbinders, and cigar-makers.

Female activism was especially visible among garment and textile workers. Confronted with persisting attempts by employers to increase piecework, hours, and speed, and to undermine wages, conditions, and co-operative action, women, bolstered in some instances by such unions as the International Ladies' Garment Workers, the Amalgamated Clothing Workers of America, and the Industrial Union of the Needle Trades Workers, took to the picket lines in both decades.[163] Their actions were not without success, especially in the late 1930s. The hard-fought contests between labour and capital, between craft and industrial and Canadian and international unions, and between the Co-operative Commonwealth Federation and the Communist Party for the loyalty of workers provided experiences crucial for female unionists. Shopfloor activists in the left-wing Industrial Union of the Needle Trades, for example, showed what could be achieved when there was a significant effort to engage women's loyalties.[164] These years produced a generation of outstanding public figures, like Madeleine Parent of the United Textile Workers of America and Becky Buhay and Annie Buller of the Communist Party, whose lives were devoted to the cause of workers. Less visible women laboured quietly on the shopfloor, learning lessons that contributed to the strengthening of the labour movement during the Great Depression and the Second World War. Like the young women who attempted to join the Great Trek to Ottawa in 1937 in protest against unemployment, and the Vancouver telephone operators who stayed out during the General Strike of 1919, ordinary labourers were contributing to a collective history that would eventually generate a new consciousness of women's capacity for radical action.[165]

Yet for all their enhanced union involvement, low-paid women, tied to domestic duties, without a long tradition of organization, and often with only limited help from established unions, could only make small gains. Too frequently, male-run unions distrusted female workers as dangerous low-wage competitors and weak members. Unions' unwillingness to promote female leaders, and their persisting indifference or hostility to issues that touched women workers most directly, notably equal pay for equal work, helped ensure that many industrial women would look elsewhere for solutions to the problems of the workplace.

To be sure, governments, especially in the 1920s, did usher in legislative initiatives such as minimum wage laws that appeared to promise some protection. Right from the onset, however, benefits could be uncertain. Laws requiring companies to make special provisions for female workers or barring women from certain hours of employment both nourished the notion that women were inferior employees, and therefore worth less, and handicapped women in their competition with male workers. Whatever promise legislation offered was further undermined by appointed officials who, for all their good intentions, often feared to offend powerful business interests, and by the wiliness of offenders of every kind, from small hairdressing concerns to department store giants like Eaton's, the Hudson's Bay Company, and the Robert Simpson Company.[166] Other official initiatives bore still less fruit. British Columbia, under pressure from an influential feminist lobby led in the provincial legislature by Mary Ellen Smith, went so far in the 1920s as to introduce acts suggested by the League of Nations' International Labour Office. These, including "one forbidding night work for women except in family business, another forbidding night work for people under the age of eighteen, and a third setting the minimum age for industrial employment at fourteen for boys and fifteen for girls,"[167] were never proclaimed, awaiting as they did similar legislation by other provinces. The state, even when well-intentioned, was at best an uncertain protector. While wages and conditions were somewhat improved in some industries, it is also clear that the principle of a living wage for women was never accepted by most legislators and employers.

In the 1920s and 1930s it was more likely than ever that women would spend some part of their lives in the paid work force. There they would have opportunities to form the non-familial associations and attachments that had long linked male workers directly to larger economic, social, and political forces. Men's traditionally closer contact with institutions such as businesses, unions, and governments, not to mention saloons, hotels, and clubs, had allowed them to claim to mediate on behalf of the less experienced female part of the population. Though often critically restricted, as with the jobs and the clubs they could not enter, by the 1920s more women than ever before could gain access to sources of information and influence external to the family. They could also collaborate in unions and professional associations and in the workplace itself with other women. In the joys and the sorrows of these exchanges, female workers learned more about themselves, other women, and the place of their sex in Canadian society. Whereas exploitation and a second-class status could more easily be obscured or ignored or conceived of as a purely personal problem within the context of the family, it was more difficult, although never impossible, to deny the blatant contradictions between the ideology of democratic capitalism and the reality of one sex's subordination in a segmented labour market. The initial optimism associated with white-collar and professional employments and the impact on women and men alike of the Great Depression and the Second World War, however, postponed recognition of and handicapped challenges to the sexual politics of the labour market. These would come later. In these decades most women preferred to counteract the dissatisfactions of public life by attempting to construct fulfilling private worlds with spouses, families, and friends.

NOTES

1. For a discussion of some of these employments see Susan Mann Trofimenkoff, "One Hundred and Two Muffled Voices: Canada's Industrial Women in the 1880s" in *Rethinking Canada: The Promise of Women's History*, edited by Veronica Strong-Boag and Anita Clair Fellman (Toronto: Copp Clark Pitman, 1986).

2. For a discussion of the integration of paid work into the family home see Veronica Strong-Boag, "Keeping House in God's Country: Canadian Women at Work in the Home" in *On the Job: Confronting the Labour Process in Canada*, edited by Craig Heron and Robert Storey (Kingston and Montreal: McGill-Queen's University Press, 1985). For the importance of a wife's contribution and the problem of underreporting in an earlier period see also Bettina Bradbury, "Women and Wage Labour in a Period of Transition: Montreal, 1861–1881," *Histoire sociale/Social History* (May 1984): 115–31.

3. Terry Copp, *The Anatomy of Poverty* (Toronto: McClelland and Stewart, 1974), 31.

4. Glenbow, Papers of the Victorian Order of Nurses . . . Calgary, Box 1, *Annual Report* (1928), handwritten.

5. From Series D8–85, *Historical Statistics of Canada*, 2nd ed., edited by F.E. Leacy (Ottawa: Statistics Canada, 1983).

6. Ruth Roach Pierson, *"They're Still Women After All": The Second World War and Canadian Womanhood* (Toronto: McClelland and Stewart, 1986), 9.

7. On the problem of under-reporting see Bradbury, "Women and Labour," especially 124, note 31.

8. For an important discussion of this phenomenon see Graham Lowe, "Women, Work and the Office: The Feminization of Clerical Occupations in Canada, 1901–1931" in *Rethinking Canada*, and his "The Administrative Revolution in the Canadian Office: An Overview" in *Work in the Canadian Context*, edited by K. Lundy and B. Warme (Scarborough, Ont.: Butterworths, 1981).

9. Marjory MacMurchy, *The Canadian Girl at Work. A Book of Vocational Guidance* (Toronto: Thomas Nelson and Sons, 1920), vi and 1.

10. Ellen M. Knox, *The Girl of the New Day* (Toronto: McClelland and Stewart, 1919), 5.

11. On this aspect of feminism in the interwar years see Veronica Strong-Boag, "Pulling in Double Harness or Hauling a Double Load: Women, Work and Feminism on the Canadian Prairies," *Journal of Canadian Studies* (Fall 1986): 32–52.

12. Constance Lynd, "Women's Independence for the Sake of the Race," *Woman's Century* (Oct. 1919): 16.

13. "Prejudice Retards Women," *Maclean's* (Feb. 1, 1922): 38.

14. SAB, Violet MacNaughton Papers, box 32, folder 52(2), MacNaughton to Irene Parlby, Nov. 22, 1938.

15. See F.E. Bailey, "Women Bring Too Much Sex into Business," *Chatelaine* (July 1930): 5, 41; Arthur P. Woollacott, "Is the School-Marm a Menace?" *Maclean's* (Dec. 1, 1936): 19, 44, 46; Amy Bowman, "Mirandy and Elevator," *Saturday Night* (May 3, 1919): 6; Mona E. Clark, "Are Brains a Handicap to a Woman?" *Canadian Magazine* (Feb. 1928): 27; Frank Bunce, "You're the Boss," *Chatelaine* (Sep. 1936): 8, a fictional telling of the same tale; Mona Clark, "A Woman in Business is Still at Heart a Woman," *Canadian Magazine* (Jan. 1928): 27; Marjorie Elliot Wilkins, "Women and their Homes," *Saturday Night* (May 15, 1937): 32; "Women Don't Change," *Saturday Night* (July 1, 1939), front page editorial; see the accusation referred to in Mary Aikman, "The Nature of Women's Employment" (M.A. thesis, McGill University, 1937, 22; "Women in Medicine . . . say Men," *The Canadian Doctor* (April 1936): 12, 35–37; Jean Graham, "The Woman

Employee and the Canadian Bank," *Journal of the Canadian Bankers' Association* (July 1919): 363–69; "Jobs for Wives?" *Maclean's* (Oct. 1, 1939): 50; *Report* of the First Annual Provincial Convention of the Women's Social Credit Auxiliaries to the Alberta Social Credit League (1939), 19; W.S. Press, "Should Women Earn Pin Money?" *Maclean's* (April 1, 1930): 60; Maude Petitt Hill, "Should Women and Men in the Same Profession Marry?" *Chatelaine* (June 1930): 8; Harriet Parsons, "Youth Replies," *Canadian Home Journal* (June 1936): 45–64. One prominent observer of Canada in these years concluded that there existed "a strong Canadian prejudice against women in the professions, re-inforced by an almost universal belief that no woman should keep up her work after marriage." J.B. Brebner, "Canadianism," *Canadian Historical Association Report* (1940): 13.

16. This seems also to have been the case in the U.S., a reflection of the visibility of this part of the female work force in both countries. On the U.S. see especially Lois Scharf, *To Work and To Wed: Female Employment, Feminism and the Great Depression* (Westport, Conn.: Greenwood Press, 1980), chap. 4.

17. See MacGill, "What of the Wage-earning Wife?" *Chatelaine* (March 1930): 9; "The Jobless Women," *Chatelaine* (Sept. 1930): 5; and "Married Women and School Teachers," *Western Home Monthly* (Sept. 1925): 25, 49, 50. See also Cora Hind, "Quiet Hour," *Western Home Monthly* (Jan. 1922): 31, 36; Harriet Parsons, "Can Youth Afford to Marry?" *Canadian Home Journal* (May 1936): 14–15, 45, 47.

18. For a discussion of these two arguments in the Canadian context see Veronica Strong-Boag, "'Ever a Crusader': Nellie McClung First-Wave Feminist" in *Rethinking Canada*. For initial formulation of the distinction, in the case of the U.S. in particular, see Aileen Kraditor, *The Ideas of the Woman Suffrage Movement, 1890–1920* (New York: Norton, 1981).

19. Gwethalyn Graham, "Women, Are They Human?" *Canadian Forum* (Dec. 1936): 22. See also the thrust of the argument by Nellie McClung, "Can a Woman Raise a Family and Have a Career" (1927) reproduced in *Manitoba History* (July 1984): 32–34.

20. Quoted in Susan Walsh, "Equality, Emancipation and a More Just World: Leading Women in the B.C. CCF" (M.A. thesis, Simon Fraser University, 1983), 108.

21. "Women Worked Then," *Free Press Prairie Farmer* (July 6, 1932): 4. On men taking women's work see also "The Broad View," ibid., 4.

22. Mederic Martin, "Go Home Young Woman," *Chatelaine* (Sept. 1933): 10.

23. Agnes Macphail, "Go Home Young Woman? Ha! Ha!" *Chatelaine* (Oct. 1933): 13, 53. For support for her point of view see the letters to the editor, "Can You Shackle Woman Again?" ibid. (Nov. 1933): 26, 44.

24. Lydia M. Parsons, "Work and Professions," *Yearbook of the National Council of Women of Canada* (1929): 108–10.

25. *Montreal Star* (Jan. 3, 1930): 21.

26. *Hansard* (1932): 2145.

27. See ibid. (1935): 3689 and Kathleen Archibald, *Sex and the Public Service* (Ottawa: Information Canada, 1970), passim.

28. J.M. Bliss and L. Grayson, eds., *The Wretched of Canada* (Toronto: University of Toronto Press, 1971), 9.

29. It is important to remember that women too could be vociferous opponents of equality in the workplace, especially for married women. Many were ready to resign on marriage. See, for instance, the case of social worker Ethel Parker in Toronto: TPLBR, Ethel Parker Papers, copy of letter from E. Dobbs Parker, Director, Division of Social Welfare, to Mr. A.W. Laver, Commissioner of Public Welfare, July 22, 1931. Charlotte Whitton, the Director of the Canadian Council on Child and Family Welfare, for example, insisted that the true place of married women was in the home. Married women met little sympathy from her. See Patricia Rooke and R. Schnell "'An Idiot's Flowerbed': A Study of Charlotte Whitton's Feminist Thought, 1941–1950" in *Rethinking Canada*. Critics of restrictions on their sex were hard put not to label such women as "mugs." See Marjorie

King, "Women are Mugs," *New Frontier* (1936), quoted in Dorothy Livesay, *Right Hand Left Hand* (Erin, Ont.: Press Porcepic, 1977): 125, 127–28. Yet, feminists, like King, frequently appreciated too the powerful effect of social conditioning in producing conservative views. For a useful assessment of female opposition to sexual equality in more recent times see Karen Dubinsky, *Lament for a "Patriarchy Lost"? Anti-feminism, Anti-abortion, and R.E.A.L. Women in Canada* (Ottawa: CRIAW/ICREF, 1985) and Andrea Dworkin, *Right-Wing Women* (New York: G.P. Putnam's Sons, 1983). It seems clear that many married women, and those who hoped to emulate their state, have seen female employment as a direct threat to their home life and personal security.

30. Alice Kessler-Harris, *Out to Work: A History of Wage-Earning Women in the United States* (New York: Oxford University Press, 1982), 254.

31. See also ibid., 272.

32. See Veronica Strong-Boag, "'Wages for Housework': Mothers' Allowances and the Beginnings of Social Security in Canada," *Journal of Canadian Studies* (Spring 1979): 30–31. See also Megan Davies, "'Services Rendered, Rearing Children for the State': Mothers' Pensions in British Columbia 1919–1931" in *Not Just Pin Money*, edited by Barbara Latham and Roberto Pazdro (Victoria: Camosum College, 1984).

33. Dora Nipp, "'But Women Did Come': Working Chinese Women in the Interwar Years" in *Looking into My Sister's Eyes: An Exploration in Women's History*, edited by Jean Burnet (Toronto: Multicultural History Society of Ontario, 1986), 187.

34. See Lilian Petroff, "Contributors to Ethnic Cohesion: Macedonian Women in Toronto to 1940" in *Looking into My Sister's Eyes*.

35. "Sunday Dinner for Tourists" in *Ten Lost Years*, edited by Barry Broadfoot (Toronto: Doubleday, 1973), 30. See also Apolonja Kojder, "Women and the Polish Alliance" in *Looking into My Sister's Eyes*, 101, who observes that one "result of the economic crisis was role reversal, with the wife out working and the man at home." Given commonplace prejudices against immigrants in employments, with the conspicuous exception of domestic service, Poles and other foreign-born women were likely to find paid household employment when their men could not compete with native-born job-seekers.

36. "'I Can Help You Pay Those Bills Jack—,'" *Family Herald and Weekly Star* (Dec. 5, 1923): 24. See also "How I Earn Money at Home and in This Way Make Up for Henry's Shrinking Salary," *Canadian Home Journal* (Feb. 1921): 35; "This Woman Earned $65.00 a Month—Right at Home," *Western Home Monthly* (Jan. 1927): 1; "And I Make $4.00 a Day Besides Doing All My Own Housework," *National Home Monthly* (Jan. 1925): 29.

37. See, for example, Marjorie Griffin Cohen, "The Decline of Women in Canadian Dairying" in *The Neglected Majority*, vol. 2, edited by Alison Prentice and Susan Mann Trofimenkoff (Toronto: McClelland and Stewart, 1985).

38. In the U.S. it appears that women's income was often considered essential among the middle classes to bridge the gap between an acceptable and an unacceptable standard of living. A second wage was increasingly necessary if the rising expectations of what constituted a middle-class lifestyle were to be met. Some of the ads for the Auto-Knitter seem to suggest that a similar development was occurring in Canada. See also the observation of one Anglican commentator who noted that "in this day when luxuries of past years are considered necessities more money is needed." Mrs. Constance Payne, "Married Women in Industry," *The Canadian Churchman* (Aug. 21, 1930): 540. On the U.S. see Winifred Wandersee, *Women's Work and Family Values 1920–1940* (Cambridge: Harvard University Press, 1981): especially chap. 1, and Scharf, *To Work and To Wed*, chap. 7.

39. Jane Synge, "The Transition from School to Work: Growing up Working Class in Early Twentieth Century Hamilton, Ontario" in *Childhood and Adolescence in Canada*, edited by K. Ishwaran (Toronto: McGraw-Hill, 1979): 249–69.

40. E.A. Bott, *Juvenile Employment in Relation to Public Schools and Industries in Toronto* (Studies in Industrial Pyschology 2, University of Toronto Studies, Psychological Series, 1920), 48.

41. Ibid., Case 2, p. 90. Not all girls were as happy or accepting of this situation. See the case of the eighteen-year-old, whose unhappiness about being forced to leave high school helped drive her to suicide. "Case 8" in R. M. Franks, "A Genetic and Comparative Study of Depressed Female Patients in the Toronto Psychiatric Hospital" (M.A. thesis, University of Toronto, 1929).

42. Ibid., 91.

43. TPL, Shirly Vessor in "Toronto Between the Wars," typed transcript, 5.

44. See, for example, Byrne Hope Sanders, "Do Women Assume Too Much: A Question of the Spinster's Responsibilies," *Chatelaine* (Nov. 1929): 16.

45. See the case, for instance, of Sadie Tait whose support of her widowed mother helped make it impossible for her to take courses to improve her standing in philanthropic work for the United Church. UCAVC, United Church, Women's Missionary Society Papers, Home Missions, Department of the Stranger, Box 106, file 5, Sadie Tait, Quebec City, to Mrs. J.M. West, Toronto, Oct. 25, 1929.

46. Canada, *Census* (1931), XII, "Housing in Canada," 476.

47. Helen Potrebenko, *No Streets of Gold: A Social History of Ukrainians in Alberta* (Vancouver: New Star Books, 1977), 193–96.

48. East End (Creche) Day Nursery [Toronto], *Annual Report* (Jan. 1, 1926), 12.

49. Livesay, *Right Hand Left Hand*, 269.

50. Susan Walsh, "Equality, Emancipation and a More Just World: Leading Women in the B.C. CCF," 202–3.

51. Gertrude Pringle, "Is a Business Career Possible For a Married Woman?" *Canadian Magazine* (March 1927): 30.

52. See, for instance, B.C., *Annual Report of the Department of Labour* (1927), L72.

53. "Loafing Husband," *Free Press Prairie Farmer* (Feb. 7, 1934): 5.

54. Virginia Coyne Knight, "Only a Super-Woman Can Juggle Both a Family and a Career," *Chatelaine* (July 1928): 21, 56, 61.

55. See Mercedes Steedman, "Skill and Gender in the Canadian Clothing Industry, 1890–1940" in *On the Job*. For an assessment of the modern successors of the familiar "putting out" system, which seem to differ little in their effect on women, see Laura Johnson, *The Seam Allowance: Industrial Home Sewing in Canada* (Toronto: Women's Press, 1982).

56. A useful discussion of the informal recruitment network that stresses the role of the foreman is Daniel Nelson, *Managers and Workers. Origins of the New Factory System in the United States 1880–1920* (Madison: University of Wisconsin Press, 1975), chap. 5.

57. See Canada, Royal Commission on the Textile Industry, *Final Report* (1938), 15 and "Christie-Brown Plant Has Undergone Thorough Clean-up Since Change," *Financial Post* (Aug. 14, 1925).

58. See Mary Mason Riopel, "A Private Viewing. A Memory of Norman Bethune," *Canadian Forum* (Feb. 1986): 18, 20–24.

59. James Struthers, *No Fault of Their Own: Unemployment and the Canadian Welfare State 1914–1941* (Toronto: University of Toronto Press, 1983), 17.

60. Ontario Sessional Papers, 1925, *Fifth Annual Report of the Department of Labour*, Employment Service of Canada, Hamilton Women's Section, 13.

61. "A Line Around the Block" in *Ten Lost Years*.

62. Lowe, "Women, Work and The Office," 120, note 16.

63. On the dual labour market see ibid.; David M. Gordon, *Theories of Poverty and Underemployment: Orthodox, Radical, and Dual Labor Market Perspectives* (Lexington, Mass.: D.C. Heath, 1972); Richard C. Edwards, Michael Reich, and David M. Gordon, eds.,

Labor Market Segmentation (Lexington, Mass.,: D.C. Heath, 1975); Marcia Freedman, *Labor Markets: Segments and Shelters* (Montclair, N.Y.; Allanheld, Osmun, 1976).

64. See Genevieve Leslie, "Domestic Service in Canada, 1880–1920" in *Women at Work: 1850–1930* (Toronto: Women's Educational Press, 1974) and Strong-Boag, "The Girl of the New Day: Canadian Working Women in the 1920s," *Labour/Le Travail* (Fall 1979): 137–39.

65. See Enid M. Price, "Changes in the Industrial Occupations of Women in the Environment of Montreal during the Period of the War, 1914–1918" (M.A. thesis, McGill, 1919).

66. Ontario, Sessional Papers, 1920, *Fourth Annual Report of the Superintendent of the Trades and Labour Branch, Department of Public Works (1919)*, "Report of the Toronto Employment Bureau," 50.

67. Between 1926 and 1939, for instance, the gross national product fluctuated wildly, beginning at $5.1 billion, rising to a high of $6.1 billion in 1929, falling to a low of $3.5 billion in 1933, and only recovering to $5.6 billion by 1939. Drawn from "Series F1-13," *Historical Statistics of Canada*.

68. In 1921 and 1931 the service category contained 71.15 percent and 82.23 percent of all ten to thirteen-year-old working "women" and 42.24 percent and 41.46 percent of all working women over sixty-five.

69. Ontario, Sessional Papers, *Annual Report of the Ontario Department of Labour* (1921), "Report of the Toronto Bureau of the Employment Service of Canada," 40.

70. SFUA, taped interview with Anita Anderson by Sara Diamond, 1979.

71. Ontario, Sessional Papers, *Annual Report of the Ontario Department of Labour* (1924), "Report of the Ottawa Bureau of the Employment Service of Canada," 40.

72. See the efforts of Ontario technical schools to overcome the "a commonly accepted notion that girls who become household employees lose caste" in Mr. F.S. Rutherford, "What Technical Schools Have Done to Meet the Recommendations of the Royal Commission on Technical Education," *Labour Gazette* (1928): 473. See also Pierson, *"They're Still Women After All"*, chap. 2, "Government Job-Training Programs for Women, 1937–1947" with Marjorie Cohen.

73. Ontario, Sessional Papers, *Annual Report of the Ontario Department of Labour* (1928), 30.

74. SFUA, taped interview with Sara McKinnon by Sara Diamond, 1979.

75. See, for example, the personal histories of the one hundred women interviewed in Toronto venereal clinics in 1922. OPA, Pamphlet 1922, no. 55, Mildred Kensit, "Result of Survey of Venereal Disease Patients in Hospital Clinics in the City of Toronto During the Months of July and August, 1922" for the Canadian Social Hygiene Council.

76. This plan included proposals for a sixty-hour work week, with a ten-hour day, wages equal to those prevailing in the locality, time off, a private room and facilities for entertainment, compulsory accident and health insurance, and adequate training centres. For this effort and others see Harriet Parsons, "Codes for the Kitchen," *Chatelaine* (March 1936): 4, 54, 72–73. See also Emilia Houlton, "Standardization of Domestic Workers," *Woman's Century* (Feb. 1920): 25.

77. Parsons, ibid., 54.

78. See the strike of Toronto waiters against the hiring of cheaper waitresses, *Labour Gazette* (April 1922).

79. For a description of conditions see E.E. Hancox, "What Hotel and Cafeteria Life Means to the Worker," *The Worker* [Toronto] (Oct. 31, 1925), and F.P. Grove, *Search for America* (Ottawa: Graphic Press, 1927), chaps. 3–7.

80. See SAB, Saskatchewan Department of Labour Papers, La I58(1) especially the reports of Inspectress M. Gladys Halbert.

81. Ibid., Halbert to Mr. Withy, Chief Factory Inspector, Feb. 7, 1921.

82. "An Objectionable Little Creep," *Ten Lost Years*. See also a similar case, Mary MacFarlane, "Recollections of a Wrinkled Radical," *Canadian Woman Studies* (Winter 1986): 100.

83. Ibid.

84. The life of the young waitress, Florentine, in Gabrielle Roy's *The Tin Flute* (New York: Reynal and Hitchcock, 1947) provides a realistic portrayal of the opportunities for human contact.

85. Joy Parr of Queen's University is now engaged in an important longitudinal study of women in Paris employments from 1910 to 1950. See "Rethinking Work and Kinship in a Canadian Hosiery Town, 1910–1950," *Feminist Studies* (Spring 1987).

86. Ontario, Sessional Papers, *Fourth Annual Report of the Superintendent of Trades and Labour Branch Department of Public Works* (1920), 47.

87. Mary MacLeod Moore, "London Letter," *Saturday Night* (June 28, 1919): 26.

88. See, for example, "Samples of Wages and Hours of Labour for Miscellaneous Factory Trades," *Labour Gazette*, Supplement (Jan. 1930): 40–95.

89. Gail Cuthbert Brandt, "The Transformation of Women's Work in the Quebec Cotton Industry, 1920–1950" in *The Character of Class Struggle: Essays in Canadian Working-Class History*, edited by Bryan D. Palmer (Toronto: McClelland and Stewart, 1986), 127.

90. Catherine Macleod, "Women in Production: The Toronto Dressmakers' Strike of 1931" in *Women at Work*, 318. See also Steedman, "Skill and Gender in the Canadian Clothing Industry, 1890–1940" on deskilling.

91. B.C. *Annual Report of the Department of Labour* (1921), 50.

92. "United Garment Workers Union Helps Boss to Impose Worsened Conditions," *The Worker* (Sept. 28, 1929). These new machines and procedures were part of the continuing introduction of the "scientific management and industrial efficiency" movement into Canadian operations. For a valuable study of this development in the pre-World War I period see Craig Heron and Bryan D. Palmer, "Through the Prism of the Strike: Industrial Conflict in Southern Ontario, 1901–14," *Canadian Historical Review* (Dec. 1977): 423–53.

93. The use of such "incentive" practices appeared in the nineteenth century but their introduction was intermittent and uneven. For a helpful discussion of some of the issues related to these practices see Nelson, *Managers and Workers*, chap. 3. For evidence of their increased use in Canada in the 1920s and 1930s see the strike files of the federal Department of Labour for the period. On one industry in particular see Steedman, "Skill and Gender in the Canadian Clothing Industry" in *On the Job*.

94. See the argument of a special investigator for the Price Spreads Commission and YWCA staff member, Winifred Hutchison: "Stripped of the beneficence which the word 'bonus' suggests it resolves itself into the system of keeping piece rates so low that the wages had to be made up by a bonus to the minimum required by law." Canada, Royal Commission on Price Spreads, *Report* (1935), VII: 4813.

95. Canada, Price Spreads Commission, *Report*, Testimony of Annie S. Wells, VII: 4410. See also "Working for Eaton's, 1934" in *The Dirty Thirties*, edited by M. Horn (Toronto: Copp Clark, 1972).

96. Parr, "Women's Employment, Domestic Gender Divisions and Labour Exchanges Among Households," 4.

97. Canada, Royal Commission on the Textile Industry, *Report* (1938): chap. IX.

98. See Ontario, Sessional Papers, *Report of the Ontario Department of Labour* (1925), "Report of Inspectress G.E. Hornell," 49.

99. Ibid. (1927), 51. For a discussion of changes in the factory environment see Nelson, *Managers and Workers*, chap. 2.

100. Nova Scotia, Royal Commission on Wages, Hours of Labour and Work Conditions of Women in Industry in Nova Scotia, *Report* (1920), 11.

101. For a useful reminder of the uneven application of mechanization and the continuing importance of hand labour for an earlier period, but which is also relevant to some degree for these decades, see R. Samuel, "Workshop of the World: Steam Power and Hand Technology in mid-Victorian Britain," *History Workshop* (Spring 1977): 6–72.

102. Ontario, Sessional Papers, *Annual Report of the Ontario Minimum Wage Board* (1923), 27.

103. Ontario, Sessional Papers, *Annual Report of the Ontario Department of Labour* (1930), Mrs. E. Scott, 69.

104. Series D86–106, *Historical Statistics of Canada*.

105. See Lowe, "Women, Work and the Office" and Jackson and Gaskell, "White Collar Vocationalism: The Rise of Commercial Education in Canada" (unpublished paper, 1984).

106. See Joan Sangster, "The 1907 Bell Telephone Strike: Organizing Women Workers" in *Rethinking Canada*.

107. M.V. Speers, "Some 'Don'ts' for A College-Trained Girl," *Maclean's* (July 1, 1925): 59.

108. Dora M. Sanders, "Women Won't Be Free," *Maclean's* (Aug. 15, 1933): 8.

109. Gabrielle Carriere, *Careers for Women in Canada. A Practical Guide* (Toronto: J.M. Dent and Sons, 1946), 20–21.

110. University Women's Club of Winnipeg, *The Work of Girls and Women in the Department Stores of Winnipeg* (1914).

111. MacMurchy, *The Canadian Girl at Work*, 12.

112. "A Big Place for Women in Business Says President of Gay Stores and Vice-president of Almy's, Montreal," *Dry Goods Review* (July 1921): 49. See also the success story of a woman buyer in "Woman Buyer Has Unique Career," ibid. (Feb. 1924): 80–81.

113. E.D. Dunlop, "Cream for the Men—Crumbs for the Women," *Woman's Century* (Dec. 1919): 62.

114. Ibid., 31.

115. Ibid., 5.

116. See table 2, Strong-Boag, "'The Girl of the New Day'," 147.

117. "Does Shirley Temple Know?" in *Ten Lost Years*.

118. Ontario, Sessional Papers, *Annual Report of the Trades and Labour Branch* (1920), 49.

119. MacMurchy, *The Canadian Girl at Work*, 15.

120. For some of the debate that surrounded this program see "University Women in the Business World," *Financial Post* (Dec. 24, 1926): 10, and the arguments between Margaret Thompson, head of Western's department of secretarial science, "Pays to Use Best in Buying Brains" and Mrs. E. Cooper, chief of stenographic division of Maclean Publishing, "College Training Not Key to Success," ibid., 10–11.

121. Quoted in "Philistia," "Canadian Women Who Are Doing Things," *Woman's Century* (April 1921): 33.

122. For an illustration of such stereotypes see R.M. Dawson, *The Civil Service of Canada* (London: Oxford University Press, 1929).

123. There were comparable efforts after World War II. See Pierson, *"They're Still Women After All"*, chap. 2, "Government Job-Training Programs for Women," with Cohen, 82–83.

124. See the description of such abuses reported to union organizers in "Store and Office Workers unite to form new union" *Toronto Star* (1934) quoted in Livesay, *Right Hand Left Hand*, 115–16.

125. "Modern Girl—And Her Parents!" *Canadian Congress Journal* (Jan. 1931): 40.

126. From the poem "Depression Suite," Livesay, *Right Hand Left Hand*, 178.

127. See Alison Prentice, "The Feminization of Teaching" in *The Neglected Majority*, vol. 1, edited by Susan Mann Trofimenkoff and Alison Prentice (Toronto: McClelland and Stewart, 1977).

128. See "Average Annual Salaries of School Teachers, by Provinces, 1925–1927, or latest year reported," *The Canadian Year Book* (1929): 909.

129. Glenbow, M233, Muriel Clipsham, "Alberta School Teacher 1926–1934" (1935) typescript, 19.

130. "Teaching from *Eaton's Catalogue*" in *Ten Lost Years*.

131. "Nobody Ever Thanked Me," ibid.

132. "News Notes of Queen's," *Queen's Quarterly* (Jan., Feb., March, 1926): 376.

133. For a description of this program see PAC, Papers of the Montreal YWCA, v. 14, folder "YWCA—Montreal Education, Courses and Seminars. Educational Department Reports 1933/4," Norah Christie, "T.A. Graduate Dec. 1933," typescript.

134. Ibid., v. 14, folder "YWCA Montreal. Education, Courses and Seminars. General Education—Correspondence 1932–3," E. Frances Upton, R.N., Ex. Sec. and Registrar, Association of Registered Nurses of the Province of Quebec to Hazel McCallum, Nov. 30, 1932.

135. See the efforts to win provincial registration in B.C. in Jo Ann Whittaker, "The Search for Legitimacy: Nurses' Registration in British Columbia 1913–1935" in *Not Just Pin Money*.

136. PAC, Papers of the Montreal YWCA, v. 16, folder "YWCA—Montreal. Education, Courses and Seminars. Training Attendants Courses—Correspondence 1924–9," Miss M. Bertha Boyer to Friend, *TAAC Register*, April 25, 1929.

137. Ibid., May Munro to the Educational Association, Aug. 3, 1928.

138. See Kathryn McPherson, "Nurses and Nursing in Early Twentieth-Century Halifax" (M.A. thesis, Dalhousie University, 1982) and Barbara A. Keddy, "Private Duty Nursing Days of the 1920s and 1930s in Canada," *Canadian Woman Studies* (Fall 1986): 99–102.

139. See K. McPherson, "At the Hospital" in *Working Lives: Vancouver 1886–1986* (Vancouver: New Star Books, 1985).

140. See Margaret Street, *Watch-fires on the Mountains* (Toronto: University of Toronto Press, 1973).

141. See Marion Royce, *Eunice Dyke: Health Care Pioneer* (Toronto and Charlottetown: Dundurn Press, 1983).

142. See J. M. Gibbon and Mary S. Mathewson, *Victorian Order of Nurses for Canada 1897–1947* (Montreal: Southam Press, 1947).

143. See Nora Robins, "Women and Libraries with Particular Reference to the Canadian Library Association" (paper prepared for History 421, Concordia University, 1980), and Meyme C. Althouse, "The Librarian's Job," *Chatelaine* (Sept. 1931): 40–41.

144. See Patricia Rooke and R.L. Schnell, *Public Person, Private Woman* (Vancouver: University of B.C. Press, 1987) and James Struthers, "A Profession in Crisis: Charlotte Whitton and Canadian Social Work in the 1930s," *Canadian Historical Review* (June 1981): 169–85.

145. Struthers, "'Lord Give Us Men': Women and Social Work in English Canada 1918–1953," Canadian Historical Association *Historical Papers* (1983): 101.

146. Ibid., 97.

147. Ibid., 98.

148. See ibid., 106–107.

149. See, for example, Marie McNulty, "Canadian Portias," *Echoes* (May 1921): 28–29; Georgie Paterson Lane, "She is Canada's Youngest Woman Judge," *Maclean's* (May 1, 1929): 81–82; "Dr. Belle Wilson," *Western Woman's Weekly* (Jan. 1, 1921): 5; "Women in the Pulpits," *Woman's Century* (Oct. 1920): 3; M. Pennell, "Interesting Canadian Women," *Canadian Magazine* (May 1927): 25; H.M. Ridley, "Canada's First Woman Inspector," ibid. (Nov. 1923): 46–52; M. Pennell, "Interesting Canadian Women," ibid. (June 1927): 27, 36; ibid. (Sept. 1927): 25, 30; "Women on the Wing," *Chatelaine* (Aug. 1931): 15; Edith Bayne, "Women and Their Work," *Maclean's* (Jan. 1, 1920): 96; "People Who Do Things," *Saturday Night* (Feb. 15, 1936): 20; Edna Kells, "Women and Their

Work," *Maclean's* (Sept. 15, 1927): 72; Edith M. Cuppage, "She Wasn't a 'Type,' So She Became a Directress," ibid. (May 1, 1921): 64; W.A. Schafer, "One Ontario Woman Funeral Director," *Canadian Furniture World and the Undertaker* (Oct. 1921): 57; Edna K. Wooley, "A Woman Undertaker," ibid. (Jan. 1920): 69.

150. See also Mary Hallett, "Nellie McClung and the Fight for the Ordination of Women in the United Church of Canada," *Atlantis* (Spring 1979): 2–16.

151. D.G. Bell, "Merle Foster Creates Art Out of Mud, and Her Sister Makes It Pay," *Maclean's* (Oct. 15, 1923): 53.

152. Rebecca Coulter, "The Working Young of Edmonton, 1921–1931" in *Childhood and Family in Canadian History*, edited by Joy Parr (Toronto: McClelland and Stewart, 1982), 143.

153. See PAC, MG 28 I10, Papers of the Canadian Council on Social Development, v. 140, file "League of Nations' Traffic in Women and Children, U.S. Central Authority," various deportation reports.

154. "Two Years of Shame" in *Ten Lost Years*.

155. Ontario, Commission on Unemployment, *Report* (1916), 180.

156. PAC, Papers of the Montreal YWCA, v. 32, folder, "Young Women's Christian Association. Montreal. Reports. Annual Reports and Individual Department Reports 1931," "Annual Report . . . 1931 of the Montreal YWCA," 6.

157. *Hansard* (1936), 4027.

158. See Rebecca Coulter, "Young Women and Unemployment in the 1930s: The Home Service Solution," *Canadian Woman Studies* (Winter 1986): 77–80.

159. For examples of this see "Eight Hours per Day for Houseworkers," *Western Labor News* (April 4, 1919): 1; *Labour Gazette* (March 1921); the case of Vancouver domestics in the 1930s: SFUA, taped interviews with Anita Andersen and Marion Sarich by Sara Diamond, 1979.

160. See Manitoba Provincial Archives, MG10 B21, Papers of the Commercial Girls Club of Winnipeg, "Commercial Girls' Club," Oct. 9, 1931.

161. Apolonja M. Kojder, "In Union There is Strength: The Saskatoon Women Teachers' Association" *Canadian Woman Studies* (Fall 1986): 82–84.

162. See Doris French, *High Button Boot Straps: Federation of Women Teachers' Associations of Ontario, 1918–1968* (Toronto: Ryerson Press, 1968), and Pat Stanton, "Validating Women's Work Through 'Grass-Roots' History: Bertha Adkins—A Case Study," *Canadian Woman Studies* (Winter 1986): 82–85.

163. On the activities of these three rival unions, the first two branches of American unions and the latter a Communist creation, see Steedman, "Skill and Gender in the Canadian Clothing Industry, 1890–1940" in *The Bitter Thirties in Quebec*, edited by Evelyn Dumas (Montreal: Black Rose Books, 1975) and Macleod, "Women in Production: The Toronto Dressmakers' Strike of 1931."

164. Steedman, ibid., 163.

165. See "Camp Boys' Trek," *BC Workers' News* (June 14, 1935): 3, and Elaine Bernard, "Last Back: Folklore and the Telephone Operators in the 1919 Vancouver General Strike" in *Not Just Pin Money*.

166. On the problems with this legislation see Strong-Boag, "The Girl of the New Day" and Margaret Hobbs, "'Dead Horses' and 'Muffled Voices': Protective Legislation, Education, and the Minimum Wage for Women in Ontario" (M.A. thesis, University of Toronto, 1985). On these particular department stores in Saskatchewan see SAB, La LA I117, Saskatchewan Department of Labour, Correspondence and Reports of the Minimum Wage Inspectors.

167. Diane Crossley, "The B.C. Liberal Party and Women's Reforms, 1916–1928" in *In Her Own Right*, edited by Barbara Latham and Cathy Kess (Victoria: Camosun College, 1980), 214.

CHAPTER 3
COURTING, MARRYING, AND OTHER ADVENTURES

Tinker, tailor, soldier, sailor,
Rich man, poor man,
Beggarman, thief,
Doctor, lawyer, Indian chief.

I love coffee, I love tea,
I love the boys, and the boys love me.
Tell my mother to hold her tongue,
She had a boy when she was young.
Tell my father to do the same:
He had a girl and he changed her name.

These and a host of other such rhymes were chanted by girls from one end of the Dominion to the other.[1] The number of prune pits in a bowl, the turns of a rope, bounces of a ball, petals on a flower, could all foretell, so it was hoped or feared, individual fate. While male culture developed a multitude of songs to celebrate or condemn life in the mines and on the fishing boats and the farms,[2] female folklore and verse told relatively little of paid work. Girls and adult women were more likely to summon up thoughts of lovers, husbands, and babies. This fascination reflected the fact that most female Canadians not only expected to marry but took it for granted that marriage would provide satisfaction, security, and purpose.

Wives and husbands were presumed to pool resources in working partnerships that enabled them to create the homes and families that signalled adulthood in their society. While this relationship was, on the one hand, based on practical economics, it also promised important emotional benefits. Strong affections, rooted in common hopes and experiences, bound many couples tightly together. Popular films, radio, and magazines also encouraged some young women to anticipate romantic passion, an emotion more easily maintained while courting than during the more mundane days of joint housekeeping. At least as important in meeting women's desires for love were children. In their nurture mothers found many of the joys of marriage.

TABLE 1

AVERAGE AGE AT FIRST MARRIAGE FOR FEMALES, BY PROVINCE, 1921–1941

	1921	1931	1941
Prince Edward Island	26.5	25.7	22.8
Nova Scotia	24.8	24.9	22.4
New Brunswick	24.3	24.7	22.0
Quebec	25.1	26.4	23.9
Ontario	24.7	24.9	22.7
Manitoba	24.0	25.2	23.0
Saskatchewan	22.4	23.8	22.4
Alberta	22.6	23.6	22.2
British Columbia	23.8	24.8	23.3
Range	4.1	2.1	1.9

Source: From Ellen Gee, "Fertility and Marriage Patterns in Canada 1851–1971" (Ph.D. thesis, University of British Columbia, 1978), 221, table 38.

In the 1920 and 1930s, a romantic consumerism that centred on families headed by male breadwinners dominated public discussion of women's adult lives. Remaining happily single and exploring the potential of same-sex relationships were never presented as real options. Yet, if an active heterosexuality ending in marriage became harder to resist, free spirits and critics never disappeared. In the face of all conditioning to the contrary, some women constructed lives independent of male sexuality and as filled with joy and pain as those of any of their marrying sisters.

Although the ultimate outcome for girls was largely taken for granted, Canada had almost as many specific traditions about courting and marrying, or not doing so, as it had regions, rural and urban areas, and ethnic groups. A hint of these can be found by examining age of marriage. Between 1921 and 1941, for instance, residents of Prince Edward Island, Quebec, Manitoba, and British Columbia were likely to marry somewhat later than those in other jurisdictions, although the differences between provinces had been declining since the nineteenth century.

The experience of rural and urban women was also dissimilar. In 1931, for instance, 12.4 percent of women aged 45 to 49 years of age in urban areas remained single as compared with only 7.1 percent in rural areas; ten years later the figures were 13.8 percent and 7.1 percent. This situation was reversed for men of the same age: 17.1 percent were unmarried in rural areas in 1931 as compared to 11.5 percent of urban males; in 1941 the situation remained much the same with 17.0 percent and 12.0 percent respectively.[3] Such differences tell a good deal, not only about the availability of suitable members of the opposite sex, but the presence too of alternate means of independence and fulfilment, notably paying jobs for women in the cities.

TABLE 2

PERCENT SINGLE AT AGES 20-24, 25-34, AND 45-54 FOR FEMALES, BY ETHNIC GROUP, 1931

	20–24	25–34	45–54
British	65.3	27.3	11.6
French	66.9	30.1	11.6
Western European	56.5	19.8	6.2
Eastern European	41.4	8.2	1.5

Source: Gee, "Fertility and Marriage Patterns in Canada 1851–1971," 213, table 37.

Ethnic origin could be another influential factor. Canadians of British and French background tended to remain single longer than those of western European and, especially, eastern European origin. Such differences continued traditional patterns that had long seen western Europe with higher ages of marriage and numbers of unmarried persons than eastern Europe. The influx of immigrants from the latter region was a significant factor in reducing the average age of brides and grooms and the number of single people of both sexes in Canada in these years.

Education and family earnings were still other influences on the tendency to marry, with higher levels encouraging postponement for some and spinsterhood for others.[4] Variations in the sex and age ratios of individual populations also helped give rise to distinctive results. Too many or too few of either sex of the "right" age could sharply differentiate one community from another and dramatically alter an individual's future. Nevertheless, as Ellen Gee has concluded in her major study of fertility and marriage in Canada, the 1920s and 1930s also saw the convergence of different traditions and the emergence of a common Canadian pattern. The net result was a female population that, as a whole, was increasingly likely

TABLE 3

PERCENT SINGLE AT AGES 20-24, 25-29, AND 45-49 AND AVERAGE AGE AT FIRST MARRIAGE, FOR FEMALES, 1921-1941

Year	Percent Single			Average Age at First Marriage
	20–24	25–29	45–49	
1921	56.9	28.7	11.1	24.3
1931	63.1	32.4	10.3	25.1
1941	61.0	32.9	11.2	23.0

Source: Gee, "Fertility and Marriage Patterns in Canada 1851–1971," 168, table 28.

to wed at least once and most of whom married in their early to mid-twenties.

The Great Depression helped reverse only for a short time the decline begun by 1891 in women's age of marriage. The same effect was also visible for men whose average age at marriage swung from 28.0 years in 1921 to 28.5 in 1931 and to 26.3 in 1941. Unchanged was the steady decrease, characteristic of the twentieth century in general, in the age difference between wives and husbands, falling from an average 3.7 years in 1921 to 3.3 years two decades later. Marital partners were more likely to be younger and more similar in age. The precise implications of these trends are impossible to know, but they contributed to a marital environment in which there was a good deal of uncertainty about optimal fertility, economic stability, individual authority, and female participation in paid labour. In the 1920s and 1930s, even by the broadest demographic indicators, Canadian marriages were no longer exactly what they had been a generation before. What this meant, women, and the men they married, would have to work out.

Census figures provide only a brief glimpse into the intimate world of human relationships. They do not, for example, reveal the number or the nature of unmarried couples sharing a common residence. Yet, a formal exchange of vows was neither a legal nor a spiritual advantage for Canadians lacking property or faith. Others lived together without benefit of clergy because they were in no position to do anything else: partners might be already married or otherwise unwilling. These common-law relationships were criticized by contemporaries, but too little evidence has survived for them to be assessed separately here.[5] Their existence is, however, part of the underside of heterosexual coupling that, like prostitution or incest or wife beating, had different implications for women and men and that bears recollection in any study of the "legitimate" institution.

For many Canadians, courting remained a family-centred affair. To a large degree, young women and men met in settings close to home and chaperoned by members of the community. Longer periods of schooling, including, for a very few, university, and of employment for women were slowly increasing the pool of possible suitors. High schools across the Dominion and universities like Dalhousie, Manitoba, and the University of British Columbia held dances, teas, and lectures that assembled unprecedented numbers of youthful suitors, giving them ample opportunity to appraise members of the other sex.[6] Co-ed groups like the Student Christian Movement brought together like-minded young women and men such as CGIT enthusiast Mary Austin and prospective missionary James Endicott.[7] Well-supervised tea dances, like those where John George Diefenbaker courted his first wife Edna Brower in Saskatchewan, provided introductions and dates for both working people and students.[8] These occasions offered some girls a wider range of prospective mates but most families attempted to control the outcome with curfews, locations designated off-limits, and the demand that serious candidates ultimately be brought under their scrutiny. Such pressures combined with their own inclinations to ensure that relatively few women married outside their own social group.

Women's most obvious resources in an unequal marriage market were their looks and sexuality. Beauty contests such as the one initiated at the Canadian National Exhibition in 1937 left little room for doubt where female assets lay. Unfortunately for women's peace of mind, their main attractions were regarded as far from permanent. According to the youth-conscious culture of these decades, beauty and erotic appeal deteriorated with age and required constant attention from childhood on. Older women were believed to be at a substantial disadvantage. A body over forty, they were reminded, did not "show up well in a room full of flappers" and the comparison "in many instances . . . opened the door to divorce."[9]

Female Canadians in general were, however, encouraged to believe as never before that the years' harsh toll could be minimized and their appeal as dates and spouses preserved or enhanced. Ordinary housewives and their sisters in shops, factories, offices, and institutions became the marketing targets of a broad range of new goods that promised solutions to the dilemma of how to maintain women's most prized assets. Advertisers of personal care products, for example, gave unprecedented attention to the sanitizing of the female body or, as it was known in the trade, "Shame on You" copy.[10] Lysol disinfectant eliminated obnoxious female genital odour.[11] Odorono Cream Depilatory dissolved the disfigurement that afflicted "ten in twelve girls."[12] Pepsodent Tooth Powder helped girls really "rate."[13] Listerine cured the bad breath or, in the new jargon of the day, halitosis, that sent boyfriends packing.[14] Once thoroughly cleansed, the modern woman was ready for makeup. Where previously facial creams and lipsticks had generally been rather discretely advertised and were viewed as not quite respectable, at least if used in any obvious quantity, by the 1920s a woman was labelled a "perfect flop" if she didn't take "due heed of the warnings in the magazine ads."[15] Up-to-date styles—in the 1920s darkened eyes and bee-stung mouths were a special focus of attention, and in the 1930s high coloured lips and cheeks received more emphasis—were identified as the keys to "poise and self-confidence."[16]

Just as shocking to the traditionally minded was the new acceptance of smoking. In the 1920s, Canadians saw the first mass advertising for cigarettes and lighters directed specifically at a female market. One Canadian-owned firm reassured nervous customers, "*Every* United Cigar Store offers to Ladies, as well as to the Men, a courteous, intelligent and helpful service from *all* employees, at *all* times."[17] Cigarettes, like makeup, may have become a sign of the "smart" woman but, if such ads are any indication, Canadian women remained nervous puffers.

Not so new, although more prevalent than ever and constantly reaffirmed in films and periodicals, was advice to follow fashion's dictates in clothes. Pattern books, newspaper ads, and store catalogues, like the dress of movie star favourites, brought dropped waists, short skirts, and cloche hats to popular notice in the flapper decade. In the 1930s, longer skirts, helped to an earlier retirement by the shortages of World War I, recovered favour, along with padded shoulders, narrow waists, and large hats. In both decades bras, girdles, and garter belts replaced front- and back-laced corsets, and nude shades of silk and the fashion for bare legs damaged the market for heavier hosiery.

Even if one had the inclination, it was not easy to follow these trends. Makeup, for example, could be expensive and Canadians were a thriftier and poorer lot than those to the south. Whereas the average American woman was reckoned in 1932 to spend $12.32 annually on cosmetics, her Canadian cousin spared an average $3.39.[18] Those with money might part with much more. A survey of co-eds at the University of British Columbia in 1937, for instance, revealed an average expenditure of $6.70 per month on cosmetics, an amount far beyond the budget of ordinary Canadians.[19] As advertisers made very clear in copy that blanketed the Dominion, purchases were essential to successful womanhood. Ideal femininity was in this way transformed into a purchasable commodity, the possession of which promised success in the marriage market.

Yet no woman could remain easily confident of her attractiveness. Boyfriends, husbands, children, friends, and doctors were regularly summoned forth to criticize. As one ad for Palmoline Soap bluntly put it, "I learned from a beauty expert how to hold my husband—and why so many women fail."[20] Lifebuoy typically featured a mother exclaiming, "I was startled by my young son's remark—believe me, I'll never risk my personal daintiness again!"[21] Reminders such as that by Calay Soap that "You are in a Beauty Contest every day of your life"[22] nagged women in both decades. Some potential consumers bitterly resented this flow of unsolicited advice. One farm reader labelled such exhortations for beauty "rubbish," pointing out how little spare time women had: "Beside raising a family, looking after chickens, cows and garden, . . . [women] often are expected to help with the hay as well as in the fields."[23] The persistence, nevertheless, of marketing strategies that exploited women's potential for guilt, shame, and uncertainty suggested that not all observers were able to maintain their equanimity. So long as women were routinely socialized to regard their own appearance as the key to emotional satisfaction and social standing, they would be susceptible to warnings from beauty products of every kind.

While female attractiveness, or lack of it, preoccupied a host of observers, commentators were much more circumspect when it came to the direct mention of sex. Women were made up and dressed up to travel the marriage route as expeditiously as possible, but the sexual itinerary itself was left deliberately vague. Girls regularly remained in the dark even about menstruation, a subject that mothers frequently found intensely embarrassing.[24] Different generations found it hard to break the conventions that silenced them, and many a girl readily recalled never hearing "a word of warning or instruction from my mother."[25] Some information could be gathered from playgrounds, friendly whispers, and barnyard animals, but female culture in general seems to have included little explicit sexual advice, except sometimes for wives. Most women had "to stumble along" about the details and the functioning of both their bodies and those of men.[26]

Such female ignorance provoked concern from more liberal thinkers. To an overwhelming degree, these advisers were preoccupied with marital sexuality; premarital, extramarital, or homosexual contacts were ignored or condemned. Women, and men, who understood their bodies better were to help guarantee more stable marriages; this was the foremost purpose of heightened sexual sophistication. Arguing that "it is . . . on the sexual side of the union that most disasters occur," Alfred Tyrer, the leading Canadian counsellor on sexual matters, recommended for couples "A CHART TO SHOW THEM THE WAY."[27] Lack of erotic response in women was attributed "to an entirely false education by unfortunate family influence or wrong religious teaching in childhood."[28] Human love was hailed as natural, indeed "sacramental";[29] masturbation and different positions for intercourse as completely normal. Even the household stand-by, *Eaton's Catalogue,* in marketing *Married Love* and *Enduring Passion* by Marie Stopes, *Modern Marriage* by a Dr. Griffith, and an anonymously authored *Marriage Manual* under the category "Health and Sex Books," hinted that many Canadians regarded existing practices as far from ideal.[30]

Although such guidance manuals had been circulating, albeit privately and circumspectly earlier, a very few people of means in these years had almost unprecedented access to psychoanalysis with its particular approach to sexual dysfunction. A Dr. Ruth MacLachlan Franks, for instance, established a Toronto practice in psychology and psychiatry in the 1930s.[31] In the 1920s, another Toronto therapist, Dr. Margaret Strong, introduced young women like Mary Elsie Austin, the future wife of the Methodist and United Church missionary to China, James Endicott, to the frank discussion of sexual problems. As a result, their son concluded, "for their day, the communication on sexuality was remarkably open and free."[32] Sex experts, insisting on the legitimacy of female erotic feelings and the importance of sexual communication between wife and husband, found larger audiences than ever before. Nevertheless, unsettling as such advice was to some who prized purity and reticence in women, these would-be therapists were fundamentally conservative. To a substantial degree they confirmed the message being broadcast in the advertising of personal care commodities. Both therapists and advertisers placed a high value on a perfected sexuality as a solution to personal problems and faulted the individual not the society for failure to find happiness. Monogamous marriage, sharply differentiated sex roles, and motherhood remained largely untouched shibboleths.[33]

For all the innovative aspects of the therapeutic and commercial interest in female sexuality, it continued to be irrevocably tied to reproduction. In the minds of most women and most public commentators on sexual issues, female fertility persisted as a social and moral problem of some magnitude.

Unfortunately, although infertility worried many,[34] it was rarely discussed publicly, not surprisingly, perhaps, since the inability to parent was frequently a matter of personal despair and shame and public pity.[35] On the other hand, the possible moral and social consequences of contraception and abortion provoked highly visible debates among doctors, clergy, and general social critics. The resumption in the decline of the Canadian birthrate that had begun in the mid-nineteenth and only briefly halted early in the twentieth century worried English-speaking nationalists who feared that the "best" elements in society (i.e., the white Protestant middle class) were failing to reproduce themselves.[36] The two sexes were rarely faulted equally. In particular, the emerging concensus about the presence of strong sexual feelings in women made them potentially all the more culpable when the "natural" outcome of intercourse was thwarted.

Despite the fact that Canadians in general were taking steps, and had been for some decades, to curb fertility, it remained difficult throughout these years for women to break the silence that surrounded contraceptive techniques, to challenge the belief that "only bad people talked about these things."[37] No Canadian female leader emerged to equal the stature of Marie Stopes in Great Britain or Margaret Sanger in the United States. There were instead a number of prominent male supporters, notably A.R. Kaufman, a Kitchener industrialist, who funded the Parents' Information Bureau from 1929. By the end of the 1930s, he supported over fifty nurses carrying contraceptive information across Canada. Although no woman wielded influence on such a scale as Kaufman, a good many were prepared at the local level to dare the penalties of the Criminal Code, in force since 1892, for providing or promoting birth control methods. In Saskatchewan, Violet McNaughton, the women's editor of the *Western Producer*, conducted a lively correspondence on the subject with sympathizers.[38] In British Columbia, Vivian Dowding took help to the women of the interior.[39] In Ontario, clubwoman Mary Hawkins championed Hamilton's first birth control clinic in 1932 and nurse Dorothea Palmer went on trial in September 1936 for taking contraceptives door-to-door in Eastview on the Quebec border.[40] One provocative assessment of the Canadian birth control movement has suggested that a political campaign led by men motivated primarily "by a desire to reduce the perceived differential in fertility between the middle classes, and the socially dependent poor and 'mentally defective'" can be distinguished from a "feminist agitation" that had "as a primary concern . . . giving individual women better control and authority in their homes. . . ."[41] While such a distinction does not hold hard and fast in every case, female birth controllers such as McNaughton and Dowding showed a sensitivity to the plight of helpless mothers that few men could equal.

Most female birth controllers did not, however, achieve even local prominence. They exchanged information quietly amongst themselves and wrote Stopes, Sanger, and the sympathetic Canadians they knew for information.[42] The action of Calgary resident Mrs. Jean McDonald, for example, in giving married women friends and hapless girls advice and help with unwanted pregnancies was not unusual.[43] Finnish women working as domestics in Toronto turned in the 1920s to a fellow countrywoman who ran a job exchange. As one immigrant remembered, "We didn't make an issue of it. People just trusted each other and didn't want any harm to come to anybody."[44] The threat of pregnancy was a powerful catalyst for some, stirring up strong feelings of identification with others of their sex. Such was the case in British Columbia in 1929 when Ruth Bullock was "astounded" to find herself pregnant after only four months of marriage. The situation deteriorated steadily when her husband "kept assuring me that this baby would be my baby, that I had let him down and that therefore I would have to bear the full responsibility for this child." Although she admitted to having had a "very arrogant and unsisterly attitude to many, many of the women I had met," this experience helped transform the twenty-one-year-old Bullock into a firm supporter of birth control and women's rights.[45]

In the early 1920s, public advocacy of birth control remained, as it had begun, the particular preserve of the left—anarchist, socialist, communist, and feminist sexual radicals, hardly a combination with which most respectable Canadians cared to associate. By the 1930s, however, the economic disaster threatening many families inspired a much wider range of public support. In 1929, with the onset of the Depression, the women's branch of the Saskatchewan section of the United Farmers of Canada asked for the legalization of birth control and the creation of clinics. In 1932 the National Council of Jewish Women recommended removing the legal ban on birth control, and a similar resolution was passed a year later by the United Farm Women of Alberta.[46] The United Church went so far as to point out that,

> Seeing that maternity always involves an expedition down to the very gates of death, the Christian man will recognize that the wife, by virtue of her personality, has a right to determine in fellowship with her husband the occasions and frequency of such experiences. And the same considerations also indicate a right to determine by voluntary and conscientious choice rather than by accident, the occasions which marital privilege may find a consequence in procreation.[47]

Confronted with the harsh reality of the Great Depression and massive private initiative in birth control, Anglicans at the Lambeth Conference of 1930 gave "tepid acceptance" to contraception, and the Catholic Church acquiesced in the "rhythm method."[48] Such reversals confirmed the value of controlling fertility, an idea that Canadian couples of various faiths had been acting upon for some time.

Faced with unwanted pregnancies, not all women were prepared finally to welcome a child. Both married and single women turned on occasion to abortion and, much less frequently, infanticide. Their resort to such solutions spoke volumes for their desire to control their fertility and for the refusal of a large part of the medical profession to provide safe alternatives.[49] Canadians had long been accustomed to the sale of abortifacients under a variety of guises in newspapers, and these years brought no change. Drugs, bleeding, and forced dilation of the cervix were employed by women who, despite admonitions from doctors who designated fertilization as the key date, used "quickening" as a measure before which it was not immoral to attempt to "put oneself right." The number of successful abortions cannot be known but, in 1930, a doctor from Toronto General reported that about forty percent of "incomplete abortions" in the public wards were self-induced. He described a typical case in which a woman assumed "a squatting position with a mirror propped upon the floor in front of her and attempt[ed] to push the instrument [slippery elm, catheter, knitting needle, crochet hook, etc.] into the cervical canal."[50] When such home remedies failed, women turned to abortionists. Again their exact numbers will never be known, as official abortion statistics by and large reflected only those women who did not survive or required hospital attention—that is, suffered medical complications from a mishandled abortion. The fact that abortion deaths were increasing not only relative to all maternal deaths in the 1930s but in absolute numbers as well indicates the continuing importance of this traditional backup form of fertility control.[51]

Despite the problem of substantial underreporting, a breakdown of the thirty-nine abortion cases reported to the attorney-general in British Columbia between 1930 and 1939 is revealing. As Angus McLaren and Arlene Tigar McLaren have suggested, "The typical woman in the interwar period having recourse to abortion was the older, married woman who already had children. . . . At least ten percent had previously aborted and one stated she had induced sixteen previous miscarriages."[52] Single women were likely to diagnose their condition too late and be harder put to identify remedies. The stigma attached to illegitimate births, the number of which almost doubled as a percentage of total live births from 1921 to 1939,[53] reminded all women that the penalties for sexual expression, even in a supposedly more liberated age, were paid overwhelmingly by one sex.[54]

The especially desperate turned to infanticide. There were the cases of a forty-year-old mother of a large family in Beausejour, Manitoba, who in 1933 admitted drowning her baby because of "family quarrels"[55] and a forty-eight-year-old married woman who was accused of incinerating a newborn in Medicine Hat in 1934.[56] The frequency of such incidents must remain even more of a mystery than abortions, but their presence even in small numbers in published accounts suggests the depths of distress to which those without protection could be driven.

The fact that women ultimately faced very different consequences from a relationship with the opposite sex necessarily affected both courtship and marriage. Girls were in the awkward position of being encouraged to desire boyfriends and eventually a husband without committing themselves to any premarital physical intimacy. Not surprisingly, under the pressure of their own and their boyfriends' desires and unprotected by sex education or birth control, many had babies rather sooner than they had anticipated. Caught short, they might enter one of many institutions for unwed mothers, usually run by churches, or seek anonymous refuge in privately run nursing homes that existed in all large Canadian cities. More often than not, however, they married the father, usually "the person they had been courting with."[57] For a short while, when the baby arrived early, the newlyweds provided gossip for the community, but their situation readily became indistinguishable from that of their neighbours. Other marriages were postponed for years, especially in the 1930s while couples saved money to set up housekeeping. The pressure on women to quit paid work after the wedding had the understandable effect of raising the average age of marriage during the Depression. In time, however, most Canadians exchanged vows.

For women, marriage could involve traumatic intimacy with a virtual stranger or be the logical extension of years of familiar contact. In any event, as the much heralded culmination of a woman's hopes, the ceremony itself was frequently fraught with anxiety. This was all the more likely since a certain romantic fantasy and a substantial dose of unreality was attached to the act of becoming a bride, especially for the middle class. Every June brought a host of lyrical tributes such as,

> The morning before the wedding ceremony should be the bride's very own to beautify and adorn herself and to see visions and dream dreams of the days to come. . . . And now she is ready to march to the strains of Lohengrin's "Here Comes the Bride," a gracious figure, the last word in modernity from the shining crown of her shingled head to the soles of her comely feet. It is small wonder that the radiant groom is of the opinion that to be seen in her company is to earn the ill-concealed envy of all right thinking men.[58]

No doubt many girls dreamed of just such a trip to the altar. The fact that its expense was well beyond most people's purses did not prevent wishful study of the brides who adorned the social pages of every newspaper and magazine.

Although the more radical opted for a civil ceremony, double rings, and hyphenated names,[59] and there was talk in the most "advanced" circles of "companionate" or "trial" marriage before children,[60] most women desired some religious recognition of their new state, a permanent commitment, and a ring and new name for the bride alone. The exchange of vows before a priest, minister, or rabbi was often a public celebration with plenty of time to joke, gossip, and reaffirm kin and community ties. In 1922, for example, an Old-Order Mennonite marriage included children hiding the bride's shoe, to her pretended consternation, the groom distributing cigars, and the bridal party joining together in a singsong. After a "very friendly social time" and a "Shivaree" that serenaded the new-lyweds with "noise makers, tin pails, tubs,"[61] until its instigators were pla-cated by cigars and cookies, the couple went to bed. Like numerous young people, they ignored the fashion for honeymoons and stayed home to take up immediately the duties of married life.

The Mennonite bride had the advantage of entering into married life in familiar surroundings, with someone known since childhood. Quite dif-ferent was the experience of a Macedonian would-be newlywed who recalled a bleak introduction to Toronto: "When I come over here I'm lost. I never even know my husband." Despite her apprehension, vows were exchanged soon after her arrival. Old world customs that prescribed "week-long celebrations which included processions and receptions held by the parents of the bride and the groom respectively . . . gave way to a spartan celebration."[62] Japanese and Armenian women chosen as "picture brides" by men who had immigrated to Canada years earlier, and whom they had never seen, had every reason to fear the future. Desperate situ-ations led some to conclude, like one seventeen-year-old refugee from the Ottoman Empire, that "there was no love in those days. No. The man needed the woman and the woman needed the man. That's why they mar-ried."[63] The newcomer was left to work out as best she could the meaning of her new relationship. The combination of a strange land and a strange man helped make the first few years of marriage heavy going for many young women.

Immigrants were especially likely to encounter threats to traditional ways of thinking and acting but they were far from alone. The entire cus-tomary basis of marriage itself seemed in question. Whereas households in general, and especially those on farms and in fishing communities, had long relied in very visible ways on the day-to-day co-operation of spouses in the production of goods for exchange for cash and for use by the family itself, these habits were in decline, with groups like the Mennonites con-spicuous exceptions. By 1921, for instance, a majority of Canadians lived in urban areas. There the contributions of husbands, wives, and children to their mutual maintenance changed, sometimes dramatically. Whereas men had previously often toiled in close proximity to and even within the family residence, by the 1920s increasing numbers spent large parts of each week, not infrequently twelve hours a day, in and on the way to paid labour and received an individual wage. Girlfriends and wives too could find employments outside the home, albeit less well paid. Women's access to waged labour, added to their newly-won right to vote, seemed to under-cut the traditional role of men as heads of families, a role that depended on men's greater participation in the political system and the labour mar-ket. The unsettling prospect of a revolution in marital relationships fueled hostility to so-called working wives in these years.

And yet the purely domestic alternative for women posed new problems as well. Homes were more and more divorced, both physically, as in the case of suburbs, and ideologically, especially but by no means only for the middle class, from the official or public place of "work." As family members went their own ways, the contribution of each to their mutual survival not only changed but, in the case of middle-class women, was rendered nearly invisible. In private homes, despite all the hullabaloo accompanying domestic innovations such as electricity, refrigeration, and linoleum, all of which remained far from universal, women were heavily occupied in tasks that were all the more fatiguing because they were so often unrecognized and unremunerated. By taking in boarders or cultivating kitchen gardens, for example, most housewives worked hard to supplement the often insufficient cash income of the male "breadwinner." Their labour was also required to transform wages into goods and services to maintain the family. Children might help, but their time was frequently absorbed by longer periods of compulsory schooling. Moreover, children of all ages were believed to be more in need of maternal care than ever before. Absent as they were for long hours of waged or salaried work, husbands rarely participated in and often failed to observe or to appreciate what went on at home. For them it was first and foremost a location that was *not* a workplace. It became all too easy to ignore women's efforts or to reckon them largely as a form of voluntary personal service to husband and offspring that above all reflected well on the earning capacity and character of the male breadwinner. The fact that involvement in the public labour force was paid and work in the home was not helped to confirm an invidious distinction between male and female contributions. Women attempted to counter damaging assessments of the significance of their labours for the marital establishment but, like men, they were uncertain how to interpret and deal with new conditions. No one could say for certain just what was the future of marriage.

Not surprisingly, explanations often addressed immediate sources of disarray. The Great War, for instance, was frequently cited as an especially disruptive influence. One mother wrote despairingly of the situation facing her daughter:

> We thought the war would have done great things for B . . . but indeed the effect seems to have been quite the reverse. Since his return he has been drinking heavily, and has been horrible to M . . . in every way. She could get a divorce if she wished but she has not the money, in the first place, and she dreads the publicity for the children's sake.[61]

But causes could rarely be pinpointed so precisely. Whether it was because of the war, the flapper, or the Great Depression, Canadians only knew that domestic relationships had changed, and too often seemingly for the worse. Ill-matched spouses emerged, for instance, as a stock-in-trade of plots of novels of the period. Wives, as in the case of Madge MacBeth's *Shackles* (1926), Mazo de la Roche's *Jalna* (1927), and Laura Salverson's *The Dark Weaver* (1937), and husbands, as with Arthur Stringer's *The Prairie Mother* (1920), Douglas Durkin's *The Magpie* (1923), and Sinclair

Ross's *As for Me and My House* (1941), were portrayed as victims of marital regimes that were fundamentally flawed. Many films of the period were equally preoccupied with trouble between spouses.[65] The frequency with which divorce, for instance, was a topic of cinematic interest worried Canadians who felt domestic matters were difficult enough without the further example of wrong-headed models of behaviour, many emanating from a morally suspect American film industry.[66]

Anxious as they were about women's place in Canadian society, feminists were deeply troubled by the future of modern marriage. Unfortunately, their ability to understand developments in the 1920s and 1930s was handicapped by their temptation to generalize from a small sample of privileged women who disappointed them by, for the most part, not providing a new generation of female leaders. Moreover, feminists failed to appreciate the transformation of housewives' work in an increasingly consumer-oriented society. Nellie McClung, for instance, summed up her bleak assessment of the economic changes affecting middle-class urban women thus:

> Indeed life has pretty well taken women's work away from them in cities and towns, and many of them have found no substitute, no moral equivalent.
>
> To be relieved from the manual work of baking, dressmaking, sweeping, cooking, and to use the time and energy thus liberated to play endless games of bridge, run aimlessly to teas and matinees, beauty parlors, fortune-tellers; to over-eat and undersleep; having no definite aim in life, but to be entertained, is a poor bargain to make with life, and the net result must appear on the wrong side of the ledger.[67]

But feminists were by no means the only critics to focus, to the exclusion of other groups of women, on upper-middle-class city-dwellers with their unprecedented access to domestic technologies and their smaller families. Few understood how the dynamics of a modern capitalist economy relied on different services from women and men. Representatives of organized labour could be similarly perplexed by what they believed to be the "Lost Legion of Dissatisfied Wives," "Cinderellas of the suburbs and Cleopatras of the counties" who "doped or daydreamed" themselves "out of all reason."[68]

An untiring legion of anti-feminists also interpreted new conditions to mean that a married man gave "up everything while the woman gain[ed] everything"[69] and that, "if marriage entailed for the woman the upkeep of a husband and children . . . marriage would have ceased long ago because no woman in the circumstances would be such a fool as to marry."[70] Such commentators feared that the modern home was being reduced to either little more than a convenient meeting place for wage-earning spouses or the site of female parasitism in the case of stay-at-home wives. In both situations, the core of domestic relationships was presumed to be almost entirely sexual. Little else was believed to bind together working couples, and male breadwinners and their non-wage-earning wives appeared to be exchanging financial support for intercourse and, eventually, heirs, although few critics put it quite this bluntly.[71] In any event, women's behaviour was believed to be at the heart of the problem. When they worked for pay, they were blamed for failing to offer husbands and offspring sufficient spiritual and emotional nurture. On the other hand, if they remained at home, critics were only too likely to believe that wives were wasting their own time and their husbands' money and spoiling themselves and their children. The recurring attacks on wives that passed for humour in popular magazines warned female readers "to be passive, loving, and submissive," lest they incur the "rightful" wrath of husbands unwilling to share privilege and power.[72] Whether they were homemakers or wage earners, women were regularly scapegoated for all the failings of modern marriage.

Despite disquiet on every side about the state of marital relationships, women were directed relentlessly to the pursuit of husbands. One editor observed the "veritable epidemic of confessional stories [that] deal with . . . the conflict of a woman torn between home and professional desires." A sceptical observer of contemporary society, she questioned the authenticity of endings in which women solved every problem by giving up their independence and returning meekly to domestic responsibilities: "we have a sneaking suspicion that it is consideration for a man-edited publication that leads so glibly and so unerringly to that conclusion."[73] Solutions for real-life women were much less simple. While paid work was no panacea, it had undeniable benefits. As Nellie McClung recognized, the possibility of wages meant that wives were "less apt to endure conditions that [were] distasteful. . . ."[74] Women with a decent independent income did not have to accept the absolute nature of male privilege. They could demand a better deal.

Since traditional views of marriage did not easily encompass female independence, many Canadians, particularly men, found it difficult to accept the idea of so-called working wives. One young school teacher with an "assured tenure of position for life" found herself battling an unemployed fiancé in the depths of the Great Depression. Concluding that a four-year engagement was long enough, she argued that they could be "happily married" on her income alone. Her "terribly unhappy" young man rejected that practical suggestion, saying "he could never look himself in the face again, that he is not going to have men call him 'the supported man.'"[75] Her United Church adviser admitted that this was a typical, if unfortunate, response from "young men from many stations of life and in many parts of the country." Women, he admitted, were much more likely to be flexible.[76] This difference is not entirely surprising since, for all the widespread reticence about acknowledging the connection between economic and marital power, the traditional sexual hierarchy was much more difficult to maintain when the long-time subordinate was potentially financially independent.

Acutely sensitive to the implications of women's economic position in these years, feminists developed their own version of the wages for housework argument of a later day. The 1920s in particular saw recurring criticism of husbands who refused wives some financial recognition of their services. Right after the war, the National Council of Women, for example, debated "The Right of Women to a Portion of Their Husbands' Income."[77] A few years later, in 1922, the Ontario Provincial Council of Women petitioned the government that, "as the wife is the business partner of her husband in conserving if not producing the wealth that supports the family, she shall be recognized as an equal partner in the marriage relationship and be entitled to a definite income."[78] A supporter of the club movement summed up women's sense of injustice:

> It is of course true that it is generally the man who earns, but it is equally true that his earning capacity depends upon his wife, upon her skill as housekeeper, upon her power to take her share in the organization of their family life. . . . It would be vain to pretend that women do not feel these things [the failure to share the income], they feel them very acutely—and difficult though the adjustments must necessarily be, men especially must face these questions, in the interest of sincere comradeship, of an honest partnership in marriage and of happier homes.[79]

The opposing view "voiced so frequently that women are supported" was in turn condemned as an "untruthful absurdity"[80] by Canadian feminists such as Dr. Augusta Stowe Gullen, daughter of the suffrage pioneer Dr. Emily Howard Stowe.

Although women as a group never won formal recognition of the real work they performed in the home, the introduction of mothers' allowances for those in distress in the 1920s and 1930s owed a great deal to feminist identification of the larger problem. Respectable middle-class housewives who complained that they were "nothing but . . . working housekeeper[s]—without a salary"[81] were not beyond making the connection between the situation of all women at home and that of impoverished single mothers. Just as in a later day, it was understood by at least some observers that only marriage stood between many women and the need for public and private assistance.

The recurring attacks on women's right to waged labour and the chronic widespread unemployment of these decades meant nonetheless that marriage continued in fact to be, as one observer put it, women's "most certain means of livelihood."[82] This blunt assessment summed up the hard reality that prompted counsellors in both decades to urge girls to train for marriage as they would for any occupation. Home economics at all levels was justified in just this way. Some recommendations went further still. Pointing out that ninety percent of women wanted to be married and "marriage as a business investment is a good thing for women," a contributor to the nation's leading magazine for women argued they should be allowed to apply "for wifehood as men apply for work," in other words propose.[83]

Logical as it might appear, such a hard-nosed suggestion was hardly likely to be taken up since it went against conventional propriety and, albeit in a rather different fashion, called into question, much as did wage-earning women, the prevailing sexual hierarchy. Even during the worst days of the Great Depression, the sensible practice of Dutch treat was rejected by many for just this reason. As one young woman wrote: "Evidently it does something to a man when the girl makes grand gestures instead of him. And I guess we girls still react to caveman stuff. We like a boy who puts us in our place, and won't let himself be wheedled."[84] Women were encouraged to appear weddable and, not so incidentally, beddable, but not to reverse the natural order by seizing command at critical moments. This reticence was all the easier when age discrepancies between dates and spouses regularly made men at least harbour the appearance of more experience and authority than their girlfriends.

For all the constraints facing women in their dealings with men, they were held to be largely responsible for failed relationships. After noting that women had more invested in marriage, lacking as they did any other focus for existence, a father, for instance, urged his daughter and others to "play their cards" shrewdly in dealing with men.[85] Almost superhuman forbearance was required of women. To tether men, identified as "polygamous by nature," women had to be constantly alert to male needs, well-dressed and made-up, but never too demanding lest husbands get "that love-strangled feeling."[86] Society put the interests of even peevish and difficult husbands before those of their long-suffering wives.[87]

Female self-sacrifice might go to considerable lengths, as indicated by the approving comments on the remorse suffered by one battered wife who at first attempted to get her husband, a graduate of the University of Toronto, arrested.

> After a night's reflection she was filled with horror at what she had almost done. The idea of what her mother would have said, and the man's mother, was more than she could bear, while the prospect of a future without the erring husband looked pretty black in the cold light of second thought. She even admitted that she deserved the slaps he had given her.[88]

Another woman, confessing that her husband had given her "black eyes several times," found more sympathy from a female columnist who suggested joining a women's group and threatening to call in a justice of the peace. Finally, however, this adviser too had to conclude that it was better not to leave "if your life is at all bearable" since "it is difficult for a woman to support three little children and the court would not consider your troubles sufficient grounds for divorce."[89] Shame at society's condemnation of "their" bad management and fear of being without financial support supplied women with a potent glue for marriage. Although there is no reason to believe that battering was unusual,[90] spousal violence remained for the most part a matter of private embarrassment rather than legal redress. Cases that came to the attention of the general public and the judicial system were most often the minority that ended in extreme injury or death, usually of the wife.[91] Even then, as suggested by the two-month sentence of a man convicted of beating with a fence post his terrified wife who had been sleeping with the cattle through a prairie winter, justice was far from even handed.[92] The trivialization of "spanking" and violence in general in what passed in some quarters in these years as humorous accounts of courtship and marriage suggests how much a certain amount of domestic violence was taken for granted.[93]

Although a few wives resorted to suicide and even to the murder of their husbands,[94] most struggled hard to cope without such drastic remedies. A Victorian Order nurse reported the solution of one battered wife who endeavoured to keep her family fed with her large garden. The unemployed husband, in search of money for liquor, was caught trying to make off with a sack of marketable potatoes. His wife, all patience and fear gone, "struck him a terrific blow in the eye. It was the first time she had tried this method." The nurse summed up the moral approvingly: "he is now a humble man and has never abused anyone since. This story is for the benefit of married women."[95] As this observation suggests, marital violence could provoke a powerful sense of sisterhood. Such a sentiment could also envision co-operative solutions as in the case of one woman's proposal that foreshadowed modern-day transition houses. She envisioned "a lovely place where mothers could take their children when the husband does not behave well to her and them; where the children would be well taken care of and the mother allowed to do something for their support."[96] Unfortunately such safe houses were forty years and more in the future. Until then, women had, for the most part, to find their own solutions.

The great majority of women probably endured assaults and made the best of things, finding satisfaction in their children and attributing their husbands' conduct to crop failure, unemployment, just plain bad luck, or, worse, to their own shortcomings as wives. Yet the seemingly unending progression of difficult times in the 1930s brought some families near the explosion point. One Saskatchewan native wrote to Violet McNaughton, outlining the effects of continuing stress:

> I am at my wit's end to know what to do. It is almost impossible to go on living like this but I can't see any way out. I hate to leave and anyway I'm not able to work and I have E . . . to think of. We have been married 21 years on the 24th of this month so it seems a great pity to break it up now. I've seriously thought of getting outside advice but I've only E . . . for a witness and it would hurt her dreadfully to say anything against her Dad. She is very fond of him when he is not so bad tempered. I do so pray we get a crop this year. I'm sure it will mean the end for us if we don't. The eternal rages are simply sapping my health away and even E . . . is frightened at times whereas before he was careful not to let her see he was angry.[97]

TABLE 4
NUMBER AND RATE OF DIVORCES, 1921-1940

Year	Number	Rate per 100 000 Population	Year	Number	Rate per 100 000 Population
1921	558	6.4	1931	700	6.8
1922	543	6.1	1932	1 007	9.6
1923	505	5.6	1933	931	8.8
1924	540	5.9	1934	1 123	10.5
1925	550	5.9	1935	1 432	13.2
1926	608	6.4	1936	1 570	14.4
1927	748	7.8	1937	1 833	16.6
1928	790	8.0	1938	2 228	20.0
1929	817	8.2	1939	2 073	18.4
1930	875	8.6	1940	2 416	21.3

Source: Series B75–81, *Historical Statistics of Canada*, edited by F.H. Leacy (Ottawa: Statistics Canada, 1983).

Faced with such unresolvable situations, women sought to separate from and divorce their husbands. Yet, whatever the husband's conduct, blame for broken marriages was largely laid at the woman's door: she was too independent;[98] she should have had babies to bring the couple together;[99] and so on and so forth. Although the numbers of divorces seem slight by the standards of the 1980s and low relative to both the United States and Great Britain of that day, contemporary social critics were extremely concerned about their rising levels, which they associated with moral decay, social breakdown, and American influence.[100]

Before the Great War, only New Brunswick, Nova Scotia, and British Columbia possessed divorce courts, but Alberta, Saskatchewan, and Ontario created their own in the 1920s and 1930s. The only option in other provinces was an appeal to parliament for a statutory divorce, an expensive process that favoured the well-to-do. Until 1925, a female petitioner to the courts or parliament had to prove desertion as well as adultery while husbands had only to prove the latter.[101] In 1930, Ottawa abolished the requirement that a wife sue for divorce in the province in which her husband resided, but this change applied only if she had been deserted for more than two years and her spouse was guilty not only of adultery but had "willfully deserted her."[102] Even this limited relief, the fruit of long feminist agitation, drew opposition from those who interpreted relaxation of any kind as "a disorganizing and corrupting force."[103]

Such criticism was dismissed as irrelevant by thousands of Canadians who lived daily with an unhappy union. One such wife wrote *Maclean's* for legal advice, explaining:

After much consideration, I have decided that a divorce is our only remedy. Can you tell me how to secure one with the least possible publicity? . . . We met in the hectic days of 1917. I was a V.A.D. [Voluntary Aid Detachment nurse]; he a captain in the army, and after less than a fortnight's acquaintance we were married. I married to escape the interference of my mother; he to secure a housekeeper. How could such a marriage be anything but a failure? We came to Canada to make a fresh start. My husband bought a farm and went to live on it alone. . . . I could not endure the loneliness and inconvenience of the life. . . . Our relations have been getting worse instead of better. We do not speak for days at a time except when absolutely necessary. He is even more anxious for a divorce than I—offers to provide for the boy and me on a generous scale. I will not agree to this—at least not for myself. It is not necessary. I have a little money and have become a fully qualified nurse since coming to this country. We do not look upon divorce as a great wrong, especially in this case, when it means happiness for everyone concerned.[104]

The answer this writer received was equally matter-of-fact: the province in which she resided issued divorces with relatively little publicity and she was to send her address if she needed a recommendation for a lawyer.

Unfortunately, not all marital disasters could be solved so expeditiously. Given legal costs, the restricted grounds for petitioning, and the stigma attached to divorce, many of those determined to leave their spouses voted with their feet, sought legal separations, and, in some instances, filed for divorce in the United States.[105] Whatever they chose to do, women were deeply concerned about inequitable property settlements and child custody.[106] Many understood only too well that neither their labour nor their commitment to their children would necessarily be fairly recognized. Nor could whatever protection the law allowed be guaranteed since delinquent spouses easily crossed into other jurisdictions with both property and children. Such considerations kept many wives home long after all semblance of a good marriage had evaporated.

The consequences of dependence upon the essentially arbitrary authority of the husband drove some wives to label their relationships "bondage."[107] Nor did they ignore the implication of messages propagated by modern advertisers regarding female duties. Even those who counted themselves far from radical questioned why men should be permitted a host of sins from "expanding waistlines" to "receding hairlines" while "magazines and newspapers are full of sinister warnings to wives these days" about losing their beauty and thus their marriages.[108] Such insights may not have been universal, but their repetition in various forms indicates that many women were far from being satisfied with the marital status quo. Unfortunately, as was also recognized, it took two people, both wife and husband, to bring about change. And as women knew only too well, "there are very few men big enough to form a real partnership with a woman, to appreciate her work and to stand shoulder-to-shoulder with her in the responsibilities of the home."[109] Masculine prerogatives were too valuable to be given up easily.

And yet for all the dilemmas of marriage for women, it attracted the majority of Canadians. To be sure, recognition of its liabilities came largely with experience and long after alternate choices could easily be made. Yet many Canadian women found deep satisfaction and abiding affection with their husbands, despite the shortcomings of an institution that gave so many advantages to men that in effect there were frequently two different marriages, hers and his.[110] At the base of successful marital relationships, as one prairie farm wife argued, lay a strong sense of partnership:

> For example, take our district last summer. The women all raised poultry, had good gardens, and when fall came, their work dressed all the youngsters and besides that there was still something left to buy other useful things in the home. The husband with his share of the profit paid store bills and old accounts, and by co-operation the home prospered.[111]

In such households, women functioned as "Partners, Not Doormats," a situation that contributed maximally to family survival and female contentment as well.[112]

The desire for and the reality of an equal union in which spouses co-operated in an equitable sharing of duties and rewards surfaced regularly in female writing. Some authors, although by no means all, believed that this co-operation included male participation in housework.[113] For many, like the following writer, flexibility in sex roles was identified as a key to success:

> I've helped outside with anything I lay hands on, and have milked up to six cows myself when the good man was away or busy. I get help with washing and other housework when he is not busy. And I can leave him to do a baking of bread and take care of six children when I go anywhere.[114]

A certain disregard for the boundaries between "her" and "his" work was most readily managed in situations like that of private farms, as above, or family businesses where spouses laboured in close proximity and easily became familiar with the range of tasks essential to collective survival. The wives of doctors, mounties, and small merchants often lived adjacent to offices, jails, and shops. They were as likely as not to be found lending a hand with patients, prisoners, or customers as washing the kitchen floor or making dinner. Such contact could foster considerable happiness, as with nurse Rose Kent Doolittle whose physician husband's office was on the side of their house. She recalled that, "it was great fun working with him. You get a kind of nice feeling, you know, when you've done everything you can do to make things go as they should."[115]

Recognition of mutual dependence did not necessarily rely on constant association. Women married to mounties, doctors, missionaries, salesmen, lumbermen, fishermen, and fur trappers, for example, might well spend a good part of their married life separated from their husbands.[116] The strength and the skill to manage alone, sometime isolated from other human help, could inspire recognition of the contribution each partner brought to the marriage. Such was the case, for example, in Northern Labrador where Elizabeth Goudie forged a strong attachment to her spouse Jim who returned from his traplines to deliver a new baby. Not only that, for, as Elizabeth reminisced, "Jim took over for me. He did the cooking, baked the bread, did the laundry and scrubbed the floor."[117]

Well-satisfied spouses often co-operated in more than work and immediate family duties. A shared commitment to religion and politics strengthened many a couple. A host of husband-wife teams, such as Lucy and James Woodsworth, Mary and James Endicott, and Violet and John McNaughton, maintained each other's courage in the face of political and religious critics.[118] Less well-known couples, such as two active union supporters, a former teacher and an employee of B.C. Telephone, also found that "sharing opinions politically" kept them close in spirit and affections as well.[119] Women in the Lake Cowichan Women's Auxiliary to the International Woodworkers of America and the Ukrainian Labour Temple Association were among many to win respect and confirm a sense of shared purpose when they stood with striking husbands in clashes against lumber and mining bosses on Vancouver Island and in Northern Alberta.[120]

Marriages did not have to be egalitarian to be happy. It was possible, and much celebrated in the media, for wives to find sufficient reward as their husband's second-in-command, close adviser, and loyal supporter.[121] The 1939 Canadian tour of Their Majesties King George and Queen Elizabeth gave one female observer a change to reflect on

> the marvellous lesson the Queen taught us wives and mothers. . . . Because she is primarily a wife and mother does she excel as Queen. Ever forgetful of self, always so ready with praise and encouragement, graciously receiving all homages but to relay them to the King; Her Majesty shows us that, although the Queen, she is first His Majesty's most loyal subject and helpmate. Too many of us women have let the successes of our feminine campaigns fog the fact that no group or corporation, let alone the family, can properly function unless there is but one head. Let us encourage, guide and uphold rather than strive to gain or divide the authority in our homes, for only then can we expect the smooth running that generates happiness.[122]

The old metaphor that compared a family and a kingdom, a father and a king, was valid for some couples. It undoubtedly worked best when, as Labrador's Elizabeth Goudie recalled, the reign was mild and beneficent:

> It was the custom for the man to run the home, the women took second place. A woman could have her say around the house but about the main things in life, the man always had his say. His word went for most everything. Women accepted this and

> thought nothing about it. They were not hard men; they were
> kind. They were not very hard to please, so a woman could sew
> and cook and look after her family; that was the most that was
> expected of the wives.[123]

As long as men were perceived as living up to their side of the implicit bargain that Goudie's comment suggests existed, then women could well reckon themselves happy. Like the Mennonite bride who enjoyed the predictability of the wedding ritual, such wives could enjoy the approval of society in general and the psychological and emotional, not to mention economic, benefits of male leadership.

Probably most successful relationships represented a complex mixture of admitted and disguised superiority and inferiority. Marriages blessed with a sense of mutual regard and common purpose could prevail over bad times and less than perfect spouses. A woman counted herself happy enough when, despite years of suffering and drudgery, a normally inarticulate husband could yell from his labours with the cows across to her as she emptied the wash tub: "I kinds [sic] like you. Thought I'd tell you. I just happened to think of it!"[124] Such exchanges were far from the romantic fantasies that flourished in films and ads, but they conveyed volumes to the individuals concerned. While romance formed part of the expectations of many girls who could hardly avoid the message communicated by pulp novels, full length features, and appeals for sweet breath and shining teeth, a good man and a good marriage were finally often a great deal more prosaic.

Groomed for marriage, as they were practically from birth, not all women either sought or found husbands. A number lost prospective marital partners during World War I. A few chose religious vocations. Others for one reason or another never made the suitable male contacts. Still another group chose not to marry for lack of interest in the institution or in men or for love of jobs or other women. For most, spinsterhood was a result of a slow accumulation of individual acts rather than one early conscious decision. This is hardly surprising, as unmarried women, as with the main character in the short story "A Wedding Dress" by Morley Callaghan, were regularly dismissed as pitiful creatures who were emotionally flawed.[125] By remaining unwed they were only too liable to be caricatured as sour, "unfulfilled and empty."[126]

The implications of women's choice whether to marry evoked considerable public interest, as the debate between one self-styled "Businesswoman" and another "Spinster" in *Maclean's* in 1931 indicated. The former, a forty-year-old with twenty-one years' experience in business, began the discussion by insisting that older women could not equal men in business where they faced insecure futures. Other benefits of the single state were equally uncertain. "Sexual promiscuity," for instance, like "companionate marriage," favoured men who could shop around, leaving unwanted lovers. Women themselves were dismissed as incapable of real friendships and thus no substitute for families. Especially noticeable in all her complaints was the near lack of interest in a man other than as a source of financial security. Much more important was the absence of a child, as the following confession revealed: "I am very, very lonely. Sometimes in the night I dream of little fumbling arms around my neck, and I am crying when I awake."[127]

Two months later, a fifty-year-old "Spinster" with twenty-seven years as a teacher, bookkeeper, and policewoman replied. She pointed to mothers' allowances and wife-beating as proof that "marriage is not a cure-all" and argued that many of women's professional difficulties stemmed largely from male opposition to their presence in business. In her experience, women had proved more capable of "loyal friendship and good sports-manship" than men. She concluded with the observation "I have no quar-rel with men. I like them when they have a becoming humility. But many of them have been spoiled and a spoiled man, like a spoiled child, is unhappy himself and makes everyone else miserable."[128] "Spinster's" com-ments were applauded two weeks later in the same magazine by "A Wife," who with her five children, car, house, and bad-tempered husband, would happily have traded places with her businesswoman sister.[129]

In all these sallies, two major points were at issue. Could a woman sup-port herself alone and were there emotional alternatives to a husband and children? Given the reality of women's wages, which in all occupations were significantly lower than men's, and discriminatory pension plans, women had some cause to worry about financial security. And yet, just because they were cheaper to hire, they might very well find employment when men could not. In some towns like Paris and Dundas, Ontario, where the knit mills preferred female workers, thrifty women could afford to set up comfortable independent households.[130] Middle-class women who found white-collar and professional jobs, especially in areas that were strongly sex-typed such as the primary school grades, hospitals, and, increasingly, clerical employments, also had some hope of paying their bills, albeit frequently with reduced salaries during the Great Depression. For those who were fortunate and industrious, the prospects for some form of economic independence, although not the equal of their brothers', existed more than ever before.

A few options were far from new. Women had long chosen religious vocations in preference to marriage. Ever since the days of Marie de l'In-carnation and Jeanne Mance in New France, nuns and lay sisters had dis-covered material security, emotional or spiritual nurture, and even, on occasion, opportunities for advancement within the Catholic Church. Orders like the Sisters of Providence, St. Joseph and St. Anne, and the Ursulines continued to offer English-speaking women useful opportunities to serve their communities as teachers, nurses, and social workers. A smaller number entered three Anglican religious orders: the Sisterhood of St. John the Divine, founded in Canada, the Community of the Sisters of the Church, established in England, and the Society of St. Margaret, with American roots. Presbyterians and Methodists and, after 1926, United

Church members also worked as deaconess nurses, teachers, social workers, and missionaries across the country. Like the Catholic orders they imitated, these "foot soldiers" of Protestantism laboured in the shadow of an
ordained male clergy who harnessed their energy without according them
equal status.[131] The admission of an occasional woman to the ministry, as
with the unmarried Lydia Gruchy to the United Church in 1936,[132] could
not counter the fact that female religious workers were in service to essentially male hierarchies.[133] While Catholic nuns still had a vital role to play
in the provision of social services, deaconesses were in decline by World
War I. In Protestant society, church-bound efforts were increasingly
superseded by secular services and religious workers by lay professionals.
In English Canada, single women desiring to serve their society had better
paying and higher status alternatives than the churches would allow.

New opportunities helped give rise to an unprecedented generation of
outstanding single women in everything from politics to the arts to the
professions. Individuals like Agnes Macphail, Charlotte Whitton, Mazo
de la Roche, Cora Hind, Ethel Johns, Eunice Dyke, Anne Savage, Florence
Wyle, Frances Loring, Emily Carr, Monica Storrs, and Hilda Neatby[134]
carved out lives that were the equal of or better than many of their more
conventional contemporaries. Some, like Cora Hind and Emily Carr, had
been affected by the suffrage agitation, but most came to maturity in the
1920s and 1930s when issues of professional legitimacy and the exact
shape of new political rights absorbed their energies and shaped their
characters. They tested their society's commitment to equality, supposedly
enshrined in the franchise and the right to enter universities and the
professions.

Such women would probably have been extraordinary in any generation, but they stood out all the more in these decades because few Canadians knew what to expect of the public performance of talented spinsters.
Their pioneering was far from easy. Devoted as any might be to issues as
diverse as prison reform, relief administration, Canadian culture, wheat
policy, health care, art education, artistic expression, missions, or the life
of the intellect in general, not one could avoid being judged first and foremost, and often harshly, as a representative of her sex. Agnes Macphail,
like Judy LaMarsh some four decades later, became unwittingly a spokes-
person for women's rights, despite the fact that she had expressed no special interest in the matter before her election to Parliament. The painters
Emily Carr and Anne Savage and the sculptors Florence Wyle and Frances
Loring struggled to be taken seriously as artists and to avoid dismissal as
mere female dilettantes. Ethel Johns and Eunice Dyke battled to win public
health nurses the respect accorded male professionals. De la Roche, Storrs,
Hind, and Neatby made their way in the male-dominated areas of literature, missions, commodity reporting, and academe despite being, as
Neatby, a Saskatchewan university professor, observed, "the wrong
sex."[135] A number like Whitton, Carr, Macphail, and Neatby refused male
suitors because they saw no way of reconciling heterosexual relationships

with their need for independence. As Macphail summed up the situation, "*the person* could not be subjected."[136]

In choosing the harder, but rewarding, path of their ambitions rather than traditional matrimony, many were strengthened by influential female relatives. Macphail looked to her outspoken, independent grandmother Campbell as her "guiding spirit."[137] De la Roche found crucial support in her cousin Caroline; Hind in her Aunt Alice; Johns, Savage, and Neatby in their mothers; Carr and Neatby in their sisters. A good number such as Whitton and Macphail depended on intimate female friends for the emotional reassurance and physical assistance in the practical details of life that allowed them to plunge back into highly competitive and frequently unfriendly male worlds. Lifelong female companions like Whitton and Margaret Grier, de la Roche and Caroline Clement, and Loring and Wyle provided a security and love found only in the best of marriages. Having, as they so often did, a positive experience of being mothered, such women went on to serve as surrogate mothers in a host of settings. For Storrs there were children in Guide and Scout companies; for Dyke and Johns there were young nurses; for Savage and Neatby there were nieces and nephews. De la Roche went so far as to adopt two toddlers; Storrs took in two refugee boys as foster sons. Such lives were far from the parched and stunted effigies caricatured by an unkind press. These women might not have found ways to accommodate their aspirations to companionship with a man within marriage, a fact that was hardly surprising given the prevailing expectations about the role of the wife, but they did not lack compensating satisfactions. To be sure, like all people, their lives were not without regrets—Macphail would have liked her own children; Neatby bitterly resented academic discrimination; Carr found dogs kinder than her Victoria neighbours—but such disappointments were minor compared to the hostility and dismissal of a world that placed inordinate value on heterosexual coupling and female deference. Over the long term, their achievements went far beyond mere survival, although that sometimes seemed hard enough, to leave a worthy heritage for subsequent generations of independent-minded women.

NOTES

1. For a wonderful introduction to singing games, skipping rhymes, ball bouncing, clapping games and songs, foot and finger plays, counting out rhymes, taunts and teases, tricks and treats, silly songs, riddles, endless songs, tongue twisters, charms and omens, answer back songs, etc., see *Ring Around the Moon* (Toronto: McClelland and Stewart, 1977) and *Sally Go Round the Sun* (Toronto: McClelland and Stewart, 1969), both by the doyenne of Canadian folklore, Edith Fowke.

2. See the selection, for instance, by Phil Thomas, *Songs of the Pacific Northwest* (Saanichton, B.C.: Hancock House, 1979).

3. Ellen Gee, "Fertility and Marriage Patterns in Canada 1851–1971" (Ph.D. thesis, Univesity of British Columbia, 1978), table 36.

4. Ibid., table 34.

5. See, for example, Henrietta Muir Edwards, "Report of the Committee on Laws for the Business and Professional Women of Canada," National Council of Women of Canada *Report* (1920): 124–29.

6. See Paul Axelrod, "Moulding the Middle Class: Student Life at Dalhousie University in the 1930s," *Acadiensis* (Autumn 1985): 84–122.

7. Stephen Endicott, *James G. Endicott: Rebel Out of China* (Toronto: University of Toronto Press, 1980), chap. 6.

8. Simma Holt, *The Other Mrs. Diefenbaker* (Toronto: Doubleday, 1982), chap. 2.

9. Constance Kerr Sissons, "An Older Wive's Tale," *Chatelaine* (Aug. 1931): 14.

10. "More 'Shame on You' Copy," *Marketing* (Aug. 25, 1934): 2.

11. "THE SERENE MARRIAGE . . . ," *Grain Growers' Guide* (Sept. 1932): 2.

12. "Pick any 12 Girls—10 Have to be Told," *Chatelaine* (May 1928): 29.

13. "That Girl Has Plenty of Ump-ph!" *National Home Monthly* (Sept. 1938): 31.

14. "Many Men Came and Went in Her Life," *Western Home Monthly* (Jan. 1925): 41.

15. Lorna Slocombe, "Are You a Good Date?" *Chatelaine* (Sept. 1938): 18.

16. "When Summer Sun Tans," *Canadian Magazine* (July 1932): 42.

17. "For Ladies Too," *Canadian Homes and Gardens* (Dec. 1927): 93. Emphasis is in the original.

18. Kathleen Murphy, "What Price Pulchritude?" *Maclean's* (March 15, 1932): 24.

19. Lotta Dempsey, "It's News," *Chatelaine* (March 1937): 84.

20. "'I learned from a beauty expert how to hold my husband—and why so many women fail,'" *Chatelaine* (Feb. 1932): 27. See also the ad by Lux, "How to Annoy Your Husband," *Free Press Prairie Farmer* (Nov. 1938): 43; "'Suddenly I realized my husband was ASHAMED OF Me,'" *Western Home Monthly* (July 1929): 31.

21. "'I Was Startled by My Young Son's Remark—believe me, I'll never risk my personal daintiness again!'" *Free Press Prairie Farmer* (Oct. 1938): 49.

22. "You are in a Beauty Contest every day of your life," *National Home Monthly* (Jan. 1932): 56.

23. "Rubbish I Say," *Free Press Prairie Farmer* (Jan. 21, 1925): 17.

24. See the comments in Eliane Leslau Silverman, *The Last Best West: Women on the Alberta Frontier 1880–1930* (Montreal: Eden Press, 1984), chap. 3.

25. "Success Cheering," *Free Press Prairie Farmer* (May 17, 1933): 5.

26. Quoted in Silverman, *The Last Best West*, 41.

27. Alfred Henry Tyrer, *Sex, Marriage and Birth-Control. A Guide-book to a Satisfactory Sex Life in Marriage* (Toronto: MacMillan, 1936), xiv, emphasis in original.

28. Ibid., 91.

29. Ibid., xv.

30. *Eaton's Catalogue* (Fall-Winter 1937–38), 253.

31. See Isabel Turnbull Dingman, "First Aid for the Married," *Chatelaine* (June 1938): 10–11, 37.

32. Stephen Endicott, *James G. Endicott*, 63.

33. See the typical criticism of free love in "Feminine Clamour for Free Love," *Saturday Night* (Nov. 26, 1927), front page editorial, and Tyrer, *Sex, Marriage and Birth Control*, passim.

34. Unfortunately, there is no historical study of this problem in Canada. It is, however, a useful reminder of the significance of infertility in human history to consult Angus McLaren, *Reproductive Rituals: Perceptions of Fertility in England from the Sixteenth Century to the Nineteenth Century* (London: Methuen, 1984), especially chap. 2.

35. On the concern with morality see, for instance, the statement of the United Church, Records and Proceedings, 1932, Board of Evangelism and Social Service, "The Meaning and Responsibility of Christian Marriage," 276–86.

36. For an important discussion of this phenomenon see Angus McLaren and Arlene Tigar McLaren, *The Bedroom and the State: The Changing Practices and Politics of Contraception and Abortion in Canada, 1880–1980* (Toronto: McClelland and Stewart, 1986).

37. Quoted in Kathryn Ogg, "'Especially When No One Agrees': An Interview with May Campbell" in *Not Just Pin Money*, edited by Barbara Latham and Roberta Pazdro (Victoria: Camosun College, 1984), 140.

38. See ibid., 28–30.

39. See Mary F. Bishop, "Vivian Dowding: Birth Control Activist 1892–   " in *Rethinking Canada*, edited by Veronica Strong-Boag and Anita Clair Fellman (Toronto: Copp Clark Pitman, 1986), 200–07.

40. McLaren and McLaren, *The Bedroom and the State*, 99–103 and chap. 5.

41. Dianne Dodd, "The Canadian Birth Control Movement 1929–1939" (M.A. thesis, University of Toronto, 1982), abstract.

42. McLaren and McLaren, *The Bedroom and the State*, part 1.

43. Glenbow, Jean McDonald papers, Appendix to Mrs. Jean McDonald's Autobiography, by Mollie LaFrance (Daughter).

44. Quoted in Joan Sangster, "Finnish Women in Ontario, 1890–1930," *Polyphony* (Fall 1981), 59.

45. SFUA, taped interview with Ruth Bullock by Sara Diamond, 1979.

46. Ibid., 69–70.

47. United Church, Records and Proceedings, 1932, Board of Evangelism and Social Service, "The Meaning and Responsibility of Christian Marriage," 280.

48. McLaren and McLaren, *The Bedroom and the State*, 130–31.

49. Ibid., chap. 2.

50. Dr. W.A. Dafoe, "The Types and Treatment of Abortion," *Canadian Medical Association Journal* (June 1930): 794.

51. McLaren and McLaren, *The Bedroom and the State*, 50–51.

52. Ibid., 42. See also the accounts of three married working-class women in Vancouver, "'I Could Have Had a Baby a Year'" in *Working Lives: Vancouver 1886–1986*, edited by the Working Lives Collection (Vancouver: New Star Books, 1985), 104.

53. Jacques Henripin, *Trends and Factors of Fertility in Canada* (Ottawa: Statistics Canada, 1972), 328.

54. On the situation facing the unwed in French Canada, which seems not all that different from that elsewhere in the country, see Andrée Levesque, "Deviant Anonymous: Single Mothers at the Hôpital de la Misericorde in Montreal, 1929–1939," Canadian Historical Association *Historical Papers* (1984). On discrimination in nineteenth-century Canada see Peter Ward, "Unwed Motherhood in Nineteenth Century English Canada," ibid. (1981).

55. "Admits Drowning Baby," *Free Press Prairie Farmer* (July 26, 1933): 9

56. "Must Stand Trial for Baby Slaying," ibid. (Dec. 12, 1934): 9.

57. Quoted in Silverman, *The Last Best West*, 45

58. See Mab, "As a Bride Adorns Herself," *Chatelaine* (June 1928): 34. See also Mary E. MacPherson, "The Bride Furnishes her Home," ibid. (June 1930): 19, and Isabel Morgan, "The Lovely Bride," *Saturday Night* (May 2, 1931): 16.

59. See Gloria Queen, "Why I Had a Civil Marriage," *Chatelaine* (March 1935): 16, 49, 50.

60. See Judge Ben B. Lindsey, "Are Marriage Vows Sacred?" *Maclean's* (April 15, 1923): 37. See the criticism of its effect on women in Emily Murphy, "Companionate Marriage: From the Point of View of Mother and Child," *Chatelaine* (May 1928): 3, which seems somewhat similar to the critique of the so-called sexual revolution of the 1960s and beyond.

61. Allan M. Buehler, "The Old-Order Mennonite Wedding and Highlights of Their Social Life" in *Explorations in Canadian Folklore*, edited by Edith Fowke and Carole Carpenter (Toronto: McClelland and Stewart, 1985), 80–83.

62. Lillian Petroff, "Contributors to Ethnic Cohesion: Macedonian Women in Toronto to 1940" in *Looking into My Sister's Eyes*. See also the case of Maria Orletsky reported by Helen Potrebenko, *No Streets of Gold: A Social History of Ukrainians in Alberta* (Vancouver: New Star Books, 1977), 171–72, 127–28.

63. Quoted in Isabel Kaprielian, "The Saved: Armenian Refugee Women," *Canadian Woman Studies* (Winter 1986), 7.

64. PAC, International Council of Women Papers, folder 497, E— C— to Lady Aberdeen, March 27, 1921. On the effect of the war see also "Sister Jean," "Have We Like Sheep All Gone Astray?" *Saturday Night* (May 15, 1920): 21; Arthur B. Baxter, "I Say to Canadian Girls 'Have Patience'—and to Our Returned Men, 'Pull Up your Socks,' " *Everywoman's World* 9 (Oct. 1919): 7, 42; Mrs. Harold Peat, "My Soldier Husband," *Maclean's* (Dec. 1918): 110–12; Ethel Chapman, "While Greater Issues Go By," ibid. (May 1918): 100–5. See also, Veronica Strong-Boag, *The Parliament of Women* (Ottawa: National Museum, 1976), chap. 8.

65. See Mary P. Ryan, "The Projection of a New Womanhood: The Movie Moderns in the 1920s" in *Our American Sisters: Women in American Life and Thought*, edited by Jean E. Friedman and William G. Shade (Lexington, Mass.: D.C. Heath & Co., 1982), and Molly Haskell, *From Reverence to Rape: The Treament of Women in the Movies* (New York: Holt, Rinehart and Winston, 1973).

66. See H.F. Angus, ed., *Canada and Her Great Neighbour: Sociological Surveys of Opinions and Attitudes in Canada Concerning the United States* (Toronto: The Ryerson Press, 1938), chap. 5 "Motion Pictures."

67. Nellie McClung, "Was Marriage Easier Then? Yes!" *Chatelaine* (Dec. 1935): 30.

68. "Women Want Too Much," *Canadian Congress Journal* (April 1929): 40. See also "The Marriage Partnership," ibid. (March 1928): 39, 40

69. James Wedgwood Drawbell, "What Did Your Husband Give up for Marriage?" *Chatelaine* (Aug. 1938): 18, and "Doctor on Color and Marriage," *Saturday Night* (June 10, 1922): 30.

70. F.E. Bailey, "Do Wives Give More Than Husbands," *Saturday Night* (May 1930): 9. See also the agreement voiced by "A Successful Wife" in a letter to ibid. (July 1930): 34; R.F. Faryon, "If I Were A Woman," *Chatelaine* (April 1932): 19; Faryon, "A Man's Side of It," *Maclean's* (Sept. 1, 1932): 30; Faryon, "Women are Like That," *Chatelaine* (Oct. 1932): 12; M. Forsyth, "Does It Pay a Man to Marry? No!" *Maclean's* (July 15, 1928): 14.

71. For the essence of this viewpoint see M. Forsyth and B. Sandwell, "Does It Pay a Man to Marry?" *Maclean's* (July 15, 1928): 14, 15, and "Doctor on Color and Marriage," *Saturday Night* (June 10, 1922): 30.

72. See J.G. Snell, "Marriage Humour and Its Social Functions, 1900–1939," *Atlantis* (Spring 1986): 85.

73. Alison Craig, "The Farm Wife and Home Department," *Free Press Prairie Farmer* (Oct. 22, 1919): 13.

74. N. McClung, "Was Marriage Easier Then? Yes!" *Chatelaine* (Dec. 1935): 13.

75. "Question," "The Business of Living" edited by Percy R. Hayward and Grace Sloan Overton, *Onward* (June 24, 1933): 198.

76. "Answer," ibid. See also the concern with the threat to "male psychology" in letters objecting to married working women in Harriet Parsons, "Youth Replies," *Canadian Home Journal* (June 1936): 45–46.

77. "Co-Workers and Co-Spenders," *Woman's Century* (Oct. 1920): l.

78. Augusta Stowe Gullen, "Ontario," National Council of Women, *Annual Report* (1922): 51; see also "Should Husbands Pay Their Wives Salaries," *Everywoman's World* (Feb. 1920) reprinted in *Canadian Woman Studies* (Winter 1978–79): 89–90.

79. "Co-Workers and Co-Spenders," *Woman's Century* (Oct. 1920): 1. See also Mollie Bawn, "What Price Wives?" IODE *Echoes* (June 1926): 16, and Margaret Patterson as quoted in Loraine Gordon, "Doctor Margaret Norris Patterson: First Woman Police Magistrate in Eastern Canada—Toronto—January 1922 to November 1934," *Atlantis* (Fall 1984), 101.

80. Stowe Gullen, "Ontario," NCWC *Report* (1923), 31.

81. "The Marriage Partnership," ibid., 39.

82. Isabel Turnbull Dingman, "Can She Manage Alone?" *Chatelaine* (April 1932): 12.

83. Constance Templeton, "Let the Woman Propose," *Chatelaine* (May 1934): 22.

84. Isabel Turnbull Dingman, "They Won't Let the Woman Pay," *Chatelaine* (March 1934): 43.

85. Garrett Elliott, "What I Wish For My Daughter," *Chatelaine* (May 1934): 14.

86. Anne B. Fisher, "Live With a Man and Love It," *Chatelaine* (Sept. 1937): 12. See also Reg R. Faryon, "Why Husbands Stray," ibid. (Aug. 1933): 13.

87. See E.G., "Why I Spoil My Husband," *Chatelaine* (May 1931): 17, and Albert A. Townsend, "When a Husband is Peevish," ibid. (Sept. 1932): 20.

88. Isabel Turnbull Dingman, "Mending Rifts in Home Sweet Home," *National Home Monthly* (Sept. 1937): 50.

89. "Don't Allow Beatings," *Free Press Prairie Farmer* (Jan. 28, 1925): 18.

90. Modern studies suggest that wife-battering is widespread among all classes of society. See, for example, Patricia Kincaid, "The Omitted Reality: Husband-Wife Violence in Ontario and Policy Implications for Education" (Ed.D. thesis, University of Toronto, 1981), and Linda McLeod, *Wife Battering in Canada: The Vicious Circle*, prepared for the Canadian Advisory Council on the Status of Women (Ottawa: Minister of Supply and Services, 1980).

91. See, for instance, "Alberta Farmer Kills Wife, Son and Self" when she was going to divorce him, *Free Press Prairie Farmer* (June 26, 1935): 1; "Given Prison Term for Death of Wife," ibid. (Nov. 27, 1935): 11; "Murder Charge Laid Against Gonor Man," ibid. (April 1, 1936): 10; "Held on Charge of Killing Wife: Gilbert Plains Farmer Arrested After Wife Found With Her Throat Slashed," ibid. (July 12, 1933): 1; "Farmer Admits He Killed Wife," ibid. (Jan. 24, 1934): 3.

92. "Wife Beater Gets Two-Month Term," ibid. (Aug. 17, 1932): 25.

93. See, for example, Walter Haefeli, Jr., "Gentlemen Don't Spank," *Maclean's* (Feb. 1, 1935): 12; Lady R. Torrington, "Woman Worship," ibid. (Sept. 15, 1932): 12, and F.E. Bailey, "The Art of Being Courted," *Chatelaine* (Jan. 1931): 8. The latter, for example, found it a subject of amusement that "Every so often a young gentleman in less refined circles than ours takes a razor to his young lady . . . and we are put to the expense of his trial and execution. I don't say that he is justified but . . . it would have been better not to provoke him, or any other man."

94. See R. M. Franks, "A Genetic and Comparative Study of Depressed Female Patients in the Toronto Psychiatric Hospital" (M.A. thesis, University of Toronto, 1929) and his

"The Pathogenesis and Prevention of Suicide" (Ph.D thesis, University of Toronto, 1936) for some examples of suicide. For relatively rare examples of wives murdering husbands, see "Poison Found Cause of Farmer's Death," *Free Press Prairie Farmer* (Oct. 30, 1935): 4; "Doukhobor Farmer Shot in Bed by Wife," ibid. (Sept. 4, 1935): 11; and "Woman Accused of Killing Husband," ibid. (Dec. 12, 1934): 32.

95. Glenbow, Victoria Order of Nurses, Calgary Papers, Box 1, *Annual Report for 1929* (handwritten).

96. "Refuge for Wives," *Free Press Prairie Farmer* (Aug. 9, 1933): 5.

97. SAB, Violet McNaughton Papers, v. 13, folder 22, Mrs. —— to McNaughton, May 16, 1938.

98. See Madge MacBeth, "Until Love Dies or the Courts Us Do Part," *Chatelaine* (Nov. 1928): 3.

99. See Anne B. Fisher, M.D., "Live With a Man and Love It," ibid. (Jan. 1938): 19.

100. See, for example, M. Grattan O'Leary, "Divorce," *Maclean's* (April 1, 1930): 3–4, 87; Social Service Council of Canada, *Some Aspects of the Divorce Situation As It Affects Canada, A Report Prepared for the Use of the Committee 1921–22* (Toronto: Publication of the Committee on the Family, 1922); Constance Travers Sweatman, "Why Doesn't She Divorce Him?" *Western Home Monthly* (April 1927): 49; and Helen G. MacGill, "Checking the Divorce Menace," *Chatelaine* (April 1931): 28.

101. O'Leary, "Divorce," 4.

102. D.C. McKie, B. Prentice, P. Reed, *Divorce: Law and the Family in Canada* (Ottawa: Statistics Canada, 1983), 46.

103. *Some Aspects of the Divorce Situation As It Affects Canada*, 37.

104. "*Maclean's* Question Box" conducted by Edwina Seton, *Maclean's* (April 1, 1926): 77.

105. See, for instance, the case of a "Canadian Olympic star" who went to Reno for six weeks to divorce a Toronto husband, in Dora M. Sanders, "Are We Honest About Divorce?" *Maclean's* (March 1, 1932): 11, 32–33.

106. See, for example, the concerns expressed by correspondents seeking advice in "Distressed," *Free Press Prairie Farmer* (Jan. 7, 1925): 4; "Answer Department. Legal," ibid. (July 13, 1932): 23–24; ibid. (July 27, 1932): 27; ibid. (Sept. 7, 1932): 26; ibid. (Sept. 21, 1932): 22; ibid. (Oct. 5, 1932): 26.

107. A Wife, "This Bondage," *Maclean's* (Oct. 1, 1931): 11, 46.

108. Florence N. Webb, "Sauce for the Gander," *Maclean's* (July 15, 1932): 10.

109. Nancy Leigh, "Wages and Wives: Why Not Put the Home on a Business Basis?" *Chatelaine* (April 1929): 23.

110. For a modern discussion of this phenomenon see Jessie Bernard, *The Future of Marriage* (New York: Bantam, 1973), chap. 1.

111. "Business Partners," *Free Press Prairie Farmer* (Feb. 19, 1936): 5. See also Emily Murphy, "What is Wrong with Marriage?" *Western Home Monthly* (July 1928): 7, 58 on the importance of friendship.

112. Margaret Pennell, "Partners, Not Doormats," *Maclean's* (Nov. 1, 1932): 11.

113. See, for example, "Should Men Help with Housework," *Grain Growers' Guide* (July 1, 1927): 17–18; Rose Paynter, "Man—the Home Maker," *Western Home Monthly* (Feb. 1923): 43.

114. "Helping Each Other," *Free Press Prairie Farmer* (Oct. 5, 1932): 4.

115. A. Peterkin and Margaret Shaw, *Mrs. Doctor: Reminiscences of Manitoba Doctors' Wives* (Winnipeg: Prairie Publishing Company, 1976), 88. See also Joy Duncan, ed., *Red Serge Wives* (Edmonton: Co-op Press, 1974), and Fredelle Bruser Maynard, *Raisins and Almonds* (Toronto: Paperjacks, 1973).

116. For an important discussion of this phenomenon see Isabelle St. Martin, "Family Separation: The Case of the Women Left Behind" (submitted to the History Department, Concordia University, in partial fulfillment of the requirements for a Master's degree, June

30, 1980). For a case study of women married to lumbermen who spent most of the week in the woods see Sara Diamond, "A Union Man's Wife: The Ladies' Auxiliary Movement in the IWA, The Lake Cowichan Experience" in *Not Just Pin Money*.

117. Elizabeth Goudie, *Woman of Labrador* (Toronto: Peter Martin Associates, 1975), 44.

118. See Grace MacInnis, *J.S. Woodsworth: A Man to Remember* (Toronto: Macmillan, 1953), Stephen Endicott, *James G. Endicott: Rebel Out of China* and correspondence between Violet and John in SAB, MacNaughton Papers.

119. SFUA, taped interview with Effie Jones by Sara Diamond, 1979.

120. See Sara Diamond, "A Union Man's Wife," and Anne B. Woywitka, "A Pioneer Woman in the Labour Movement" in *Rethinking Canada*.

121. See "The Brilliant Man's Wife," *Saturday Night* (March 12, 1927): 50; Leslie Roberts, "The Wife of a Politician," *Chatelaine* (May 1931): 9

122. Louise Forrest, "The Queen's Example," *Maclean's* (Sept. 15, 1939): 3.

123. Goudie, *Woman of Labrador*, 50.

124. Quoted in "Editorial Page," *Chatelaine* (Aug. 1935): 2.

125. See M. Callaghan, "A Wedding Dress," *Canadian Nation* (March-April 1929): 12.

126. Henriete Fragonard, "Women Who Never Marry," *Saturday Night* (Dec. 13, 1924): 35. See also Madge MacBeth, "So Women Really Pay," *Maclean's* (May 1, 1922): 66.

127. A Businesswoman, "This Freedom," *Maclean's* (July 15, 1931): 48.

128. A Spinster, "A Reply to 'This Freedom,' " *Maclean's* (Sept. 15, 1931): 17, 44–45. (Oct. 129. A Wife, "This Bondage," *Maclean's* (Oct. 1, 1931): 11, 46.

130. On Paris see Joy Parr, "Rethinking Work and Kinship in a Canadian Hosiery Town, 1910–1950," *Feminist Studies* (Spring 1987), and on the case of one female worker in Dundas see Patricia Bird, "Hamilton Working Women in the Period of the Great Depression," *Atlantis* (Spring 1983): 130–31.

131. See John D. Thomas, "Servants of the Church: Canadian Methodist Deaconess Work, 1890–1926," *Canadian Historical Review* (Sept. 1984): 370–95.

132. See Mary Hallett, "Nellie McClung and the Fight for the Ordination of Women in the United Church of Canada," *Atlantis* (Spring 1979): 2–16.

133. For a provocative study of the relationship of Catholic nuns in Quebec to the male church see Marta Danylewycz, "Changing Relationships: Nuns and Feminists in Montreal, 1890–1925" in *The Neglected Majority*, vol. 2, edited by Alison Prentice and Susan Mann Trofimenkoff (Toronto: McClelland and Stewart, 1985).

134. See Margaret Stewart and Doris French, *Ask No Quarter: A Biography of Agnes Macphail* (Toronto: Longmans, Green and Co., 1959); Patricia Rooke and Rudy Schnell, "'An Idiot's Flowerbed'—A Study of Charlotte Whitton's Feminist Thought, 1941–1950" in *Rethinking Canada*; Mazo de la Roche, *Ringing the Changes: An Autobiography* (Toronto: Macmillan, 1957); Kennethe Haig, *Brave Harvest: The Life Story of E. Cora Hind* (Toronto: Thomas Allen, 1945); Margaret Street, *Watch-fires on the Mountains: The Life and Writings of Ethel Johns* (Toronto: University of Toronto Press, 1973); Marion Royce, *Eunice Dyke: Health Care Pioneer* (Toronto and Charlottetown: Dundurn Press, 1983); Anne McDougall, *Anne Savage: The Story of A Canadian Painter* (Montreal: Harvest House, 1977); Rebecca Sisler, *The Girls: A Biography of Frances Loring and Florence Wyle* (Toronto: Clarke Irwin, 1972); Marie Tippett, *Emily Carr* (Toronto: Oxford University Press, 1979); Doris Shadbolt, *The Art of Emily Carr* (Toronto: Douglas and McIntyre, 1979); W.L. Morton with Vera K. Fast, eds. *God's Galloping Girl: The Peace River Diaries of Monica Storrs, 1929–1931* (Vancouver: University of British Columbia Press, 1979); and Michael Hayden, ed., *So Much To Do, So Little Time: The Writings of Hilda Neatby* (Vancouver: University of British Columbia Press, 1983).

135. Hayden, *So Much To Do, So Little Time*, 21.

136. Stewart and French, *Ask No Quarter*, 31.

137. Ibid., 25.

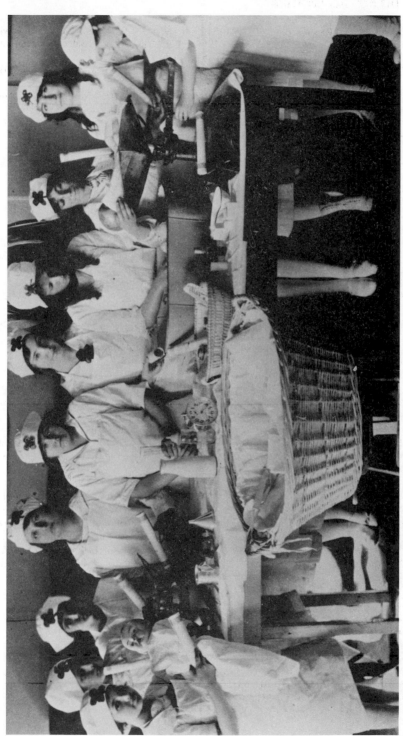

Since mothers were believed to be too often behind the times, indifferent, or otherwise preoccupied, Canadian girls were directed to classes in modern housewifery that reaffirmed women's responsibilities for domestic life. (Manitoba Archives, N9342)

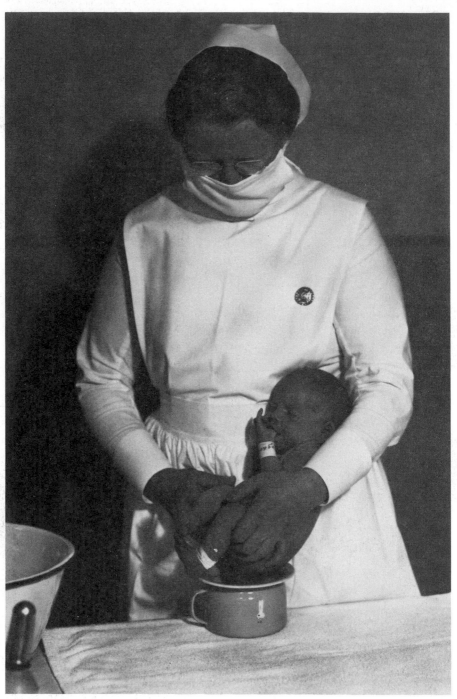

As this nurse demonstrates, very early potty training was to mark up-to-date and conscientious child rearing. Babies like this one and many mothers often had other ideas. (Eugene Michael Finn/NFB/National Archives of Canada/PA-803178)

Like girls across the country, especially in poorer families, this Toronto youngster might well spend hours caring for younger sisters and brothers. Her opportunities for play and education were often directly tied to the extent of such duties. (United Church Archives, Victoria University)

Field work was a matter of course for many women on marginal farms. Like this woman on a Saskatchewan homestead, few could afford to concentrate their activities within the home. (United Church Archives, Victoria University)

Switchboards were the "high tech" of the 1920s and 1930s but, for all such "glamour," the closely supervised, physically taxing, and repetitive work they offered was all too reminiscent of blue-collar industrial employments where, incidentally, the wages might well be better. (Eaton's Archive)

Even when they could not protest on picket lines or in parades, women, such as these in the radical Women's Labour League, expressed their practical solidarity with the oppressed, in this case poor Cape Breton coal miners fighting the wage-cutting efforts of the powerful British Empire Steel Corporation. (Manitoba Archives, N9343)

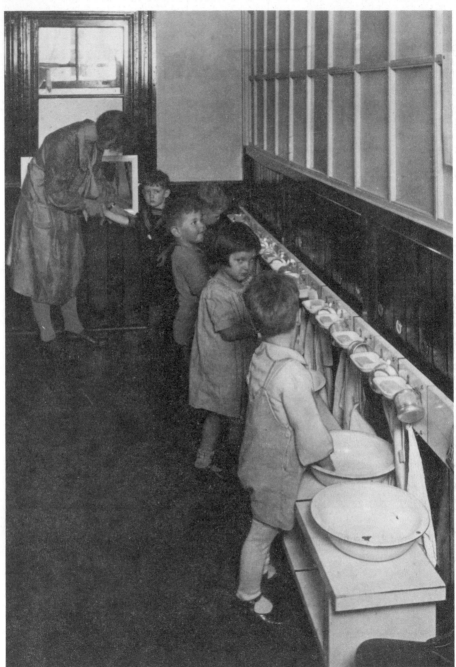

"Scientific" nursery schools like the St. George Institute for Child Study, shown here, modelled ideal child-rearing behaviour for attentive middle-class mothers in the 1920s and 1930s. Poor mothers and their offspring, like the Dionnes, encountered the advice of child psychologists more haphazardly, unless they found themselves the clients of child welfare agencies. (University of Toronto, Rare Book Room, Blatz Papers)

Agnes Macphail (1890-1954), the Grey County teacher and rural activist, challenged conventions that denied most women the opportunity for independent participation in the making of public policy. The stern dignity of this portrait reminds us how much courage it took to demand equality for women. (PAC 21562)

Alberta feminists Nellie McClung (first row centre left) and Emily Murphy (first row centre right) welcomed Emmeline Pankhurst (first row centre) to Edmonton as a British representative of an international feminist sisterhood to which they too felt they belonged. Tours by feminism's leaders and visits by a host of more anonymous supporters regularly reminded Canadians that they were far from alone in the fight for equal rights. (Provincial Archives, Victoria, B.C.)

More searching than your mirror
... *your husband's eyes*

Over 20,000 beauty experts for that reason insist that clients keep skin radiantly young by using an olive and palm oil soap. Palmolive is the only large-selling soap made of these oils.

"IF ALL the women who seek to hold their husbands would first hold their good looks, editors of beauty columns wouldn't get such a large mail ... and there would be greater chances for happiness." That's the warning addressed to women by leading beauty specialists.

❖ ❖ ❖

Neither a great amount of time nor large sums of money are necessary to keep looking your best. But intelligent home care, every day, *is* necessary. Don't think that means hours of primping. It means the best natural skin cleansing you can obtain. And beauty experts are unanimous in their recommendation of Palmolive facial cleansing.

Two minutes. That's all it takes. A simple washing of face and throat with the lather of this olive and palm oils soap. Then, powder, rouge, if you wish. But foundation cleansing, first.

Won't you try this method, endorsed by more than 20,000 experts, as the wisest step toward keeping that school-girl complexion? Use Palmolive ... twice every day ... faithfully. Then see what your mirror reveals. See what your husband's eyes reveal.

"When you are in doubt as to the claims a soap makes, look at the label. Can you tell what's in that soap? Then why take chances? Use Palmolive—which is recommended by those who KNOW."

Carsten, Europe's Distinguished Beauty Expert.

Retail Price
10c

PALMOLIVE

Commercial ads everywhere hammered home the close connection between female attractiveness and husbands' loyalty. The test of male scrutiny, here represented in two visuals and "20,000 experts," was one that no "true" woman could afford to fail. (*Chatelaine*, May 1932)

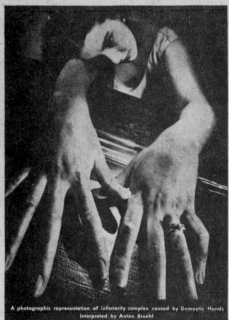
In their campaigns to increase consumption, advertisers regularly employed the current language of "pop psychology." Here a dramatic reference to an "inferiority complex" captured women's vulnerability in a commercial society that nurtured activity in men and narcissism in women. (*Chatelaine*, Jan. 1932)

Husbands' financial power and wives' deference to their wishes were matter-of-factly asserted by many advertisers such as Lux. The fact that many women were the family authority in money matters was handled very circumspectly on the few occasions when it surfaced in ads. Male power was rarely publicly questioned. (*Chatelaine*, Feb. 1934)

A host of advertisers like Lysol reserved their "shame on you" copy for Canadian wives whom, it was hoped, would boost sales in their efforts to forestall male criticism. Male shortcomings in hygiene or appearance were rarely if ever addressed. (*Chatelaine*, March 1928)

The proliferation of ads like this from Dominion Life and other insurance companies capitalized on women's fears of the long-term consequences of low wages. Women had only to look about them to see the female elderly living lives made cramped and miserable by inadequate support. (*Chatelaine*, Feb. 1932)

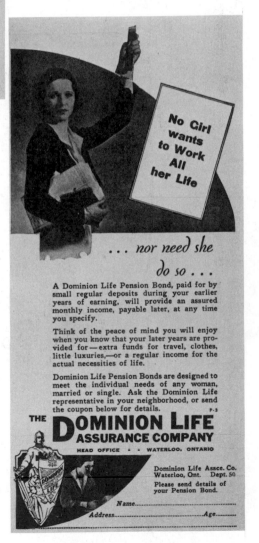

Despite the claims of Rinso and its competitors, backbreaking labour remained characteristic of most washdays. In most houses, women struggled manually with heavy loads of deeply soiled cottons, wools, and linens. No wonder washing headed the list of hated chores. (*Chatelaine*, Feb. 1934)

CHAPTER 4
KEEPING HOUSE

Once courtship and marriage had culminated in homes and families, wives and mothers were expected to take over as emotional and practical mainstays of the private realm while husbands and fathers normally functioned as breadwinners in the public world. Women's increased presence in the paid labour force and their enfranchisement in the political system in the 1920s and 1930s did almost nothing to change this fundamental allocation of duties. Indeed, much of the feminists' case for suffrage had rested on the pledge that women's work at home would in no way be neglected.[1] Very few Canadians questioned that, whatever duties women might have in the world at large, as income earners, voters, volunteers, activists, and so forth, they were secondary to their efforts as housewives and mothers.

This is not to argue that the precise nature of women's domestic exertions was unquestioned or unchanging in these two decades. As this chapter suggests with regard to the work of home maintenance, and the next with respect to childbirth and child rearing, women encountered and contributed to domestic regimes whose practices and assumptions seemed far from certain. A fundamental transformation—from an economy based on thrift, a multiplicity of small domestic producers, and resource extraction and primary manufacturing, to one based on consumer credit, large-scale production separated from the family residence, and secondary manufacturing and tertiary industries—was underway, although it neither began nor finished in these decades. Nor was the impact of this change spread equally throughout the nation's homes. Many families residing on farms or dependent on employment in resource industries or locked into ill-paid waged labour in the cities were hard put to update their operations: for them the need for thrift and domestic production remained urgent. But Canadians with relatively stable, skilled, white-collar, and professional employments readily became the beneficiaries of heightened consumer credit and mass production.

City-dwellers were the first to experience the modernization of domestic regimes. Improvements in public and private transit increasingly took men to more distant workplaces for most of the day and schools commandeered children of useful ages for long hours, leaving women at home with the very young. Isolated in large degree from other adults, their task was to transform the cash income of the male breadwinner and, not so incidentally, their own labour, into the comforts of home. Whereas, in the past, the majority of homes had been centres of production and labour that engaged at least part of the energies of most family members, households, particularly among the middle class, now slowly emerged as centres of consumption and labour dependent, to an increasing degree, on female energy alone.

Even middle-class Canadians, however, entered slowly, and often incompletely, into the world of modern homes equipped with electricity, central heating, indoor plumbing, and major appliances. The recurring threat of hard times and stubborn domestic traditions meant that old homes and habits were not easily refurbished. Household arrangements became a complex mix of what had to be suffered for lack of economic alternative, what was retained because of affection or custom, and what modern additions could usefully be integrated into existing regimes. Across the Dominion, individual housewives co-ordinated resources that demanded everything from hard physical labour to considerable mental ingenuity.

Not surprisingly, given average annual wages that in 1929, for example, were $1 200, and conservative estimates of the minimum budget required to maintain an average Canadian family, $1 430 in the same year,[2] domestic survival often relied on credit. This had long been commonplace at local merchants who allowed customers to run up accounts to be settled when crops were sold or wages received.[3] What was unprecedented in these years was the appearance of consumer credit on a scale that was specifically designed to encourage purchase of a wide range of personal and household items, most notably the automobile[4] but also everything from refrigerators to linoleum to toilets. In 1916, Guaranty Securities Corporation, later Continental Guarantee Corporation of Canada Ltd., opened the first sales finance company in Canada and it soon faced a host of Canadian-owned and American branch imitators such as the Traders' Finance Corporation, which operated in Manitoba from 1920, and the Industrial Acceptance Corporation, which came north in 1923. These companies assisted retailers in offering instalment and credit programs by assuming part of the liability. Merchants such as Eaton's and Simpson's widely advertised their own "Home Lovers' Clubs," "Budget Clubs," and "Plans" to prospective clients.[5] Consumers were also able to arrange their own financing. In 1928, Central Finance Corporation became the first registered small loan company, and its success quickly attracted competitors.[6] Caisses populaires and credit unions sometimes offered loans other than mortgages to members, but of the chartered banks only the Bank of Commerce had entered the personal loan field in a significant way by World War II. Despite the conservatism of the country's foremost financial institutions, the creation in 1927 of the Canadian Credit Institute, with its enthusiasm for professional standards, signalled the emergence of consumer credit as a major commercial enterprise.[7] Not all businesses, however, aimed at corporate respectability. Operating at especially usurious rates of interest were loan sharks, which, as the House of Commons heard in 1939, escaped whatever minimum regulation governed other classes of lenders.[8] Even the relatively respectable incorporated lenders, sometimes referred to as "borax houses," could take people to the cleaners, charging rates that could easily lead to garnisheed wages and repossessed goods.[9]

For all its dangers, the expansion of consumer credit was accompanied by considerable optimism. Champions argued that it encouraged thrift in those with modest incomes who otherwise would dissipate funds "in a variety of minor expenditures."[10] The writer of the winning essay for a scholarship from the Canadian Bankers' Association in 1930 summed up the most optimistic case for the defence:

> If instalment buying enables many who otherwise would have continued the daily round of monotonous labour to obtain some share in the larger life from which they are now excluded, if it pays the way to the comforts of home life, if it relieves the back-breaking toil of the farmer, if it brings comfort into the home and brightness to the lives of those who have suffered, if it accomplishes only some of these great things, who is there to deny that it has atoned for its shortcomings?[11]

Equally visible were the benefits to Canadian business. Few observers of the credit revolution in these years failed to acknowledge that, without the extension of financing, there would have been far fewer sales.[12]

Data are not complete for 1931 but, ten years later, the census confirmed how important debt financing had become. Credit accounted for 28.4 percent of sales in all stores: 25.1 percent of purchases in the food group of retailers, 30.8 percent in the general merchandising group, 41.7 percent in the automotive group, 17.7 percent in the apparel group, and a massive 65.9 percent in the furniture, household, radio group.[13] A MacLean-Hunter survey of housewives taken in 1945, when many Canadians had pent-up savings to spend, suggested that credit had come to be taken for granted in many homes. Over a fifth of respondents, for instance, intended to pay for heating stoves, water heaters, refrigerators, washing machines, vacuum cleaners, sewing machines, pianos, and dining room and bedroom furniture on the instalment plan.[14] While old habits of thrift died hard, and persisting high levels of unemployment meant strict economy for the majority of Canadians, what might be termed a credit revolution was helping to change not perhaps "the attitude or the norm towards credit but rather the definition of what constitutes the basic needs of the population . . . the consumption norm—the standard package of goods and service which each family wishes to possess."[15] Underway in the 1920s and 1930s were the elaboration and promotion of credit mechanisms by which Canadians could purchase goods that were otherwise beyond their reach. The home and its female managers were at the centre of this rising tide of expectations.

Demand for credit was fueled by a marked increase in the sophistication of Canadian advertising in both decades.[16] More sophisticated approaches to the consumer reflected the maturing of an industry that saw the incorporation of the Association of Canadian Advertisers in 1917 and its subsequent efforts to rationalize agencies' relationships with merchandisers, and periodicals and newspapers, and to educate members of the advertising industry.[17] One 1938 survey of the evolution of marketing tactics summed up some of the changes:

> Thirty years ago . . . advertising in Canada lacked much that produces its colour, its costs, and its controversies today. It was unblessed by motion pictures, glamour girls, comic strip technique, vitamins, rural free delivery, candid cameras, electric gadgets, cosmetics, radio, taint scares, and advertising clubs with their truth crusades.[18]

These developments coincided with the discovery first of "Mrs. Consumer" and then of the child as a potential customer.[19] Modern theories of psychological motivation were increasingly applied to make direct appeals to such buyers' emotions.[20] A so-called normal feminine personality emerged. As the leading index to Canadian advertising put it:

> Women as a whole are more suggestible than men. They are more influenced by their emotions and by the ideas which are associated with, but not directly conveyed by, the illustrations, words and other symbols used in an advertising message. For this reason, human-interest copy, or the liberal use of illustrations, especially illustrations which tell the story, are especially desirable in advertising to women. Text is relatively less important, for it is not easy to make a strong appeal to the emotions by means of words. . . . Evidence of facts and figures is ordinarily useless.[21]

The outcome of such marketing assumptions was especially visible in the merchandising of cosmetics, but home furnishings and food products did not escape. The Canadian advertising industry proudly took responsibility for "a domestic revolution" that was abetted by its strategy of "Glorifying the Fireside" and "Glorifying the Personality."[22] Like it or not, Canadian women and the homes they superintended were at the centre of a celebration of consumerism in which, as Stuart Ewen has suggested for the United States, "in response to the exigencies of the productive system of the twentieth century, excessiveness replaced thrift as a social value."[23] Modern advertisers promised women that desires for a better life could be satisfied through purchases rather than through reform or rebellion. The independence and freedom demanded by feminists were trivialized and stripped of moral content to become merely opportunities for personal self-indulgence.[24] The intended beneficiary was not so much the female population as capitalism.

Certainly Canadian business was convinced that modern advertising tactics were essential in stimulating demand. The manager of Toronto's 1900 Washer Company spoke matter-of-factly of turning to "direct-to-consumer advertising," the installment plan, and free trial offers as ways of countering women's resistance. A good market for his product was created, he argued, as a direct result of such initiatives.[25] Approaches to domestic management that did not rely on each family making individual purchases were routinely condemned. Private clothes washers, for instance, were pressed on consumers in preference to commercial and co-operative laundries by claims that home cleaning was cheaper and the only way "to destroy all vermin and pathogenic organisms."[26] Consumers' Gas used advertising, more particularly by its Home Service Department, to counter what it viewed as the insidious "'modern spirit' which induces women to neglect home duties and depend on the corner bakery for supplies, instead of taking pride in turning out her [sic] own dainties, and in as much as the kitchen range is the chief consumer of gas, this competitor is not to be lightly reckoned with."[27] Escalating domestic purchases easily became integral to corporate planning. After World War I, for instance, Canadian General Electric found its sales of power-generating equipment slumping as demand for electricity weakened. In a deliberate policy of increasing the market for electric power, and thus for its generators, it targeted housewives for sales of electric appliances that in turn would act as "good load builders."[28]

Few consumers could avoid massive marketing campaigns that celebrated everything from household cleaning equipment,[29] baby foods,[30] and furniture,[31] to plumbing and heating supplies,[32] on radio and billboards, in store windows, and in publications of every description. The intended impact of this self-conscious and expensive onslaught was captured by a prize-winning poem submitted in a contest run by a home furnishing dealer in western Canada:

My Re-Made Kitchen

My old kitchen was drab and dreary,
When night time came I was so weary,
A thousand steps unnecessary
I made from dawn 'til dark.

My new kitchen is bright and cheery
With every unit gay and airy,
At dinner I am always merry,
My days are all a lark!

With space galore and cabinets many
Electric helpers all and any
And yet I didn't waste a penny
I need them all and how!

Now all my home seems recreated,
My old kitchen was so out-dated
My friends exclaim with breath abated
A perfect work-shop now![33]

Patronizing as they might be about the susceptibility of female consumers to their blandishments, businesses were also extremely conscious about public relations. Women were deliberately catered to and, not so incidentally, flattered by efforts to seek their advice and approval. In 1930, for instance, the women's magazine *Chatelaine* set up its own Institute as a domestic demonstration and research bureau for the benefit of female consumers.[34] Canadian General Electric advertised its Hotpoint Range as "Designed by Women for Women."[35] Prominent figures like Judge Helen MacGill were asked for their advice on marketing to their sex.[36] The recognition that women might understand their own needs best was reflected in arguments such as that by the jam giant E.D. Smith and Sons of Winona, Ontario, that "Women Should Write Copy Addressed to Women"[37] and by the creation in 1933 of the Toronto Women's Advertising Club by the female president of the Margaret Pennell Advertising Agency.

Corporate sensitivity to the opinion of female buyers was heightened by women's leadership of a fledgling consumer movement and their search for alternatives to the choices presented to them by businesses eager to maximize profits. Unused as they might be to the barrage of advertising, Canadian women learned quickly to be critical observers of hype, exaggeration, and contradiction. By the 1930s critics were abundant. At a 1937 Brampton, Ontario, protest meeting against advertising, for example, "one woman said she would never buy a certain brand of corn syrup because she was so sick of hearing about it on the radio."[38] Revelations of corporate malpractice such as those by a Department of Labour investigation into "An Alleged Combine in the Bread-baking Industry in Canada" in 1931 and by the Price Spreads Royal Commission in 1935 helped keep consumers alert. The well-publicized Price Spreads *Report* condemned the operations of many manufacturers and merchandisers as including:

> false and misleading advertising and marketing; misleading statements as to quality of products, including design of goods likely to confuse or deceive rather than inform the consumer; uncertainty of specificities and formulae of manufactured goods; adulteration; substitution of cheaper or inferior goods; harmful or poisonous ingredients; exorbitant prices for essentially simple and inexpensive products, when sold under a brand or trade mark; short weight and unjust scales; and deceptive packages and containers.[39]

In a study prepared for the Royal Commission, the National Research Council had discovered, among other offences, that many goods labelled wool and cotton blends contained very little wool, that others identified as silk and wool contained only synthetic silk, and that many products labelled "pure silk" had none of this expensive material whatsoever. Similarly, electric lights advertised as burning for 1000 hours failed on average after 662 hours. Labels carried fictitious company names. Fruit boxes and wine bottles concealed false bottoms. So-called pure cotton was abundantly laced with filler. And the list did not end there.[40] Experience with a few of these sharp practices made many housewives understandably sceptical about corporate claims.

Frauds could also be dangerous. Not until 1927, however, did the federal Department of Health have authority to deal with the misbranding of drugs. When its overworked staff could manage to build up sufficient evidence, it prosecuted offenders against public safety, as with its case against "one firm [that] sold a radio-active jar for $40.00. Water was placed inljthe jar and left overnight, when it presumably became activated by the imaginary radio-active substance contained in the walls of the jar."[41] Despite the threat posed by such chicanery, a generally short-sighted approach to cost-saving by federal governments kept food and drug regulation generally a low priority.[42] As the traditional guardians of their families' health, women had to make their way amidst a minefield of competing and misleading claims for cures for everything from cancer to TB to painful menstruation.

Quality was not the only problem. More than anything else, consumers were likely to be up in arms over what they regarded as unfair pricing. The shortages and spiralling costs of everything from butter to sugar to potatoes during World War I made many women extremely conscious about the need to intervene directly in the marketplace.[43] Although protest appears to have died down in the 1920s, the hardships of the 1930s drove women to reassert consumers' right to a fair price. In 1932, Jewish housewives in Toronto picketed kosher butchers whose religious monopoly kept prices higher than in gentile shops.[44] Six years later, the Housewives' Association of Toronto boycotted dairies that had raised milk prices.[45] As the president of the city's Women's Advertising Club observed, the protest was forceful:

> The women were explosive, sang songs proclaiming "We want milk for ten cents," cheered, shouted and applauded violently, not to mention pledging themselves by a standing vote to boycott butter until the price goes down to 30¢ per pound.[46]

Toronto women were not alone in their anger. In 1938 the B.C. Housewives' League battled the Retail Merchants' Association over its support of a bill to prohibit the sale of any trademarked or branded good at less than the price established by the manufacturer.[47] Experiences such as these prepared women to assume a major role in assisting the federal Wartime Prices and Trade Board after 1941 in monitoring prices. This prominence in turn would give rise to a new national women's organization, the Consumers' Association of Canada, in 1947.[48]

Criticism of business went beyond pickets and boycotts to search for alternate ways of meeting household needs. In the heady days after the 1918 armistice when change seemed in the air, recommendations for transforming the domestic world abounded. Prairie women in particular, influenced by the co-operative experiments of the farm movement, turned to co-ops. In 1918, Regina women formed a Saskatchewan Women's

Co-operative Guild to support a co-op store. Somewhat later, a co-op purchasing group for coal and bulk commodities was formed in Moose Jaw. Yorkton activists established a rural women's guild. Such initiatives were troubled by capital shortages and administrative inexperience but by 1941 support was sufficient to establish a Provincial Women's Co-operative Guild Council for Saskatchewan.[49]

Other kinds of joint initiatives were proposed as well, especially in the years immediately after the Great War when optimism about domestic advances was at its height. In Toronto in 1919, for instance, the United Women Voters listened to speakers extol the advantages of community kitchens:

> Why should a more or less untidy kitchen, a weary woman, and since all women are not good cooks, an oft-times badly-cooked meal, constitute a home? Why should the meals have to be even prepared in the house to preserve the home atmosphere? Wouldn't the time be less wearisomely and more acceptably spent in attending to the dainty service of the food which would with Community Kitchen service be brought to the home, hot and delicious, in containers used for that purpose? Would the fact that there would be no dishes to wash destroy anyone's appetite?[50]

Another Toronto observer of "domestic discontent" was still more ambitious in her proposals "to reduce work, to make use of outside help such as that of laundry, bakery, nursery school, to organize paid help in the house for certain parts of the work, and to organize the neighbourly interchange of responsibility for the children in the evenings."[51] Such urban feminists had obvious advantages in contemplating the creation of common services but their rural counterparts also hoped to ease domestic labours. Right after the war, Saskatchewan's organized farm women, for example, got busy investigating the possibility of a community laundry to spare housewives the hard labour of the family wash without having to resort to the expense of individual washing machines.[52]

But for all their promise, such collective remedies to the problems of women's domestic workload ran full-tilt into Canadians' attachment to the ideal of family intimacy and privacy, an attachment fostered by advertising and businesses whose prospects depended on a mass market of individual purchasers. Such resistance helped ensure that the major, but not insurmountable, practical difficulties facing co-ops, including raising capital, redesigning existing physical plants, and coming up with cost-competitive as well as sociable domestic services, proved overwhelming. By the mid-1920s feminist hopes for reconstructing domesticity along more co-operative lines had largely faded. In the absence of co-operative solutions on a sufficient scale to meet their needs, housewives turned, when they could, to the opportunities promised by enhanced consumption. The lifestyle advertising that was so much a feature of these years enkindled alluring daydreams. It remained to be seen, however, whether mass production serving the interests of a patriarchal capitalism could offer women freedom and independence.

In the heady days after the Great War, women were ready to insist that they alone could not "do everything" that needed to be done in the home.[53] They needed help. Assistance from husbands and children was one solution. If women's pages in newspapers are any guide, one sign of a good husband was his willingness to do his share wherever it was needed. Many women would have agreed that "if a man wants his home perfect, let him help to make it so. Let him remember when he comes in tired from his work his wife . . . will be equally tired."[54] Men committed to more egalitarian marriages were most likely to "help out," but there is little evidence that many questioned the traditional division of labour that left women responsible for the home. The problem, of course, as modern commentators have also appreciated,[55] was how to encourage more flexibility about behaviour appropriate to the sexes. One frequent response in these years focussed on the socialization of children. As an article entitled "Dolls for Small Boys" in the *Farm and Ranch Review* suggested, male helplessness in domestic matters was largely a product of traditional training that could be overcome if Canadians allowed "our children to grow up naturally. If the small boy wishes to play with dolls, let him, he won't then be so useless when he is a father."[56] Yet, while members of some families pitched in to help regardless of sex, most did not. Girls and their mothers, not boys and their fathers, remained the domestic workers par excellence.

Until the coming of that better world of mass consumption or the male helpmate, women had to find ways to make do with the domestic environment as they found it, which was often far from satisfactory. Despite the inauguration in May 1925 of an up-scale magazine, *Canadian Home and Gardens*, that celebrated housing renovation and innovation as signs of an evolving national culture,[57] residential housing, the setting for most female labour, remained much less than ideal in these years. The Great War had reduced housing starts dramatically and worsened already inadequate conditions. Matters were so bad that in 1919 a National Industrial Conference convened by Ottawa in the wake of the Winnipeg General Strike condemned "land speculation, poor and insufficient housing, and high rents"[58] across the country as contributing to social distress and unrest. Intermittent good times in the 1920s, aided to a very limited degree by a federal housing loan program administered by municipalities, increased the number of annual dwelling starts from 30 100 in 1921 to a high of 43 100 in 1929. In some areas such as Vancouver, the "low cost of land, building materials and finished houses made home ownership a reality for many people."[59] Ironically enough, federal assistance did little to help poorer householders. As one leading town planner put it, "the houses were acquired by Civil Servants and such who would have found some kind of decent housing in any case."[60] When the number of dwelling starts dropped to 34 700 in 1930, reached a low of 14 600 in 1933, and recovered to only 37 300 by 1939, despite population increase over the same period, prospects for affordable decent housing fell still further. Only in 1941 did starts exceed those reached in 1929.[61]

In the 1930s, even relatively fortunate cities such as Vancouver saw doubling up and overcrowding as families struggled to cope with deteriorating conditions. In Halifax in 1932, for instance, 370 families were discovered living in 192 condemned houses while many more shared toilet facilities and sinks or taps in far from sanitary conditions.[62] Housing surveys undertaken in Montreal, Ottawa, Toronto, and Winnipeg in the early 1930s similarly uncovered a "serious shortage of low-rent dwellings with modern conveniences," yet these very cities were described as comparing "favourably with others in the Dominion."[63] The federal government responded to these revelations with the Dominion Housing Act of 1935, replaced three years later by the National Housing Act, to provide relatively low-cost home-building loans, and the Home Improvement Plan of 1936 to help finance renovations.[64] And when they could, families at every income level were likely to initiate their own round of home improvements. Yet, as in the 1920s, government assistance plans had limited impact on wage-earning families who, both as tenants and owners, experienced steadily worsening conditions during the Great Depression.

The housing of rural families tended to be especially bad, particularly in the more recently settled Prairie Provinces, where electrification and indoor plumbing were late arrivals. Farm wives in need of water or power regularly substituted their own labour for amenities that even poorer urban women had come to expect. While sod shacks had become rare by World War I, to be replaced by frame and brick buildings, prairie farm residences remained small. For example, in 1921 68 percent of Saskatchewan's rural households lived in four or fewer rooms, in 1931 64 percent and in 1941 61 percent.[65] Substantial investment in farm implements and machinery rather than domestic amenities, "together with the inaccessibility of building materials and fuel in a relatively cold climate" led to more overcrowding in prairies houses than in long-settled rural areas of the Maritimes, for instance. Atlantic coast farm homes were larger, although here too household expenditures were frequently limited by men's decisions regarding farming practices. In 1931, for example, New Brunswick farms averaged both more machinery and fewer rooms and household appliances than those in Nova Scotia.[66] Inevitably, housewives' regimes were affected.

In both urban and rural areas, pressure on living quarters was increased by the prevalence of lodgers. In 1931, 10.4 percent of rural and 17.5 percent of urban home owners rented out accommodation as did 12.0 percent of rural and 19.1 percent of urban tenants, figures that provide a telling commentary on the burden of shelter costs.[67] Space was all the more limited when several families shared resources. In 1931, for example, the nine provinces reported from 4 percent to 9 percent of their households were multiple-family.[68] Extra residents meant still more to do for housewives. But as two pioneers of Flin Flon, Manitoba, remembered, boarders might be taken in stride, and even enjoyed: "It just means having an extra mouth to feed. I'd throw a few more dumplings in the pot, wash some extra clothes, make another bed. What's one more to care for when you're already doing the work?" Moreover, "having boarders was never a dull moment, all those young men. They meant extra work for the money but some of them was [sic] just like members of the family."[69] For all the additional labour involved, boarders eased budgets and often made housekeeping a good deal more sociable.

The increased trend to tenancy, associated with the rise in the number of apartment dwellers, also helped set the basic conditions of housewifery. Multiple dwellings for instance, were much less likely to have either formal play space for children or gardens for supplementing purchased supplies.[70] The standard housing for working-class people in 1931 was described by real estate and trust companies handling rental properties in Canadian cities as:

> equipped with electric lighting, running water, and water closet. Nearly all had a bathroom and electricity or gas available for cooking. Houses generally were heated by hot air or hot water systems while steam was employed to a considerable extent in flats and apartment dwellings, particularly in Western Canada. Stoves were still widely used for heating flats in a number of Eastern cities. In the large majority of cases, the typical workmen's dwelling was of pre-War construction and finished inside with softwood floors and trimmings. The average amount of floor space ranged from 600 to 900 square feet in Eastern Canada but was roughly 100 square feet less in Western cities.[71]

This restricted area served a family of five or so as well as, in many cases, their lodgers. Even this modest picture was frequently optimistic, failing to summon up a reality that included, among many variations, exceptionally low-cost rentals in St. John, New Brunswick, where floor space was commonly still more limited and bathrooms unusual. Nor could it conjure up the conditions facing mother-led families whose housing conditions were expressly excluded from the 1931 survey. Such marginal households were far more likely to enter a private, low-cost housing market rarely served by real estate agents and trust companies.

For all its shortcomings, families often had to pay dearly for rental accommodation. Rents advanced throughout much of the 1920s, particularly in western locations, finally to fall between 1930 to 1934.[72] Wage increments, when they came, could rarely keep up with housing costs. Population increase combined with low earning levels to exert steady pressure on low-priced housing. Families on relief, especially in cities like Calgary and Vancouver with little stock of older housing, were especially likely to be penalized by overcrowding and limited facilities.[73] By way of contrast, the situation of middle-class tenants was substantially better. Almost all better quality residences included "standard bathroom plumbing fixtures in addition to electric light and gas or electricity for cooking."[74] Electric refrigerators were also commonplace while the less well-to-do had to supply their own ice-boxes.

Not surprisingly, Canadians were willing to make considerable sacrifices in order to possess their own homes. This often took the form of doing without sinks, flush toilets, refrigerators, furnaces, and even running water in owner-occupied dwellings; such amenities were more likely to be present in rental accommodation.[75] Home ownership was positively correlated not only with income levels but with the age of the male breadwinner. Older couples might have both accumulated savings and wage-earning children to help purchase property. It was just during the years when mothers were coping with young children that they were most likely to be tenants, a situation adding to the general stress of child rearing.

Congestion and pollution in the inner city encouraged families to look for cheaper, more spacious accommodation. The marked advance in public transportation and, more particularly, in the number of private automobiles, from 196 367 registrations in 1919 to 1 191 914 in 1939,[76] aided the suburban development of Canadian cities. Those employed in Vancouver proper, for instance, increasingly chose to live in the old suburbs of South Vancouver and Point Grey, both of which amalgamated with the city in 1929, or even Burnaby to the east that also housed increasing numbers of Lower Mainland residents. In keeping with both the greater distances that were likely to separate families from services of every kind and the shortcomings of public transportation on the urban periphery, middle-class women began to take up chauffeuring as an additional responsibility.[77] Less well-to-do women lacking private transportation might have had to give up the mobility and sociability of the city core in exchange for greater privacy and more space. Families seemed willing to make these changes: by 1945 an estimated 42.9 percent of prospective home-buyers wanted to locate in the suburbs.[78] This trend to urban decentralization placed considerable pressure on the community's collective resources and increased the attractiveness of the private services and goods being marketed by business.

Essential to women's hopes for their homes was the increasing availability of electricity and other innovative sources of energy. "Emancipation" and "New Freedom" became the common refrain of advertisers trumpeting electricity's virtues.[79] Canadians were ready to be convinced. The number of residential users rose steadily from 764 900 in 1920 to 1 623 700 in 1939.[80] By 1941 69.1 percent of occupied dwellings had electric lighting, with another 30 percent illuminated by kerosine or gasoline and .4 percent by gas.[81] While the use of oil and gas was still extremely limited, it too accustomed consumers to think in terms of domestic innovation. Homes, it seemed, could share in the advances that new energy sources promised industry.

Wherever they lived, women adjusted operations and expectations to cope with available floor space and household equipment. Inevitably, standards, styles, needs, and resources varied tremendously from one family to another but, whether they lived in rural shanties or comfortable suburban residences, the great majority of women found more than enough to do. Only a tiny minority could afford to purchase most goods and services that were necessary for family maintenance, and even the informed management of heightened consumption could be a time-consuming business for responsible householders. Paradoxically, however, with the shift in women's domestic work patterns, observers tended not to recognize the contribution of housewives as "real labour." Whereas when the home was clearly a centre of production, as on the family farm, women's role as domestic organizers and labourers was admitted, if undervalued, housewives' function in the modern community was generally unclear to most observers. Children were at school much of the day; goods could be purchased in stores; furnaces, electricity, plumbing, and appliances changed and, to some ways of thinking, eliminated burdensome domestic toil. Largely ignored were the facts that child care comprised a good deal more than sending youngsters off to be educated, that consumption was time-consuming, fatiguing, and required skill, and that modern conveniences did not so much end housewifery as upgrade domestic standards and transform the nature of individual tasks. The result helped spawn the myth of the underemployed and essentially lazy modern homemaker.

Reality for Canadian women was far different. The maintenance of homes required large amounts of both paid and unpaid work from their female inmates. Despite a pervasive domestic ideology that attempted to drew a firm line between the home and the marketplace, many housewives, while nominally unemployed, produced both goods and services for sale. For many Canadians, the instability of male incomes made cash-producing activities a fact of household life.[82] The incorporation of paid work into domestic routines appeared relatively commonplace in both the 1920s and 1930s, a good index of how tough times were not restricted to the Great Depression. Both before and after the introduction of mothers' allowances, beginning in 1916, single mothers, for instance, routinely turned their hand to whatever home-based money-making they could find.[83]

These initiatives were not the preserve of the desperately poor and, if women's pages in newspapers are any guide, money-making was never far from readers' minds in both country and city. The *Farm and Ranch Review*, for example, addressed women in "Making Farm Hobbies Pay," an article that surveyed the prospects for marketing flowers, livestock, poultry, rabbits, and foxes.[84] Dairying continued to occupy many farm women as it had for decades, although by the interwar years factory production under male supervision had taken over much of the liquid milk, butter, and cheese industries.[85] Detailed exchanges of information among female correspondents on breeds, breeding, and care of poultry in the *Free Press Prairie Farmer*, like the creation in 1923 of an Egg and Poultry Pool by the United Farm Women of Alberta and the appointment of a member of the Women's Section of the Grain Growers as president of the

Saskatchewan Egg and Poultry Pool,[86] reflected women's involvement in yet another income-producing endeavour. The comment of one female honey-producer in 1935 summed up the importance of women's contributions when the staples of grain and beef failed in long droughts and poor markets:

> A few hives of bees are a great standby in a period of depression for not only do they produce honey under most unfavourable weather conditions but the product is easily disposed of. If cash is scarce, honey is readily accepted in exchange for other necessities.[87]

Not all women's cash-producing endeavours were visibly discrete from those of other members of their households. Across the country, women made direct contribution to family enterprises where men were the titular breadwinners. Female farmers joined in sowing and harvesting. Women in Maritime fishing villages "daily set out and turned the fish on the stages, and, on the return of the boats each day, aided the men in cleaning and preparing the fish for preserving."[88] Even when the products of female labour could not find a market, they might well ensure family survival. This was true, for example, of Indian women in British Columbia in the 1930s who, when all else failed, "were able to return to traditional subsistence pursuits such as the gathering of plant foods and the collection of shellfish to sustain their children and themselves."[89]

In cities and towns women also ran the equivalent of small home businesses in supplying lodgings, child care, and laundry. Variations on the putting out industry were commonplace. Advertisements for the Auto-Knitter by a Toronto hosiery company, which promised to buy a purchaser's entire output of socks, stockings, toques, and sweaters, offered a solution to the constant dilemma of accommodating domestic duties to the need for more cash. One Saskatchewan homemaker was depicted as earning the magnificent sum of $65.00 a month "when things looked black."[90] Another ad featured a woman acknowledging matter-of-factly the effects of postwar inflation: "How I Earn Money at Home and In This Way Make Up for Henry's Shrinking Salary."[91] Home-knitters added to the family coffers without calling into public question the role of the male breadwinner.

For most women, however, the bulk of domestic labour remained unpaid. Although the entirety of women's work in various classes and cultures is difficult to capture, it included most generally (besides childbirth and child rearing, which are considered in the next chapter) management, shopping, cooking, and cleaning.[92] Domestic management entailed the coordination of household and family finances and schedules. In home economics classes, which had been springing up since the 1890s, girls were encouraged to become up-to-date administrators through conscientious budgeting, more psychological know-how, and informed consumerism. Women's pages of every newspaper carried the same message, as did public health nurses and social workers into the homes of the poor. Their instruction helped introduce female Canadians to a new vocabulary of weights and measures, exotic foods and new cooking techniques, and social science interpretations of human behaviour. The impact of calls for change could be powerful but resistance to innovation was also strong. At least as important in women's domestic training was the effect of individual traditions and material circumstance.[93] Under the pressure of custom and need, housewifery, for all admonitions to the contrary, largely remained an inexact science.

Nor did schools normally teach the most critical aspect of domestic management, "making do." Yet this skill was fundamental to the economy of families from one end of the country to the other. Such was the case in the coal mining towns of Cape Breton where a miner's wife, stretching a male wage that was far from adequate during World War I and that fell still more in the 1920s, earned her reputation as "the greatest financier in the world."[94] While some husbands, in a practice that irritated numerous wives, monopolized financial management, doling out whatever cash they believed sufficient, the majority either shared budgeting or allocated the greater part of their wages to their wives, withholding only enough perhaps to pay for smokes or lunches or an occasional beer. For most women, the responsibility for budgeting meant, as it did for a Vancouver Island resident, the need to economize "as much as you could. . . . Well when your sheets started to wear out, you tore them up the middle and put a seam down the middle and hemmed the sides. . . . You patched . . . you canned, you jammed. . . . You had to be very ingenious . . . to stretch your dollar."[95]

Nor was financial ingenuity necessarily limited to household tasks. Wives in Nova Scotia's fishing communities, for instance, "assisted directly in the business by keeping the books for their husbands' boats."[96] Married women knew only too well how essential to family survival were their dairying, sewing, quilting, preserving, and gardening efforts. Frugality and ingenuity were all the more crucial to family management in the absence of a male breadwinner. Such absences were nothing new to Canadians. Fur trading, fishing, logging, whaling, policing, missions, and a host of other occupations had long required lengthy periods away from home.[97] Nor was it all that unusual for men to desert their families altogether when self-respect and optimism were at their lowest ebb or alternate prospects rosier. The wives and mothers left behind often struggled to manage. Ida Hopkins, for instance, whose husband was a commercial fisherman on the Pacific Coast, remembered:

> I learned the meaning and the reason for the remark, "Screaming Fishwife." The fathers were away for days at a time, out in storm and wind. The mothers were left alone with not only the worry about their husbands but the responsibility of bringing up the family alone. Sometimes a darned good scream relieved a lot of pressure.[98]

As this wife and many others knew, planning the particulars of family survival was much easier with a good husband present to lend support.

Women had shopped for their families for years, pouring through catalogues, bargaining for supplies with local merchants. In the past, goods were likely to be produced locally and judged on the merits of close observation of product and producer, brands were few and those well-known, and choice of merchant and purchase limited and well-understood. These familiar patterns were changing. To be sure, housewives in outlying areas still relied on Eaton's and Simpson's to clothe their families and furnish their homes, and husbands, more often than wives, left farms and homesteads to go to town for supplies. Just as importantly, many women continued to clothe and feed their household with only limited assistance from commercial products. New habits, however, were slowly taking root particularly in the cities under the impact of the forces of mass production and a cash economy.

A notable part of the change was the emergence of store chains and supermarkets. Names like Kresge's, Safeway's, Red and White, Loblaw's, Woodward's, Tamblyn's, Dominion's, and Piggly Wiggly, were becoming household standbys. Up-to-date retailers made paper bags, car-loading, cash registers, "go carts" or "gliders,"[99] and sales slips a familiar part of shopping.[100] One by one, meat counters were transformed with the addition of refrigeration, meat slicers, computing scales, and meat choppers.[101] Loss leaders and coupons flourished to entice customers away from old loyalties. The pages of the *Canadian Grocer* in these years reveal an industry eager to try out the power of artful visual displays, the most effective placement of goods, and the influence of high-powered advertising. A wider variety of nationally advertised products such as McLaren Peanut Butter, Heinz Cooked Spaghetti, Bee Hive Golden Corn Syrup, and Jello Gelatin replaced homemade and bulk-food alternatives and helped homogenize the shopping experience in big cities from one province to another. Drug and grocery chains and national brands offered consumers an almost unheard of selection of goods in surroundings that were more sanitary than ever, if also standardized. New buyers had to choose between multiple brands of soaps, cereals, condiments, cleaning powders, and even baby foods. Finding one's way among these selections required levels of discrimination heretofore unnecessary. And as the revelations of government studies suggested, buyers needed to have their wits about them to avoid fraud.

Shopping was also in the process of becoming increasingly feminized, and the common pattern became female clerks serving female customers. The male salesforce was less visible, engaged in administration or with products whose interest, as with men's clothing, or cost, as with major appliances and automobiles, more frequently involved consultation with male purchasers. Male breadwinners, on the other hand, were inclined to leave day-to-day and general household shopping to their wives. Merchandisers set forth a public world of consumption in which women would spend more and more time. Women could find in department stores and their competitors the prospect of excitement and indulgence, much like, although on a lesser scale, that available on radio and in the movies. Daydreams of a better life flourished along side a reality that, for the vast majority of Canadians, was far removed from that which they glimpsed on celluloid or store shelves.

A great deal of shopping activity revolved around the need to feed the household. Many women continued to preserve large amounts of fruit, vegetables, and meat, constructing a diet that coincided to a substantial degree with what was locally available. Seasons remained a major influence upon a family's eating habits with root vegetables, for instance, predictable on tables eight months of the year. In Labrador Elizabeth Goudie evolved a routine as a young bride that many of her contemporaries would have understood: catching trout for winter meals, hunting birds in the spring, and fishing for salmon in the summer. Partridge berries, blackberries, bakeapples, wild raspberries, red currants, squashberries, and marshberries were picked wild with dandelions and willowleaf to join cultivated potatoes, cabbage, carrots, beets, and turnips in a menu that in good times was nourishing as well as varied.[102] Rural newspapers were full of instructions on preparing farm animals for the table, as with advice from one farm wife: "when getting ready to pluck a fowl have two pails of water, one hot and one cold. First dip [the] fowl into hot water, then into cold and you can pluck it without tearing the skin."[103] It was taken for granted that many Canadian housewives had butchering skills.

Recipes were sought and exchanged as newcomers struggled to cope with local produce and custom and those who could tried to share in the availability of more numerous and exotic products, everything from citrus fruit to fresh fish, commercial ice cream to ketchup. An emerging awareness of the significance of vitamins and calories for physical health and development, especially for children, also spurred interest in experimenting with unfamiliar products and preparations.[104] Innovation was still further encouraged by the introduction of cooking programs in schools and on radio. In the 1930s, for instance, Kate Scott Aitken, later a Conservative MP, hosted a radio show and travelling cooking schools for Canada Starch Limited. In one 1938 broadcast she stressed the larger significance of cooking:

> You're a creator, an artist and a manufacturer when you lay on the table a meal balanced, not too expensive, lovely to look at, and delicious to eat. When you toss your family a scrappy meal, put together carelessly because you think such work is belittling, then you're falling down on your job—woman and you're a fraud. . . .[105]

Standards for nutrition and presentation undoubtedly increased under the impact of new products and prodding from would-be authorities like

Aitken but, as the fierce competition for awards in baking at agricultural fairs regularly demonstrated, a reputation as a good cook had long been prized.[106]

For most housewives, the need to prepare regular and substantial meals superseded thoughts of experimentation and tasteful presentation. Women facing the arrival of a threshing crew or even the less labour-intensive combine operations, like those confronting a tableful of boarders, had little time to experiment with new methods of food preparation. The unrelenting pressure of work, even when significantly abated by a shift in the technology of the male workplace, was well summed up by one Saskatchewan resident:

> The combine is surely a great invention. No more big supplies of food to be stored up for hungry threshers. No more getting up at half past three in the morning to prepare breakfast for fifteen or twenty hungry men and perhaps to be awake for an hour before getting up time, for fear you'd oversleep. Now I get up at half past five, have breakfast at six, the men go to the field. . . . With the old method of threshing, there came wet weather, you had a crew on hand for perhaps several days. . . . You were supposed to feed them. When the old crew were working, they expected lunch in the middle of the forenoon; likewise the same in the afternoon. With the combine that all changed. . . . There were no lunches between meals. . . . The three meals were plenty.[107]

For such women, even when blessed by a combine, the sheer quantity of food needed normally meant a reliance on tried and true recipes rather than innovations garnered from cooking columns and radio broadcasts.

Some changes in kitchen technology in these years did, however, lend themselves to new menus. This was particularly true of the introduction of the mechanical refrigerator and the increasing sophistication of the cookstove. Such products nevertheless remained expensive, and the great majority of families waited long to make their purchase and updated appliances with considerable caution. Eaton's Spring/Summer 1926 catalogue introduced the first ice-box identified explicitly as a refrigerator but still constructed of wood. Enamelled steel models appeared only in 1933. Rather than being advertised in the appliance section, they were located with furniture and, more particularly, kitchen cabinets, of which they were evidently seen as a more specialized variety. Not until the Fall/Winter catalogue of 1939–40 was the electrical refrigerator presented unequivocally as a domestic appliance, following sewing machines and completely separated from other furniture. Ads for fridges also began to appear in Fall/Winter as well as a Spring/Summer catalogues, a timing that suggested they had previously been viewed as pre-eminently a hot weather convenience. Despite their slow appearance in catalogues, ads for electrical refrigerators had run in the fashionable *Canadian Homes and Gardens* since the 1920s. By 1941, refrigerated facilities had made major inroads into urban households, as table 1 suggests. Food preparation, menus, and shopping could

TABLE 1

REFRIGERATION FACILITIES IN OCCUPIED DWELLINGS IN SELECTED CITIES OVER 30 000, 1941

| City | Tenant/ Proprietor (T/P) | Refrigeration facilities | | |
		(T/P)	Mechanical	Ice	Other/None
Halifax	T	17.2	47.5	0.3	35.0
	P	36.8	42.5	0.4	20.3
Montreal	T	24.2	65.8	4.9	5.1
	P	32.6	59.0	3.8	4.6
Ottawa	T	47.8	42.1	0.9	9.2
	P	54.9	38.2	0.4	6.5
Toronto	T	42.8	44.5	0.2	12.5
	P	46.5	43.4	0.1	10.0
Winnipeg	T	45.9	30.8	0.3	23.0
	P	41.0	37.3	0.1	21.6
Edmonton	T	26.2	16.2	0.6	57.0
	P	25.9	19.4	0.4	54.3
Vancouver	T	27.8	12.5	1.4	57.0
	P	29.6	16.1	0.9	53.4

Source: Canada, *Census* (1941), IX: 81, table 17a, "Refrigeration facilities in occupied dwellings, cities of 30,000 and over."

shift substantially with the addition of reliable refrigeration. Yet, for the majority of Canadians, even those in urban areas of Central Canada favoured by relatively cheap electricity and higher standards of living, the ice-box, the cold cellar, and more make-shift arrangements prevailed until well after World War II, and the opportunities to construct new menus remained restricted.

In some ways the 1920s and 1930s seemed the heyday of Canadian stoves, which came in a wide and colourful variety of shapes and sizes. Like early kitchen cabinets, they frequently encompassed a range of functions including storing water, heating rooms, and housing utensils. Electricity made slow headway against wood and coal despite the attractions of high speed units, limited supervision, and easier cleaning.[108] Not until its Fall/Winter 1929–30 catalogue did Eaton's introduce an electric stove, the "Canadian Beauty" Rangette, which offered two burners and an oven for $24.50 and required no special wiring. Sales were presumably fairly limited since no subsequent advertisement appeared until the 1936 Spring/ Summer edition when the price fell to $17.50. Despite a proliferation of ads for electrical stoves in *Canadian Homes and Gardens*, they evidently never penetrated Eaton's intended market to any significant degree. Nevertheless, by 1941, 39.6 percent of all dwellings had electric stoves, although this included only 7.4 percent of farm homes in comparison with 77.0

percent of houses in cities over 30 000.[109] Whatever their specific type, stainless steel and enamel stoves saved time spent in blacking and cleaning their cast-iron predecessors. This potential for releasing women from labour was reduced, however, when new purchases allowed and indeed promoted—with the encouragement of manufacturers and nutrition experts—more elaborate menus with their longer and more complicated preparations.[110] Little wonder too that books and newspaper columns on cooking became standard fare for housewives who could no longer automatically look to domestic traditions for precise guidance on handling the newest technological additions.

The domestic appliance revolution in these years shifted aspirations more than actual practice. For the most part, housewives had to make do with routines familiar to their mothers and grandmothers. Only occasionally could they taste the innovations promised by modern marketing. A 1945 MacLean-Hunter survey entitled *Canada's Market in Home Equipment* suggested, however, that consumer priorities had been critically influenced. Refrigerators and cookstoves were high on the list in both number and dollar volume of purchases planned after the end of hostilities. The survey claimed, for example, that nearly 28 percent of all families would buy a mechanical refrigerator right away. One in five housewives was in the market first of all for a new cookstove, of which 40 percent were to be electric and about the same number coal or wood.[111] When they had the opportunity to make their preferences known, Canadian women were no longer content to live without the conveniences of modern manufacturing.

For most, however, there was no alternative in the 1920s and 1930s. Menus, like much else in their lives, remained wedded to the exigencies of a domestic economy that had little to spare. In part this was a reflection of gender politics. There was almost always, for instance, considerable reluctance to shift expenditure from farm machinery and stock to the improvement of the female workplace. To the chagrin of rural wives, male work was considered more important and more difficult and so "the kitchen is often the last place on the farm to turn modern."[112] Faced with such prejudices, it was difficult for housewives to update practices. More critical, however, to the maintenance of old ways in cooking, as much else, was sheer lack of cash. This was especially true for families during the 1930s, but many Canadians in both decades were relieved enough to find food regularly on their tables without expecting anything new in the way of variety or presentation. The miners' wives of Cape Breton whose budgets could barely feed their households in 1917 would have understood full well the desperation of a nursing mother in Alberta who lived on bread and potatoes for days at a time and the Saskatchewan family of five subsisting on bread and tea in the 1930s.[113] And their situation was far from unique. In the summer of 1932, for instance, in a season when conditions might have been expected to be better than they were at other times of the year, substantial numbers of Canadians were drawing relief: 12 to 13 percent of the population in Calgary, 13 percent in Edmonton,

8 percent in Medicine Hat, 20 percent in Lethbridge, 17 percent in Greater Vancouver, 12 percent in New Westminster, 37 percent in Port Alberni, B.C., 47 percent in Fernie, B.C., 20 percent in Greater Winnipeg, 10 percent in Brandon, 20 percent in Regina and Saskatatoon, and so on.[114] Although it meant survival, public aid was far from generous. The Saskatchewan Relief Commission, for instance, established a monthly maximum food budget "for a family of five at $10 plus one 98–pound bag of flour."[115] Ontario's relief offices rarely sanctioned purchase of cheese or fish or eggs. Sources of vitamin C such as tomatoes were hard to get anywhere. In 1933 a Red Cross dietitian had a good but far from unusual cause for despair in observing that even "a well-informed Ontario municipality . . . adopt[ed] a scale of relief food allowances based apparently on wholesale prices."[116]

Despite such self-evident limitations on women's ability to manage household budgeting, administrators of government and private assistance were only too likely to zero in on domestic mismanagement as a cause for distress. Toronto's director of the Visiting Housekeepers' Association, for instance, preferred a voucher system to cash relief since, "When investigated, these [complaints about relief levels] usually reveal that the mother is lacking in knowledge of the simplest principles of cooking. . . ."[117] Despite critics who blamed the victim, housewives regularly showed considerable ingenuity in stretching, borrowing, and scavenging supplies. For all their dedication, however, they sometimes had to watch children grow weak through lack of nourishment. Lectures on greater efficiency, like knowledge of modern appliances and more nourishing menus, did little good for those for whom wages were too low and unemployment too frequent.

Domestic management, shopping, and cooking, for all their worries, were often the preferred part of housewives' days. Cleaning was a more tedious necessity but even here the imaginative or the lucky could find innovative solutions to the dilemma of keeping families and homes neat and unsoiled. As with much else, they found ready counsellors in the advertisements of the period. Rinso, they were told, would make their clothes whiter than white; sponge mops would eliminate dirt in a jiffy; battleship linoleum would make floor spills a minor inconvenience; Standard's plumbing fixtures would ensure bathroom purity. Also potentially helpful were trends in house design that favoured greater casualness, simplicity, and efficiency. Built-in kitchen cupboards, counters at higher levels, the elimination of the formal dining room and sitting room, and the introduction of basement rumpus rooms, when supplemented by improved wiring and plumbing and modern appliances, could usher in new levels of comfort and convenience.[118]

Few advances did away altogether with domestic labour, but its nature sometimes could, or appeared to, change radically. A survey of several hundred women across Canada by the Chatelaine Institute Consulting Board, for instance, held powdered soaps and flakes and electric washing machines responsible for reducing the amount of wash sent out, eliminating the need for overnight soaking of dirty garments, and making washing schedules more flexible.[119] The shift to electric and gas stoves spared women "the scouring of pans to remove the soot" and the determined but often futile efforts to dissipate the "'sooty' kitchen odor [that] permeated every corner of every room."[120] The decades' high hopes for its domestic labourers were captured in an editorial in *Canadian Homes and Garden*s in 1927:

> There is a certain magic to housekeeping these days—the magic of electricity—over which I confess I never cease to marvel. Your modern housewife leaves the dishes within a machine, pops the dinner into an oven, laundry into a washer, and jumps into a roadster with never a thought except for the rubber of bridge and the round of golf which she is away to enjoy for an afternoon. She returns to find the washing done, her china and crystal sparkle, a six course dinner is ready for serving.[121]

As contemporaries frequently recognized, such expectations were far from realistic even for those who could afford electric irons, dryers, stoves, and so forth,[122] but this failed to deter either enthusiastic advertising or the hopes of women for whom every respite was a luxury.

Nevertheless, for all the promise of new commodities, nothing finally replaced the need for human labour, as the steady demand for domestics illustrated. Female servants whose numbers increased whenever bad times robbed women of other job alternatives were, as had always been the case, much prized. During the Great Depression in particular, more Canadians who maintained a middle-class income were able to purchase help extremely cheaply. A Westmount matron remembered phoning an employment agency that supplied with no difficulty a chef for $40 a month, a personal maid for $30, a first domestic maid for $25 and a second for $15, all with room and board, and a laundress for "two dollars a day, and she scrubbed by hand and ironed by hand and she lived at home."[123] In such favoured cases cleaning was more a matter of management than physical exertion. Yet, even when employees were abundant, workers' resistance to this occupation, householders' own desire for privacy, and the promise of new domestic technology were undercutting old habits. The use of domestics did not disappear without regret and resistance. One forty-year-old wife with five children complained, for instance, "I used to have a woman come in one day a week to do the washing and heavy cleaning, but John brought me a washing machine and I don't have her now."[124] Like many other "lucky" purchasers of large appliances, this middle-class woman was now all the more isolated from other adults for much of the day. If you believed corporate advertisers and many husbands, housewives, thanks to new products, benefited from having relatively little to do. In fact wringer washing machines, like other innovations, still demanded a heavy input of physical labour from their mistresses.

Exertions were of course harder still for those who had resort neither to human nor mechanical servants. In the mid-1920s, a homemaker recalled her washing routine for the magazine of the Canadian Trades and Labour Congress:

> My soap solution and boiling water starch I prepare on Mondays, and to make the soap solution I shred half a pound of soap into a basin and pour on a quart of boiling water. This I stir until the soap is dissolved. It then only requires reheating before being used.

She next sorted out the different types of clothing, soaked those that were most soiled, boiled the whites, and set out two tubs, one for washing and one for rinsing. Blueing and starching were two additional steps in an exercise that dominated the beginning of the week in many households and all week long in the winter when drying clothes were hung everywhere.[125] The prevalence of these time-consuming steps was suggested by the steady appearance of clothes boilers in Eaton's catalogues throughout these years. No wonder most Canadian women appeared to hate wash day with a passion that few other chores evoked or that by 1945 one in four housewives was in the market for a washing machine, particularly of the electric wringer type.[126]

Women's responsibility for household maintenance in everything from management to cleaning had, as always, the potential for isolating the homemaker, leaving her for long hours without adult company. On the one hand, modern consumer society relied to a significant degree on domestic privatization, on individual families making individual purchases without sharing. Yet isolation, as pioneer women had discovered, could be intensely alienating. Nor did it actually serve business, which depended on the exchange of information about and competition for new products. For many reasons, ready communication with the world outside the private home was essential and, in these years, the radio, the telephone, and the passenger car met this need as never before. By 1941, 77.8 percent of all occupied dwellings included a radio: 60.6 percent of those in rural areas and 90.6 percent of those in cities over 30 000.[127] Department store catalogues, like the pages of popular magazines, were jampacked with ads expounding the virtues of battery-operated and electrical machines. The home might be a solitary enterprise but purchasers could tune in on a rich world of broadcast.

Loneliness on the domestic frontier could also be countered by the magic of long distance telephones. By 1939 Canadians rented over 949 000 residential telephones and over 50 000 extension phones.[128] As Bell Telephone appreciated, the implications for family satisfaction were enormous. A typical advertisement featured a wife rejoining, " 'I'm not lonely now, Peter' " when her out-of-town husband called home on night rates.[129] Just as the rural dwellers who fought hard for electrification understood, the phone was the first line of defence against the terrors of isolation.

The home became all the more attractive when modern inventions permitted easy exit from its confines. The private car offered the prosperous new mobility. The dramatic increase in passenger automobile registration, despite the collapse of the economy, from 251 900 in 1920 to 1 191 900 in 1939 touched women directly.[130] The massive advertising campaign directed at them in *Canadian Homes and Gardens* and *Mayfair* in the 1930s in particular suggests how critical the car was to be in the creation of a middle-class lifestyle based on private suburban, servantless homes. A full-page ad for Packard in 1937 was typical in celebrating the change in female routines portended by the coming of the automobile:

> No, I don't run a dress shop, manage a tea room, or go to an office.
>   I'm just a wife. But if you think that means I'm any Sally-sit-by-the-fire, then you ought to follow me through one of my days! I drive to the station twice a day, taxiing my lord and master. I shuttle the children to school, to parties, to dancing class. I drive to the stores, the bank, the Club. I see the world every day—through a windshield.[131]

The speaker's suggestion that the possession of a car saved the modern homemaker the tedium of days spent solely at home is revealing. With motorized transport she had no need to envy her wage-earning sister. Not only did the private automobile offer the escape from the house that the servant had also demanded, it helped change the very nature of female duties. Women's days were more and more taken up as a "chauffeur-in-skirts." The hours freed by electrical appliances could be dissipated in a dozen new ways, most notably in thrall to children's leisure and educational activities.

Such opportunities would have been welcomed by less fortunate homemakers. When unemployment soared, markets collapsed, and crops failed, they were lucky to keep even radios and telephones, not to mention cars, which easily deteriorated into Bennett Buggies drawn by horses. In Saskatchewan, for example, the number of rural telephones dropped from 71 616 in 1930 to 39 488 four years later. Nor could farmers afford to recharge the batteries for the radios that had quickly become a standby of domestic life.[132] Such deprivations returned many women and their families to the state of isolation that the pioneers had endured.

For all the hyperbole associated with mass production, household labour took up large amounts of female energy and time. Women's champions understood this reality. Violet McNaughton, founder of the Saskatchewan Women Grain Growers, typically observed, "Prairie men may work hard, there may be chores early and late, but never later than the woman, besides there is eight hours rest per day on many of the implements. I would rather disc than bake any day."[133] Nellie McClung made much the same point still more dramatically:

> On the farms before electricity and labour-saving devices lightened their loads, women's work obsessed them. Their hours were endless, their duties imperative. Many broke under the

strain and died, and their places were filled without undue delay. Some man's sister or sister-in-law came from Ontario to take the dead woman's place. Country cemeteries bear grim witness to the high mortality rate in young women.[134]

Another westerner, Emily Murphy, summed up the situation more pithily with her observation that female Canadians were to "be a combination of Mary, Martha, Magdalen, Bridget, and the Queen of Sheba."[135] Women, when they were able to express an opinion, knew full well that their sex carried its share and more of the world's work. Pride in the extent of their labours kept some women from seeking public relief in bad times but awareness of the extent of their contributions made others equally unembarrassed about requesting assistance when need was great. Whatever happened, many women intended to remain survivors.

While their suffering and deprivation was no less real for it, poorer women were likely to be perceived positively in their struggle to cope. As the institution of mothers' allowances indicated, they accommodated to cultural ideals merely by remaining at home with their children. In contrast, men without markets for their products or their labour were only too readily perceived as failures whether by the community, their wives, or themselves. In Saskatchewan, the father of historian Hilda Neatby floundered as a doctor and a farmer. While Neatby senior retreated into his books, his wife kept the family together and endorsed her children's ambitions.[136] Another male breadwinner, who was much loved but "not good at making money" as a merchant, possessed a fundamental liability that went a long way to making his "a matriarchal household, intensely female."[137] Both the doctor and the merchant were appreciated and protected by their families but for others the results of economic failure could be desperate. A P.E.I. native who worked hard, fishing when he could as well as keeping up a big house and garden so his wife could take in summer tourists, was driven in shame and despair first to bootlegging and then to suicide. His wife in contrast had the reassurance of being held in considerable esteem by her children and her neighbours as someone who "kept the world turning, every day of her life."[138] Ironically enough, bad times were likely to highlight women's management just as they undercut the economic basis of male authority.

Families hard hit by economic disaster, whether in the coal towns of Cape Breton in the 1920s or the wheatfields of the Prairies in the 1930s, frequently relied all the more heavily on women's capacity to make do, to stretch a shrinking dollar. In a multitude of individual strategies, they did everything from giving up on commercial foods "to go back to less expensive methods of food preparation,"[139] to finding uses for the flour bags they might have thrown out in better days, to transforming old coats into quilts, to keeping bees to cut down on sugar purchases, to expanding gardens and picking more wild berries, to experimenting with a host of ways of adding to cash income.[140] While in many cases male roles and identities were threatened to their core by unemployment and lost crops and markets, the traditional sphere of the domestic economy and its female managers assumed more prominence and importance. Their greater responsibilities broke the health and spirit of some women but the resolve and energy of others kept families from total disaster and made homemakers in many instances the "Heroines of the Depression."[141]

NOTES

1. See, for example, Nellie McClung, *In Times Like These* (Toronto: University of Toronto Press, 1972), chap. 4.

2. John H. Thompson with Allen Seager, *Canada 1922–1939: Decades of Discord* (Toronto: McClelland and Stewart, 1985), 138.

3. For the experience of a prairie general merchant see Fredelle Bruser Maynard, *Raisins and Almonds* (Toronto: Doubleday, 1972).

4. See Canada, Royal Commission on Banking and Finance, *Report* (1964), 201.

5. See "The Budget Club," *Canadian Congress Journal* (March 1938): 5; "What Is a 'CASH PRICE?'" ibid. (June 1938): 6; and "Psychology of Installment Buying," *Dry Goods Review* (Jan. 1925): 101. See also Norman Macphee, Assistant Sales Manager, Goblin Electric Cleaner Co. Ltd., "The Installment Plan is Indispensable," *Canadian Furniture World* (Nov. 1937): 19, 26–27, 31; Alex Moss, "Says Installment Selling Is Increasing," *Dry Goods Review* (Feb. 1926): 73–74.

6. See E.P. Neufeld, "Changing Relative Importance of Suppliers of Consumer Credit in Canada" in *School of Consumer Credit in North America: Proceedings of Conference* (University of Toronto, May 1970). On the function of sales finance companies see also Wilbur Plummer and Ralph A. Young, *Sales Finance Companies and Their Credit Practices* (New York: National Bureau of Economic Research, Studies in Consumer Instalment Financing, 1940).

7. W.J. Dunlop, "Foreword," *Credits and Collection in Canada* (Toronto: Ryerson Press, 1947).

8. Canada, House of Commons, *Debates* (1939), III: 3203–5, the Honourable J.L. Ilsley.

9. See A.A. Synder, "Installment Houses Must Revise Their Methods to Survive," *Dry Goods Review* (Nov. 1931): 10, 56.

10. Eric Hehner, "Instalment Credits: A Case for Retail Stores," *Marketing Organization and Technique*, edited by Jane McKee (University of Toronto Press, Political Economy Series, no. 7, 1940), 50. See also Alfred Reeves, "Ten Advantages of Installment Buying from the Consumer's Standpoint," *Marketing* (Oct. 2, 1926): 201.

11. Philip H. Adams, "Instalment Buying—Its Advantages and Disadvantages in Relation to Banking, Commerce and the Community," *Journal of the Canadian Bankers' Association* (Oct. 1930): 63.

12. See Warren Galloway, "Financing the 'Pay-as-You-Use' Consumer," *Saturday Night* (Jan. 6, 1940): 7, 9.

13. Canada, *Census* (1941), X: 374–77, table 12.

14. *Canada's Market in Home Equipment* (Toronto: McLean-Hunter, 1945), 8.

15. Gerald Fortin, "The Social Meaning and Implications of Consumer Credit" in *Consumer Credit in Canada*, edited by J.S. Ziegel and R.E. Olley (Proceedings of a Conference on Consumer Credit in Saskatoon, University of Saskatchewan, Saskatoon, May 2–3, 1966).

16. For an important study of the relationship of advertising to modern capitalism in the U.S. that is nevertheless relevant for Canada in these years as well see Stuart Ewen, *Captains of Consciousness: Advertising and the Social Roots of the Consumer Culture* (New York: McGraw-Hill, 1976).

17. Florence E. Clotworthy, "Guarding of Advertisers' Interests is Successful Objective of A.C.A.," *Marketing* (Oct. 1938): 32.

18. "30 Years of Canadian Advertising As Revealed in Newspaper Files," *Marketing* (Oct. 15, 1938): 15.

19. Ibid., 16–17. See also Mrs. Christine Frederick, "How to Advertise to Women Buyers," ibid. (Nov. 1, 1921): 742, 744, and H.N. Casson, "Twelve . . . Tip No. 11— Appeal More to Women Than Men," ibid. (April 1, 1922): 306, 308.

20. See also Dr. Arthur Gates, "Does the Average Man Understand You?" *Marketing* (Sept. 1, 1920): 513–14, 516, 518, 201, and Elmer Wheeler, "Don't Sell the Steak—Sell the Sizzle," *Canadian Grocer* (April 15, 1939): 24, 33.

21. Lydiatt's Book, *"What's What in Canadian Advertising"* (Toronto: Marketing Publishers Ltd., 1922), 331.

22. "30 Years of Canadian Advertising . . . ," *Marketing* (Oct. 15, 1938): 48.

23. Ewen, *Captains of Consciousness*, 25.

24. See especially ibid., chap. 6, "Consumption and the Ideal of the New Home." See also Ruth Schwartz Cowan, "Two Washes in the Morning and a Bridge Party at Night: The American Housewife between the Wars" in *Our American Sisters: Women in American Life*, edited by Jean Friedman and Wm. Shade (Lexington, Mass.: D.C. Heath, 1982).

25. H.H. Morris, "How the Washing Machine Market Was Created," *Marketing* (Aug. 1, 1920): 425–27.

26. "Selling Washing Machines for Home Use," *Canadian Furniture World and the Undertaker* (April 1919): 31.

27. Margaret Brown, "Demonstrations and Recipes Build Goodwill for Gas Company," *Marketing* (July 10, 1926): 20.

28. "C.G.E.'s Twenty Years of Progress as an Advertiser of Household Utilities," *Marketing* (Nov. 28, 1936): 9. See also the efforts of Ontario Hydro, "Greater Use of Electricity Promoted by Ontario Hydro-Electric," *Marketing* (May 2, 1936): 2–3, and B.C. Electric's promotion of clothes washers in *Western Woman Weekly* (May 22, 1920): 9.

29. "Housecleaning Campaign Brings in New Business," *Canadian Grocer* (March 9, 1934): 12.

30. "National Baby Week, May 2–7," *Canadian Grocer* (April 15, 1938): 28.

31. "Creating Demand to Sell More and Better Furniture," *Canadian Furniture World and the Undertaker* (July 1921): 39–40.

32. "'Giant' Plumbing-Heating Campaign is Announced," *Marketing* (Jan. 23, 1937): 1.

33. "Remodelling Kitchen Contest Paves the Way for Profitable Sales of Kitchen Equipment," *Canadian Furniture World* (Nov. 1932): 11.

34. See "Announcing the Chatelaine Institute," *Chatelaine* (Feb. 1930): 22, and "The Director of the Chatelaine Institute," ibid. (March 1930): 24.

35. "New Freedom is Yours," *Canadian Homes and Gardens* (May 1930): 9.

36. See her lecture to the Advertising and Sales Bureau of the Vancouver Board of Trade, "Women Want to Know 'How Much' and 'Where to Get It'," *Marketing* (Oct. 15, 1927): 304.

37. John Watson, "Women Should Write Copy Addressed to Women," *Marketing* (Feb. 27, 1932): 102.

38. "'Consumer Movement' Menace Gathering Force in Canada," *Marketing* (Dec. 18, 1937): 1. See also the remarks by one mother of three, "How a Housewife Views Some Current Trends in Advertising," *Marketing* (Feb. 25, 1933): 3.

39. Canada, Royal Commission on Price Spreads, *Report* (1935), 234.

40. Ibid., 236–37. See especially chap. 8, "The Consumer."

41. PAC, Canadian Council on Social Development, Papers, v. 411, folder 178, "Department of Health," typescript mimeo, n.d [c. 1930], 8.

42. See Janice Dicken McGinnis, "From Health to Welfare: Federal Government Policies Regarding Standards of Public Health for Canadians, 1919–1945" (Ph.D. dissertation, University of Alberta, 1980).

43. See, for instance, the *Annual Reports* of the National Council of Women both during and after the war for their persisting attention to the problems of the cost of living.

44. See Dorothy Kidd, "Women's Organization: Learning from Yesterday" in *Women at Work: Ontario, 1850–1930* (Toronto: Women's Educational Press, 1974), 331–61.

45. "When Women Investigate Prices," *Chatelaine* (July 1938): 14, 43–45.

46. Mabel Crews Ringland, "'No Consumer Movement in Canada!' Oh, No!" *Marketing* (Feb. 26, 1938): 7.

47. See "B.C. Housewives League and R.M.A. to Do Battle Over Price Legislation," *Canadian Grocer* (Sept. 15, 1938): 1, 48.

48. Only after 1961 did its membership include men.

49. See Glenbow, *History of the Saskatchewan Women's Co-operative Guild* (n.p., n.d.).

50. "Address on Community Kitchen. Given by Mrs. Oag at a Meeting of the United Women Voters," *Woman's Century* (April 1919): 37.

51. Margaret Fairley, "Domestic Discontent," *Canadian Forum* (Nov. 1920): 45.

52. See Veronica Strong-Boag, "Pulling in Double Harness or Hauling a Double Load: Women, Work and Feminism on the Canadian Prairies," *Journal of Canadian Studies* (Fall 1986): 32–52.

53. Katherine Hale, "Some Problems of Peace," *Woman's Century* (May 1919): 15. See also the argument in B.C.B., "Domestice Service—The House Mother," *Woman's Century* (March 1919): 24–26.

54. Rose Paynter, "Man—the Home Maker," *Western Home Monthly* (Feb. 1923): 43.

55. See Penney Kome, *Somebody had to do it. Whose Work is Housework?* (Toronto: McClelland and Stewart, 1982).

56. "Mater," "Dolls for Small Boys," *Farm and Ranch Review* (Oct. 20, 1919).

57. See the editorial by J. Herbert Hughes, *Canadian Homes and Gardens* (Oct. 1925): 9.

58. Quoted in Canada, *Census* (1931), XII, *Housing in Canada*, 435.

59. Gillian Wade, "Modest Comforts" in *Working Lives* (Vancouver: New Star Books, 1984), 109.

60. PAC, Papers of the Canadian Council on Social Development, v. 19, Folder "Child Welfare - P.E.I. 1930," Alfred Buckley to Charlotte Whitton, Dec. 13, 1930.

61. Series S198-202, *Historical Statistics of Canada*, 2nd ed., edited by F.H. Leacy (Ottawa: Statistics Canada, 1983).

62. *Report of the Halifax Citizens' Committee on Housing, 1932*, quoted in *Housing in Canada*, 436.

63. Ibid., 438.

64. See H.G. Robinson, "Fifty Millions for Modernization," *Canadian Homes and Gardens* (Dec. 1936): 17–29, for one optimistic account of the Home Improvement Plan. Such mention in this magazine directed at upper-middle-class householders suggests, however, its limitations. For an important preliminary assessment of the HIP and its affirmation of traditional sex roles, see Margaret Hobbs and Ruth Roach Pierson, "'When Is A Kitchen Not a Kitchen?'" *Canadian Woman Studies* (Winter 1986): 71–76.

65. Saskatchewan, Royal Commission on Agriculture and Rural Life, *Report* (1952), 27.

66. *Housing in Canada*, 456.

67. Ibid., 504.

68. Ibid., 496.

69. Quoted in Meg Luxton, *More Than a Labour of Love: Three Generations of Women's Work in the Home* (Toronto: The Women's Press, 1980), 174.

70. *Housing in Canada*, chap. 10.

71. Ibid., 516.

72. Ibid., 507.

73. See chap. 11 "The Housing of Relief Families, 1936," ibid.

74. Ibid., 516.

75. Ibid., 530.

76. Series T147–194, *Historical Statistics of Canada*.

77. See the explicit reference to these duties made in ads for Packard and other cars in *Canadian Homes and Gardens* during these years, for instance, "Listen to the Plea of the Family Taxi-Driver," *Canadian Homes and Gardens* (Oct.-Nov. 1936): 48.

78. *The Housing Plans of Canadians* (Toronto: MacLean-Hunter, 1945), 15.

79. "Emancipation," *Canadian Homes and Gardens* (March 1930): 59; "New Freedom is Yours," ibid. (May 1930): 9.

80. Canada, *Census* (1941), 63.

81. Series P29–33, 63–74, in *Historical Statistics of Canada*, 1st ed., edited by M.C. Urquhart and K.A.H. Buckley (Cambridge: Cambridge University Press, 1965).

82. See, for example, Marjory MacMurchy, *The Canadian Girl At Work* (Toronto: King's Printer, 1919), chap. 18, "The Girl at Home."

83. See Veronica Strong-Boag, "'Wages for Housework': Mothers' Allowances and the Beginnings of Social Security in Canada," *Journal of Canadian Studies* (Spring 1979): 24–34.

84. "Making Farm Hobbies Pay," *Farm and Ranch Review* (May 1931): 26–27, 35.

85. Marjorie Griffin Cohen, "The Decline of Women in Canadian Dairying" in *The Neglected Majority*, vol. II, edited by Alison Prentice and Susan Mann Trofimenkoff (Toronto: McClelland and Stewart, 1985).

86. Amy J. Roe, "Interesting Farm Women," *Grain Growers' Guide* (Oct. 1, 1926): 31.

87. "Start With One Hive," *Free Press Prairie Farmer* (May 29, 1935): 4.

88. Nanciellen Davis, "Women's Work and Worth in an Acadian Maritime Village" in *Women and World Change*, edited by Naomi Black and Ann Baker Gottrell (Beverly Hills: Sage Publications, 1981), 101.

89. Marjorie Mitchell and Anna Franklin, "When You Don't Know The Language, Listen to the Silence: An Historical Overview of Native Indian Women in B.C." in *Not Just Pin Money*, edited by Barbara Latham and Roberto Pazdro (Victoria: Camosun College, 1984), 27–28.

90. "This Woman Earned $65.00 a Month—Right at Home," *Western Home Monthly* (Jan. 1927): 1.

91. "How I Earn Money At Home And In This Way Make Up for Henry's Shrinking Salary," *Canadian Home Journal* (Feb. 1921): 35.

92. For a discussion of the problems of assessing women's work in the home historically see Veronica Strong-Boag, "Keeping House in God's Country: Canadian Women at Work in the Home" in *On the Job*, edited by C. Heron and Robert Storey (Kingston and Montreal: McGill-Queen's University Press, 1985).

93. See Barbara Riley, "Six Saucepans to One: Domestic Science vs. the Home in British Columbia 1900–1930" in *Not Just Pin Money*, 171.

94. J.B. McLachlan quoted in David Frank, "The Miner's Financier: Women in the Cape Breton Coal Towns, 1917," *Atlantis* (Spring 1983), 138.

95. SFUA, taped interview with Jeanne Ouellette by Sara Diamond, 1979.

96. M. Patricia Connelly and Martha MacDonald, "Women's Work: Domestic and Wage Labour In a Nova Scotia Community," *Studies in Political Economy* (Winter 1983), 56.

97. For an excellent discussion of this phenomenon see Isabelle St. Martin, "Family Separation: The Case of the Women Left Behind" (M.A. thesis, Concordia University, 1980).

98. Ida Hopkings, *To the Peace River Country and On* (Richmond, B.C.: The Author, 1973), 126, quoted in St. Martin, "Family Separation."

99. Known today more pedestrianly as grocery carts.

100. See B.T. Huston, "Milestones in 50 Years Progress of Grocery Retailing," *Canadian Grocer* (June 26, 1936): 10–11, 49; "Merchants of Fifty Years Ago Recall Customs and Methods That Are Here No More," ibid. (June 26, 1936): 70–71, 74, 76; "Comes Natural to the Women," ibid. (Oct. 29, 1937): 12

101. "'Market Store' Represents Main Development in Meats in Past 50 Years," *Canadian Grocer* (June 26, 1936): 88.

102. Elizabeth Goudie, *Woman of Labrador* (Toronto: Peter Martin Associates, 1975), 24–25 and passim.

103. "We Amuse Her," *Free Press Prairie Farmer* (Jan. 14, 1925): 16.

104. See Kathleen Murphy, "Nutritious Foods—Nature Sealed," *Canadian Magazine* (April 1931): 37.

105. PAC, Kate Scott Aitken Papers, v. I, Broadcast, Jan. 20, 1938. On the emphasis on high standards see also Marianne Masson, "January Suggestions," *Canadian Magazine* (Jan. 1934): 20.

106. See David C. Jones, "'From Babies to Buttonholes': Women's Work at Agricultural Fairs," *Alberta History* (Autumn 1981): 26–32.

107. Mrs. James McPherson, "Farm Women Praise the Combine," *Grain Growers' Guide* (April 15, 1930): 19.

108. See the ad from CGE Hotpoint, "New Freedom is Yours," *Canadian Home and Gardens* (May 1930): 9.

109. Canada, *Census* (1941), IX: 59, table 12, "Principal cooking fuel in occupied dwellings, 1941."

110. On some of the implications of changes in stove technology see Ruth Schwartz Cowan, *More Work for Mother: The Ironies of Household Technology from the Open Hearth to the Microwave* (New York: Basic Books 1983), especially chap. 3.

111. *Canada's Market in Home Equipment* (Toronto: MacLean-Hunter, 1945), 6.

112. "In A Modern Farm Kitchen," *Free Press Prairie Farmer* (July 6, 1932): 14. See also Strong-Boag, "Pulling in Double Harness or Hauling a Double Load."

113. M. Horn, ed., *The Dirty Thirties* (Toronto: Copp Clark, 1972), 236, 242.

114. Ibid., 254–55.

115. Ibid., 279.

116. Margaret S. McCready, "Relief Food Allowances in Ontario," *Public Health Journal* (May 1933): 221.

117. Marjorie Bell, "Planning Minimum Food Budgets," *Public Health Journal* (May 1933): 212.

118. *Canadian Homes and Gardens*, which began publication in May 1925 and continued throughout the 1930s, is an invaluable guide to just what was possible domestically for those who could afford the price.

119. "How Do You Wash Your Clothes," *Chatelaine* (March 1931): 21, 75.

120. "She Had Lost All Interest in Life," ad by Winnipeg City Light and Power, *Western Labor News* (Jan. 23, 1920): 7.

121. "Next Month with *Canadian Homes and Gardens*," *Canadian Homes and Gardens* (May 1927): 13.

122. See, for example, the criticism of exaggerated claims in Eustella Burke, "The Magic of Electricity," *Canadian Homes and Gardens* (June 1927): 44–45, 64, 67.

123. "Buying a Human Being" in *Ten Lost Years*, edited by Barry Broadfoot (Toronto: Doubleday, 1973), 6.

124. A Wife, "This Bondage," *Maclean's* (Oct. 1, 1931): 11.

125. "Managing the Family Wash," *Canadian Congress Journal* (Jan. 1926): 41.

126. *Canada's Market in Home Equipment* (Toronto: MacLean-Hunter, 1945), 6.

127. Canada, *Census* (1941), IX: 81, table 18, "Occupied dwellings with specified conveniences 1941."

128. Series S323–331, *Historical Statistics of Canada*, 1st ed., 559.

129. "I'm Not Lonely Now, Peter," *Canadian Homes and Gardens* (Aug. 1932): 40.

130. Series S222–235, *Historical Statistics*, 1st ed., 550.

131. "'So I'm a Stay-At-Home, Am I?'" *Canadian Homes and Gardens* (June 1937): 45.

132. Saskatchewan, Royal Commission on Agriculture and Rural Life, *Report* (1952), 32.

133. Saskatchewan Archives Board, Violet McNaughton Papers, v. 35, folder 72, McNaughton, "The Prairie Woman," handwritten, n.d.

134. Nellie McClung, *The Stream Runs Fast*, quoted in Linda Rasmussen et al, *A Harvest Yet to Reap: A History of Prairie Women* (Toronto: The Women's Press, 1976), 82.

135. Emily Ferguson, *Janey Canuck in The West*, quoted in *A Harvest Yet to Reap*, 57.

136. See Michael Hayden, ed., *So Much To Do, So Little Time: The Writings of Hilda Neatby* (Vancouver: University of British Columbia Press, 1983).

137. Fredelle Bruser Maynard, *Raisins and Almonds*, 61 and 159.

138. "Just Tired of Waiting" in *Ten Lost Years*.

139. "Prairie Women," *Free Press Prairie Farmer* (Sept. 14, 1938): 23. See also the reports from the Home Economics Committee of the United Farm Women of Alberta in Jane Allen, "Home-loving Hearts," ibid. (March 1, 1933): 4.

140. See "Plan to Utilize Empty Flour Bags Will Sell Housewives More Flour," *Marketing* (Oct. 16, 1937): 4, and "Quick Yeast Starter," *Free Press Prairie Farmer* (July 11, 1934): 4; "Two Coat Quilt," ibid. (June 29, 1938): 4; "Sisters Under the Skin," ibid. (Feb. 7, 1934): 4.

141. See the letters to the Canadian Council on Child and Family Welfare in "Heroines of the Depression," *Canadian Congress Journal* (Dec. 1933): 19–20.

CHAPTER 5
MOTHERING

So far as most Canadians were concerned, motherhood was taken for granted as marriage's logical outcome for the female sex. Women of every background were socialized from childhood on to discover personal fulfilment and purpose in childbirth and child rearing. As the following poem, saccharine in expression but commonplace in sentiment, illustrates, motherhood was to do much to compensate women for other shortcomings in their lives:

Why Should I Envy Her?

My neighbour's house has gracious, flowing lines,
Low built, deep sloping roof and all
That makes a house a home to love.
Wide casement windows, chimneys tall
Oak beams crisscrossed along its mellow front,
Roses in cluster round the quaint blue door,
A terraced garden rich with blossoms gay.
Why should I envy her? My neighbour's poor!

There's hunger in her eyes; her hands hold naught
Though decked with costly pearls and jewels rare,
But I am rich whose home is but a cot!
I have no need of priceless gems to wear,
For both my hands are full and full my life.
I've jewels sweet, that laugh and cry and play,
A man, whose very soul is mine to keep.
I would not have my neighbour's life one day!

Why should I envy her? My neighbour's poor!
No babies romp about the quaint blue door.
Homage men pay her—homage to her gold!
Why should I envy her? I've wealth untold![1]

Whatever else happened, proper performance of maternal duties gave women cause for personal pride and public approval.

Pregnancy and care of offspring remained first of all of intense personal interest to parents, but the society at large and, increasingly, the state were also presumed to have a major stake in their outcome. Whereas communities had always exerted a variety of positive and negative sanctions on the conduct of mothering, increasingly elaborate public health, welfare, and educational bureaucracies staffed by powerful professionals now influenced more directly than ever women's experience of parenting. Motherhood in Canada was very far from being either simple or natural, involving as it did a complex and changing blend of private initiative and public intervention.

The choice to parent provoked widespread debate in these years as Canadians struggled to understand how traditional sex roles, opportunities for women, desires for intimacy and affection, and the state's interest in good citizenship could be reconciled. The controversy over the necessity and morality of birth control was only the most visible expression of a larger issue that engaged the thoughts of many citizens.[2] While Canadians in general agreed that pregnant women and mothers needed additional health care, nutrition, and support and that babies needed regular medical attention, a sufficient material environment, and opportunities for education,[3] there was no consensus on the best means of achieving these conditions. Answers ranged everywhere from a conservative Malthusianism that went so far as to advocate sterilization of the "unfit" to a demand for a socialist revolution that would ensure an equitable distribution of the nation's resources to all mothers. The great majority of prospective mothers sought solutions somewhere between such extremes, attempting to work out more or less satisfactory compromises between the feasible and the preferred.

Many households, for instance, had long depended on children and wives to augment the cash income and labour of male breadwinners. No wonder then that pregnancy and young offspring were a near certain recipe for financial difficulty or even disaster for poorer households. In their efforts to match family size with available resources, women, when they could, regularly tried to "put themselves right." For them abortions were a fact of life. However, attempted abortions were not always successful, nor were all women who were faced with an unwanted pregnancy able to choose this alternative. Like one prairie woman who feared the loss of income she made from selling brushes, what they could not change they endured: "there will be another baby this winter. . . . I thought I had that problem licked as Gordon was 3 in April, but I guess as long as one lives with men there is apt to be babies. I sure don't want any more."[4] Such hard-pressed mothers were in no position to devote themselves to the intricacies of modern child rearing. The persistence of bad times throughout both decades made some families unable or unwilling to meet all the heightened standards of modern parenting advocated by child care professionals. They continued to hope for the best and cope with the worst.

More couples than previously, however, were successful in choosing to bear few or no children. The general fertility rate, that is the annual number of births per 1000 women aged 15 to 49 years of age, went from 128.1 in 1921, to 99.5 in 1931, to 89.1 in 1941, a drop from 1911 to 1921 of

1.4 percent, from 1921 to 1931 of 22.3 percent, and from 1931 to 1941 of 10.5 percent.[5] Some Canadians, notably urban-dwellers and the British- and native-born were especially likely to experience a drop in fertility, but from 1921 on "the Canadian provinces embarked on a path of convergence" that would produce a "Canadian pattern" of high marriage rates and relatively low marital fertility.[6] Women of all ages joined in this shift to fewer children in these two decades but the decline was especially noticeable in the age group over 30. Between 1921 and 1931 and 1931 and 1941, the fertility rate of women aged 30 to 34 years of age fell 20.0 percent and 18.7 percent; that of women aged 35 to 39, 19.0 percent and 25.1 percent; that of women aged 40 to 44, 23.9 percent and 30.6 percent; that of women aged 45 to 49, 30.2 percent and 35.7 percent.[7] Women were having fewer babies and producing them over a shorter period of time. In 1921 the mean age of childbearing was 25.8 years, in 1931 it dropped to 25.1 years, and in 1941 fell to 24.7 years, maintaining a decline that has continued through the 1980s.[8] Especially noticeable here as well is the fact that the disastrous decade of the 1930s was in no way an anomaly; rather it was in keeping with the continued overall decline in fertility. In fact, the 1920s saw a much more dramatic drop in childbearing, a reflection more particularly of changed views of ideal family size.

Critical to Canadians' reduction in their birth rate was their conception of a desirable standard of living. As Winifred Wandersee has noted with regard to the United States, "rising expectations were a part of the economics of family life."[9] To a large degree, Canadians of every income level in the 1920s shared in a heightened emphasis on consumption that could only be satisfied by going into debt, increasing cash income, or reducing family size. In order to grasp some part of the promise of mass consumption, budgeting on necessities was tightened, goods were bought on time, wives went out to work, and the number of babies was more regulated. One young mother, for instance, whose husband earned significantly above the average wage, claimed to have nursed her daughter longer to save on food bills. The prospect of additional child care expenses, in addition to the costs of having a Caesarean section, drove this couple to attempt to achieve their desired standard of living by limiting themselves to one baby.[10] Another wife came to the same conclusion after her assessment of the amount of money and domestic work needed to maintain a larger family.[11] Canadians such as these wanted a better share than they yet had of the postwar world "fit for heroes" promised by politicians[12] and of the domestic improvements marketed to heroes' wives by capitalists.

Also at issue was the matter of a "fair deal" for their sex advocated by the women's movement. While relatively few individuals actively identified themselves as feminists in these years, many more were deeply influenced by presumptions that feminism had fostered and defended. Notable among these was the belief that women had the right to demand the improvement and protection of the private sphere through state action, the right to expect recognition of their contribution to the family economy, and the right to legal equality with their husbands.[13] These aspirations were far from being satisfied. Women pointed, for instance, to the lack of affordable obstetrical services as evidence that motherhood was more honoured in the breach than the observance. One prairie farm wife went so far as to propose a "baby moratorium" until medical assistance was made available.[14] In her rage at the near-death of a patient in childbirth, a nurse

> made the Dr. let [the patient's] husband help right thro where they usually call for two nurses. He had 3 children before, 2 hospital cases and one instrument case at home and they never let him thro a door before. He could just say over and over I never thought it was anything like that and I sure hope he remembers it for a while . . . It's a pity the men and the priests didn't have their turn.[15]

Even when women could not demand some greater control of their bodies on their own account, others like this nurse were there to demand it for them.

The continuing absence of effective state support for women facing the problems of childbirth and child rearing also helped make some feminists conclude that demands of maternity were not easily, if at all, reconcilable with female autonomy and self-respect.[16] The writer Mary Quayle Innis, for example, summed up the contradictions between society's expectations and the reality of motherhood in the fictional character of a depressed cleaning woman who longed to marry off her last child: "She was one of the women who should never have had children, at least not the children of a man she didn't like."[17] In real life, persistent efforts at family regulation spoke volumes for some women's determination to assert their own claims within marriage. At least equally important was the recognition that, without limiting fertility, no woman could fill "the demanding twentieth-century role of romantic wife and conscientious mother and possibly would lose her husband."[18] So long as the burden of parenthood remained so potentially threatening and so frequently unshared, women were prepared to go to considerable lengths to control their fertility.

There were also women on the left, in the 1930s in particular, who demanded liberalization of the laws on contraception and situated birth control firmly within "a class perspective and a materialist analysis which stressed the right of working-class families to make their own decisions about family size, and the need for relief from the economic and physiological burdens of constant childbearing for working-class women."[19] For some such critics of contemporary affairs, the decision not to have children represented an explicit condemnation of the social order. One member of the Housewives' League in British Columbia, for instance, chose to stop after her first because, as she told her husband, "I can't see them brought up, and educated and finding work under this system."[20] While such explicit political acts were not common, disenchantment with a system that permitted breadlines and unemployment had its own contribution to make to women's determination to limit the number of births.

Women's competence as decision-makers over marital fertility and as parents was far from being unquestioned. Embedded in contemporary misogynous literature was the assumption that mothers both had too much power and wielded it inappropriately. Harkening back to supposed better days when "women were women and men were men," anti-feminists, among whom doctors were some of the worst offenders, painted horrendous pictures of a modern world "of selfish materialism, when women would sooner kiss the cold clammy nose of a lap-dog than the tender baby fingers of a little child"[21] and of "society women who did not nurse their babies in order that they might be free to enjoy themselves."[22] Women's detractors dismissed protection of a preferred standard of living as an insufficient justification for remaining without children.[23] Mothers who claimed rights "to freedom and amusement" were blamed for all the shortcomings of modern society.[24] Any woman who refused maternity was damned as "a traitor to the race and a coward and a skulker in the battle of life and should be branded and despised accordingly."[25] Critics, mindful of the latest trumpetings of the social sciences, insisted that procreation was basic to the female personality. Suppression of this natural instinct would only result in neurotic individuals "who try by all sorts of substitute activities, from teaching to dog-fancying and bridge to avoid the real issues."[26] Ironically enough, women who dedicated themselves too thoroughly to parenting also heard criticism from the same source. In 1933 one expert in "Humanology" identified a major problem in the creation of a "mother fixation" by the overly attentive adult.[27] Another concluded, "if your child is a problem child, probably you are a problem mother."[28] Such maternal failures, according to another commentator, deserved "a good sound smacking"; only then might they perform their duties adequately.[29]

External attempts to regulate the critical parent-child bond invariably reviewed the credentials of the average Canadian mother. Eager tutors in medicine, education, and social work contrasted their superior professionalism with maternal amateurism. Experts complained:

> the trouble is that the home today is the poorest run, most mismanaged and bungled of all human industries. . . . Many women running homes haven't even the fundamentals of house management and dietetics. They raise their children in the average, by a rule of thumb that hasn't altered since Abraham was a child.[30]

They claimed that such a lack of expertise resulted in mortality, disease, and dysfunction among Canadian children, and they placed the responsibility for failure later on in life squarely upon the mother.

Canada's poor showing internationally in infant and maternal mortality helped fuel such calumnies. Lives were at stake. At issue, too, as child care professionals well knew, was a transfer of domestic authority. Female power and prestige in nineteenth- and twentieth-century Canada were tied to women's role in reproduction and early socialization. Attacks on women's credibility as nurturers of infants and small children undermined the customary basis for women's self-esteem and public value. The benefits of expert supervision in terms, for instance, of the early identification of remediable defects such as rickets were nevertheless substantial. Child care experts had much to offer that women wanted. In exchange, however, women had to surrender power over themselves and their offspring. It was an authority they would not easily recover, however much their faith in experts proved misplaced.[31]

Women's receptivity to would-be advisers was enhanced by a postwar celebration of maternalism that challenged declining birth rates, especially among the middle class, and the worldly ambitions of the "new woman." Advertisers of every kind used children to help sell products and appreciated full well that youngsters' needs could supply entry into individual homes.[32] The extensive coverage given the Dionne quintuplets and the British princesses, Elizabeth and Margaret Rose, also supplied powerful models for prospective mothers. At a more formal level, press, pulpit, clinic, and school reaffirmed familiar efforts to direct girls to motherhood as the career par excellence. National survival was depicted as dependent on women's acceptance of their "proper" role. Pro-natalists such as Benito Mussolini were cited in defence of the view that women who refused to bear children were more concerned with the state of their figures than that of the race. Their selfishness was identified as condemning western civilization to military and economy inferiority.[33]

In pregnancy, so it was claimed, lay womanly fulfilment. Occasional talk of companionate marriage and professional employments for women faltered before the insistence that being a mother was "the highest of all professions" and "that no power of imagination on the part of women who have no children can succeed in placing them in the same position as the mothers."[34] Flattery and hyperbole such as this obscured the limitations of the maternal role and downplayed the significance of career alternatives. Women so socialized were anxious consumers of information on how they might better meet the challenge of modern parenting.

At the same time, traditional methods of coping with the strains of motherhood were condemned by experts. Women's customary networks of exchange on everything from infant health to adolescent tempers were no longer seen as sufficient to the needs of the new age. A typical warning reminded mothers not to "try out fancy theories learned over the back fence or other unreliable sources. There are good books on the subject of bringing up your child."[35] One short story, entitled "The Girl Who Didn't Love Babies," summed up the case for a new-style mothering in its contrast between Marion and her friend Ruth. The former who knew little of babies before her marriage turned to books and professionals for guidance and refused advice from local women. The result was six children, all healthy testimonials to up-to-date methods. Ruth, on the other hand, who had a great deal of previous experience with youngsters, persisted in her reliance on tradition and counted only one puny child to her credit. For readers of the latest information on child development the lesson was self-evident.[36]

Education for mothering was not new in Canada in the 1920s and 1930s, but the extent of the assault by child care experts was unprecedented.[37] In the forefront of professionals' intrusion into mothers' lives was the federal Division of Child Welfare, captained until 1934 by the dynamic Dr. Helen MacMurchy. Thousands of its "Little Blue Books" on home and child care were sent free to women who feared the costs of ignorance. Popular demand necessitated a succession of printings and editions. Imitators followed. In 1926 the Canadian Council on Child Welfare sponsored a nine-month package of "Pre-natal Letters" that were widely advertised in the dominion's family magazines. By 1930, over 30 000 of these sets had been posted. The Council in addition co-operated with provincial departments of health in mailing a series of "Pre-school Letters" to mothers eager to secure the most up-to-date child-rearing advice. Information was also available through pamphlets from the Canadian Red Cross and the Victorian Order of Nurses as well as publications from the Metropolitan Life Insurance Company, including a free layette pattern. Such initiatives were complemented by hundreds of "little mother" classes, expectant mothers' clinics, well-baby clinics, better baby contests, and baby welfare centres. Advice from every quarter was informed by an unshakeable confidence in the universality of the maternal role, the centrality of the mother-child bond, and the indispensability of external advice to the optimal functioning of the modern family.

The case for updating child care practices was communicated still more widely in regular newspaper and magazine features on children. Columns entitled "Your Baby and Mine" (*Halifax Herald*), "Mother and Baby" (*Family Herald and Weekly Star*), "What of Your Child?" (*Chatelaine*), and "The Well-Baby Centre" (*Canadian Home Journal*) raised child care and child problems to unprecedented public prominence. Advertisements for condensed milks, baby foods, and children's medicine, clothes, and and toys became the stock-in-trade of the mass circulation press. Canadian physicians added to the avalanche of paper by publishing child care manuals. By the 1920s, babies had become the mainstay of both industries and careers.[38]

Whatever the changing fashions in advice to mothers, women continued to want babies. In some ways more than marriage itself, pregnancy and motherhood marked a critical passage to new duties, to a new period in women's lives. After several miscarriages, Phyllis Knight was glad to give birth to her son, hoping it meant that she and her Ali could cease their wanderings and "lead a more normal life."[39] For her and other women, babies were a powerful sign of normality. Children also called forth some of women's deepest feelings of love and responsibility and in many cases supplied essential company and consolation. Their love and attention could make up for a host of deficiencies in circumstances and husbands. In a typical expression of sentiment, one homemaker on the northern frontier wrote, "I did not dread the coming of winter though now the baby tied me to the house for he was a great amusement." [40] Bad husbands could be made at least minimally endurable. As a prairie columnist wrote to an unhappy wife: "In them [her children] you will find consolation. . . . Bad as it is you doubtless prefer your present situation, plus your children, than never to have married."[41]

For all the national and personal celebration of parenthood, its beginning in pregnancy was far from being a matter of general discussion. Images of expectant women were almost never seen in the press and indeed it seems that women in the months prior to birth were normally expected to disguise their condition as much as possible and not to draw attention to themselves by any more public display of their person than was absolutely necessary. So strong was reticence that public health nurses had to insist that:

> For no reason except illness, should the expectant mother shut herself indoors. True men and true women hold the highest esteem for the maternal state, and surely the opinion of others does not matter! Moreover, thanks to the sensible clothing of today, pregnancy is not obvious.[42]

Yet, for all the fact that patterns for pregnancy garments did appear from time to time in women's pages, expectant mothers remained reluctant to identify themselves even to VON nurses, let alone more generally.[43] As one woman remembered of her second pregnancy, "You were even ashamed to say that you were pregnant."[44] However much babies were looked forward to, it was difficult to ignore that pregnancy was a direct result of a sexual act. This might elicit expressions of rough humour, especially from men, and was a matter of some embarrassment to women.

Shyness about their condition may have been more widespread among middle-class urban-dwellers, who aspired to a certain gentility that made pregnancy all the more a taboo subject, than among rural and working-class Canadians, whose living arrangements and labours exposed them more regularly to the "facts of life." Such was the case with farm women who admitted quite matter-of-factly to planning pregnancy with reference to seasonal labour needs.[45] Yet, whatever their situation, many women tended to be reticent when it came to public display or discussion. The more fortunate found that pregnancy knitted them even more firmly into a world of female relatives and neighbours where they might find sympathetic advisers and helpers.[46] Others who lived in new cities or far from family and friends had to deal alone with bodily changes that might be far from understood. The novelist Kathleen Strange, for example, who regarded herself as "a very modern young woman," had "no intimate friends" in her new prairie home and felt "bewildered, and sometimes frightened, at the prospect of what was going to happen to me."[47] The Prenatal packages sent out by the federal Department of Child Welfare were designed to help with just such situations.

Pregnancy readily exacerbated fears about economic and personal survival. An additional child sometimes placed whole families in jeopardy. And the prospect of multiple births could make poorer women hysterical with anxiety.[48] Women's auxiliaries to hospitals like Vancouver General discovered that new mothers in the hard-hit 1930s were especially likely to "depend entirely on the Auxiliary for the clothing of their babies, and in some cases additional nourishment for themselves."[49] Testimony to B.C. provincial royal commissions investigating health insurance and maternity benefits at the end of the First World War and again at the onset of the Great Depression repeatedly confirmed the desperate plight of mothers whose resources could not extend to proper medical care for themselves and their infants.[50] The founder of Victoria's Free Child Welfare Clinic concluded bleakly:

> Again and again I knew of expectant mothers, married women, who had abortions procured or attempted through the dread, not of pains of childbirth, but of the expense that would be incurred at the birth of the child and after. Abortions have been brought about and lifeless premature children born, or else children deformed or under normal have been born due as much to nervous depression and worry on the part of the mother as to the attempt at prevention.[51]

The story was much the same in all regions of the country.

Continuing high levels of maternal and infant mortality gave harsh witness to far from satisfactory conditions. Maternal deaths nationally did not drop below the 1921 figure of 4.7 per thousand live births until 1938 when they fell to 4.3 as a result of sulfanamide drugs and improved public health care. In the intervening years they had risen as high as 5.8 in 1930. The neonatal death rate was 43 per 1000 live births in 1921, rose to 48 in 1926, and then dropped relatively steadily to 30 in 1940.[52] While these trends were in the right direction, the number of fatalities was especially high in larger cities and a good deal higher than in many countries of western Europe, a fact that prompted recurring public health campaigns.

Not even Canada's sad showing internationally, however, made the great majority of doctors willing to share the care of parturient women with midwives. Those traditional custodians of female health remained unlicensed in the majority of provinces despite the evident need for their services.[53] For all the prejudices of physicians, women continued, when they could, to seek familiar assistance from midwives, especially in rural and remote areas. Over 95 percent of one Newfoundland outport's births before 1945, for instance, took place at home. This community "always had one midwife, who was usually middle-aged or older, married with children of her own, but who had received no formal training except advice and the experience from some older midwife, and occasionally the advice of a medical person."[54] In Cape Breton, midwives served the close-knit Scottish and Indian communities.[55] Extensive immigration or urbanization often disrupted the community networks upon which midwives depended but, even in newly settled areas such as Alberta, women like Mrs. Charles Brown, who possessed a certificate from the Obstetrical Society of London, England, were there to aid friends and neighbours.

Between 1904 and 1939, Brown delivered 156 babies in the Cochrane and Didsbury areas of the province.[56] Even in rapidly expanding cities like Vancouver, it remained possible to find traditional assistance. Between 1925 and 1929, for instance, this city recorded at least 1 743 deliveries by midwives out of a total of 19 730.[57]

And right across the country, in small and large centres, Victorian Order, private duty, public health, and missionary nurses delivered babies when purses were slim and doctors absent.[58] Nor was it unusual to find these female professionals co-operating with local women. In 1923 the superintendent of Manitoba's Public Nursing Service described how midwives practised extensively in isolated areas of the province, especially among new Canadians. When rural public health nurses were introduced in 1919, they often found their predecessors eager to receive instruction. "In one case, where a nurse was conducting a confinement, five midwives came in unannounced to watch proceedings."[59] In the 1930s in a small village north of Toronto, a retired public health pioneer, Eunice Dyke, "admired the skill and resourcefulness of the local midwife who lived a busy life in her own household in addition to the nursing duties that fell to her lot."[60] Working as they did so often with their own sex and the chronically poor, nurses often had good reason to question doctors' determination to keep specialized obstetrical techniques, such as forceps and anesthetics, solely their own preserve.

One critic, more sympathetic than most, described midwife competitors as:

> women, good-hearted souls and all that sort of thing, practising maternity work and calling themselves maternity nurses, and they have absolutely no such qualifications; they know absolutely nothing about the work. They don't know about sterilizing; they don't know the first rules of procedures. . . . They happen to drop in at a neighbour's house when a case is coming off.[61]

Midwives were sometimes just as unqualified as this comment suggested but, just as often, they brought to childbed invaluable experience with many more cases than the few normally offered interns in hospitals. Whatever their lack of professional qualifications, such women were cheap, potentially extremely helpful with domestic duties, and often reassuringly familiar when compared with their more scientific rivals. Parturition remained a chancy business at the the best of times, but frequently no more at home than elsewhere. Indeed so long as the pregnancy was normal and hospitals remained centres of infection and intervention, domestic surroundings and experienced, if unlicensed, care might be a very sensible solution. This was especially true when too many doctors, as one associate professor of obstetrics at the University of Manitoba observed, "often looked upon [obstetrics] as the most drab and arduous as well as the least interesting of the . . . branches of medicine."[62]

Women were well aware of childbirth's dangers. Sometimes they were fatalistic about their chances, like one prairie woman who wrote:

> I'm going to have a baby next July. . . . I do not feel at all well. . . . I feel so blue, and can sit down and cry for an hour, except I'm ashamed to do that very often. Ah well, one of my neighbours has 13 children and she is still alive, so, why shouldn't I survive?[63]

Most women wanted the best remedies available to relieve the pains of childbirth. Patients in these years constituted a powerful lobby on their own behalf:

> The modern young woman approaches her confinement in an altogether different frame of mind [from her mother and grandmother]. When the pioneer woman was taken in labour, she knew there was no help forthcoming, and that she would have to see it through as best she could. . . . Not so with the modern young woman who has probably never experienced greater pain than that caused by having a tooth filled, or her ears pierced. For weeks and months before her confinement, she has heard whisperings of twilight sleep, chloroform, ether, and nitrous oxide, and how Mrs. So and So was given an anaesthetic and her baby taken away. Therefore after a variable time in labour she declares that she can stand this no longer, and firmly demands that she be given something at once.[64]

Whatever doctors thought of women's independence and initiative, expectant mothers like the author of the best-seller *The Viking Heart* (1923), Laura Salverson, were sometimes prepared to go to considerable lengths to reap the benefits of new technology. In her case she travelled 1500 miles from her Manitoba home to try out "twilight sleep," a combination of morphine to deaden the pain and various drugs, notably scopolamine, to induce forgetfulness.[65]

For just the same reason, women pushed hard for better prenatal and hospital care. As one settler from Peace River put it,

> I think we should have hospital treatment and a doctor whether we can afford it or not. . . . If the men want the highway gravelled or something else to make life easier for them they just howl until they get it. The only thing we women can do is to kick up a fuss until we get some consideration during confinement cases.[66]

The common predicament of pregnancy kept women raising money and demanding maternity assistance in cash or kind from provincial governments. The cottage hospitals funded largely by the Women's Missionary Society of the United Church, for instance, helped expectant mothers in isolated districts in northern Canada and the Prairies. A good part of the motivation for such initiatives was summed up by the Secretary of Medical

Missions in a letter to two nurses at the United Church hospital in Gypsumville, Manitoba. Referring to the difficulties her own mother had encountered in settling in Ontario, she concluded, "I think of her and I hear her as she told me many a time how she cried herself to sleep every night for several years, and if I can make life a little happier and brighter for some lonely mother or child on the frontier I will feel that I have not lived in vain."[67] This secretary's sentiments would have been well understood by the working- and middle-class women in hospital auxiliaries across the country as well as those who joined together in B.C. to testify before provincial commissions in 1919–21 and again in 1929–32 on behalf of medical assistance to expectant mothers.[68] Motherhood and its dangers regularly prompted cross-class examples of women helping women.

Women's desire for improved treatment and doctors' determination to monopolize delivery assistance increased the likelihood of professional supervision and hospital confinement. As the House of Commons' Special Committee on Social Security learned, however, as late as 1936, 26 313 or 13.13 percent of all births occurred without a physician in attendance. Four years later, 22 330 births or 9.77 percent still failed to find a doctor. The great majority of these confinements—98.59 percent in 1936 and 97.55 percent in 1940—occurred outside of institutions, presumably largely at home.[69] As table 1 indicates, this location was the same for the majority of Canadian mothers. The shift to hospitalization was not interrupted by the Great Depression but the national figures do conceal a large measure of provincial variation. In P.E.I. in 1926 and 1940 respectively, for example, only 2.7 percent and 26.2 percent of births occurred in hospitals, a reflection in large part of the rural nature of much of the province. This compared to much more urbanized British Columbia where 48.3 percent and 84.4 percent of live births occurred in institutions in 1926 and

TABLE 1

PERCENTAGE OF LIVE BIRTHS IN HOSPITAL IN CANADA, 1926–1940

Year	%	Year	%
1926	17.8	1934	30.0
1927	19.3	1935	32.3
1928	21.5	1936	34.5
1929	24.5	1937	36.4
1930	26.6	1938	39.4
1931	26.8	1939	41.7
1932	27.5	1940	45.3
1933	28.5		

Source: Canada, House of Commons, Special Committee on Social Security, Health Insurance, *Report of the Advisory Committee on Health Insurance*, appointed by Order-in-Council, P.C. 836, Feb. 5, 1942, p. 309.

1940. And yet Alberta, which also had a large rural population, went from 33.5 percent to 72.9 percent in the same years, a reflection of the importance of the cottage hospital movement supported by the United Farm Women of Alberta and the Women's Institutes.[70] This trend to physicians in attendance and hospital delivery was taken up by women, both individually and collectively, because they hoped it offered them a longed-for opportunity to take advantage of modern advances and control the dread consequences of dangerous and painful pregnancies. If there were any hope of remedy, tragic deaths like that of Christine Morrison who, six months into her pregnancy in 1934, started having convulsions and bleeding at the mouth but lived beyond the help of any Cape Breton hospital, were too instructive to ignore.[71]

Women might deliberately choose to deliver themselves into medical custody but, once there, they found it extremely difficult to determine the details of the process they were to experience. In particular, hospitalized births helped secure the position and authority of the medical profession. In a highly ordered and hierarchical environment, physicians could restrict the aspirations of subordinates and patients more easily than in public clinics and patients' homes. The situation in Vancouver, and more particularly at its largest health care institution, Vancouver General Hospital or VGH as it was familiarly known, is instructive in this regard. By the end of the First World War the time had passed in the city when

> No self-respecting woman, however much she dreaded the coming ordeal of maternity or the upsetting of her household, resultant upon its advent, would entertain for a moment the suggestion of going to the hospital. The hospital was only for the outcast and the unfortunate.[72]

Elsewhere in the country too, hospitals were discovering a largely new clientele in respectable expectant mothers.

Although by the interwar years obstetrics had become a profitable business for doctors, practice and procedures were undergoing considerable change. Obstetrics had been late emerging as a specialty, and it remained in Vancouver, as in Canada and North America generally, a lowly cousin of more glamorous fields such as surgery and research. Just as inauspicious was its predilection for surgical as well as chemical and endocrinological solutions to labour problems.[73] For medical students, inadequate training in obstetrics remained a continuing problem. VGH, for example, only offered its interns two months on the maternity wards; if students wished more they had to arrange to trade assignments with their colleagues. In general, the balance of internship training in no way reflected the relative importance of obstetrics to medical careers. In his address to the Toronto convention in 1928, the president of the American Association of Obstetricians, Gynecologists and Abdominal Surgeons damned existing programs in his field in both Canada and the United States. He pointed out that McGill's and Toronto's university medical schools, among many others, allocated surgery much more time on the curriculum, despite the fact that obstetrics formed the backbone of most general practices.[74]

In spite of the low status of obstetrics, attendance at childbirth was essential in building clientele for general practitioners. GPs delivered the majority of babies and they guarded this privilege. Zealous attempts to exclude non-medical and often female competition meant that in the 1920s and 1930s an overwhelmingly male profession presided over women in childbirth. Not only were there very few female doctors, but obstetrics as a field was, ironically enough, especially difficult for women to enter. Hospital internships and residencies were a special problem. In 1939 Vancouver General typically allowed only one female intern and the city's other large hospital, St. Paul's, permitted none whatsoever, despite its management by the Sisters of Providence.

Such shortcomings in training and recruitment help account for regular complaints in the medical literature about the "meddlesome midwifery" of obstetrician and GP alike.[75] "Meddling" could take many forms, from the use of X-rays to administration of anesthetics and substances such as pituitrin to produce more rapid contractions, from artificial induction of labour to versions (turning the child manually in the womb), from episiotomies (cutting several inches through the skin and muscles of perineum, the area between the vagina and anus) to the use of low, mid, and high forceps, from Caesarean sections to the use of manual or chemical means to extract the placenta. Such substances and techniques presented problems even to the relatively skilled practitioner, and yet, for a number of reasons, they were tempting and their use increased throughout these decades. Most obviously, they proposed solutions to long-standing medical complications in pregnancy, but, significantly they also promised to save time for the "busy practitioner"[76] and to assert his authority over the timing and experience of delivery. As doctors also pointed out, they responded as well "to the pleadings of the patient and the relatives to 'do something.'"[77] Whatever the cause of intervention, the associated mortality and morbidity rates worried many doctors, some of whom, like those in Montreal's Royal Victoria Maternity Hospital, were eager as a result to label themselves "conservatives."[78] Unfortunately, it is impossible to know how much intervention contributed to rates of maternal death and disability. Many procedures, for example, added to the possibility of hemorrhage, but this in turn might be countered by new blood transfusion techniques. The consequences of other innovations like X-rays were not always obvious for some time.

Obstetricians and gynecologists believed that unsupervised GPs were especially likely to attempt unsuitable interventions. As one way of bringing them under more control, they encouraged hospital births. Ironically, however, by bringing women into an environment where the staff and the equipment, and thus the opportunity and temptation, for greater intervention were more readily available, specialists contributed to the potential for over-medicalization. For example, elaborate preparation procedures—shaving, enemas, and Lysol washes for example—and the insistence on stirrups, arm straps, and a lithotomy position in which the patient lay on her back with her legs in the air—came to be taken for granted as part of the normal environment of the modern hospital in these decades.[79]

The procedures recommended upon the onset of labour captured physicians' desire for passivity on the part of patients. The expectant mother's hair was arranged in "two tight braids"; the area around the vagina was shaved and bathed with soap, water, and Lysol. She was given only a liquid diet, "even though she does not ask for it" and was to excrete every hour. In the meantime, she was checked regularly for her own and the baby's pulse rate.[80] In the delivery room itself she was surrounded by doctors, nurses, and students, commonly strangers, hidden in gowns, caps, and masks. She herself was similarly disguised with elaborate draping. At this point, the woman and her physician faced a number of options that varied not only with her condition but with shifting fashions in obstetrics and the relative skill and knowledge of those in attendance.

Chloroform and ether, old stand-bys from the 1840s, continued to be used into the 1930s. Their use was, however, tightly regulated since the possibility of damage to liver and kidneys was by then recognized. Twilight sleep had been used in Canada since its development in Germany in the early twentieth century, but its potential for causing vertigo and delirium in the mother and narcotizing the baby limited its popularity. Also available to doctors were rectal anaesthesia and a combination of nitrous oxide and oxygen. The latter seems to have been especially popular. For all its usefulness and success, however, it definitely required the presence of an anaesthetist. This added not only to the number of strange attendants surrounding the patient but also to her bill at VGH and other institutions. Only with the introduction of spinal anaesthetics in the 1940s would choices change substantially and, even then, the additional expense remained. As it was, hospital experience for many was a memory of "an anaesthetic above my nostrils. Then—oblivion"; perhaps pain again, and then being "put to sleep again, taken into the delivery room, and there the baby artificially extracted."[81] In such situations women were not so much active participants as drugged observers or worse.

The extent of medical intervention could also vary from private to public wards. At least in Vancouver, staff doctors appear to have been rather more conservative than private practitioners. One report, examining VGH records for 1934, 1935, and 1936 made this point about induction, arguing that,

> when one is dealing with a private patient, . . . there is a real urge to make it truly successful, to get it over with. Patients are not much impressed with the idea of going home and coming back and, as a result, the doctor gets the blame; it is rather poor advertising.

This staff doctor believed that patients should not in fact be induced solely because they were at term, but he noted that VGH's Chief of Obstetrics disagreed with him.[82] This self-proclaimed conservatism changed markedly once it came to a discussion of low forceps, admittedly much less serious than the mid or high variations. Usually done "for the benefit of the intern on the service," their employment was supervised by a resident or staff member. The author believed that more patients might be delivered this way since "it wouldn't hurt . . . and it would be a great help to the intern who is soon to embark in private practice." With his own primipara cases he preferred "prophylactic low forceps and median episiotomy" as a matter of course.[83] Despite this predilection, he observed that "instrumental deliveries are far more common on the private than on the staff side." Even then they made up a small part of the case load at VGH. Between 1934 and 1936, 1 253 of 1 519 confinements, or 82.49 percent, were assessed as normal; there were 129 cases of low forceps, 27 of mid-forceps, 20 of version, 45 Caesarean sections, and 45 breech deliveries.[84]

This staff doctor's preference for instrumental intervention helped, however, change the percentage of so-called "normal" deliveries over the longer period from 1933 to 1941 when only 13 359 of 18 539, or 72.2 percent, were so identified at Vancouver General. Especially noticeable was the increase in the resort to Caesareans, from 2.5 percent to 3.3 percent, mid-forceps, from 3.4 percent to 4.4 percent, and low forceps, from 14.0 percent to 18.9 percent of normal deliveries.[85] What stood out as well was the difference, not always large but almost always present, between private and public patients. In almost every case the degree of medical intervention, including the very dangerous, if "glamorous," C-section,[86] was greater with the former group. Explanations vary. Patients anticipating difficulty may have made additional efforts to raise funds to pay for confinement and doctors' fees. Certainly more and more women in Vancouver were turning to private or semi-private accommodation over these years. What cannot be ignored, however, is the fact that interventions added to medical fees and incomes while simultaneously asserting the supremacy of the professional. They also commonly shortened the length of delivery, a boon sometimes to a weary mother but always to a busy practitioner. Nor is the fact that most cases were delivered by GPs without significance. Obstetricians regularly condemned them for attempting treatments beyond their experience or understanding.[87]

Vancouver General itself, like institutions elsewhere, made some attempt to regulate doctors' regimes. The increase in the incidence of C-sections, for example, prompted a rule requiring the prior consent of the general superintendent or one of his assistants. In other developments the hospital concurred. The steady increase in episiotomies, from 8.7 percent of all patients, 14.4 percent of private patients, and 1.7 percent of public patients, to 34.6 percent, 38.3 percent, and 25.2 percent respectively in the period from 1933 to 1941 reflected a trend that was becoming normative in North American hospitals.[88] It is also quite clear that episiotomies were being democratized over these years; they became matter-of-course for the so-called "normal" delivery wherever it occurred, in private room or public ward.

Once the baby arrived, and if the hospital was not overcrowded, the woman might rest in the delivery room under observation for an hour. Should there be bleeding, pituitrin and ergometrine would be given; hemorrhage, with its threat of shock, brought the administration of intravenous fluids by a specialist. After her pulse returned to safe levels and there were no other signs of distress, she would be returned to her room where the extent of comfort and nursing care depended on a private or public location. The increasing employment of registered nurses, still assisted by students, especially in the 1930s, also brought changes to patient care. That transformation, with its promise of a more knowledgeable staff, helped convince expectant mothers to choose hospitals for their confinements.

Once in her own bed, the patient could not expect unregulated access to her new baby. The modern hospital imposed a strict regimen based on the most up-to-date strictures about successful child care. Breast-feeding was a central dictum, but some procedures, such as the recommendation that it was "most important" not to nurse the baby for at least six to eight hours after delivery, very likely made it more difficult.[89] The attempt to inculcate regular habits from the start may have had the same effect, as with the standing orders for an efficient obstetrical department that recommended feedings at precise four-hour intervals for three days and "only fifteen minutes" at a time with the mother. Later, twenty minutes were to be allowed on the same schedule.[90] At VGH the baby was then carefully tagged and distinctively stencilled with the family surname by exposure to a sun-lamp, continuing the objectification that the mother had experienced.

Mothers' activities also remained closely regulated. They were to recline in bed until the fifth or sixth day, only then to sit up if all was well. Not until five or so days later were they allowed out of bed for limited periods. They were not to leave the hospital for twelve to fourteen days. VGH seems to have observed this rule throughout these years, despite the circulation problems it might have caused the patient, the added risk of infection, and the contribution such stays made to the institution's chronic problem with overhospitalization. On the other hand, it may be that mothers without urgent domestic responsibilities looked forward to such respites from labour. Once home, the model patient was to continue consultations with her doctor and public health nurse. The reality for many women, however, was an immediate return to postponed duties and tasks. Domestic labour and family budgets also made medical visits a low priority for many families, especially in the days before medicare.

Throughout the course of treatment, women and their relatives undoubtedly demanded the full range of up-to-date procedures that might in any way ease childbirth. For them, like the professionals they consulted, there were trends and fads. However much they might shop around, pro-spective mothers were finally expected to deliver themelves into the hands of their doctors. Women's acquiescence was ensured by repeated assur-ances from public health authorities and the popular media that experts knew best and that doctors alone could guarantee the happy outcome of pregnancy. In general, while the safety of mother and child was presented as a legitimate concern, a woman's right to some say over the course of childbirth was not. The influential hospital dictum that "no information regarding baby other than 'favourable' is to be given mother by the nurse,"[91] represented a common enough attempt to control the flow of information and thus to determine the process itself. This was in no way unique to Vancouver. As the chairman of the Maternal Welfare Committee of the Canadian Medical Association concluded in 1934, "co-operation is more to be desired than self-reliance" in the nation's mothers.[92]

After the birth, experts continued to watch anxiously lest women fail the initial challenge of breast-feeding. To counteract extensive advertising campaigns by commercial milk companies such as Carnation and Cow Brand, counsellors insisted that "only the mother who is the whole mother by giving her baby his birthright in natural feeding . . . can experience sat-isfied maternity."[93] Maternal satisfaction being inseparable from infant sur-vival, the experts were right. Pasteurization or sterilization of cows' milk was far from widespread and cooling facilities were at best uncertain. Babies weaned before eight or nine months experienced high rates of infant mortality, especially in the summer.

The continuing sales of commercial milk products and the inclusion of sections on formula preparation in major child care manuals nevertheless suggest that many babies spent little or no time on the breast.[94] The alter-native was the elaborate preparation of milk, water, sugar, or gruel mix-tures proposed by nutritionists, or home-grown recipes. Whatever the choice, the average home, without electricity or refrigeration, frequently lacked adequate facilities for safe sterilization and preservation. Still, for all the obstacles in their way, women displayed considerable ingenuity in nourishing their babies. These strategies might be very successful, as the experience of one Labrador woman makes clear:

> She could not nurse her babies. She had to get a bottle for them. What she used for food was flour. She took the dry flour and packed it in a white cloth and boiled it for four hours. Then she [would] grate it up and make a pap like a real thick gravy. She boiled it again and added sugar, a little butter and a little salt. She raised eight children like that until they were ten months old. . . . Some of them grew up to be old men and women.

Such resourcefulness was matter-of-factly summed up by a niece of this woman: "When put to the test we could always manage."[95]

Once the choice between breast and bottle had been made, the modern baby was subject to rigorous scheduling. One typical Toronto psychologist asserted that, while "it formerly was believed that mother instinct or mother love was the simple and the safe basis for the problems of training, it is now known that a much more reliable guide is the kitchen time-piece."[96] Children raised under such a regime were to be better adapted, it was hoped, to the mechanical rhythms of school and work and, ulti-mately, were to be better citizens.

Mothers following professional advice were to establish precise elimi-nation routines. Bowel movements were clearly a potential battleground between mother and child since training was to begin at about four months and be nearly complete by one year. Adaption to this strict timetable was encouraged, when necessary, by the judicious use of enemas, catheters, and cathartics. Bladder control was permitted to develop somewhat later, but the two-year-old was expected to be largely continent except at bed-time. Whatever emotional upsets such advice produced, the benefits of early training were self-evident to mothers sewing and washing large num-bers of cloth diapers by hand.

Children raised with guidance from professionals were expected to have their emotions similarly regulated by perceptive parents. Letter Nine of the Pre-natal series issued by the federal Division of Child Welfare set out typ-ical instructions: "Remember that a baby is born without habits. Teach him only good ones. . . . If you pick him up each time he stirs, you will teach him to cry whenever he is lying down."[97] Babies were to be cuddled when nursed, but at times when their schedule called for sleep they were to be left firmly alone since, "the less a baby is handled the better."[98] Over-cud-dling could produce a spoiled child or one imperfectly prepared for the realities of modern life. Dubious mothers were informed sternly that:

> It is well that a growing infant should cry a little every day. The benefit derived from crying is due to the muscular movements involved. The baby should be made to cry every day by slapping him on the buttocks, for besides his exercise obtained in this way, it keeps the lungs well expanded. In fact, in the newly born it is the cry that expands the lungs; consequently he should be made to cry at this early stage several times a day at first.[99]

Similarly, the physical comforts of pacifier and thumb were proscribed as "unclean" childish habits that deformed children's jaws and teeth. Mothers were warned repeatedly that youngsters' future welfare depended on their ability to subjugate just such immediate gratifications.[100]

In contrast, the same professionals who advocated firm control over weaning, elimination, sleep, and sucking were relatively casual about the masturbation that had disturbed an earlier generation. Modern-minded counsellors stressed that exploration of the body was natural. "Undue interest in sex organs" was linked to overly tight clothing or improperly washed genitals rather than immorality per se, and simple distraction by means of a toy or another activity was recommended as a remedy.[101] Old solutions of "slapping" and "tying . . . in bed" were discouraged since they focussed unwanted attention on the child's actions.[102] Repression by adults would only foster unhealthy interest and sexual disturbance later on in life. In this way, mothers were encouraged to accept infant sexuality as a normal stage in human development.

Child-rearing guides took a similarly liberal view of punishment. Spanking was condemned for inspiring a sense of injustice and grievance. Parents who used corporal discipline were dismissed as irresponsible. Instead, authorities urged mothers to seek the underlying cause of the trouble. Two leading Toronto pediatricians argued: "Usually the bad child is a sick child, the illness being either mental or physical or both and the remedy is not to be found in corporal punishment."[103] Restraint in the use of force, the "primitive urge for revenge that lies dormant in every human being," was essential to modern parenting.[104] In other words, parents who desired to control their offspring were urged first to control themselves.

Isolation was recommended as effective alternative discipline when the constant affirmation and inculcation of good habits failed. Above all, mothers were reminded that the child "should and can be educated to derive no satisfaction from repeated offences against the standards of the community."[105] By regular conditioning, all children could learn polite behaviour and thus mature without trouble to themselves or others, except to mothers who were required to spend numerous hours mastering the psychological tools of the new child rearing in the hope of producing such perfected progeny.

The pragmatic tone of the advice literature in the interwar years was rooted in the relativism of the modern social sciences. Behaviour was presented as neither intrinsically bad nor good. Moral judgments that had informed past generations were treated as products of particular environments and truth became merely "the morals of the age."[106] Psychologists rejected much of the idealism, sentimentalism, and emphasis upon the child's essential spiritual goodness that had influenced an earlier generation of mothers.[107] And, at least in Canada, Freud's stress on the importance of the subconscious was almost ignored in the enthusiasm for the work of behavioural psychologists like John Watson.[108] The infant as machine succeeded the idealistic image of the child as flower,[109] and mothers across Canada were urged to take the business world as their model.[110]

A North America-wide child study movement also provided Canadian mothers with an unprecedented opportunity to see theories in action in model institutions. The Laura Spellman Rockefeller Memorial Foundation and the Metropolitan Life Insurance Company funded two "scientific" nursery schools at Toronto and McGill universities to investigate the personality of normal children while simultaneously providing instruction to parents and their offspring.[111] Unlike other day nurseries, creches, and kindergartens with which they are often confused, such nursery schools served a select middle-class population, often associated with universities. As this clientele had generally kept its young children at home under the supervision of a servant or of a non-wage-earning mother, the schools established in 1925 were relatively new alternatives for parents of children between the ages of two and five. In the 1920s, new ideas about child raising, together with safer health conditions generally, made some mothers willing to trust youngsters to such alternate institutions.

This was particularly true in Toronto where the appointment of Dr. William E. Blatz, a psychologist and physician who had trained in that city and Chicago, ensured the long-term survival of the St. George's School for Child Study, unlike McGill's nursery school which folded in 1930. His forceful personality and flair for publicity convinced progressive middle-class mothers to support Toronto's program, and his influence extended to parents beyond St. George's itself. With his colleagues and disciples, Blatz contributed extensively to the periodical literature on children, directed a wide variety of provincial and national child welfare efforts, constructed programs for the Dionne quintuplets in the 1930s, and in the 1940s helped the British and Canadian governments create wartime day nurseries. For many years the Toronto group around Blatz dominated the Canadian child study movement with no obvious rivals for public attention or official recognition.

St. George's began with eight children but quickly won a long and insistent waiting list. Mothers willingly paid significant tuition and incidental fees to offer their children the special benefits of the new instruction. They also joined parent education groups, modelled on those of the Child Welfare Association of America, to learn scientific child care. These groups, which began with an enrolment of sixty-eight in 1925, had grown to include 189 members ten years later, even though fees and homework for regular meetings required a substantial commitment. Members of parent education groups tended to come from smaller middle-class Toronto families. In 1927–28, for instance, forty-seven parents reported that they had only one child, forty-four had two, twenty-one had three. Only fourteen reported more than three and none more than six. Prior to their marriages, twenty-four mothers had been teachers, nine nurses or members of the Voluntary Aid Detachment, which had provided nursing service during World War I, twenty-eight businesswomen, two lecturers, two demonstrators, one instructor, three doctors, one barrister, two dieticians, two editors, two social service workers, one musician, one tutor, one librarian, and seven students. Only one, a fur finisher, claimed an identifiably working-class occupation. On the other hand, thirty claimed no wage-earning occupation whatsoever before marriage. All of these mothers were expected to invest large amounts of time and energy in the program, not only through discussion with other parents but by compiling detailed charts on the home activities of their children. In very many ways they were hardly typical Canadian parents.[112] Nonetheless, the Toronto experiment was followed with interest across the country, influencing the mothers' meetings and discussions held in situations as far removed from comfortable homes as Halifax's Jost Mission and Day Nursery with its clientele of domestic servants and their children.[113]

At St. George's, mothers took their children to school each morning by 9:30 and sometimes served as assistants to the teachers later in the day. At that time they had ample opportunity to observe the orderly and predict-able patterns that were supposed to characterize the modern child's life. With this training, in conjunction with parent education courses, it was hoped mothers could correct the home's customary bad habits. In devot-ing this much time and thought to the details of rearing relatively few off-spring, they were in many ways the apotheosis of the modern mother. Encouraged to develop a strong sense of maternal mission, such women dedicated much of their days to matching the standards of child rearing they were told would not only solve many of the problems of modern society but would fulfill them as mothers in the process.

Yet not all Canadians accepted the claims of William Blatz and his behav-iouralist colleagues. Traditions related to child care were guarded tena-ciously by parents from every walk of life. While institutions and publications concerned with children were heavily influenced by Blatz's theories, there remained those who denounced the modern child specialist as the "New Ogre Which Threatens Home Life."[114] Novelist Clara Rothwell Anderson spoke for the unconverted when she observed little Angus, who:

> soothed by the soft tones, slept calmly in peaceful ignorance of present-day methods of baby management which would require that he rend the air with his cries until he received sufficient lung expansion for this evening, after which he would of his own accord, cease his physical culture exercises and fall into a quiet, unbroken sleep.[115]

A B.C. mother also typified the sceptical consumer with her observation, "Although I grew up in a big family I didn't really know anything about child rearing—except the basics. But then, who does? Certainly not the people who write these silly psychological books on child care."[116] Such responses, frustrating professionals from one end of the country to the other, were summed up by one Halifax public health nurse: ". . . everyone is met with the argument that the mother, or grandmother, or great-grand-mother did thus and so—hence it is right."[117] But not all mothers were confident, outspoken, or independent. Eager to reduce infant mortality and anxious about their responsibility for social maladjustment, women were susceptible to pressure from well-meaning, if sometimes self-serving, advisers who urged them to reject midwives, home births, folk remedies, and care by rule of thumb.

While most parents were at liberty to reject or accept advice, many saw their authority over their children eroded. Especially vulnerable were mothers who by reason of illness, death, or unemployment found them-selves dependent upon the emerging welfare state or older charities. Wid-ows under the mothers' allowances acts and parents on relief found themselves subject to intervention by child care professionals employed by state bureaucracies as well as private philanthropies.[118] Oftentimes, the assistance was so urgently required, as with the case of one desperate mother who, before the inauguration of Ontario's assistance plan, had to place her three small sons separately with neighbours while she went to work as a domestic, that any loss of parental authority seemed well worth the cost.[119] A good number on mothers' allowances, missing the help they might have had from husbands, appreciated the advice they were offered, whether it was regarding money problems, health concerns, or "wayward" boys and girls.[120] Hard times in and out of the Great Depression also made mothers swallow what one prairie resident called her "stubborn, selfish pride" and take material assistance even if it were accompanied by unsolicited instruction.[121] Yet, since modern social welfare bureaucracies were still in their infancy, and the resources of public and private charities—and thus their capacity to intervene—were spread especially thinly when distress was greatest and applicants largest in number, meddlesome supervision could often be easily avoided by Canadians.

One family, however, was world famous and could not escape systematic scrutiny. On May 28, 1934, Canada's most newsworthy babies were born: the Dionne quintuplets. Yvonne, Annette, Cécile, Emilie, and Marie were the first known set of identical quintuplets to survive for more than a few days. They soon captured headlines the world over. Their parents, Oliva and Elzire Dionne, and their small farm near Callander, Ontario, immediately attracted curiosity seekers and fortune hunters. The fragility of the quints, the limited resources of the Dionnes, and the threat of commercial exploitation provoked state intervention. In northern Ontario, far from the centres of the child study movement, a unique scientific laboratory with five genetically identical female subjects came into being. Canadians' experience with advice literature and nursery schools since the war led them to accept the child study experiment that began in 1934.

Unlike the middle-class parents who patronized the nursery schools and the uncertain mothers who leafed through pages of child-rearing advice, the Dionnes were firmly rooted in Catholic, agrarian, and French-Canadian traditions that offered sure guidance to the obedient. Up to May 1934, Oliva and Elzire had met the requirements for exemplary parenthood according to their faith and their culture: five living children, all nourished and housed without recourse to public assistance. In comparison to many of their neighbours during the 1930s, this showed good fortune and management. Their farmhouse, without indoor plumbing or electricity, and their time-honoured familial customs were hardly, however, calculated to win the approval of the experts who soon flocked to attend Canada's greatest tourist attraction. A press largely sympathetic to the professionals helped mobilize sentiment against the Dionnes who became a symbol for all that was backward and irresponsible about Canadian families.

Their loss of traditional parental authority reproduced in an exaggerated form the plight of many parents who came under the enforced supervision of public authorities. Too poor to defend themselves or to care adequately for the babies in their first vulnerable months, the Dionnes surrendered guardianship of the sisters to the Ontario government in July 1934. The following spring the quints were made wards of the Crown until their eighteenth birthday. In September 1934, still in uncertain health, the babies were moved from the family farmhouse to separate accommodation in a specially equipped hospital. There a professional regime was set in motion that would last until their parents recovered the children in 1938.

Ironically, the instigator of Canada's most famous "child laboratory" was a country doctor who seemed far removed from the scientific investigation of childhood. Dr. Allan Roy Dafoe was, however, prone to the professional's arrogance when dealing with parents. In addition, he had a connection with the world of child study through his brother, Dr. William Dafoe, a prominent Toronto obstetrician. William in turn summoned Dr. Alan Brown,[122] the head of Toronto's Hospital for Sick Children, one of the inventors of Pablum, and Canada's most prominent pediatrician. Under Brown, a rigorous regime of cleanliness and diet was followed. His concern for germs, weight charts, strict scheduling, and scientific feeding gave him little in common with the Dionnes but made his advice typical of that which Canadian mothers had been receiving since World War I.

In reaction, the Dionnes clung to their own traditions. Elzire, for example, "believed in plump babies and . . . fed her other children on thick soups, rice, potatoes, quantities of well-cooked vegetables, fresh bread, and unpasteurized milk."[123] She opposed the scientific feeding prescribed by Brown and regarded the quints as painfully thin. Bolstered by public opinion and a sympathetic government, the medical regime, however, prevailed against the mother's wishes. One nurse put the professional case very plainly in her summing up of Elzire's deficiencies:

> The young woman did not think that the advice and the counsels of solicitous aunts and of well-meaning and helpful neighbours who had borne many a child of their own, were in any way wanting in expediency and aptitude. She had no idea that her other six children, of whom one had died young, could not have passed with an altogether clean sheet of health, had they been submitted to a medical examination during at least the first part of their childhood. It is not very easy for the layman to detect the first symptoms of rickets and malnutrition which may later develop into crooked legs, pigeon chests and listless anemia. Nevertheless, in her case as well as in so many thousands of similar instances, practical precautions to safeguard from prenatal disturbances could have been thought out and inaugurated. If she had realized and recognized the need of proper prenatal care, not only for her own relief and comfort but to lessen the risks to her expected offspring, her five babies might not have been born so prematurely nor to such a degree afflicted with the worst curse of infancy—rickets.[124]

To nurse de Kiriline, the Dionnes were proof that parents should be guided only by counsels "recommended and supported by the doctor, such as those given at well-baby clinics and in authorized baby books."[125] Elzire was judged unfit by a jury of child care experts. The arrogance of the professionals drove a wedge between the Dionne family and the quintuplets. For this schism, with its lifelong, unhappy repercussions, the parents were to hold the child care experts totally responsible.

In 1936 Canada's leading child psychologist supplanted Dr. Brown as the decisive authority in the quints' lives. Like Brown, Dr. William Blatz showed little respect for traditional parenting. The enforced non-intervention of the parents allowed him full rein to test the theories he had been developing based on middle-class Toronto children, a world and more away from a Northern Ontario Catholic farm family. The observational studies he initiated at "Quintland" were undertaken in company with a control group of seventeen children at St. George's. Blatz visited regularly and his ideas were implemented by a nurse with training in child study and, eventually, a pre-school teacher. They introduced a program that, in its minute-to-minute routines, followed the model being proposed for other Canadian parents. With five children, rigorous scheduling was an especially attractive means of ensuring order. Habit reinforcement through repetition and praise was all-important. Insofar as possible, the girls were to be treated rationally and scientifically. In the process, traditions fell by the wayside. The quints were not misled by stories of Santa Claus. Corporal punishment was forbidden. Childish resistance was met firmly and, it was hoped, unemotionally, with an isolation room awaiting mischief-makers. The "old-fashioned" obedience and conformity preferred by the Dionnes was ignored.

Just as with families across the nation, however, professional advice was not followed in every detail in the case of the five sisters. One nurse, for instance, thought Blatz "a little severe" and to compensate treated the sisters with extra warmth.[126] Two Roman Catholic French Canadians, one a teacher and the other a nurse to the quints, were, despite instruction at St. George's School, highly suspicious of the secular, materialistic, and Anglo-American orientation of modern child study. This opposition placed them squarely in the camp of the Dionne parents as supporters of a more traditional mode of child rearing. Nor were they alone. The Dionnes found powerful allies in the Franco-Ontarian nationalist movement that, by 1938, had sufficient political strength to force Blatz's withdrawal. From then on, Catholic family values were impressed upon the quints. A religious order replaced the psychologist as supervisor of the children's education.

Yet the early years, when the parents were effectively supplanted by experts, were the most publicized of the quints' lives. During this time, thousands of photographs and stories of the undeniably attractive sisters flooded the newsstands, and quint movies and dolls spread the arguments for modern child care practices around the world. The result, as canny advertisers soon enough appreciated, was a powerful model for Canadian mothers. Brown, Blatz, and their fellow professionals could hardly have hoped for better publicity. For the power of the quints, unlike the nursery school or even the advice literature known mostly to middle-class parents, superseded the fact of class and drew mothers from many backgrounds to modern conventions in child care.

Whether or not they were in agreement with or knowledgeable about new theories in child development, mothers assumed major responsibility for the outcome of parenting. Placing, as many did, their highest hopes and dreams on their children's futures, they struggled to find some combination of practices that was feasible in light of their own traditions, modern expertise, and material circumstance. Not surprisingly, a happy compromise was not always easy to discover. One social work professional, like others who worked day-to-day with the consequences of insufficient income, provided a sympathetic summary of the predicament facing the poor:

> On low incomes you can only attempt to heat one room—the mother has to cook and wash with the children underfoot as the rest of the house is too cold for play. The younger and the older are mixed—squabbling, temper tantrums, and frayed nerves are inevitable. Whatever order exists, is maintained by fear. Under such circumstances, I have tried to puzzle out how and when a mother should dry the wash. The choice seems to be between letting it drip on the children and work in the daytime, or on the husband and the wife in the evening. With a scarcity of garments one cannot wait for weather to clear. The garments have to be worn the next day.
>
> Doubling up and crowding are on the increase with makeshift kitchens and sleeping accommodation. . . . I have found that the air in such kitchens has made me choke all during my visit. There is no vent for the gas plate. . . .
>
> In overcrowded quarters the children do not get adequate sleep. The little ones are either kept up til the older ones go to sleep, or are awakened by them and made fussy and restless. The parents either have to go to bed when the children do or keep the children up if there are no separate sleeping and living quarters.
>
> One point of view towards housing comes from practical experience and while we know quite as well as every one else that some families could and should manage a good deal better than they do, to actually work in homes with these conditions makes for a less critical attitude. One is not quite so sure how he would come out himself after years in such an environment. The majority of families call forth admiration for their management and maintenance of ideals.[127]

Women caught up in such circumstances would have to await better times before they could act on even their best intentions, not to mention on the advice of the better off.

While children sometimes consigned mothers to poverty and to pain, they were also frequently their chief consolation. The death of a child at birth or later was never easily borne. Kathleen Strange, for example, never forgave herself for leaving her invalid stepson Freddie who, despite looking "so much better" and being under good care, died before she could return from a brief holiday.[128] Like many other mothers, she had to bear other tragedies as well. A short while later after the death of her first daughter at birth, she wrote:

> It is impossible for me to describe the anguish that was now mine. I could not cry. I did not cry even when finally . . . I returned to my own home. . . . It was not until months afterwards that the stemmed-up tide of tears was loosened and I was at last released from that awful stony grief. . . . It was a long time before I could bear to look upon the tiny garments I had so happily prepared a short while before.[129]

The survival of other children did not always make loss easier to bear. In Labrador, Elizabeth Goudie expressed her anguish at the death of her youngest of three: "the family chain was broken by the death of our little one. We would go to the table for meals and his place was empty and when we went to bed at night, it was the same thing. We spent a very lonely spring."[130] The high infant mortality rates that persisted throughout these years meant that many parents, however careful, had to deal with the death of a child.

From long experience, women took what consolation they could from each other and from religion. Nellie McClung wrote, in a way that many would have understood, to a friend who had just lost a young daughter: "Your darling little girl is somewhere safe with God, and her little life on earth, so filled with joy and love, has in some way accomplished its mission, and now goes on, in a brighter, better world to complete fulfilment."[131] Kind words and acts from other women could not compensate for bereavement but they comforted mothers in their reminder that others shared their special preoccupation with children and that surely a kindly saviour or god would protect their loved ones.

After World War I, as the media and bureaucracies dealing with youngsters steadily extended their influence, it became increasingly difficult to bear or rear children in isolation. Wittingly or not, mothers' influence over their children's behaviour and development was apt to be judged by the standards of middle-class child care professionals. The result for some Canadians was a strengthening of their store of shared experience; for others the impact of professional advice was paid in the hard coin of alienation and despair. Not all would or could match a portrait of normality that was overwhelmingly white, middle-class, Anglo-American, and Protestant in character. Finally, however, the majority of women continued to look to childbirth and child rearing as providing perhaps the most significant moments in their lives. More than careers or husbands, children were likely to enshrine women's hopes and dreams for a better future. That challenge preoccupied large numbers of female Canadians from at least their early twenties into their forties.

NOTES

1. Helen Shackleton, "Why Should I Envy Her?" *Chatelaine* (Sept. 1931): 42.

2. See Angus McLaren and Arlene Tigar McLaren, *The Bedroom and the State: The Changing Practices and Politics of Contraception and Abortion in Canada, 1880–1980* (Toronto: McClelland and Stewart, 1986), especially Part 3.

3. See, in particular, the arguments presented in the influential "Blue Book" series produced by the federal Division of Child Welfare, including *Beginning a Home in Canada* (1922), *How to Build the Canadian House* (1922), *How to Make Outpost Homes in Canada* (1922), *Canadians Need Milk* (1923), *How We Cook in Canada* (1922), *How to Manage Housework in Canada* (1922), *How to Take Care of Mother* (1922), *How to Take Care of the Family* (1922), *How to Take Care of the Children* (1922), *Household Accounting in Canada* (1922).

4. SAB, Violet McNaughton Papers, v. 19, Thelma Sanders to McNaughton, June 20, 1937.

5. Ellen Gee, "Fertility and Marriage Patterns in Canada 1851–1971" (Ph.D. dissertation, University of British Columbia, 1978), 45.

6. Ibid., 161.

7. Ibid., 86.

8. Ibid., 237.

9. Winifred D. Wandersee, *Women's Work and Family Values 1920–1940* (Cambridge: Harvard University Press, 1981), 9.

10. "Just One Baby?" *Chatelaine* (March 1931): 15, 69.

11. See Katherine Hale, "Some Problems of Peace," *Woman's Century* (May 1919): 15.

12. On some of these expectations see Ramsay Cook and R.C. Brown, *Canada: A Nation Transformed* (Toronto: McClelland and Stewart), chap. 1.

13. On the determination to use the power of the state to rectify abuses in the private sphere see Veronica Strong-Boag, "'Ever a Crusader': Nellie McClung, First-Wave Feminist" in *Rethinking Canada: The Promise of Women's History* (Toronto: Copp Clark Pitman, 1986), 178–90. See also Strong-Boag, "Pulling in Double Harness or Hauling a Double Load: Women, Work and Feminism on the Canadian Prairies," *Journal of Canadian Studies* (Fall 1986): 32–52.

14. "Women Must Act," *Free Press Prairie Farmer* (May 16, 1934): 6, and "Baby Moratorium," ibid. (April 4, 1934): 5.

15. SAB, Violet McNaughton Papers, L.C. Shoebridge to McNaughton, March 30, 1934.

16. See Hilda Ridley, "A Re-evaluation of Motherhood," *Dalhousie Review* (July 1929): 211, and "An Endowment of Motherhood?" ibid. (April 1926): 81.

17. Mary Q. Innis, "Wedding Days," *Canadian Forum* (Feb. 1932): 103.

18. McLaren and McLaren, *The Bedroom and the State*, 26.

19. Joan Sangster, "Canadian Women in Radical Politics and Labour, 1920–1950," (Ph.D. dissertation, McMaster University, 1984), 86.

20. SFUA, taped Interview with Effie Jones by Sara Diamond, 1979.

21. "Something to Do for the Modern Mother," *Canada Lancet* (Oct. 1922): 151.

22. Dr. Hastings quoted in "Child Welfare," *Canada Lancet* (Sept. 1918): 13.

23. See Frances Hope, "The Economy Baby," *Chatelaine* (May 1932): 24.

24. "Pity the Poor Parent," *Saturday Night* (Sept. 15, 1923): 25.

25. Dr. Woods Hutchinson, "The Saner Kinder Worship of the Race," *Maclean's* (March 15, 1920): 70.

26. Louis C. Bisch, "Women Not Inferior to Men," *Maclean's* (Aug. 15, 1927): 36.

27. R.S. Hosking, "Humanology," *Canadian Comment* (Aug. 1933): 28.

28. Evelyn Seeley, "Debunking the Mother Myth," *Chatelaine* (Feb. 1936): 4. See also the opinion of the Director of McGill University's Nursery School, "The Nursery School as a Ground for Young Children," *McGill News Supplement* (March 1927): 27–30, and Dr. Geo. Davidson, *Panel Discussion on Mental Hygiene*, B.C. Board of Health, V, 5 [c. 1939], 38.

29. "Mother and Child," *Saturday Night* (Aug. 31, 1929): 15.

30. B. Atlee, "The Menace of Maternity," *Canadian Home Journal* (May 1932): 9.

31. Doctors' opposition to midwifery is a case in point. See Suzann Buckley, "Ladies or Midwives? Efforts to Reduce Infant and Maternal Mortality" in *A Not Unreasonable Claim*, edited by Linda Keeley (Toronto: Women's Press, 1980).

32. See, for instance, "Reach the Home Through Children," *Dry Goods Review* (Nov. 1929): 30.

33. "Western World's Low Birth Rate," *Saturday Night* (Aug. 4, 1928): 2.

34. Dr. H. MacMurchy, *How To Take Care of the Children* (Ottawa: King's Printer, 1922): 4, and Dr. W.W. Chipman, "Preparing Women for the Greatest of Professions," *Maclean's* (Oct. 15, 1921): 58.

35. *The Canadian Mother and Child* (Ottawa: National Health and Welfare, 1940): 122. See also K. McAllister, "The New Mother," *Chatelaine* (July 1932): 40, 57.

36. Margaret Bartlett, "The Girl Who Didn't Love Babies," *Western Home Monthly* (March 1920): 38, 39.

37. See Veronica Strong-Boag, "Intruders in the Nursery: Childcare Professionals Reshape the Years One to Five, 1920–1940" in *Childhood and Family in Canadian History*, edited by Joy Parr (Toronto: McClelland and Stewart, 1982) from which much of this discussion is drawn.

38. Strong-Boag, "Intruders in the Nursery," 161–63.

39. Phyllis Knight, *A Very Ordinary Life*, quoted in Isabelle St. Martin, "Family Separation: The Case of the Woman Left Behind" (submitted to the History Department, Concordia University, in partial fulfillment of the requirements for a Master's degree, June 30, 1980), 29.

40. Kathrene Pinkerton, *Wilderness Wife*, quoted in St. Martin, ibid.

41. "What Shall I Do?," *Free Press Prairie Farmer* (March 22, 1933): 15.

42. Stella Pines, "Preparing for the Great Adventure," *Chatelaine* (Oct. 1928): 19.

43. See Norah H. Lewis, "Reducing Maternal Mortality in British Columbia: An Educational Process" in *Not Just Pin Money*, edited by Barbara K. Latham and Roberta J. Pazdro (Victoria: Camosun College, 1984), 347.

44. Quoted in Eliane Silverman, *The Last Best West: Women on the Alberta Frontier 1880–1930* (Montreal: Eden Press, 1984), 66.

45. See "Play Twenty Games," *Free Press Prairie Farmer* (Dec. 28, 1932): 5.

46. See, for instance, Hilda E. Murray, *More Than 50%* (St. John's: Breakwater Press, 1980), "Pregnancy, Birth and Babyhood."

47. Kathleen Strange, *With the West in Her Eyes: The Story of a Modern Pioneer* (Toronto: Macmillan, 1945), 164.

48. VCA, Papers of the Vancouver General Hospital, Series C, v. 22, clipping, F.G. Addam, "General Hospital's Labor of Love," *Daily Province* (c. April/May 1932).

49. "Report of Women's Auxiliary," *Annual Report of Vancouver General Hospital* (1931): 31.

50. Much of the following discussion of childbirth is drawn from Veronica Strong-Boag and Kathryn McPherson, "The Confinement of Women: Childbirth and Hospitalization in Vancouver, 1919–1939," *BC Studies* (Spring/Summer 1986): 142–74.

51. PABC, B.C., Royal Commission on State Health Insurance and Maternity Benefits, Hearings, Brief #56, Arthur G. Price, Oct. 23, 1930.

52. B51–58, *Historical Statistics of Canada*, 2nd ed., edited by F.H. Leacy (Ottawa: Statistics Canada, 1983).

53. On the efforts of middle-class reformers to get assistance for pregnant women see Suzann Buckley, "Ladies or Midwives? Efforts to Reduce Infant and Maternal Mortality."

54. G.J. Casey, "Traditions and Neighbourhoods: The Folklife of a Newfoundland Fishing Outport" (M.A. thesis, Memorial University of Newfoundland, 1971), 119.

55. See Dr. C. Lamont MacMillan, *Memoirs of a Cape Breton Doctor* (Toronto: McGraw-Hill Ryerson, 1975), 111–12 and 152–53. My thanks to Margaret Mullins for drawing my attention to this account.

56. See Glenbow, Papers of Mrs. Charles Brown.

57. W.N. Kemp, "The Still birth Problem in Relation to Iodine Insufficiency," *Vancouver Medical Association Bulletin* (Dec. 1933): 58.

58. See, for instance, Barbara A. Keddy, "Private Duty Nursing Days of the 1920s and 1930s in Canada," *Canadian Woman Studies* (Fall 1986): 101.

59. A. Wells, "In Rural Districts," *Public Health Nurse* (March 1923): 131.

60. Marion Royce, *Eunice Dyke: Health Care Pioneer* (Toronto and Charlottetown: Dundurn Press, 1983), 224.

61. PABC, GR707, Royal Commission on State Health Insurance and Maternity Benefits, Transcript, Testimony of Mrs. Sadie Moore, 314.

62. O. Bjornson, "An Obstetrical Retrospect," *Canadian Medical Association Journal* (henceforth *CMAJ*) (Dec. 1925): 1236. A May 1929 *CMAJ* editorial by H.M. Little of the Montreal Maternity Hospital critiqued contemporary obstetrical surgical procedures and claimed "Obstetrics is still in the large majority of cases a matter for the home," "What's the Matter with Obstetrics?" 646. This opinion was supported by the international statistics for midwife deliveries often reported in the journal. For example McGill professor of Obstetrics and Gynecology J.R. Goodall's article, "Maternal Mortality" cites an Aberdeen, Scotland inquiry into maternal mortality that discovered the institutional maternal death rate to be five times greater than that for midwives, and doctors' rate two times greater. *CMAJ* (Oct. 1929): 447–50. In "Cross-cultural Practices" in *Women Confined: Towards a Sociology of Childbirth* (London: Billing and Sons Ltd., 1980), the sociologist Ann Oakley places the "home-hospital" debate in an international framework. Comparing Britain, with high rates of hospitalization, to the Netherlands, which supports midwife-assisted home-confinements, Oakley demonstrates that the "correlation between the rise in hospital delivery and falling maternal and perinatal mortality rates cannot be taken as cause and effect" (p. 25), and that home birth has been a central feature of improved maternal health in many societies.

63. SAB, Violet McNaughton Papers, v. 16, folder 37, Mrs. C. Langerok to McNaughton, Dec. 27, 1935.

64. O. Bjornson, "An Obstetrical Retrospect," 1238. See also "Maternal Mortality and the Practice of Obstetrics," *CMAJ* (Feb. 1929): 180–81 for its comments on pressure from patients and their families.

65. Laura Salverson, *Confessions of an Immigrant's Daughter* (Toronto: University of Toronto Press, 1981, 1939), 375. In the U.S. the promise of twilight sleep produced a determined public campaign by prominent women to ease the lot of their sex. There appears to have been no such outcry in Canada. See Judith Walzer-Leavitt, "Birthing and Anesthesia: The Debate Over Twilight Sleep," *Signs* 6, 1 (1980): 147–64.

66. "Doctorless Babies," *Free Press Prairie Farmer* (Feb. 21, 1934): 5.

67. UCAVC, Women's Missionary Society, Home Missions, Medical Work, Manitoba Conference, Box 119 (Box 5), File 59, Mrs. H. H. Kipp to Miss Margaret Mustard and Miss Anette Sinclair, Dec. 3, 1929.

68. See Strong-Boag and McPherson, "The Confinement of Women," 159–60.

69. Canada, House of Commons, Special Committee on Social Security, Health

Insurance, *Report of the Advisory Committee on Health Insurance*, appointed by Order-in-Council, P.C. 836, Feb. 5, 1942, 311.

70. Ibid., 309.

71. See MacMillan, *Memoirs of a Cape Breton Doctor*, 113–14.

72. Dr. A.S. Munro, "The Hospital—Past, Present and Future," *Proceedings* of the First Convention of the Hospitals of British Columbia (1918), 11.

73. On these associations see R.W. Wertz and D.C. Wertz, *Lying In: A History of Childbirth in America* (New York: The Free Press, 1977).

74. Dr. Palmer Findley, "The Teaching of Obstetrics," *American Journal of Obstetrics and Gynaecology* (henceforth *AJOG*) (Nov. 1928): 611–24. For more information on the training of Canadian GPs and its shortcomings see S.E.D. Shortt, "Before the Age of Miracles: The Rise, Fall, and Rebirth of General Practice in Canada" in *Health, Disease and Medicine*, edited by Ch. D. Roland (Toronto: Hannah Institute for the Study of Medicine, 1982).

75. See, for example, M.R. Bow, "Maternal Mortality as a Public Health Problem," *CMAJ* (Aug. 1930): 169–73; Robert Ferguson, "A Plea for Better Obstetrics," *CMAJ* (Oct. 1920): 901–4; J.R. Goodall, "Maternal Mortality," *CMAJ* (Oct. 1929): 447–50; E.D. Plass, "The Relation of Forceps and Caesarian Section to Maternal and Infant Morbidity and Mortality," *AJOG* (Aug. 1931): 176–99; and E. Johns, "The Practice of Midwifery," *Canadian Nurse* (Jan. 1925): 11.

76. *CMAJ* (July 1920): 678.

77. Ross Mitchell, "The Prevention of Maternal Mortality in Manitoba," *CMAJ* (Sept. 1928): 293.

78. W. Bourne, "Anaesthesia in Obstetrics," *CMAJ* (Aug. 1924): 702–3.

79. See M.T. MacEachern, *Hospital Organization and Management* (Chicago: Physicians Record Co., 1935). MacEachern was the General Superintendent of VGH from 1913 to 1923.

80. MacEachern, *Hospital Organization*, 866–75.

81. Strange, *With the West in Her Eyes*, 182. See also the revealing stress on passivity in delivery in the badly written fictional account, Arthur Stringer, *Prairie Mother* (New York: A.L. Burt Co., 1920), chap. 1

82. W.K. Burwell, "Report from Staff (Gynaecological Division) of Vancouver General Hospital," *Vancouver Medical Association Bulletin* (June 1937): 193.

83. Ibid., 195.

84. Ibid., 196.

85. F. Sidney Hobbs, "Maternity Statistics," *CMAJ* (Jan. 1943): 49.

86. Burwell, "Report from Staff," 196.

87. See Robert Ferguson, "A Plea for Better Obstetrics," which claimed that 30 percent of the work of gynecologists was created by bad attention in delivery. Another contributor to the leading Canadian medical journal claimed that 60 percent of gynecological cases were directly due to poor obstetrical practice, "Effects of Popular Gynecological Procedures on the Future Child-Bearing Women," *CMAJ* (Sept. 1924): 797–803.

88. Calculated from Hobbs, "Maternity Statistics," 50, table 2. See Wertz and Wertz, *Lying In*, 141–43.

89. MacEachern, *Hospital Organization*, 283.

90. Ibid., 870–71.

91. Ibid., 869.

92. W.B. Hendry, "Maternal Welfare," *CMAJ* (Nov. 1934): 520.

93. Stella E. Pines, RN, "Preparing for the Great Adventure," *Chatelaine* (Oct. 1928): 19.

94. See especially "Breast-feeding Continues to Decline," *Canadian Child Welfare News* (Feb. 1930): 29–30.

95. Elizabeth Goudie, *Woman of Labrador* (Toronto: Peter Martin Associates, 1975), 46.

96. William Blatz and Helen Bott, *Parents and the Pre-School Child* (Toronto: Dent, 1928), viii.

97. PAC, Canada, Department of Health and Welfare, v. 992, folder 499-3-7, pt. 4, Pre-Natal Letter #9, Canadian Council on Child Welfare.

98. L.S.M. Hamilton, "Care of Mother and Babe," *Grain Growers' Guide* (May 12, 1920): 47.

99. Alan Brown, *The Normal Child: Its Care and Feeding* (Toronto: McClelland and Stewart, 1926), 223.

100. Louise de Kiriline, *The Quintuplets' First Year* (Toronto: Macmillan, 1936), 172.

101. PAC, Canada, Department of Health and Welfare, folder 499-3-7, pt. 9, Pre-School Letter #3, p. 1.

102. Ibid., 2.

103. Alan Brown and Frederick F. Tisdall, *Common Procedures in the Practice of Paediatrics* (Toronto: McClelland and Stewart, 1926), 120.

104. Mabel Crewes Ringland, "To Spank or Not to Spank," *Maclean's* (April 1, 1928): 82.

105. F.L. Johnson, "What of Your Child? Shall We Punish Our Children?" *Chatelaine* (Jan. 1930): 51.

106. Johnson, "What of Your Child? The Lies Which Children Tell," *Chatelaine* (May 1930): 23.

107. For a survival in the 1920s of these older views, see James Laughlin Hughes, *Mistakes in Teaching and Training* (Toronto: W.J. Gage and Co., 1928).

108. For the significance of Watson, see John C. Flugel, *A Hundred Years of Psychology: 1833–1933. With Additional Part on Developments 1933–1947* (London: G. Duckworth, 1951), chap. 5.

109. See the typical image of the child as machine in the best-seller: Brown, *The Normal Child*, 223.

110. See the typical recommendation in Edna W. Park, "A Shorter Day for Mother: By Housekeeping in a Business-Like Way," *Canadian Home Journal* (April 1929): 56.

111. See Strong-Boag, "Intruders in the Nursery," 166–67.

112. UTRB, William Blatz Papers, St. George's School for Child Study: Complete List of Forms, Records, etc., 1927–28.

113. See Christina Simmons, "'Helping the Poorer Sisters': The Women of the Jost Mission, Halifax, 1905–1945" in *Rethinking Canada*.

114. Josephine D. Bacon, "New Ogre Which Threatens Home Life," *Family Herald and Weekly Star* (Feb. 8, 1928): 29, 40.

115. Clara Rothwell Anderson, *John Matheson* (Toronto: Ryerson, 1923): 20. I wish to thank Margaret Hobbs for drawing my attention to this source.

116. Phyllis Knight and Rolf Knight, *A Very Ordinary Life* (Vancouver: New Star Books, 1974), 164–65.

117. Jessie L. Ross, R.N., "Attacking Infant and Maternal Mortality. 1. In a City. The Halifax Experiment," *Public Health Nurse* (March 1923): 125.

118. See Veronica Strong-Boag, "'Wages for Housework': Mothers' Allowances and the Beginnings of Social Security in Canada," *Journal of Canadian Studies* (May 1979): 24–34, for an examination of such intervention.

119. See Ontario, Mothers' Allowances Commission, *Annual Report* (1921–22), 25.

120. Ibid., (1924–25), 11.

121. "Warns Mothers," *Free Press Prairie Farmer* (Feb. 7, 1934): 5. See also "Hopes Toboggan," ibid. (Jan. 9, 1935): 5.

122. Physician-in-Chief, Hospital for Sick Children, Toronto; Professor, Diseases of Children, University of Toronto; Consulting Physician to local, provincial and Dominion Departments of Health, to New Born Clinic, Toronto General Hospital, to Woman's College Hospital, to Infants' Home, and to Riverdale Isolation Hospital; King's Jubilee

Medal, 1935; past-president and organizer of the Canadian Society for the Study of Diseases of Children: *Canadian Who's Who*, 1936–37, 128–29.

123. Pierre Berton, *The Dionne Years* (Toronto: McClelland and Stewart, 1977), 114.

124. Louise de Kiriline, *The Quintuplets' First Year*, 12.

125. Ibid., 123.

126. Mollie O'Shaughnessay, as quoted in Berton, *The Dionne Years*, 120.

127. Marjorie Bell, "Are We Exaggerating? Experiences of Visiting Homemakers," *Social Welfare* (June-Sept. 1937): 39.

128. Strange, *With the West in Her Eyes*, 164.

129. Ibid., 184.

130. Goudie, *Woman of Labrador*, 74.

131. Glenbow, Mrs. Harold Price Papers, McClung to Irene [Price], July 14, 1934.

CHAPTER 6
GETTING OLD: FORTY AND BEYOND

Adeline Whiteoak, the matriarch of Mazo de la Roche's best seller *Jalna* (1927), is simultaneously repugnant, indomitable, and much loved. Enthroned at home, surrounded by several generations of her family, the centenarian Adeline embodies contradictory messages about female longevity. On the one hand, she hates her own state of enfeebled dependence and frequently escapes into dreams of her flamboyant, energetic youth. Even in a family as relatively wealthy and protective as the Whiteoaks, very old age was a burden. And yet, for all her disabilities, Adeline stands at the core of her little community, an influential authority within the family and a powerful symbol of female survival, in distinct contrast to the men of her generation whom she outlived.[1] In the extremity of old age she still cannot be ignored. If she and her daughter Augusta, herself a woman well into old age, are any guide, female vitality extended significantly beyond menopause. Jalna's matriarchs, like other aging Canadian women, might mourn the lost attractions of youth, but the passing years also brought the harvest from a lifetime of labours and the testing of talents previously taken up with husbands and children and, more occasionally, the establishment of careers. As Margaret Atwood in *Survival* (1972) observed about the Hecate-Crone image that flourishes in Canadian literature, the older woman "is not sinister" or, one might add, pitiful or unattractive "when viewed as part of a process."[2] Readers of *Jalna* in these two decades might have understood as well that wrinkles and grey hair could be badges of a life well spent.

In the 1920s and 1930s, youthfulness was celebrated to an unprecedented degree in print, on film, and on radio. For many Canadians, especially those in larger urban centres with front row seats on the creation of a youth-oriented popular culture, it was difficult to ignore messages that denigrated the value of experience and preferred the potential of the young to the achievement of their elders. And women suffered more than men in any discussion of the consequence of age.[3] In a world that promised a new politics and a new economics after the "war to end all wars" and new opportunities for modern women that would set them apart from previous generations, old age frequently appeared to transform people and things into the obsolete and the irrevelant. The fact too that poverty often accompanied the decline of physical and mental powers gave good reason for special anxiety.

At odds with the flourishing disparagement of age, a minor refrain also emerged within the cacophony from the contemporary media. Less prevalent and less prominent, but almost always present in some form or another, were acknowledgements of a role for female elders as sources of comfort, support, and advice. Magazine short stories featured mothers, aunts, grandmothers, and older women in general aiding younger people in matters of the heart and the body.[4] Commercial advertising for household and personal care products such as Magic Baking Powder,[5] Benson's Cornstarch,[6] Sloan's Liniment,[7] and Dr. Chase's Ointment[8] employed supposed testimonials from middle-aged or elderly female users to demonstrate the products' worth. Outweighed as they always were by the celebration of youth, such salutes to female wisdom and experience surfaced just often enough to remind readers of an alternate reality. For some women, schooled in days or in ways that honoured a lifetime's accumulated deeds and reflections, and for whom the passage of time could mean self-knowledge, freedom from child bearing and rearing, and perhaps some degree of economic security, aging could bring important opportunities to exercise talents and command respect and, on some occasions, power. Like Adeline Whiteoak and her daughter, many Canadian women were far from being nonentities or ciphers after they entered their forties.

In the interwar years, women's lives aroused marked public attention at four critical points: entry into the paid work force, courtship and marriage, childbirth and child rearing, and, finally, old age. With regard to the last stage, it was the fifth decade of a woman's life that seemed the most problematic.[9] A woman's handling of this critical period, it was often suggested, would determine the tenor of the remainder of her life. And the average female Canadian, now almost past the threat of death in childbirth, had a good many more years ahead of her. At age forty she could expect to survive an average of 33.0 more years in 1921, 33.01 in 1931, and 33.99 in 1941, some year or so longer than her male counterpart.[10] Yet guidelines as to what was to occur during these decades of a woman's life were far less clear than they had seemed in more youthful years when the great majority of women were directed firmly to a timetable that emphasized the creation of new families. After age forty it was increasingly likely that this work had largely been done: husbands had long been chosen; children were often at school for much of every day and even away from home permanently. Women who had not accommodated to this preferred pattern had, by the same age, usually identified the careers that would occupy them until retirement. For them too, the years after forty raised new questions about the lives they had chosen. The fact that this transition frequently coincided with the onset of menopause added to a sense of looming mental and physical crisis, as ads for Lydia E. Pinkham's Vegetable Compound and Dr. William's Pink Pills made clear.[11] Central to this mid-life crisis was the uncertainty as to what cares, responsibilities, and pleasures were to replace the urgent and time-consuming demands of family formation and early child rearing or the launching of careers.

Women who looked to the mass media for guidance were likely to be disappointed. The overwhelming message here was that women should devote additional time to the maintenance of looks that were on the downhill slope. The persistent stress on the overriding significance of physical beauty in women's lives could hardly be anything but damaging to anyone who took it seriously. Advice columns that typically concluded, "There is no place in the world for old people, so why be old,"[12] "No man likes grey hair. . . . You know what he's thinking—that it's unbecoming and makes you look old. This idea is disastrous—for personal happiness and social or business success,"[13] and "The older a woman is, the smarter she has to be to get by,"[14] were calculated to produce a female narcissism that was the antithesis of the active, critical mind hoped for by feminists. Doing something cosmetic about physical deterioration was depicted by advertisers as a satisfying, enjoyable, and an essential job in and of itself.

In particular, modern cosmetics and toiletries, from Tangee lipstick to Pepsodent toothpaste, Calay soap, and Listerine mouthwash, were widely presented as the up-to-date solution to women's age-old problem with inadequate bodies. Ads for Lysol disinfectant, for example, informed readers that it was a sure cure for the special hygiene problems that plagued older women. With its purchase, it was suggested, "At forty, life is just beginning for the modern woman."[15] Starlettes, debutantes, and royalty made unprecedented commercial appearances, crediting their looks to the proper application of new products.[16] Beauty of an especially high calibre was no longer the preserve of the wealthy or fortunate few. By the miracle of modern science, harnessed to the forces of mass production, it was now ready to be democratized in tube or bottle. The several hundred women who flocked over two days to a play entitled "Farewell to Age" put on by the Elizabeth Arden Salon in Toronto in 1936 attested to the strength of the appeal of cosmetic preparations.[17] For the more desperate and, one might add, the well-to-do, there was also the option of eliminating unwelcome lines and wrinkles with the help of plastic surgery.[18]

Some women's appearances were undoubtedly improved through such solutions, and there is no disputing the comfort of good looks, however acquired. Nevertheless, the unprecedented emphasis on the need to remedy women's extensive physical shortcomings was also potentially damaging to female self-esteem. A generation and more of women, schooled in the lessons of the popular mass media, came to feel, especially as they got older, that they could not manage without "putting on their face." Not surprisingly too, given the preference for the sylph in modern advertising,[19] many perfectly normal individuals could believe themselves to be so far from the cultural ideal as to require the purchase of every possible remedy and even then to fall short, increasingly as the years passed, of the standard that products claimed it was possible to achieve.[20] Men, in contrast, faced no comparable pressure from the media. Indeed it was often through their critical gaze that female shortcomings were identified and catalogued.[21]

Little was new about the recognition of the importance of women's physical attractiveness for courtship and marriage, but in these decades it was tempered by a still more token acknowledgement of the value of good character or any other non-material attribute than had been true in the past. Victorian Canadians, whose advisers in matters of the heart often tended to be clergymen, had at least professed to believe that moral and mental strengths were assets to those seeking husbands.[22] Modern commercial counsellors, on the other hand, had no stake in promoting a reliance on qualities that could not be purchased at some profit to themselves.

Also unprecedented in the 1920s and 1930s was the insistence that job opportunities were highly dependent on an appearance transformed by cosmetic applications. Without artificial preparations, for example, "grey hair cheated" female workers out of jobs.[23] Women's fears about losing paid employments they desperately needed were increasingly exploited alongside anxieties about losing husbands to younger rivals if wives did not "shape up." In both cases the message was clear: women's worth in the labour and the marriage market ultimately depended on their attractiveness. Without good looks they were in danger of being judged worthless to the employers and husbands whose support both guaranteed their economic survival and often nourished their sense of emotional well-being. Well schooled in this hard lesson, the cheerful flapper Edna Brower, for example, became in time, as the first Mrs. John G. Diefenbaker,

> more and more preoccupied with the fact that she was aging, that she was no longer the slim, youthful, and attractive woman she had been when John met her. . . . She came to believe, rightly or wrongly, that only by retaining her beauty could she continue to live up to her husband's expectations of her.[24]

Hardly surprisingly, women like Edna experienced many of the problems of low self-esteem. In her case, this eventually included a diagnosis of depression, incarceration in a mental institution—Guelph's Homewood Sanatorium—and electroconvulsive therapy or shock treatment.

Even feminists who knew full-well the value of their sex could quail before the force of assaults on women's self-confidence. Nellie McClung, in a classic statement of its kind, wrote "I'll Never Tell My Age Again!!" in 1926. Although she pointed hopefully to jobs and sports for women as promising that life was more than "a beauty contest" for her sex and that "durability and strength had now entered the picture," she was finally pessimistic about immediate prospects.[25] She acknowledged ruefully that in most matters women "were wise to keep our age a secret" until the time came when "the world puts women on the same age basis as men."[26] So long as prejudice existed, "almost every mature woman worker knows she may lose her job to the lip-stick beauty, if her employer is a man."[27] Significantly, McClung did not give way to the temptation to blame women for this unfortunate state of affairs. In her mind it was the sheer prevalence of sex prejudice on the part of a male-run world that forced women to engage in essentially demeaning subterfuges such as hiding their age. Like many of her self-confident contemporaries in the suffrage generation, however, she herself showed little fear about the passage of years and gave every indication of enjoying good health and good friends well into her sixties and seventies.

An essential conflict existed between a feminist ideal that relied on middle-aged and older women for the energy, time, and talent to take on the reform of their society and a commercial culture that denigrated the same group just as it directed them to narcissistic consumption. The strength of the latter, in combination with patterns of socialization that persistently limited female horizons, was often fatal to feminist hopes. Agnes Macphail voiced typical frustration before a meeting of the Ottawa branch of the Business and Professional Women's Club:

> Women of [the] middle class today find themselves at 40 or thereabouts more alone or with women in a similar predicament. To a degree her [sic] personality may have been impaired by years of detail or vicarious living. Such women, who have been trained before marriage, or the intelligent, though untrained, with a broad social outlook, will have turned it towards study, social service, music, art, clubs or politics, but the majority [turn] toward bridge or teas. While entertaining only the utmost respect for the intelligent mother and homemaker who pulls her weight in the economic and social service works of her community, the business woman deeply resents the parasitic type, the lap-dogs of luxury, who by marriage gain economic security without contribution.[28]

Women with too much free time and too little to do did more than irritate their more active, engaged sisters. They also injured themselves. As one female critic observed:

> Everywhere we see this middle-aged woman who is among the most pitiful of all the unemployed, because she has finished her job and does not know what to do with her idle hands. She fills doctors' offices because she develops queer, imaginary diseases when she had nothing to do but to take her temperature and search her system for symptoms.[29]

In such cases illness took the place of the constructive activity favoured by feminists.

It would hardly be unusual, given patterns of medicalization identified by historians for the nineteenth century and the period after the Second World War, for maladies resulting from women's restricted horizons to be brought to the attention of medical experts.[30] In 1926 one contributor to the *Journal* of the Canadian Medical Association assessed such patients from the vantage point of Freudian psychiatry with his characterization of "the woman of middle age, who married young, who was too busy rearing her family to develop other interests and who now finds, with children grown up and married, with ample help at home, little to occupy her."[31] Except, he might as well have added, regular visits to the doctor. Unlike feminists such as McClung and Macphail who advocated activism to motivate and challenge the middle-aged of their sex, this doctor had no answer for this "female condition." Some in the medical profession were not so reticent. Canadian doctors, like those elsewhere, had a history of surgical solutions—hysterectomies and ovariotomies for example—to the problem of difficult women.[32] In time, electroshock therapy, as with Edna Diefenbaker, and, eventually, overprescription of tranquillizers would take their place, all testimonies to the ultimate inadequacy of medical explanations. Doctors' helplessness left the field open to competitors with their own cures for the "female condition." Such was the case, for instance, with a writer for *Chatelaine* who recommended "a career—not necessarily a job, but a career" or some significant intellectual challenge for women in their forties.[33] In its casual dismissal of a job (e.g., remunerated employment), this proposal, like most others, failed to deal with the critical problem of financial dependence within marriage that so many women found demeaning. It also missed the point that large numbers of older women desperately needed paid work and that discrimination against them on the basis of sex and age made it much more difficult for them to get employment.[34]

In the interwar years, a broad-based public consensus emerged suggesting that too many middle-class housewives had too much time on their hands and no idea how to use it to their own or anyone else's advantage.[35] Disillusionment, frustration, and bewilderment typified the prevailing response of women whom money or age freed from day-to-day preoccupation with house and children. This phenomenon seems remarkably similar to what Betty Friedan called in the 1960s "the problem that has no name."[36] In the 1920s and 1930s, however, the material conditions of most Canadians kept the situation from being widespread. Relatively few middle-class women were yet in a position to discover that increased opportunities for consumption and leisure were finally no substitute for lack of socially valuable labour. It would be years before many of them were able to interpret their malaise as anything more than expressions of individual failure. For all the complaints by feminists and anti-feminists alike, the lives of most older women were far removed from the situation facing the relatively small numbers of middle-class housewives whose chief worry was the absence of meaningful and dignified outlets for their talents. For many, their later years entailed a struggle to survive on inadequate incomes and with problematic shelter. As had long been true, old age often meant poverty. The low wages of many husbands, the fact that men frequently predeceased their wives, women's ability to command only relatively poor remuneration in the paid labour market, and the absence of pension arrangements for the vast majority of Canadians all added up to widespread penury.

Not surprisingly, for many women their later years brought no respite from hard work, as they endeavoured to support themselves, sometimes their immediate families, and even their grandchildren. Their efforts might bring considerable rewards. After her husband died, Mrs. Angus Campbell of Victoria, for example, was hailed as the "Dean of Women's Wear Buyers in the West" when she was well into her fifties at least.[37] Less high profile older working women also abounded, getting paid for everything from washing to baby minding at home and from cleaning to teaching elsewhere. Fifty-year-old Laura June Slauenwhite of Pine Grove, Nova Scotia, for instance, had no choice but to toil as a domestic in a nearby town after her husband died in 1930.[38] Much labour of this sort remained unreported in the census, but it is quite clear that immigrant and non-Anglo-Saxon Canadians were especially likely to be found earning some kind of cash income well past the time when others might concentrate their energies on non-remunerated employments. Unlike the parasitic housewife identified by social critics, the poor had little time for playing bridge or worrying about having too little to do.

The possibility that women might have to find paid employment later on in life was publicly acknowledged from time to time. Specialized professional training in youth, for instance, was frequently justified as job insurance should middle-class financial security not materialize in the form of a successful husband.[39] If necessary, a widow or spinster could fall back upon her teacher's certificate or nursing diploma. A smaller number of older women, undeterred by schools and universities geared to the service of youth, took the courses they needed to improve their job prospects. Such was the case with Sara Revelle, a teacher in Frontenac County, Ontario, who, after her children got older, returned to school to get a B.A. in 1916, one year after one son's graduation, and an M.A. in 1921.[40] Dedicated professionals like the nurses Ethel Johns and Eunice Dyke regularly took more training at later points in their lives so as to remain current and knowledgeable in their chosen fields. Such women always found more than enough to occupy their time.[41]

The commitment and energy older women could bring to jobs did not go entirely unappreciated. There was always a minor genre of fiction, for example, that celebrated just such heroines. Dedicated female doctors were special favourites. In one typical *Chatelaine* story, "L'il ole Miss Doc" won the respect of her rural community by her hard work and intelligence.[42] In the *Country Guide/Nor'West Farmer*, Nelia Gardner White developed the character of Doctor Jo who spent more than thirty productive years serving the Prairies and gaining the love of her patients.[43] Church magazines with their depiction of heroic missionary doctors serving in Asia and Africa also made it clear that, given the chance, older women could lead satisfying, economically independent lives.[44]

But in many cases income remained far from sufficient. Recurrent expressions of concern about finances in old age and ads from life insurance companies in women's pages of magazines and newspapers directly addressed the uncertain future facing many older women.[45] Some contributions, like one 1933 message from the Dominion Life Assurance Company, specifically raised the issue of loss of employment to younger rivals, asking "What will she do now—50—no position—nothing saved—no family?"[46] The lack of offspring to offer traditional help was regarded as especially damaging to prospects for a safe retirement. An ad from the Prudential Insurance Company in 1936, for instance, argued that "You who are without children need to make special preparation for your later years. You will require life's essentials and comforts after you have ceased to earn."[47]

The nature of that bleak future confronting those who failed or were unable to plan ahead was set out in a reminder from the Imperial Life Assurance Company, "Poor Old Folks—looks as if they'll have to go over the hill to the Poorhouse."[48] Another from the Mutual Insurance Company threatened the unprepared with "the narrow routine of a dependent relative."[49] Noteworthy in such warnings were references to the shortcomings of family support, as one columnist put it "a problem every woman has faced—or may face."[50] Women were regularly portrayed as clashing with children and in-laws over everything from housekeeping to child rearing.[51] The prospect of becoming or being regarded as an intruding "mother-in-law bogey" could only downhearten the elderly seeking a welcoming haven.[52] Sad stories like that of Annie Ambrose, who came to Canada in 1908 with her family, only to encounter bad luck that cost the life of her son in a mill accident and left her with a daughter and son-in-law who refused her a room in the midst of the worst of the Great Depression, abounded.[53]

Nevertheless, since older women were a good deal more likely than their male contemporaries to be helpful with domestic chores and might very well have had closer ties with their children, they could also be welcome guests. As child-minders and companions, they continued to make substantial contributions to their families. And yet even friendly relationships were seen as holding dangers, as with children who, in an excess of affection, were determined to prevent mothers from doing anything whatsoever, thus depriving them of "the responsibilities and tasks which they have grown to love."[54] Whatever the good intentions of the people involved, contemporaries evidently believed that living together in a two or three generation group was fraught with danger, all the more since it was recognized that dependent parents were surviving longer than ever before.[55] Of course it is difficult to know just how much Canadians in general shared such concerns, but certainly there were enough concrete reasons in terms of limited accommodation and finances, not to mention incompatible temperaments, to make living together especially difficult. The existence of provincial laws requiring children to support impoverished parents also testified not only to the presence of parsimoniously minded bureaucrats but to the lack of caring relationships among kin as well.

One alternative to the family setting was some kind of retirement home or, to characterize the accommodation for the majority in such settings, institution for the elderly. Public hospitals and poor law institutions had long served this purpose in much of Central and Eastern Canada. Even provinces with a shorter history of European settlement, such as British Columbia, continued demeaning solutions to the problem of where to house their impoverished older residents. Beginning in 1915, for example, Vancouver's municipal home for the aged, Taylor Manor, accepted single and married women and men into accommodation so dismal that it was deliberately used as a threat to discourage people from requesting relief.[56] Still more unfortunate were those confined to bleak beds for the chronically ill offered by the provincial infirmaries in Vancouver, Victoria, and near Haney, British Columbia.[57] The situation in privately run institutions, such as Vancouver's Glen Hospital, was equally or more depressing as operators strived mightily to make a profit from the bedridden elderly supported by the city. As late as 1948, "very few of the patients" at Glen, for instance, had "their own radios" and there was "practically nothing with which patients [could] occupy themselves."[58]

Not surprisingly, given straitened municipal and individual budgets, the situation for the elderly often deteriorated in the 1930s. In 1932 the Anglican sister in charge of the Church Home for the Aged in Toronto reported that

> Many of our old ladies who have been maintained by relatives are now without support. Others have lost the savings of a lifetime. We always have a waiting list, but now we find applications coming in from much younger women, those who have been forced out of the business world. . . . With our present accommodation it is impossible to take a larger number. One hardly knows what is the right thing to do.[59]

Refuges all across the country faced much the same predicament.

Of course, for those who could afford to pay their own way, there were always pleasant surroundings. Female readers of the Anglican *Canadian Churchman*, for instance, had their attention drawn to the Ellen Osler Memorial Home in Dundas, Ontario, which provided "hospitality for some fourteen elderly ladies under the most ideal conditions of family life, modern comforts, and Christian atmosphere," and St. John's House in Toronto for those "elderly women who desire quiet, congenial surroundings. Light, airy private rooms. Dining rooms with small tables."[60] In Hamilton, Ontario, fifty to fifty-two old ladies, who were able to come up with $400 upon entry, although nothing more after that, lived relatively comfortably in the Aged Woman's Home. Rooms that one contemporary study described as "attractive and homelike," providing "an opportunity for the residents to have their own personal treasures around them," together with management that maintained a friendly, clean, and relatively liberal environment, attracted a long waiting list by 1937.[61]

Institutional care was, however, often resisted to the very last as women struggled to remain with their kin or on their own. Even when the family situation was ideal or health good enough for separate residence, an independent source of income was invaluable. Without it life could become psychologically and often materially unbearable. Yet women's subordinate place in the home and the workplace entailed financial penalties that persisted throughout old age. One otherwise healthy Cape Breton widow, for instance, having lost, in the stock market crash of 1929, a fund set up by her father, resigned herself to starvation in order to save money for a decent burial.[62] Her situation was especially desperate, but many found themselves in difficult circumstances. In 1929, for example, the average annuity for Methodist ministers was $629 while their widows received only $396, amounts that were hardly sufficient to ensure a reasonable standard of living for either but consigned women in particular to a much worse situation.[63] Annuities managed by the federal government after 1908 were also discriminatory. Although both sexes had to pay $1000 into their account in order to benefit, annual payments were different. At age 70, for example, a man received $135.50, a woman $121.20. The discrepancy continued right through the upper years: at age 75 a man received $167.15 and a woman $150.60; at age 80 a man received $211.70 and a woman $192.05; and at age 85 a man received $274.85 and a woman $250.75.[64] The differences were relatively small but could mean a great deal in terms of comfort and security. Inadequate as such sums finally were for the problems of dependency in old age, they were also far beyond the means of the great majority of Canadians, who could not afford to put aside any large sum of money out of their meagre lifetime earnings. Only 7 713 annuities were issued between the onset of the federal program in 1908 and the Old Age Pensions Act in 1927.[65] As it was, even the famous could not always escape the poverty that so often accompanied old age. Marshall Saunders, the author of the best-seller *Beautiful Joe* (1894) and twenty-five other volumes, for instance, found herself reduced in the 1930s to receiving assistance from the Canadian Writers' Foundation.[66]

The desperate plight of the many who were left unprotected in their declining years led to calls beginning in the nineteenth century for a system of state pensions.[67] In 1919 the Liberal party's platform included a promise of action on old age pensions, but only pressure from two Labour members of the House of Commons caused a belated measure to pass in 1927. Relying as they did on provincial compliance, old age pensions took nine years to bring into force across the country, with British Columbia the first to sign an agreement with Ottawa in 1927. Under federal-provincial agreements, pensions were issued to needy applicants seventy years of age or over in order to bring them up to an annual income of $350, a figure in fact far below that required for a minimum acceptable standard of living. Even claims for this limited amount regularly ran into regulations that interpreted the means test in such a way as to disqualify the greatest number of applicants from receiving any, and certainly the maximum, pension. In

1934, for example, a seventy-four-year-old widow, Mrs. Victoria McKinlay of Spanish Ship Bay, Nova Scotia, was denied assistance because her unemployed, but employable, son lived with her. One widow of ninety, Catherine McNeil of Grand Narrows, Cape Breton, was similarly refused because her two single daughters, one of whom lived in Massachusetts, were deemed capable of support. A totally blind widow born in 1838, Mary MacRae, from Baddeck, Cape Breton, had to be taken in by charitable non-relatives in 1923 but still only received a pension of $12.90 a month instead of the $20.00 maximum in 1934.[68] As governments struggled to minimize their responsibilities such cases were far from unique.

Despite increasingly niggardly interpretations of regulations, requests for old age assistance, just as with mothers' allowances, far outstripped anticipated demand. In 1928 the Dominion recorded only 2 712 recipients of old age pensions but by 1939 their numbers had jumped to 186 035, a reflection, given the rigour of the means test, of the tough times facing many elderly Canadians.[69] Even the relatively small sums involved could sometimes be critical. Winnipeg's Middlechurch Home for old people reported in 1938, for instance, that as a "direct result of the Old Age Pension scheme" the elderly were able to "stay in their own homes or in boarding houses as long as they can be looked after without much care and only apply for admission . . . when they are very infirm in body or mind or almost bedridden."[70] As this observation indicates, an unintentional result of pensions was to leave institutions with populations composed more than ever before of the very old and decrepit whose care was much more demanding than that of the more fit or younger elderly who might afford to live on their own.

Yet, if aging and old age could be fearsome in prospect and reality, the years forty and up often brought a period of energetic engagement in the life of the community. Even older women with relatively few resources developed their own ways of helping out each other and their neighbours. Almost every community offered some example of a great-hearted soul, like the Scottish-born Calgary boardinghouse-keeper Mrs. Jean McWilliams McDonald[71] who, despite personal hardship, found reserves of time, energy, and sympathy for those around her. More visible, if perhaps no more important, than the tradition of informal mutual aid among the less well-to-do, were the formal co-operative efforts of middle-aged and, often but not always, middle-class women. It was this age group above all that maintained a tradition of female involvement in the larger affairs of their society.

Canada had a history of such collaboration dating from at least the mid-nineteenth century. The issue of woman suffrage was central. By World War I its symbolic significance in uniting diverse sections of the women's movement was extremely powerful. Although farm, labour, and middle-class reformers frequently developed separate agendas and fierce disagreements over the exact nature and pacing of changes needed in their society, they were unanimous in denouncing a system that gave political power solely to men. The consensus on this issue was essential in winning the suffrage campaign. It also inspired great, but finally unrealistic, expectations, in middle-class quarters in particular, about the impact of the newly enfranchised electorate. Although activism among different groups of women continued to show marked similarities in the 1920s and 1930s, no single cause, with the possible exception from time to time of peace and of the exclusion of Quebec's women from the provincial franchise until 1940[72] elicited the same widespread sense of outrage provoked by the denial of suffrage in English Canada.

In the interwar years, formal and informal coalitions in favour of birth control and equal divorce laws, wives' right to paid labour and better maternity services, and international co-operation and peace existed among women of very different backgrounds, but few of these transcended class, racial, ethnic, and provincial divisions for any marked period of time. Making connections was all the more difficult in the face of continuing resistance among almost all groups of men—farmers, labourers, businessmen, or professionals—to feminism or any type of independent female alliance. Whether in agrarian progressivism, industrial unionism, ethnic societies, or political parties, anti-feminism flourished as a powerful deterrent to active, ambitious women. Scornful, dismissive, "humorous," and generally ignorant denials of women's rights in the community at large helped undercut the effectiveness of female talent and co-operation in everything from purely women's groups to associations undertaken with men.

And yet, for all obstacles, middle-aged and older women remained a force to be reckoned with, both in their clubs and, to a more limited degree, in the male-dominated world of politics.[73] Almost without exception, female club leaders and politicians were those whose years at last permitted some freedom from the responsibilities that kept the great majority of young women close to home and family or, much less commonly, dedicated to the establishment of a career. Club executives and appointed and elected officials at every level were normally women in their forties to sixties. In most cases, although family connections or partisan loyalties may have helped a good deal, as with Cairine Wilson, the first female senator, the majority owed their prominence just as much to reputations for industry and ability.[74] Elevation to higher office was one way that society recognized and harnessed the talents of mature women. Their assumption of voluntary and unpaid executive responsibility in clubs and local, provincial, and national politics continued to make a significant contribution to the public and private life of Canada.

The majority of their activities centred, as always, on the local community where libraries, hospitals, orphanages, parks, refuges for unmarried mothers and the elderly, day nurseries, schools, museums, and art galleries still owed their creation and their maintenance largely to female efforts. In many instances too, the thrust of reform was woman-centred as with campaigns for better maternity care, mothers' allowances, equal access to homesteads, the rights of married women to paid work, equal divorce laws, day nurseries, the legalization of birth control, and protection against seducers. The third outstanding characteristic of women's work in clubs and politics was its frequently international orientation.[75] Causes as varied as the Junior Red Cross, Zionism, Armenian refugees, the Girl Guides, foreign missions, protection of women and children, prohibition, feminism, and peace challenged female Canadians to look abroad, often far abroad, as well as at home. Related to the recurring interest in world affairs was the explicitly or implicitly ethnic character of much of women's organizational and political lives. Organizations devoted to the concerns of the British, English-speaking charter group, such as the Imperial Order of the Daughters of the Empire and the Dominion Order of King's Daughters, often took their supremacy in the Canadian cultural mix for granted as they sought to Canadianize and assimilate newcomers. Their influence was challenged by other women, likewise custodians of distinctive traditions who, such as activists in the Polish Alliance Ladies' Circles, the Greek Ladies' Philoptoho Society, and the Ukrainian Women's Enlightenment Society,[76] also tried to mobilize resources in defence of treasured special identities. Finally, women's clubs and politics were often narrowly interpreted in terms of class self-interest.[77] The Women's Labour Leagues associated with the Communist Party knew this full well when they agitated for workers' rights.[78] Other associations, like the National Council of Women, were less willing to admit their class biases but they too, in their opposition for instance to the Winnipeg General Strike and their promotion of the Made-in-Canada campaigns of the Canadian Manufacturers' Association, often defended particular interests. Much the same situation existed with respect to politics. In 1930, Martha Black succeeded her husband as a Tory MP sympathetic to business.[79] Ten years later, Dorise Nielsen went to Ottawa from Saskatchewan as a Labour-Progressive MP to represent relief recipients in particular whose predicament she attributed directly to the operations of capitalism. Local, woman-centred, international in sympathy, ethnic in character, and class-bound, clubs and politics provided women without overriding responsibilities for childbearing and child rearing, that is those generally in their forties and older, with important opportunities both to socialize and to demonstrate their importance to themselves and the community at large.

During World War I, conscription, Union Government, and the limited franchise of 1917 divided women badly.[80] Differences were not easily resolved after the conflict and they made all the more difficult the familiar dilemma of finding issues that would unite women in various churches, in town and country, and of varying political persuasions.[81] The situation of the National Council of Women of Canada in the interwar years embodied this dilemma. Founded in 1893 in response to the liberal-minded, international feminism of the day, it had struggled to establish a "Parliament of Women" where all views could be heard and whose strength would lie in persuasion rather than direct action.[82] By 1914 the Council, especially through its local councils that functioned in cities from Nova Scotia to British Columbia, had considerable influence in helping to reform conditions relating to public health, education, and the welfare of women and children in general. It was, however, far from uniformly approved. The Woman's Christian Temperance Union criticized its early failure to endorse prohibition. The Imperial Order of the Daughters of the Empire doubted its patriotism and suspected its internationalism as a camouflage for pacifism. The Young Women's Christian Association condemned its failure to endorse a more evangelical protestantism. None of these organizations joined the NCWC before 1914. By World War I western farm women also were increasingly unhappy with the Council's urban, pro-business, and Central Canadian sympathies. Working-class women never felt comfortable in the Council's overwhelmingly middle-class gatherings. Radicals always censured the length of time it took to consider any issue and its failure to take direct action, as with its refusal to endorse woman suffrage until 1910.

For a time in the early 1920s, as long-time hold-outs like the WCTU, the IODE, and the Y entered as national affiliates, it seemed that old differences might be waning. Certainly the IODE's less imperialist nationalism and the Y's declining evangelical prejudices[83] made them easier company. Yet the withdrawal in the early 1920s of all the rural and western societies, including the Women's Institutes of Ontario, the Saskatchewan Women Grain Growers, and the United Farm Women of Alberta, recognized different agendas among organized women. Similarly, the sectarianism that had threatened the NCWC in its early days was also finding new recruits. The Catholic Women's League of Canada, formed in 1920, united those of one faith who showed little interest in a non-denominational body like the Council. Evangelical Protestant sentiments surfaced in the creation of the Protestant Federation of Patriotic Women set up in Toronto in 1922. Jewish women also became increasingly active, first in the Hadassah Organization of Canada, beginning in 1917, then in the Pioneer Women. Only Hadassah affiliated with the NCWC. Often closely associated with the assertion of particular religious loyalties was the affirmation among women of the importance of distinctive cultures. Women belonging to non-charter ethnic groups were increasingly visible and active in separate organizations, such as the Finnish domestic groups and the Jewish Pioneer Women of Canada, that emerged in the 1920s.[84] The agendas of such ethnic women were not easily encompassed within the mandate of traditional English-speaking bodies like the National Council and its middle-aged, Anglo-Celtic leadership. At the same time, business and professional women, long essential expert resources for Council work, devoted themselves increasingly to separate organizations such as the Federation of Medical Women of Canada and the Federation of Women Teachers' Associations of Ontario.

The National Council made several rather half-hearted attempts, including constitutional changes and a proposed girls' auxiliary, to stem its decline, but recruits remained reluctant. In the middle of the 1920s, Carrie Carmichael of Nova Scotia, a long-time member and president from 1922 to 1926, lamented "sometimes one hears murmurs of the N.C.W. having fulfilled its mission; that its line of work has been taken up by other and newer women's organizations; that its ranks are mostly composed of the older women and that we are not sufficiently aggressive in our policy."[85] The situation had not improved by the end of the decade. Again a NCWC president issued an urgent appeal for renewed effort:

> If we want to hold our position, to justify those women who worked hard to obtain the franchise, and those men who were generous enough to give it, we have to do a great deal more and give a great deal more.
>
> It isn't lack of time, or lack of money, which handicaps us, it is apathy—throw it off, and in your enthusiasm influence those around you. Don't let the "Interests" rule the land, but realize the interest of the many.[86]

Such appeals continued throughout the next decade, but the NCWC, along with its other difficulties, found too few professional or leisured women to take up its cause. The former had the skills and the information, the latter the time, to study national developments and to suggest alternative policies. Women with any combination of these attributes resisted choosing a federation that seemed both lethargic and class-bound. Part of the problem with the NCWC lay with an organizational structure that had too long favoured a small group of Eastern and Central Canadians and alienated other important sectors of the female community. Unable to capitalize on proud traditions of pioneer work and initiative, it stagnated, one organization among many. Pretensions to national hegemony rang hollow. New competitors were ready to exploit such weakness. In the past, rivals had been by-passed or incorporated, but flexibility had lessened even as goals became blurred, and the NCWC's aging leadership possessed no standard with which to unite women.

The absence of even the superficial appearance of unity that suffrage had brought to organized women contributed to the strong sense of disappointment that marked much discussion of the women's club movement in the interwar years. So far as many critics were concerned, bodies like the National Council, the IODE, the WCTU, and the Women's Institutes had failed to evolve to meet the needs of a post-enfranchisement world. Instead "an immense amount of human energy, time, expense and thought is being wasted because of an out-dated technique in organizations built for indirect influence, not for direct action."[87] Yet the very diversity and the resulting proliferation of women's clubs made the emergence of a consensus in favour of direct action all the more difficult. Instead, the tendency in these years was to the further fragmentation of the club movement as women sought to express special interests. Some of these might require direct action, as with the Ladies' Auxiliary to the International Woodworkers of America on Vancouver Island, which hid union organizers, and the Women's International League for Peace and Freedom, which boycotted shipments to Japan during its occupation of China. But many, like the Women's Canadian Clubs and the Parent-Teachers' Associations, continued long-familiar strategies of education and influence.[88] Just as in the pre-suffrage days, such tactics might not have been without impact on policy, but they were far less than optimistic feminists had hoped for.

And yet the persisting high level of co-operative activity among women, particularly during the early 1920s, was not insignificant. To be sure, as had been the case in the past, enthusiasm came in peaks and valleys. Some groups, as with the United Farm Women of Alberta,[89] proved unable to maintain early high membership levels even in the 1920s, and many more, like the National Council itself, found the 1930s with the substantial drop in revenues extremely hard going. And yet if older organizations like the UFWA and the NCWC, and also the IODE, the YWCA, and the WCTU, were in some distress in these decades, women's collective energies had not so much disappeared as sought different avenues of endeavour. Grass-roots activity often remained intense.

British Columbia is a good case in point. Under leaders born in the last half of the nineteenth century, women's clubs of every variety flourished, a testament to the local, woman-centred, internationalist, ethnic, and class sympathies that distinguished women's groups across the Dominion. In both decades, for instance, the Graduate Nurses' Association of B.C., under Helen Randall, actively championed the cause of heightened professional standards.[90] The University Women's Club of Vancouver, led by well-educated matrons like Evelyn Harris, continued to push governments for mothers' allowances, minimum wage legislation for women, and equality before the law.[91] The Vancover section of the National Council of Jewish Women, established in 1924, quickly moved to set up a Neighbourhood House that hosted English classes, Girl Guides, baby clinics, and sewing courses. In the 1930s, Council concerns included providing relief for members and opposing armament production.[92] By the mid-1920s, the Women's International League for Peace and Freedom recruited those on the west coast who were eager to discover solutions to international aggression.[93] In the 1930s the Vancouver Local Council of Women was especially active, drawing attention to the city's failure to make provision for the female unemployed, trying to arrange shelter and employment for women, assisting mothers on relief, and pressing for higher relief rates and help for those in relief camps. Such energy flowed directly from its success in linking both middle-aged liberal and socialist women such as Helen (Mrs. Paul) Smith, Helena Gutteridge, Susie Lane Clark, Dorothy Steeves, and Helen Gregory MacGill.[94] The desperate plight of the unemployed also brought women together in Vancouver in the Mothers' Council where radicals like Susie Clark and Sarah Colley, both women in their fifties during the Great Depression, voiced their condemnation of capitalism.[95]

Not all female initiatives were allied to the left. As the international situation worsened in response to fascist expansion in the late 1930s, "a host of unofficial women's paramilitary corps sprang up across Canada."[96]

Those on the west coast were especially active. Female patriots who wished to establish an independent women's military unit for Canada formed the B.C. Women's Auxiliary Driver's Club, later the B.C. Women's Service Corps.[97] At first glance these bellicose nationalists had little in common with progressive champions of the unemployed, but they shared two very important qualities: a refusal to be limited to the role of passive bystander in peace or war and a willingness to intervene directly in the politics of the day.

Admittedly, British Columbia's situation was somewhat unique in regard to female activism. It had sympathetic provincial governments for much of the 1920s, an outstanding group of well-educated women concentrated in two cities in relatively close proximity, and very active socialist and labour movements. All these factors helped keep female energies at high levels, in ways that were often immeasurably more difficult to maintain elsewhere. In the Maritimes, for example, administrations were regularly hostile, activist women were spread through a host of small towns, and the left was in a much more desperate situation. Yet even in so unfavourable a milieu, experienced female activists rallied to register voters after enfranchisement and to gain power by infiltrating the federal Liberal-Conservative Party.[98] In the 1920s, the Halifax Local Council of Women continued to speak on behalf of women and children in its campaigns for a minimum wage law for women and for equality of parents in guardianship of children and responsibility for illegitimate offspring.[99] The internationally-minded contributed a lively and powerful female contingent to the local League of Nations Society in both the 1920s and 1930s.[100] And again, as in B.C., still larger numbers devoted themselves to local charitable projects such as the Jost Mission day nursery in Halifax whose service to the poor of its community would not have survived without their efforts.[101] The level of involvement did not match that on the west coast, but there is no reason to believe that there was an absolute decline in the extent of local female activism after suffrage or that this involvement was insignificant in the life of the community.

What was largely unprecedented, both locally and nation-wide, was the number of women involved in explicitly political organizations, that is those associated with parties of every description. After the suffrage victories, many activists with long experience in various aspects of the woman's movement anticipated new political opportunities for those of their sex whom age and income freed from the daily round of domestic responsibilities. Female citizens readily became active as Liberals, Conservatives, rural Progressives, CCFers, Communists, and Social Crediters, not to mention those who were, while fewer in number, often politically vocal in causes that ranged from Zionism to Ukrainian, Armenian, and Polish nationalism. This involvement did not go unchallenged by anti-feminists who continued to question women's ability to make or enforce political decisions and to argue that good women should be fully occupied with home duties.[102] The fact that misogyny in all its forms, violent, comic, and scholarly, was regularly given a respectable and often prominent place in print, on radio, and on the screen, provided subtle and not so subtle reminders to both the brave and the fearful that women's rightful place in public and private was to be subordinate to men. Novice campaigners like the CCF's Gladys Strum in Saskatchewan shared with men "the insults of partisan politics, the sugar in her gas tank, the birds' eggs on her car seat," but they also endured special disincentives such as "the calf named after her because 'women should not be in politics'."[103] Nor did feminism's opponents moderate their views over the course of the two decades. As Nellie McClung observed to Irene Parlby in 1930, "It seems that the hostility to women in public life is not lessening, but rather growing."[104] Politically-minded women of every persuasion had always to deal with the assumption, either vocalized or implicit, that their presence was in some way an aberration and illegitimate.

Nevertheless, if anti-feminism discouraged political activities among women, it could not stop them altogether. Indeed, the difficulties of more traditional female groups in the years after the conferral of suffrage owed something to the unprecedented political participation of women. Energies that in the past might have been devoted to the IODE or the WCTU were now more likely to be directly harnessed to partisan interests.[105] To be sure, some former suffragists were attracted to purely women's parties. In Toronto a group identified sometimes as the Woman's Party or the United Women Voters surfaced briefly after enfranchisement.[106] In West Kildonan, Manitoba, a Women's Independent Political Party existed for a short time in 1920.[107] All such initiatives failed, unable to overcome partisan divisions among organized women. Feminist support for some independent educational body like the American League of Women Voters also continued,[108] but only in Vancouver in the case of the transformation of the Political Equality League into the New Era League in 1916 did this actually persist with any degree of success in these decades.[109] To a large degree, women trusted instead to their ability to sensitize male political groups to the needs of a female electorate and to the faith that they were politically more similar to some men than to women as a group. For many, this conclusion was confirmed by observing women's political behaviour in the years after suffrage. As one rural activist pointed out after the federal election of 1930:

> The outstanding impression received from this campaign has been the confirmation of my opinion that the popular method of lumping all women in one class and declaring that certain ideas and actions are "just like a woman" is fundamentally wrong. The majority of women will not support a woman candidate for any office merely because she is a woman. Why should they? Women, whether in political, social, or economic life do not think and act as a class; citizens, whether men or women, are divided into social and industrial groups.[110]

Such logic drew women into collaboration with men.

Within the parties themselves, the debate over separation versus integration was frequently fought all over again as women debated the most efficacious route to influence and authority. Before World War I, Liberal women chose to form their own parallel associations with separate provincial charters. By 1939, for instance, the Ontario Women's Liberal Association encompassed 105 clubs with some 4000 members. The National Federation of Liberal Women itself was formed in 1928 but appears to have remained rather moribund in the face of the problems of the 1930s and World War II. Conservative women were beginning to organize as early as World War I but not until 1946 did a Women's Committee become active within the national Progressive Conservative Party.[111]

The assistance of such groups, essentially that of women's auxiliaries, to the traditional parties was roundly criticized by more radical women such as Nora Henderson, a socialist alderman for Hamilton, who summed up the situation disparagingly:

> In the two main political parties the women . . . persist in perpetuating this sex cleavage by separating themselves into Women's Liberal and Conservative Associations. These are little better than women's auxiliaries to the main organizations and prevent the active women of the parties from having any real influence or power.[112]

Nor were female members of the old parties entirely indifferent to the shortcomings of their position. One old-time feminist associated with the Conservative Women of Montreal complained as early as 1928:

> The women are getting tired of being exploited. When it comes to electioneering the cry is, "all hands on deck." But, when plans are made, the women are left in the cold. Yet women do as much work as the men, and in the majority of cases do it for nothing, while most of the men in politics are paid either directly or indirectly for their work.[113]

Liberal women were sometimes equally unhappy with the attitudes of their male allies. In 1935, a party member in Toronto objected to the treatment of Agnes Macphail during the federal election:

> My blood boils with indignation as I realize that no one in the Liberal Party is voicing protest over the fact that a Liberal (and a medical man at that) is out to defeat, if he can, the election of our only woman MP, Miss Agnes Macphail. . . . I care not what her political belief is, Miss Macphail has consistently fought in the interests of world peace; for prison reform in the cause of humanity; for the farmer, our basic producer; in the interest of us all, and, in fact, for any worthy cause, and she is ever ready to cast her vote in Parliament for any good thing, as anyone may learn who reads Hansard.[114]

Frustration did not end there. In 1940 the Toronto Women's Liberal Association informed Liberal Prime Minister William Lyon Mackenzie King that they were "tired of being loyal and hardworking at election time and being passed over when it comes to handing out political appointments and of receiving so little recognition."[115]

Nor were such problems unique to the traditional parties. Farm women frequently had some experience of separate organization under experienced leaders, as with the UFWA, the Saskatchewan Women Grain Growers, and the United Farm Women of Ontario, but they too were usually underfinanced and often taken for granted by the male organizations. Such women had a strong sense of the need to organize their sex in defence of equal treatment on and off the farm, in and beyond the family. In the face of widespread indifference to the special plight of farm wives, however, they were often perplexed as to the best course of action. On the one hand, separate organization seemed essential to provide women with opportunities for discussion and the grooming of leaders. On the other hand, female groups were not always taken seriously. In 1919 the President of the UFWO asked Violet McNaughton, elected that year as president of the Interprovincial Council of Farm Women, about the prospects of merging with the male organization. So far as the UFWOer was concerned, separate structures had not meant that the women's federation was "an equal partner."[116] Instead, almost all power rested with the United Farmers itself. Yet, when the UFO at last embraced the women's organization in 1920, difficulties did not disappear. Some male UFO directors, for instance, refused to recognize women's right to be present at their meetings and worried lest women spend UFO money. The latter fear turned out to be especially ironic since "one of the first things the UFO did regarding the women's auxiliary was to take over its treasury," thus effectively crippling efforts to organize rural women.[117] Even activists with McNaughton's Grain Growers, well-known for its advanced views on the woman question, found the situation less than ideal.[118] A critic summed up the problem in writing to the influential McNaughton: "I must confess that our men, while they profess to believe in equal rights for women, seem to have mighty little appreciation of what the woman vote means and have made no effort to secure woman speakers."[119] The continuation of such neglect through the 1920s and 1930s, despite rural women's significant support for the "politics of the farm," meant that the issue of separate versus combined organizations was never entirely resolved.

In 1931, for instance, the United Farm Women of Manitoba debated once again the whole issue of separate meetings. On the one hand, "timid members" found it easier to take part at purely women's gatherings. On the other, female leaders wanted male farmers to acknowledge shared responsibility for home and family and their own members to take a full share in public life. These needs seemed to require joint gatherings.[120] Yet merging meant the effective subordination of women's interests to men's. As the hybrid of separate and integrated meetings adopted by the Manitoba women suggested, tactics for ensuring equality seemed not much clearer at the end of these two decades than they had at the beginning. In contrast, the success of the non-partisan and separatist Women's Institutes suggests that many farm women were reconciled to using traditional means of education and indirect lobbying rather than direct action through the franchise to achieve their ends.

The tension between the choice for total integration and some degree of separation was also acted out within the Co-operative Commonwealth Federation established in 1933. Right from its founding, the CCF included progressive feminists, women such as Agnes Macphail, Dorothy Steeves, Laura Jamieson, Elizabeth Kerr, Annie Hollis, Louise Lucas, Elizabeth Morton, Gladys Strum, Edith Paterson, Lucy Woodsworth, and Amelia Turner. Many had previously been active in independent farm, labour, and socialist politics, including separate female organizations such as the Women's Section of the Independent Labour Party, the Saskatchewan Women Grain Growers, and the Western Labour Women's Social and Economic Conference.[121] Within the CCF itself opinion was divided on the merits of independent organization for women. One prominent view articulated by an early member, Eve Smith, held that "women shouldn't be separated from men. The problem was not a sexual one, but an economic one, and the economic problem makes a sexual one."[122] Yet for all resistance to separatist politics and the emergence of many more female leaders than found in more traditional parties, women frequently tended to gravitate to duties that corresponded to those performed by female Conservatives and Liberals: fund-raising, organizing, and education rather than policy-making and public leadership.

This stereotypical situation was not accepted by all female CCFers, some of whom, like women in other parties, believed that too little attention was paid to their sex either in recruitment or in policy. One early solution, drawing on familiar separatist traditions, was women's committees that would serve to train "new women activists and female leadership, as well as a medium through which women's special concerns and abilities could be expressed."[123] They could be very successful. In 1937 the Saskatchewan CCF hired a female organizer who, within a year, was able to report the existence of forty-two women's groups. In Winnipeg, middle-aged women like Lucy Woodsworth and Beatrice Brigden drew on a strong sense of maternal feminism and the value of women's work for home and family to help lead the city's Women's Labour Conference. In Toronto, under experienced leaders like Rose Henderson, Jean Laing, and Elizabeth Morton, CCF women organized the Women's Joint Committee in 1936. These three left-wing members of the CCF shared a history of struggle on behalf of women and the underprivileged that dated back to World War I and before. Like their western sympathizers, they were especially conscious of the need to involve women through addressing directly their special needs, such as birth control, and their political inexperience with less authoritarian models of leadership. Unfortunately, the WJC collapsed after six months, a victim to the CCF executive's half-hearted commitment to organizing women and fear of communist influence.[124] In B.C., similarly minded women became active in the Women's Lyceum, later the Vancouver CCF Women's Council. Despite, or perhaps because of, a lengthy history of feminist activism in the province, some CCFers feared feminist influence lest it undermine primary commitment to an analysis based on class. Like their colleagues in more traditional parties, they belittled and challenged, with monotonous regularity, efforts to promote women and to raise women's issues.[125] Such opposition doomed proposals to hire a national woman organizer for the federation. For all such setbacks, the CCF gave women opportunities, both within the party structure, especially in British Columbia, and on the hustings, that Liberal and Conservative feminists could only envy.

The situation was somewhat similar in the Communist Party where powerful leaders like Annie Buller, Florence Custance, Bella Hall Gauld, Léa Robak, and Beckie Buhay gave women a high profile. Unlike the CCF, however, many came from working-class backgrounds, especially among recent British, Finnish, Ukrainian, and Jewish immigrants. Here too, despite the theoretical commitment to equality, women's rights were subordinated to the need of the party as it was perceived by a dominant male elite. In both the 1920s and 1930s, this meant the primacy of the class issue.

In the 1920s, what interest the CP had in women entailed an emphasis on organizing working-class housewives, especially those in ethnic communities such as the Finns and the Ukrainians, into the Women's Labour Leagues as fund- and consciousness-raising auxiliaries. At the end of this decade, concern shifted to the unionization of female wage earners. This change in focus from the domestic to the industrial sphere reflected the still greater subordination of female concerns per se to those of class. The embattled position of the Communists in the early 1930s, under repeated attack from capitalist defenders of the status quo, made feminist deviation all the more difficult for party loyalists. The routine dismissal of women's interest in home and family as conservative and counter-revolutionary meant an effective focus on men and their problems. As Joan Sangster has suggested, "Women did not fit easily into the transient, rough-and-ready, sleep-anywhere, hard-cut revolutionary stereotype of the CP's militant phraseology, and many women, unless graced by exceptional circumstances, had day-to-day family obligations which could not be ignored."[126] The adoption in 1935 of the politics of the Popular Front, which stressed co-operation with other opponents of fascism, including feminists, in the Canadian League Against War and Fascism (renamed the Canadian League for Peace and Democracy in 1937) and the Canadian Committee to Aid Spanish Democracy, brought more attention to women's issues such as birth control and domestic labour. Together with their continuing efforts to unionize wage-earners, Communists in the 1930s also joined broadly-based women's groups to oppose evictions and demand higher relief payments. This pragmatic combination of tactics helped attract more women into the party. Yet Popular Front policies, which might be summed up as "militant mothering,"[127] easily slipped into an uncritical sentimentalizing of women's family roles, which reflected the unwillingness of many Communists to practice a domestic equality that would allow female comrades the time and the energy to take leadership positions. Nevertheless, obedient to shifting party directives, some women carved out positions of influence that were hard to match in either the Liberal or Conservative parties. Activists like Beckie Buhay and others grew old in the service of Canadian communism, their time and energy fully occupied in the struggle against capitalism.

The distress of the 1930s also drew women, especially on the prairies, to the promise of Social Credit. Some of William Aberhart's strongest champions in the early years were female converts such as Edith Gostick and Edith Rogers, both of whom became MLAs in 1935, the latter defeating the UFA premier, John Brownlee, in the riding of Ponoka.[128] Two years later saw the creation of the Women's Auxiliaries to the Social Credit League in Alberta. Such essentially populist groups often assembled a mixture of social critics. Resolutions from the first provincial convention of the auxiliaries in 1938 that urged legislation to give domestic servants an eight-hour day, a minimum wage, and a contract, and to pension widows whose children had reached majority, for instance, would have been supported by many feminists, as would a resolution a year later asking for female police magistrates. And in 1940 the president urged her members not to "lose sight of Women's Rights, proper Legislation, to relieve the suffering of Women and Children."[129] Yet Social Credit's overall ambivalence about women's place in the modern world can be seen by contrasting a 1938 resolution, urging that married working women with employable husbands be taxed at a rate of fifty percent to support unemployed single women, with the tabling in 1939 of a resolution asking that women be placed on an equal basis before the law.[130]

Social Credit women were not to aspire to a pre-eminent place in the public realm. Their role was explicitly delimited, as the "Lady Organizer" reminded auxiliary members in 1939:

> I appreciate very much the wonderful spirit and enthusiasm of Auxiliary members, and whilst in no way wishing to curtail that enthusiasm and activity, I would like to appeal to the members never to forget they are "Auxiliary" members, and the purpose of Auxiliaries is to "help" or "assist" the groups. It would never do in our enthusiasm to reverse the order and find Auxiliaries replacing groups or groups becoming Auxiliary to the Auxiliary. If such a state existed we would be defeating the purpose for which we were organized. . . . Men, after all, even as women, like to feel important and every man still likes to feel he is boss in his own home—even if he admits his neighbour's wife is boss in his neighbour's home. The greatest co-operation will be obtained . . . if men are allowed to feel all-important in our organization and we do all in our power to assist them.[131]

The cause was different, but feminists in the other parties would have recognized a familiar unpalatable message. Their talents were to be used to one end, the promotion of essentially male-defined interests. And yet, as the comments of the "lady organizer" Edith Gostick, herself an MLA for Calgary, also suggest, women could be a forceful presence, essential to the survival of the Social Credit movement and determined to present their point of view.

Once in office, parties could choose to acknowledge such dedication through appointment to a variety of commissions, committees, and offices and nomination for miscellaneous awards. Although Canadians did not benefit, as did Americans in the 1930s, from a national leader like Franklin Delano Roosevelt who was especially disposed to acknowledge female talent,[132] a number of women seasoned in partisan and, particularly in the early 1920s, feminist politics took up posts, often but not always unpaid, that gave their sex almost unprecedented public authority. In most cases such appointments went to women in their forties and beyond in recognition of leadership in philanthropy and politics. The appointment of mature activists like Emily Murphy, Helen Gregory MacGill, Alice M. Jamieson, Laura E. Jamieson, Edith Paterson, and Margaret Norris Patterson[133] as police magistrates and juvenile court judges testified to the new power women could wield. Indeed, the existence of many appointments owed much to the energy of women themselves in their campaigns in organizations like the National Council of Women. After suffrage, senior female representatives from the party in power or from influential women's groups were regularly appointed to mothers' allowances boards, park commissions, delegations to the League of Nations and the International Labour Organization, the Board of the Canadian Broadcasting Commission, the Dominion Council of Health, the Canadian Council of Immigration, and worker's compensation boards. Honorary degrees, memberships in the Order of the British Empire, the Royal Red Cross Medal, the Jubilee Medal, and the Kaiser-I-Hind Medal were other means of honouring and acknowledging influential women. Such rewards, although they could rarely match those handed out to men, only appear inconsequential in retrospect. Their significance is too easily ignored by later generations: they often meant a great deal to the individual and her contemporaries. A grey-haired recipient might retire well-pleased with such official and public recognition of her talents and contribution to society.[134]

The rarest and most prestigious form government acknowledgement could take was appointment to the Canadian Senate. The right to such a post did not occur automatically with enfranchisement. Rather, five feminists from Alberta—Emily Murphy, Irene Parlby, Henrietta Muir Edwards, Nellie McClung, and Louise McKinney, all born between 1849 and 1878—had to go all the way to the Judicial Committee of the Privy Council in 1929 for a belated recognition as "persons" according to the British North America Act and thus the right to sit in the Upper House.[135] None of the applicants, however, all senior feminists, were well enough connected to the Liberal administration of William Lyon Mackenzie King to win nomination. In 1930 this instead went to Cairine Wilson, long active in the Women's Liberal clubs and youth groups and well-connected to a prominent, wealthy, and Liberal family.[136] Wilson was far from a nonentity, as her subsequent presidency of the League of Nations Society of Canada (1936–42) and chairwomanship of the Canadian National Committee on Refugees (1938–48) suggests, but it was specifically for her partisanship rather than the independence of spirit she later showed as an outspoken critic of anti-semitism that she won the nod from Prime Minister King. When R.B. Bennett's turn came to appoint a woman, he chose safe Conservative Iva Fallis, who had also made her mark as a partisan loyalist.[137]

Women did a good deal more than win the nod from the prime minister of the day. The 1920s and 1930s are full of examples of women, again the great majority aged forty and over, who won election to local, provincial, and, occasionally, even national office. Their full numbers in school, library, and park boards, city councils, provincial legislatures, and the House of Commons will probably never be known, but few elections passed, especially at the local level, that did not bring forward, sometimes to victory, female candidates.[138] Even a brief introduction to women elected to town and city boards and councils indicates the importance of prior experience with organized women's groups in giving candidates the knowledge, confidence, and reputation with which to win elected office. On the Pacific coast, Helena Gutteridge parlayed a long history of activism with suffrage, labour, and CCF organizations, including the Political Equality League, the Vancouver Local Council of Women, and the Vancouver Trades and Labour Council, into election as the city's first female alderman in 1937. She was re-elected at the age of sixty in 1939 and finally defeated in 1940. She quickly made her presence felt as an energetic member of city council and an ardent defender of women's right to paid employment.[139] In Regina, Mrs. Helena Walker, a graduate of Acadia and Dalhousie Universities and a former school teacher, took her first steps into public life in the Local Council of Women, the University Women's Club, and the Canadian Club. She was also involved with the Victorian Order of Nurses and the Library Board, which she eventually chaired. In 1925 she won election to the Public School Board and became its chair in 1927. She went on to serve nine years as Regina's first female alderman beginning in 1932.[140] In Winnipeg, Mrs. Margaret McWilliams, born in 1875, a graduate of the University of Toronto and a journalist and writer, was an energetic president of the Local Council of Women, the University Women's Club, the Canadian Federation of University Women, and the Women's Canadian Club, and was prominent in the city's Business and Professional Women's Club before being elected to the City Council for seven years beginning in 1933.[141]

Like the West, Ontario also produced a host of female officials in these decades, many of whom, as with Gutteridge, Walker, and McWilliams were also graduates of the suffrage campaign. Adelaide Plumptre, a graduate of Oxford and long active in the Anglican Women's Missionary Society, the National Council of Women, the YWCA, the Girl Guides, and the Canadian Red Cross, won election to the Toronto Board of Education in 1926, served as its chair in 1933, and was elected alderman in 1936. Like many of her sister officials elsewhere in the country, she defended women's interests, as with her opposition to a proposal in 1939 to abolish the position of female inspector in the public health nursing services and to retire two women, after twenty-five and twenty-eight years of service respectively, on paltry pensions of $9.00 a week.[142] The record of office-holding appears rather poorer in the Maritimes but here too women like Miss Leontine Chipman, elected to the town council of Kentville, Nova Scotia, in 1931 at least partly on her record as a clubwoman, can be found.[143] While Maritimers became active supporters of the Conservative and Liberal parties, this allegiance was rarely translated into candidacy and still less frequently into election. Whatever the cause of this situation, the marked absence of female politicians suggests that organized activities for Maritime women were more restricted to traditional charitable forms than those in Western Canada.

The situation at the provincial level conforms to this pattern. Western women, with their more direct engagement in local politics, were especially visible as candidates and, occasionally, as members in the local legislatures. No woman was elected east of Manitoba until two, including Agnes Macphail, ran successfully in Ontario in 1943. Six hailed from Alberta, four from B.C., two from Manitoba, and one from Saskatchewan. Notably, not one represented the Conservative Party, and the showing from the "protest parties"—Non-Partisan League (1), United Farmers of Alberta (1), CCF (2), and Social Credit (3)—testifies to women's generally warmer reception on the margins of Canadian politics and, perhaps too, the attraction of such politics for independent-minded women. Even those running as Liberals, notably McClung and Mary Ellen Smith, were regular critics of the traditional parties and their lack of regard for women and issues such as child welfare and peace. Noteworthy too were ages and family status. All but two were over forty at the time of their first election to office. Eleven members were either married or widowed. Two—Sarah Ramsland and Mary Ellen Smith—were initially elected to fill the seats vacated by the deaths of their husbands. None had preschool children. Finally, the majority had a great deal of experience in female organizations. McKinney had a long history of involvement with the Woman's Christian Temperance Union. Mary Ellen Smith had been regent of the IODE, president of the Vancouver Women's Canadian Club, and member of the Vancouver Local Council of Women, the B.C. Women's Institute, the Suffrage League of Canada, and the Pioneer Political Equality League. Edith Rogers was one of Winnipeg's most active clubwomen, in the Women's Auxiliary of the Great War Veterans' Association, the Political Equality League, and the Local Council of Women. Nellie McClung had long been known as an energetic WCTUer and member of the Winnipeg Political Equality League, Canadian Women's Press Club, and Women's Canadian Club. Irene Parlby was founding president of the United Farm Women of Alberta. Helen Douglas Smith's involvement included the provincial presidency of the Methodist Women's Education Club and the Vancouver Local Council of Women and a period as the supreme factor of the Native Daughters of Canada. Dorothy Steeves gained experience in the Vancouver Local Council of Women and CCF women's groups. Laura Jamieson was a leader in the Van-

TABLE 1

WOMEN ELECTED TO PROVINCIAL LEGISLATURES, 1917-1939

	Birth date	Province	Political Affiliation	Tenure
Mrs. Louise McKinney	1868	Alberta	Non-Partisan Association	1917–21
Miss Roberta MacAdams	1881	Alberta	Armed Services Representative	1917–21
Mrs. Mary Ellen Smith	1861	B.C.	Independent/Liberal	1918–33
Mrs. Sarah Katherine Ramsland	1882	Saskatchewan	Liberal	1919–25
Mrs. Edith Rogers	1877	Manitoba	Liberal	1920–32
Mrs. Nellie McClung	1874	Alberta	Liberal	1921–25
Mrs. Irene Parlby	1878	Alberta	United Farmers	1921–35
Mrs. Helen Douglas Smith	1886	B.C.	Liberal	1933–41
Mrs. Dorothy Steeves	1891	B.C.	CCF	1934–45
Mrs. Edith Gostick	1894	Alberta	Social Credit	1935–40
Mrs. Edith Rogers	1894	Alberta	Social Credit	1935–40
Miss Elin Haldorson	1887	Manitoba	Social Credit	1938–41
Mrs. Laura Jamieson	1883	B.C.	CCF	1939–45, 1952–53

couver University Women's Club, Local Council of Women, Women's International League for Peace and Freedom, YWCA, Business and Professional Women's Club, and CCF women's groups. Edith Gostick and Edith Rogers were active in mobilizing local women's groups for the Social Credit movement.[144]

These women earned credibility and learned confidence in important apprenticeships along side other women. Not all were feminists. A few did not distinguish their interests from those of men in their parties. But for many, election to provincial office was the logical culmination of careers developed in good part out of the initiatives of the first feminist movement. Not surprisingly, they were frequently noteworthy supporters of causes long dear to organized women: mothers' allowances, equal divorce laws, minimum wages, improvements in public health and child welfare, peace, and female juvenile court judges. While many retired from public life far from pleased over changes or lack of such in their society and some grew extremely dissatisfied with the shortcomings of their sex,[145] they also had cause to believe that they helped to bring in a better world for women and children.[146] Finally, however, female politicians could not overcome the resistance to female leadership in parties, both old and new, the scattering of feminist energies across a wide range of endeavour, and women's hesitation in challenging socialization that emphasized their responsibility for domestic life and their incapacity in the public sphere.

In some ways, women's situation in Canadian political life was summed

up in the persons and experience of the only two female MPs elected during these years—Agnes Macphail and Martha Black. It would be hard to
imagine two more different representatives of their sex. Macphail, the former rural school teacher, elected at age thirty-one for the United Farmers
of Ontario in 1921, devoted herself to the politics of the farm, peace,
social justice, and women's rights. For her, political life meant a commitment to equality and power for women within a transformed social system.
Black, a former businesswoman, elected at age seventy to hold her husband's seat for the Conservatives in 1935, while he recovered from a nervous breakdown, espoused northern development, a stalwart imperialism,
and cadet training. For this Yukoner, politics was one more way of affirm-
ing the existing social order, including to a very large degree the unequal
relationship of women and men.[147] Women like Black and her counterparts
in all the parties had in effect struck a deal with the patriarchal order. In
return for essentially subsidiary participation in public life, they gave their
primary loyalty to the dominant gender hierarchies. In contrast, feminists,
such as Macphail and those that shared her devotion to equality for
women, whatever their particular party label, raised troublesome questions and proved uncomfortable colleagues. Their demand for a reordering
of gender hierarchies was punished in a host of minor and major ways.
Honours, positions, and money were withheld. Isolation, ridicule, and
denial of authority were the common lot of the outspoken. Such costs
were too high to be paid by many even among feminism's most brave and
stubborn champions. In a patriarchal world it was much easier and safer
to be a Martha Black.

Not surprisingly, there was little personal understanding between these
pioneers.[148] Supporters were equally divided. One rather poetical socialist
admirer referred to Macphail's support for the Cape Breton miners against
the coal companies in the 1920s in summing up her feelings for the "Lady
from Grey County":

> One lone woman in Parliament,
> T'was Agnes Macphail;
> When the miners were hungry
> She never did fail
> To fight for the starving
> With their empty dinner pail
> God give us more women
> Like Agnes Macphail.
>   (Chorus)
> God give us more women
> Like Agnes Macphail
> God give us more women
> Like Agnes Macphail;
> When the miners were hungry
> She never did fail
> God give us more women
> Like Agnes Macphail.[149]

When Black withdrew in favour of her husband in 1940, one of "Aggie's" good friends, alderman Nora Henderson of Hamilton, set out a rather disillusioned feminist's assessment of the critical differences between the two female MPs:

> Mrs. Black has frankly stated that politics is not for women. That, apparently is what most Canadian women think, too. Mrs. Black undertook to keep Mr. Black's irons in the public fire, but now that he is able to look after them himself again she is hurrying back to keep her home fires burning.
>
> It is a sentimental touch that Canadian women just love. It leaves implications of citizenship equality untouched. It leaves Agnes Macphail, M.P., and her eighteen years of service in parliament out-rivaled by one dexterous feminine stroke.
>
> It is, in effect, the coup de grâce of womanhood, as opposed to feminism.
>
> Mrs. Black, albeit unconsciously, has on many occasions succeeded in overshadowing Miss Macphail's impersonal approach to public problems by the same method. I recall that during the early 1939 session of Parliament Miss Macphail made a careful, practical speech on the international situation. It was full of information and the realities of international politics. It was the kind of speech to which her men colleagues in the House give grudging admiration because it is the kind they might make or would like to make themselves.
>
> On the same day, Mrs. Black rose in her seat with her rosy, grandmotherly face and her snow white hair and said: "Mr. Speaker, I am a mother—I sent two boys to the Great War. . . ." She said some more but very little more that mattered. The members of the House of Commons were moved, many of them to tears.
>
> Again, it was magnificent, but it left the realities of our complicated international relations untouched.[150]

Two months' later, Macphail went down to defeat, a target of the two old parties and a victim of pro-war enthusiasm. With her passage, the politics of the suffrage generation might be said, at least symbolically, to have come to an end. Martha Black's departure was no less a testament: to the failure to win general acceptance of women's right to politics independent of their male relatives.

Like other women of her day and those who would come after her,[151] Macphail was often lonely in political life. She eagerly looked forward to the time when "half the Commons is women; yes, more than half. Wouldn't I enjoy seeing the Commons then!"[152] When few successful female politicians came in her own lifetime, disappointment sometimes turned to bitterness. She never found any satisfactory answer to her question of Violet McNaughton: "When will the women of Canada waken up? I really want to know."[153] Another of the Saskatchewan activist's correspondents, however, explained the problem in ways that Canada's first female MP would have understood:

> As women, we are all too prone to think our men more intelli-
> gent than we are in politics. Most women have heard men engage
> in boring, futile and often cantankerous political discussion, but
> instead of letting this convince them of man's equal ignorance
> with women, they have put the whole matter aside by thinking
> such things were beyond them.[154]

In public life in the 1920s and 1930s, men benefited from a "habit of
authority," which like the sense of superiority of the English regarding the
so-called lesser races,[155] was of inestimable advantage in assigning women
to and getting them to accept subordinate roles. Feminists like Macphail
and her sisters in other parties, for all their courage and persistence, would
find their lifetimes too short to counter such ingrained prejudice.

And yet the 1920s and 1930s represented a significant political advance
for women. For the first time, they were in a position to judge the practical
advantages of formal political equality. Not surprisingly, the period was
frequently one of experimentation. Female activists in all parties deliber-
ated the relative merits of separatist and integrationist tactics. Which constituted the surest route to influence? to power? Just how far would
patriarchal politics, whether in the traditional or the non-conventional parties, go to accommodate the ambitions of individual women or the needs
of their sex as a whole? Answers to such questions were not easily found
or, once found, accepted as irremediable by women who trusted to the
logic of reason and justice.

There also seemed some cause for optimism. Women achieved highly
visible firsts, as party members, officials, and candidates, and, occasionally, as aldermen, school trustees, reeves, mayors, MLAs, and MPs. Feminists like Helen Gregory MacGill could also point to reforms ranging from
mothers' allowances to minimum wage legislation to assert that "Canadian
Women have *not* Failed in Politics."[156] While the world was very far from
being transformed by female participation, it was still possible in these decades to believe that women were making progress, albeit far too slowly.

At the same time, the collapse of the international order and the world
economy in the 1930s encouraged a tendency to put women's issues aside
for the time being. Old and young, women, feminists included, were
increasingly preoccupied with the very terms of survival. For most activists, women's rights had lesser priority than what seemed to be the more
urgent problems of unemployment and peace. For some individuals this
meant a preoccupation with personal and private life. But, when they
could, many women whom age gave some respite from daily domestic
duties rallied to organizations and parties that offered some recognition for
their talents and some opportunity to shape the community. Not all their
labours were altruistic or self-conscious, but the impulse that inspired Mary
Ellen Smith of B.C., the first female cabinet minister in the British Empire,
to desire to "render much greater service to my sex" was never lost.[157]
Women in their forties and beyond might not be the favoured children of
the youth culture of these decades but they remained the custodians of an
activist tradition that favoured maturity in its leaders.

NOTES

1. Recent research is also suggesting that female longevity may hold special significance for some groups. In some immigrant communities the image of the elderly female became a "symbol of ethnicity" and survival. See, for instance, Frances Swyripa, "Outside the Bloc Settlement: Ukrainian Women in Ontario during the Formative Years of Community Consciousness" in *Looking into My Sister's Eyes: an Exploration in Women's History*, edited by Jean Burnet (Toronto: Mutlicultural History Society of Ontario, 1986).

2. Margaret Atwood, *Survival: A Thematic Guide to Canadian Literature* (Toronto: Anansi, 1972), 199.

3. See Peter N. Stearns, "Old Women: Some Historical Observations," *Journal of Family History* (Spring 1980): 44–57.

4. See, for example, Frances Fenwick Williams, "Dreams in Flower," *Chatelaine* (Sept. 1928): 20; C. Thompson, "Carrina," ibid. (Nov. 1928); 5; Frances B. Taylor, "All on a Christmas Morning!" ibid. (Dec. 1928): 6–7, 60; Lionel Stevenson, "Second Sight First," ibid. (March 1929): 10; Ellia P. Butler, "The Locked Book," ibid. (Oct. 1929); 5; Marian B. Walker, "Nets," ibid. (May 1930); Joan Sutherland, "Cross Currents," ibid. (May 1931): 8; Grace E. Campbell, "The Charm," ibid. (June 1932): 10; Margaret Craven, "Jilting is Such Sweet Sorrow," ibid. (July 1936): 14; Melanie Benett, "Day After Xmas," ibid. (Dec. 1938): 7; Margaret N. Hoffman, "When the Heart is Right," ibid. (Nov. 1939): 8; Jean L. Hinds, "The Gay Tradition," *The Country Guide* (Sept. 2, 1929): 4, 36; Temple Bailey, "The Crystal Bowl," ibid. (Dec. 1931): 3; Nelia G. White, "I Want to Live My Own Life," *Country Guide/Nor'West Farmer* (Jan. 1937): 12; Gordon M. Hillman, "Chorus Girl," ibid. (April 1939): 11.

5. "Baking Day at Grandma's," *Canadian Churchman* (April 30, 1936): 283.

6. "The best in her day—and still the best," *Chatelaine* (Aug. 1932): 39.

7. *Grain Growers' Guide* (Dec. 7, 1921): 3.

8. "I know Dr. Chase's Ointment is the best treatment for chafing, skin irritations and eczema," *Chatelaine* (Feb. 1929): 48.

9. See, for instance, "Now We Are Forty!" *Canadian Congress Journal* (Feb. 1930): 40; MAB, "The Challenge of the Forties," *Chatelaine* (Oct. 1930): 49; Marion Forster, "The Fateful Forties," ibid. (March 1935): 35; Annabelle Lee, "For the Busy Forties," ibid. (Feb. 1931): 28; Lotta Demsey, "It's News. What to Do After Forty," ibid. (May 1936): 104; "The Most Fateful Years in a Woman's Life Are Those Between 45–50," *Canadian Churchman* (Jan. 10, 1927): 42; Joan Crystal, "Face to Face with Forty," *Canadian Magazine* (Sept. 1937): 40–41.

10. Series B65–74, *Historical Statistics of Canada*, 2nd ed. edited by F.H. by Leacy (Ottawa: Statistics Canada, 1983).

11. See, for example, ads in *Chatelaine* (Oct. 1938): 50, and *The Country Guide* (July 1930): 32, for Lydia E. Pinkham's products and in *Canadian Churchman* (Jan. 20, 1927): 42 and (Nov. 1, 1928): 724, for Dr. William's.

12. "The Promise of Beauty," *Chatelaine* (Sept. 1929): 38.

13. "Don't Be Grey," ad for Mary T. Goldman's Hair Colour Restorer, *Grain Growers' Guide* (Jan. 7, 1925): 11.

14. Carolyn Damon, "Be Your Age," *Chatelaine* (Nov. 1938): 25.

15. "At forty life is just beginning for the modern woman," *Western Home Monthly* (Sept. 1923): 11.

16. See, for instance, the ad featuring Pauline Fredrick, star of stage and screen, "I'm Over 40!" *Chatelaine* (May 1932): 40.

17. "New Elizabeth Arden Salon Gets Impressive Introduction in Toronto," *Marketing* (April 25, 1936): 5.

18. See Mariella, "Compliments After Forty," *Canadian Magazine* (July 1929): 22, 24.

210 THE NEW DAY RECALLED

19. See the complaint in "A Plea for the Young Middle-Aged," *Canadian Churchman* (Sept. 1, 1927): 887.

20. See Kim Chernin, *The Obsession: Reflections on The Tyranny of Slenderness* (New York: Harper and Row, 1980); Susie Orbach, *Fat is a Feminist Issue* (New York: Berkley Medallion, 1978); and Brett Silverstein, Lauren Perdue, Barbara Peterson and Eileen Kelly, "The Role of the Mass Media in Promoting a Thin Standard of Body Attractiveness for Women," *Sex Roles* 14, 9/10 (1968).

21. The idea of the male as the active observer and the female as object of his gaze is critical to the development of much of the modern of media. See John Berger, *Ways of Seeing* (New York: Viking, 1973), especially 47.

22. See, for instance, Benjamin F. Austin, ed., *Woman: Her Character, Culture and Calling* (Brantford: Book and Bible House, 1890), passim.

23. "Grey Hair Cheated Her Out of the Job," ad for Kolor-Bak, *Chatelaine* (March 1930): 54.

24. Simma Holt, *The Other Mrs. Diefenbaker: A Biography of Edna May Brower* (Toronto: Doubleday Canada Ltd., 1982), 233–34.

25. Nellie McClung, "'I'll Never Tell My Age Again!!'" *Maclean's* (March 15, 1926): 15.

26. Ibid., 14.

27. Ibid., 15.

28. PAC, Agnes Macphail Papers, v. 7, clipping, "Asks Tolerance Between Groups," *Ottawa Journal* (March 19, 1935).

29. Dorothy Dix, "Don't Forget Friends; Think of Future," *Victoria Times* (July 22, 1939), magazine section, 4.

30. See Leah Cohen and Constance Backhouse, "Women and Health: The Growing Controversy," *Canadian Woman Studies* (Summer 1979): 4–10; Paula Fine, "Women and Shock Treatment," *Issues in Radical Therapy* (1974): 9–11; and P. Susan Penfold and Gillian A. Walker, *Women and the Psychiatric Paradox* (Montreal: Eden Press, 1983), part 2.

31. Chas. Hunter, M.A., M.D., "The Mental Factor in Disease and Its Treatment by the General Practitioner," *CMAJ* (July 1926): 752.

32. See Wendy Mitchinson, "Gynecological Operations on Insane Women: London, Ontario, 1895–1901," *Journal of Social History* (Spring 1982): 467–84 and "A Medical Debate in Nineteenth-Century English Canada: Ovariotomies," *Histoire sociale/Social History* (May 1984): 133–47.

33. Marion Foster, "The Fateful Forties," *Chatelaine* (March 1935): 54.

34. See Lotta Demsey, "It's News," *Chatelaine* (Oct. 1937): 96.

35. See, for instance, Lotta Demsey, "It's News," *Chatelaine* (May 1936): 104.

36. Betty Friedan, *The Feminine Mystique* (New York: Dell, 1974), chap. 1.

37. C.M. Storey, "The Dean of Women's Wear Buyers in the West," *Dry Goods Review* (Jan. 15, 1937): 22.

38. Margaret Conrad, "Recording Angels: The Private Chronicles of Women from the Maritime Provinces of Canada, 1750–1950" in *The Neglected Majority*, vol. 2, edited by Alison Prentice and Susan Mann Trofimenkoff (Toronto: McClelland and Stewart, 1985), 55.

39. See Ursilla N. Macdonnell, Dean of Women, University of Manitoba, "After University—What?" *Chatelaine* (June 1931): 14, 38–39.

40. Ethel Chapman, "College Women Blaze New Trails," *Maclean's* (June 15, 1921): 60.

41. See Margaret Street, *Watch-fires on the Mountains* (Toronto: University of Toronto Press, 1973), and Marion Royce, *Eunice Dyke: Health Care Pioneer* (Toronto and Charlottetown: Dundern Press, 1983).

42. Mildred Foulke Meese, "Not Without a Plan," *Chatelaine* (June 1939): 5.

43. See Nelia Gardner White, "I Want to Live My Own Life," *Country Guide/Nor-West Farmer* (Jan. 1937): 12; White, "Doctor Jo," ibid. (Nov. 1936): 9; White, "I'll Never Come Back," ibid. (March 1937): 8.

44. See, for example, the *Missionary Monthly* of the United Church.

45. See, for example, Isabel Dingman, "Supposing You Were Left a Widow?" *Chatelaine* (April 1937): 54; the ad for Mutual Life Assurance, *Canadian Churchman* (Nov. 22, 1928): 772; ad for United Bond Co. Ltd., *Chatelaine* (Sept. 1928): 37; ad for Mutual Life Assurance Co. of Canada, *Chatelaine* (Jan. 1932): 37; ad for Dominion Life Assurance Company, *Chatelaine* (May 1932): 67; ad for Mutual Life Assurance Co., *The Country Guide* (March 1931): 76.

46. *Chatelaine* (Oct. 1933): 50.

47. *Chatelaine* (May 1936): 60.

48. *Grain Growers' Guide* (Jan. 28, 1920): 38.

49. *Chatelaine* (Oct. 1933): 75.

50. Byrne Hope Saunders in *Chatelaine* (June 1932): 1.

51. See Virginia Coyne Knight, "Jane Stands By," *Chatelaine* (Jan. 1929): 20; Flos Jewell Williams, "The Blue Bowl," ibid. (Nov. 1931): 14.

52. See the fears of the mother reported in Marian Douglas, "The Mother-in-Law Bogey," *Chatelaine* (Aug. 1932): 14.

53. See PAM, Jessie Ambrose Papers, especially the letters from Annie Ambrose to Jessie in the 1930s.

54. "Putting Mother on the Shelf," *Grain Growers' Guide* (May 28, 1924): 16. See also the fictional account in "The Caretakers" by W.B. Maxwell, *Chatelaine* (Feb. 1931): 13.

55. See Maud Pettit Hill, "The Old Folks at Home," *Chatelaine* (July 1934): 24.

56. See Dennis T. Guest, "Taylor Manor—A Survey of the Facilities of Vancouver's Home for the Aged" (M.S.W. thesis, University of British Columbia, 1952).

57. See Bernice Leydier, "Boarding Home Care for the Aged: A Study of the Social Welfare Aspects of Licensed Homes in Vancouver" (M.S.W. thesis, University of British Columbia, 1948).

58. W. D. McFarland, "The Care of the Chronically Ill. A Survey of the Existing Facilities and Needs of Vancouver" (M.S.W. thesis, University of British Columbia, 1948), 44.

59. "Church Home for the Aged," *Canadian Churchman* (May 12, 1932): 294.

60. See *Canadian Churchman* (Jan. 27, 1938): 62.

61. PAC, Papers of the Canadian Council on Social Development, v. 133, folder 600, "A Study of the Community Fund and Its Member Agencies in Hamilton 1937."

62. Dr. C. Lamont MacMillan, *Memoirs of a Cape Breton Doctor* (Toronto: McGraw-Hill Ryerson, 1975), 9–11.

63. "Proceedings of the General Conference," *Western Methodist Recorder* (Oct. 1930): 4. The situation facing retired Methodist Deaconesses was little better, see John D. Thomas, "Servants of the Church: Canadian Methodist Deaconess Work, 1890–1926," *Canadian Historical Review* (Sept. 1984): 371–95.

64. PAC, Canada, Ministry of National Health and Welfare, v. 148, file 148:208–6–6 pt. 1, *Old Age Pension Pamphlet for the Use of Local Pension Authorities* (1930), 5.

65. Dennis Guest, *The Emergence of Social Security in Canada* (Vancouver: University of British Columbia Press, 1980), 36.

66. Phyllis R. Blakeley, "Margaret Marshall Saunders: The Author of 'Beautiful Joe'," *Nova Scotia Historical Quarterly* (Sept. 1971): 237.

67. See Kenneth Bryden, *Old Age Pensions and Policy-Making in Canada* (Montreal: McGill-Queen's University Press, 1974).

68. PAC, Canada, Ministry of National Health and Welfare, v. 134, file 134:208–5–2A, Old Age Pension Questionnaires.

69. Series C287–299, *Historical Statistics of Canada*.

70. Provincial Archives of Manitoba, Middlechurch Home of Winnipeg Papers, "Fifty-sixth Annual Report of the Christian Women's Union of Winnipeg 1938," 5.

71. See Glenbow, Jean McDonald Papers, "Mollie La France, Appendix to Mrs. Jean McDonald's Autobiography."

72. In fact, of course, P.E.I. did not grant female suffrage until 1922 and Newfoundland until 1925 but the issue did not appear to have raised any great agitation in either jurisdiction in these years.

73. For an important discussion of the need to reformulate the issue of power "in a form . . . compatible with women's social experience" (p. 23), see Ann Duffy, "Reformulating Power for Women," *Canadian Review of Sociology and Anthropology* (Feb. 1986): 22–46.

74. See the long overdue recognition of Wilson's talents in Veronica Strong-Boag, "Peace-making Women: Canada 1919–1939" in *Women and Education for Peace and Non-Violence*, edited by Ruth Roach Pierson (London: Croom-Helm, 1987), and Franca Iocavetta, "The Political Career of Senator Cairine Wilson 1921–62," *Atlantis* (Fall 1985): 108–23.

75. See Strong-Boag, "Peace-making Women."

76. See Apolonja Kojder, "Women and the Polish Alliance of Canada" in *Looking into My Sister's Eyes*; Eleoussa Polyzoi, "Greek Immigrant Women from Asia Minor in Prewar Toronto: the Formative Years" ibid.; and Frances Swyripa, "Outside the Bloc Settlement," ibid.

77. See Carol Lee Bacchi, *Liberation Deferred? The Ideas of the English-Canadian Suffragists, 1877–1918* (Toronto: University of Toronto Press, 1983) for the fullest discussion of the class biases of the suffrage movement.

78. See Joan Sangster, "Canadian Women in Radical Politicals and Labour, 1920–1950" (Ph.D. thesis, McMaster University, 1984), especially chap. 3.

79. See Martha Black, *My Ninety Years* (Anchorage, Alaska: Northern History Library, Alaska Publishing Co., 1976).

80. See Gloria Geller, "The Wartimes Elections Act of 1917 and the Canadian Women's Movement," *Atlantis* (Autumn 1976): 88–106.

81. Canada was not unique in this regard. In the U.S. women's groups were also badly split. There a major division was on the issue of protective labour legislation. So-called "hard-core" feminists demanded an Equal Rights Amendment that seemed to threaten protective legislation while social feminists were determined to preserve what protection the law offered wage-earning women. The question of protective legislation was occasionally raised in Canada but it did not serve as a major area of contention for women's groups as a whole. On the U.S. see J. Stanley Lemons, *The Woman Citizen: Social Feminism in the 1920s* (Urbana: University of Illinois Press, 1973).

82. See Veronica Strong-Boag, *The Parliament of Women: The National Council of Women of Canada 1893–1929* (Ottawa: National Museum, 1976).

83. See Diana Pederson, " 'Keeping Our Good Girls Good': The Young Women's Christian Association, 1870–1920" (M.A. thesis, Carleton, 1981).

84. Varpu Lindstrom-Best, " 'I Won't Be a Slave!'—Finnish Domestics in Canada, 1911–30" in *Looking into My Sister's Eyes*, and Paula J. Draper and Janice B. Karlinsky, "Abraham's Daughters: Women, Charity and Power in the Canadian Jewish Community" in ibid.

85. "Presidential Report," NCWC *Yearbook* (1924): 37.

86. "Presidential Address," NCWC *Yearbook* (1928): 24.

87. Anne Anderson Perry, "What's Wrong with Women's Clubs," *Canadian Comment* (Sept. 1933): 15. See also Alice C. Parsons, "Women of Canada . . . Wake Up," *Canadian Home Journal* (Nov. 1934): 12–13, 71, 75.

88. See Sara Diamond, "A Union Man's Wife: The Ladies' Auxiliary Movement in the IWA, The Lake Cowichan Experience" in *Not Just Pin Money*, and Strong-Boag, "Peace-making Women."

89. See Leslie M. Robinson, "Agrarian Reformers: Women and the Farm Movement in Alberta 1909–1925" (M.A. thesis, University of Calgary, 1979).

90. See Jo Ann Whittaker, "The Search for Legitimacy: Nurses' Registration in British Columbia" in *Not Just Pin Money*, edited by Barbara Latham and Roberta Pazdro (Victoria: Camosun College, 1984).

91. See Gillian Weiss, " 'As Women and as Citizens': Clubwomen in Vancouver, 1910–1928" (Ph.d. thesis, University of British Columbia, 1984), chap. 2.

92. See Eliane Silverman, "The National Council of Jewish Women: Private Lives, Public People," *Canadian Woman Studies* (Winter 1986), 51.

93. On this group see Strong-Boag, "Peace-making Women."

94. See Mary Patricia Powell, "A Response to the Depression: The Local Council of Women of Vancouver" in *In Her Own Right*.

95. See Irene Howard, "The Mothers' Council of Vancouver: Holding the Fort for the Unemployed, 1935–1938," *BC Studies* (Spring 1986): 249–87.

96. Ruth Roach Pierson, *"They're Still Women After All": The Second World War and Canadian Womanhood* (Toronto: McClelland and Stewart, 1986), 97.

97. See Susan Wade, "Joan Kennedy and the British Columbia Women's Service Corps" in *Not Just Pin Money*.

98. Ernest Forbes, "The Ideas of Carol Bacchi and The Suffragists of Halifax," *Atlantis* (Spring 1985), 125.

99. See Rebecca Veinott, "The Call to Mother: The Halifax Local Council of Women, 1910–1921" (Dalhousie University honours essay, May 1985).

100. See Strong-Boag, "Peace-making Women."

101. See Christina Simmons, " 'Helping the Poorer Sisters': The Women of the Jost Mission, Halifax, 1905–1945" in *Rethinking Canada*.

102. See P.W. Luce, "Feminine Franchise," *Saturday Night* (June 11, 1938): front page; "Women Voters as Elevators," ibid. (March 10, 1923): front page; "The 'Duty' of the Woman," ibid. (Jan. 17, 1925): front page; "Quebec Women and the Vote," ibid. (Dec. 24, 1927): 2; "The Confessions of a She-Politician," *Maclean's* (June 1, 1922): 25; William D. Tait, "Some Feminisms," *Dalhousie Review* (April 1930): 51; and Marjorie E. Wilkins, *Saturday Night* (Aug. 18, 1934): front page.

103. Quoted in Georgina M. Taylor, "Gladys Strum: Farm Woman, Teacher, and Politician," *Canadian Woman Studies* (Winter 1986), 90.

104. Glenbow, Irene Parlby Papers, McClung to Parlby, May 1, 1930.

105. On some of the consequences of this see Sylvia Bashevkin, *Toeing the Lines: Women and Party Politics in English Canada* (Toronto: University of Toronto Press, 1985).

106. On the former see Carol Lee Bacchi, *Liberation Deferred*, 129–31.

107. See Linda McDowall, "Some Women Candidates for the Manitoba Legislature," Historical and Scientific Society of Manitoba, *Transactions*, (Series III, 32, 1975–76): 9.

108. See, for example, Anne Anderson Perry, "What's Wrong with Women's Clubs?" *Canadian Comment* (Sept. 1933): 15, and Alice H. Parsons, "Women of Canada . . . Wake Up," *Canadian Home Journal* (Nov. 1934): 12–13, 71, 75. The latter mentions a Social Science Club in Winnipeg, a Women's Municipal Association in Ottawa and a Women's Civic Council in Sackville. In the late 1930s Toronto also produced a Women Electors' group who monitored civic politics: see TPLBR, Papers of the Women Electors of Toronto.

109. See Weiss, " 'As Women and as Citizens'," chap. 2.

110. Annie E. Hollis, "A Candidate's Experience," *Grain Growers' Guide* (Jan. 1931): 26.

111. See Bashevkin, *Toeing the Lines*, 100–5.

112. PAC, Agnes Macphail Papers, v. 5, folder, "Women, Role in Society 1933–1945," clipping, "Canadian Women Socially Conscious Not Politically," *Daily Sun-Times* (Owen Sound), (Jan. 19, 1940).

113. Quoted in Anne Anderson Perry, "Is Women's Suffrage a Fizzle?" *Maclean's* (Feb. 1, 1928): 7.

114. PAC, Agnes Macphail Papers, v. 4, file "Macphail—Election Campaigns 1921–1945," clipping, letter from Gayle Powell, *Globe and Mail* (Oct. 5, 1935).

115. PAC, Agnes Macphail Papers, v. 5, folder "Women in Society 1933–1945," clipping, "Toronto Association Votes for Strong Protest Note to Be Sent to Prime Minister," *Globe and Mail* (Feb. 23, 1940).

116. SAB, Violet McNaughton Papers, v. 35, folder 81, Mrs. G.A. Brodie to McNaughton, May 23, 1919.

117. Margaret Kechnie, "The United Farm Women of Ontario: Developing a Political Consciousness," *Ontario History* (Dec. 1985): 274.

118. See Bacchi, *Liberation Deferred*, chap. 8.

119. SAB, Violet McNaughton Papers, v. 37, folder 92(6), M.L. Burbank to McNaughton, Nov. 23, 1923. For similar complaints see ibid., A.L. Hollis to McNaughton, Sept. 11, 1921 and Ida Cecil to McNaughton, Jan. 29, 1922.

120. See "The U.F.W.M. Meet," *Grain Growers' Guide* (Dec. 1931): 15.

121. See Joan Sangster, "Canadian Women in Radical Politics and Labour," 160–5.

122. Quoted in ibid., 202.

123. Ibid., 214.

124. See John Manley "Women and the Left in the 1930s: The Case of the Toronto CCF Women's Joint Committee," *Atlantis* (Spring 1980): 100–18.

125. Sangster, "Canadian Women in Radical Politics and Labour," 234. See also Susan Walsh, "Equality, Emancipation and a More Just World: Leading Women in the B.C. CCF" (M.A. thesis, Simon Fraser University, 1983) for an important discussion of Helena Gutteridge, Laura Jamieson, Dorothy Steeves, and Grace MacInnis.

126. Sangster, "Women in Radical Politics and Labour," 151. On one Jewish Communist see Frances Aronsen, "Léa Robak, Plus de Cinquante Ans de Militantisme," *Canadian Woman Studies* (Fall 1986), 105.

127. See Sangster, ibid., chap. 5.

128. See John Irving, *The Social Credit Movement* (Toronto: University of Toronto Press, 1959), 59, 186–94.

129. PAA, Social Credit Women's Auxiliaries' Papers, *Report of the Third Annual Provincial Convention . . . 1940*, "Report of the President Mrs. W.T. Williams," 3.

130. PAA, Social Credit Women's Auxiliaries' Papers, *Report of the First Annual Provincial Convention of the W.S.C.A. to the Alberta Social Credit League.* See resolutions 29, 35, and 41.

131. PAA, Social Credit Women's Auxiliaries' Papers, *Report of the Second Annual Provincial Convention...1939*, "Report of the Lady Organizer for Women's Auxiliaries of Wetaskiwin," 5–6.

132. See Susan Ware, *Beyond Suffrage: Women in the New Deal* (Cambridge, Mass.: Harvard University Press, 1981).

133. See Elsie MacGill, *My Mother the Judge: A Biography of Judge Helen Gregory MacGill* (Toronto: Ryerson Press, 1955); Byrne Hope Sanders, *Emily Murphy, Crusader* (Toronto: Macmillan, 1945); D.B. Parker, "Women and Their Work," *Maclean's* (April 1, 1923): 66; "Women and Their Work," *Chatelaine* (Oct. 1930): 24; Georgie P. Lane, "Women and Their Work," *Maclean's* (May 1, 1929): 81; E.M. Chapman, "Women and Their Work," *Maclean's* (Feb. 1, 1922): 52; Loraine Gordon, "Dr. Margaret Norris Patterson: First Woman Police Magistrate in Eastern Canada, Toronto—January 1922 to November 1934," *Atlantis* (Fall 1984): 95–109.

134. See Duffy, "Reformulating Power for Women," especially 37–38 for a useful reminder of the importance of looking for other than traditional indicators of power.

135. See Eleanor Harman, "Five Persons from Alberta" in *The Clear Spirit,* edited by Mary Quayle Innis (Toronto: University of Toronto Press, 1966), and Rudy Marchildon, "The 'Persons' Controversy: The Legal Aspects of the Fight for Women Senators," *Atlantis* (Spring 1981): 99–113.

136. See John L. Scott, "Our New Woman Senator," *Maclean's* (April 1, 1930): 16, 97–98, and Iocavetta, "The Political Career of Senator Cairine Wilson, 1921–62."

137. See *Who's Who in Canada* (1943–44), "The Hon. Iva Campbell Fallis," 1538.

138. See, for example, the pathbreaking assessment of Vancouver school board candidates, of whom many of the most successful in the 1920s and 1930s were women, Jean Barman, "Neighbourhood and Community in Interwar Vancouver," *BC Studies* (Spring-Summer 1986).

139. See "Gutteridge, Helena Rose" in *In Her Own Right*, and Walsh, "Equality, Emancipation and a More Just World," especially chap. 3.

140. SAB, *EXPO '67 Honour Roll. Saskatchewan*, "Mrs. Ashley (Helena) Walker."

141. Betty Jane Wylie, "Margaret McWilliams 1875–1952" in *The Clear Spirit*.

142. "Mrs. Plumptre," *Chatelaine* (June 1937): 31. See TPLBR, Papers of the Women Electors of Toronto, Notes at Council Meeting, Feb. 15 [1939].

143. *Canadian Churchman* (March 25, 1937): 189.

144. See Harman, "Five Persons from Alberta" in *The Clear Spirit*, and Sheilagh S. Jameson, "Give Your Other Vote to the Sister," *Alberta Historical Review* (Autumn 1967): 10–16; "Smith, Mary Ellen" in *In Her Own Right;* Linda McDowall, "Some Women Candidates for the Manitoba Legislature"; Walsh, "Equality, Emancipation and a More Just World," chap. 3; "Canadian Women in the Public Eye," *Saturday Night* (Jan. 23, 1926): 27, and "Mrs. Paúl Smith," *Chatelaine* (June 1936): 79; "Jamieson, Laura Emma" in *In Her Own Right*; Connie Carter and Eileen Daoust, "From Home to House: Women in the BC Legislature" in *Not Just Pin Money*.

145. See the extraordinary anti-feminist statement in anonymous, "The Confessions of a She Politician," *Maclean's* (June 1, 1922): 25.

146. See, for instance, Diane Crossley, "The B.C. Liberal Party and Women's Reforms, 1916–1928" in *In Her Own Right*.

147. See D. French, "Agnes Macphail" in *The Clear Spirit*; Margaret Stewart and Doris French, *Ask No Quarter* (Toronto: Longmans, Green and Co., 1958); and Grant MacEwan, *. . . and Mighty Women Too: Stories of Notable Western Canadian Women* (Saskatoon: Western Producer Prairie Books, 1975).

148. See TPLBR, Anne (Peggy) Merrill Papers, Black to "Dear Peggy Anne," Oct. 26, 1922.

149. PAC, Macphail Papers, v. 6, folder "Press Clippings," "Agnes Macphail," n.d.

150. PAC, Macphail Papers, v. 5, folder "Women, Role in Society 1933–1945," clipping "Canadian Women Socially Conscious Not Politically," *Daily Sun-Times* [Owen Sound], (Jan. 19, 1940).

151. See Judy LaMarsh, *Memoirs of a Bird in a Gilded Cage* (Toronto: McClelland and Stewart, 1969).

152. PAC, Macphail Papers, v. 10, folder, "Speeches, Women Role in Society," "How Far Can Women Help Solve National Problems?" CBC, May 21, 1939, typescript.

153. SAB, McNaughton Papers, v. 17, folder 45, Macphail to McNaughton, Aug. 19, 1930.

154. SAB, McNaughton Papers, v. 16, folder 42, Mrs. Winnifred Lumb to McNaughton, Oct. 29, 1934.

155. On the importance of this psychology for British imperialism see Archibald Thornton, *The Habit of Authority* (Toronto: University of Toronto Press, 1966).

156. Helen Gregory MacGill, "Canadian Women have *not* Failed in Politics," *Liberty Magazine* (May 16, 1936): 15–16.

157. PAC, International Council of Women Papers, v. 34, folder 502, Smith to Lady Aberdeen, March 2, 1921.

CONCLUSION

The two decades between the great wars tested Canadians' commitment to equality. Just what did liberal capitalism, now more or less formally democratized with near universal suffrage,[1] hold out for women? The answer, as the preceding chapters have suggested, was something considerably less than the "land of the new day" hoped for by feminists and feared by misogynists. In the 1920s and 1930s women had to make their way in a world that, for all its appearance of innovation, remained committed to their sex's primary responsibility for the maintenance of family and home. Right from birth, female socialization was designed to produce citizens committed to domestic values that would anchor a society facing social and political unrest. While boys could be bold and bad with little regard to their future as the nation's fathers, girls had above all to be cautious and good; anything else compromised the essence of the maternal role they were expected, almost without exception, to embrace. The implications of this fundamental allocation of responsibility touched every facet of female experience. Opportunities in paid employment and public life, while they expanded in these decades, finally were critically limited by the assumption that women's over-riding duty was to shoulder almost all of the labour of the domestic sphere. The sentimentalization and even glamorization of their roles as wives and mothers should not obscure the fact that women were, with little regard for temperament or aptitude, allocated work that was regularly hard, time-consuming, and in very many cases both insecure and poorly remunerated.

Strict accommodation to the society's feminine ideal was encouraged by a host of positive and negative sanctions that were far from easy to escape, however independent the spirit. Many women might well, as Nellie McClung argued, "object to barriers, just as the range horse despises fences,"[2] but throughout life they were continually forced to take them into account. More than their brothers, female Canadians helped out at home, found horizons restricted in schooling, had fewer and less rewarding job options, were expected to assume the major part of household tasks and parenting responsibilities, could anticipate poverty in old age, and found political opportunities limited. Whether conscious or unconscious, observation and experience of such inequalities could well be instructive. Lives and ambitions were circumscribed accordingly.

Yet, while patriarchal forms and thinking handicapped Canadians from birth, women were far from being without resources. Female networks, often originating in kin but extending well into workplaces and organizations of all kinds, nurtured women's sense of self-worth and empowered them in the search for individual expression. First in the home and then in the world at large, women placed great value on personal ties and contacts. A predisposition to intimacy, rooted in patterns of socialization, helped sustain a female culture without which lives would have been poorer and harder. Associations like the Canadian Girls in Training and the Girl Guides, led by public-spirited activists, provided youngsters with important lessons in female co-operation, leadership, and community involvement. Accustomed to think well of their sex, self-confident graduates were often encouraged to search out better jobs than those offered previous generations and to find public, as well as private, outlets for their abilities. Intense friendships with other women were essential resources for a talented generation of innovators like Agnes Macphail, Dorothy Livesay, and Charlotte Whitton. Bolstered by same-sex relationships, they challenged convention and affirmed women's claim to a voice in the public affairs of their society.

In the interwar decades, a period of paid employment, frequently in the company of other women, continued to become more commonplace for female Canadians. The spread of modern offices and retail outlets offered alternatives, especially for increasingly numerous high school graduates, to familiar jobs in domestic service, manufacturing, nursing, and teaching. The innovative aspects of this widening white-collar field of endeavour frequently camouflaged familiar problems with discrimination in wages and promotion that characterized the dual labour market. Attacks upon wives' right to work, which mounted with deepening economic crisis, confirmed the inequality of women's place in the labour force. And yet, for all such handicaps, women's opportunities for independence in paid employment were unprecedented. With some combination of good luck, talent, and effort, female citizens were more likely than ever before to find either important alternatives or supplements to domestic roles.

Nevertheless, when they could, most women concentrated their resources of talent and energy on families, hoping that, over the long term, returns, whether from spouses or children, would properly recognize their contribution and ultimately shield them from the society that favoured men in so many of its operations. In many cases, accommodation to preferred behaviour was made more palatable by the prevailing emphasis on the social and personal value of motherhood and the promise of increased opportunities for household consumption, albeit often on credit. Indeed, a concentration on home and family life offered many rewards that paid employment and public activities in general frequently withheld from women, notably influence, authority, and respect comparable to that allowed men.

Many women remained intensely preoccupied with the details of day-to-day existence in the home. A host of new household and personal care products, marketed by increasingly sophisticated sales campaigns in print, on the air, and on film, clamoured for their attention. Sensitive as they were to the weight of domestic labour, women were far from indifferent to the prospect of relief. When they could, they became eager consumers of goods ranging from electric stoves to in-door plumbing. While products would be hard put to live up to their advertising, benefits could be real enough, as those wrestling with wood stoves and out-door privies well knew. Despite the greater availability of consumer credit, however, many hopes for domestic improvement were dashed against the reality of households struggling with inadequate incomes. The effects of class, race, ethnicity, and region always kept significant numbers from testing the promise of happy homes and trouble-free housework held out by modern businesses eager for profits.

The lack of change for some citizens was poignantly captured by one observer who took the 1930s in stride since "we always had some sort of Depression going for us in New Brunswick."[3] For many Canadians, hard times were likely to be normal times and those that survived learned to cope as best they could. Poor, Native, Mennonite, and Maritime outport women, for instance, often continued to rely on the returns from domestic production that had succoured generations before them. Women took pride in their talent for stretching slim resources, in their ability, as one admirer commented, to be "strong in times of toughness."[4] Traditional strengths in household management and child rearing helped keep female citizens powerful in countless difficult situations, even where male authority and self-confidence crumbled along with the breadwinner role that could not easily survive lay-offs, lost markets, and failed crops. Families across the country honoured wives and mothers as the mainstay of their existence. Such women frequently had good cause to appreciate their own worth and were content enough to loom larger than life in family histories despite public chroniclers who were determined to ignore their contribution.

Women's domestic realm might well be small but hegemony there, despite all the intrusion from advice-givers in medicine, social work, and education, was far easier maintained than elsewhere. Especially for young, inexperienced women, prospects for private happiness, enshrined in a thousand folktales, popular films, and songs, both traditional and contemporary, appeared immediate and real enough when contrasted with the possible consequences facing those who contested men's continuing claim to superiority in the public arena. This practical fact of life helped blight feminism's highest hopes. Complaints by some unhappy feminists that "women won't be free" and that they wouldn't be leaders[5] were grounded in a reality that did little at all to reward public manifestations of female independence or leadership. Freedom to explore and innovate in the wider world did not exist for the vast majority of female Canadians, constrained as they were to bear the brunt of maintaining the nation's homes and families.

At home or in the workplace, old age was a daunting prospect, all the more so when purveyors of a commercialized popular culture harped on women's need to preserve looks, without which marriages and jobs were said to be in jeopardy. More threatening still was the reality of poverty that overtook a higher proportion of elderly women than men. The adoption of old age pensions after 1927 relieved, but did not eliminate, the short-comings of accommodation and nutrition for Canada's female aged. Nevertheless, for all the financial difficulty many women experienced as they grew older, a good number also used the years after age forty to make their mark in public life. Club work was a familiar choice. The proliferation of new associations, while they reflected a lack of consensus about the best direction for female efforts, enrolled large numbers who wished to better themselves and their society. Mature women also proved their worth as judges, school trustees, town reeves, aldermen, provincial legislators, and even on occasion, senators and MPs. Whichever party they chose, political life posed the choice of segregation from or integration with men, which was never resolved. Yet if male resistance undermined the overall effectiveness of public-spirited women and if real political equality was nowhere achieved, successes were not inconsequential. The example of pioneers like Agnes Macphail and Mary Ellen Smith was not forgotten, even when it could too rarely be imitated.

In the interwar years the adventurous, the brave, and the lucky forged a long list of firsts in everything from aeronautics to undertaking. Age and material circumstance granted some women important opportunities to test their measure in public life. Not all their achievements, however, could finally offset a society's fundamental unwillingness to allocate duties and rewards fairly between the two sexes or its undervaluation of domestic labour. In the face of such intransigence, a woman easily became, as the president of the Women's Section of the Saskatchewan Grain Growers' so vividly described them, "a caged bird [that], while perhaps not consciously unhappy, beats its wings against the bars in an effort for more natural freedom."[6] For some female Canadians, the roles they lived brought on illness, depression, and even suicide. Edna Brower Diefenbaker had many counterparts in wrestling with what Betty Friedan later called "the problem that has no name."

Some among the bright and talented of their generation who could not reconcile themselves to "women's place" left home and sometimes Canada itself in search of fulfilling and meaningful work.[7] The case of the psychologist and educator Dr. Olive Ruth Russell, who faced obstacles to higher education despite winning the Governor General's Medal for General Proficiency at Albert College in 1918, but overcame them to get a B.A. in 1931 at age thirty-four from the University of Toronto and a Ph.D. two years later from the University of Edinburgh, was not unique. Dr. Russell came home to teach mathematics and guidance at Moulton College until 1942, and eventually to become executive assistant to the director-general of rehabilitation for the Department of Veterans Affairs from 1944 to 1947. Then, for all her passionate desire to stay and serve her own country, she was forced, like many others, to accept a faculty position in the United States. She very quickly became head of the department of psychology at Western Maryland College; there at least the "reactionary forces . . . and unjustifiable discriminations" she had long observed in Canada proved less strong.[8]

In these decades anti-feminism, misogyny, and fascism, closely related sets of prejudices, posed a terrible danger to free women everywhere, as progressive activists like Violet McNaughton, Nellie McClung, Agnes Macphail, and Cairine Wilson appreciated full well. A 1939 appeal from the noted American historian and feminist Mary Ritter Beard to the president of the National Council of Women of Canada, vividly conjures up the shadow under which female citizens lived. Writing on behalf of the World Center for Women's Archives in New York, Beard argued:

> In these terrible times when not only the public work that women do but their very names are in danger of being blotted out—to the great injury of tomorrow's memory . . . it must not happen that modern women, who have done so much to build up civilized behavior and enriched the thought of society, will be forgotten as Greek and mediaeval women have commonly been forgotten.[9]

Feminists like Mary Beard and her Canadian sisters shared a strong sense of history. As the American's appeal suggests, reactionary, anti-feminist influences finally meant much more to them than occasional sexist remarks and blighted personal aspirations: unchecked, such negative forces could deny women any separate existence, not only in their own time but in the memories of future generations as well. Two decades or so after enfranchisement, feminists had reason to fear that the achievements of modern women might be consigned to oblivion, just as had those of so many of their predecessors in the struggle for social justice. That possibility haunted them as they struggled to counter attacks by ultra-conservative enemies in the 1930s.

By 1939, some twenty years of experience with the franchise provided a more than adequate demonstration of female competence but also an equally instructive reminder of the depth of resistance to meaningful equality. Canada remained a long way off, as the president of the United Farm Women of Manitoba observed earlier, from granting "a square deal (something we have never had), and a fair field, and no special favour to anyone."[10] Of necessity, Canadian women had to cope as best they could with a world that made substantial demands on their resources of talent and energy, while simultaneously limiting their capacity to meet the challenges of modern living. Eventually, the contradictions between the egalitarian promise embodied in the franchise in democratic society and the reality of patriarchal prejudices would force another generation of Canadian women to rethink the equality they had supposedly gained in the 1920s and the 1930s. As the feminists of those two decades appreciated full well, equality for Canadian women lay in some future day.

NOTES

1. The great exceptions of course being the voting restrictions on orientals in B.C., status Indians generally, and women in Quebec until 1940.

2. Nellie L. McClung, "A Retrospect," *Grain Growers' Guide* (Dec. 2, 1929): 3.

3. "The Great Marriage Plot" in *Ten Lost Years*, edited by Barry Broadfoot (Toronto: Doubleday, 1973).

4. "Tougher on Women" ibid.

5. Dora M. Sanders, "Women Won't Be Free," *Maclean's* (Aug. 15, 1933): 8, 33, and G.C. Mary White, "Strayed—A Millenium," *Canadian Magazine* (July 1930): 40.

6. "Mrs. Frith's Address," *Grain Growers' Guide* (Jan. 1923): 8.

7. See the comment on the importance of emigration in the "draining off of Canada's most precious possession to the United States, . . . many young women who . . . might have been engaging in political action and furnishing that leadership, the lack of which their young country feels so keenly." Miss Scott cited in Catherine L. Cleverdon, *The Woman Suffrage Movement in Canada* (Toronto: University of Toronto Press, 1974, 1950), 277.

8. PAC, Dr. Olive Ruth Russell Papers, v. I, file 4, Russell to Dr. Walter S. Woods, Deputy Minister, Department of Veterans' Affairs, Nov. 6, 1947.

9. PAC, International Council of Women Papers, v. 76, file "Miscellaneous," Mary Beard to Mrs. Spencer, May 15, 1939.

10. Provincial Archives of Manitoba, United Farmers of Manitoba Papers, v. 15, "The President's Address," *Year Book* (1920): 80.

INDEX

Abortion: economic necessity of, 146; as response to unwanted pregnancy, 89–90

Adolescent girls: urban social activity, 32; working-class, 41, 42, 48. *See also* Education

Advertising: and aging, 100, 181; description of "feminine personality," 116; development of psychological theories of motivation, 116; exploiting female insecurity, guilt, and shame, 85–86; "feminine hygiene" products, 15; and increased demand for credit, 115–16; manipulating demand by women, 116; marketing campaigns, 116–17; seeking women's input, 118; toys, 13; and women's smoking, 85

Aging: appearance and employment, 182; community work, mutual aid, and clubs, 189–91; crisis of the fifth decade, 180; and employment, depiction in popular literature, 185; financial consequences, 185–86, 187–89; federal government annuity program (1908), 188; images, 179–80; and institutionalization, 186–87; literary depictions, 179; medicalization, 183–84; need for employment, 185; Old Age Pensions, federal government response, 188–89; and women's appearance, 100, 181. *See also* Older women

Aitken, Kate Scott: broadcaster and Conservative MP, 129

Alliance Ladies' Circles: Polish women's organization, 191

Almy, Emma: on opportunities for advancement for working women, 61

Amalgamated Clothing Workers of America, 69

Anti-feminists: birth control, 89, 147–48; Henri Bourassa, 1; on changes in domestic relations, 94; on education, 18; on female labour, 44–45; Stephen Leacock, 1, 25; Andrew Macphail, 1; on participation in political organizations, 195–96; Goldwin Smith, 1

Appearance, women's: as advantage in marriage market, 85–86; aging and, 100, 181; cosmetics, 86; and employment, 182; importance of, 19, 100, 181

Athletics, 30–32

Automobile: consequences for middle-class women, 136; increase in registrations, 136

Babies. *See* Infants

Basketball: Edmonton Grads, 31

Battered women, 93–94; difficulty in leaving violent men, 97–98

Beard, Mary Ritter: on women's history, 221

Beauty contest: Canadian National Exhibition (1937), 85

Behavioural problems: in children, attitudes toward, 22–23; poverty and, 22–23

Bennett, Prime Minister R.B., 46, 203

Berezowski, Irene: and domestic labour, 49

Birth. *See* Childbirth; Motherhood

Birth control, 88–89, 146; advocates on the left, 89, 148; and anti-feminists, 149; Lambeth Conference, Anglican Church (1930), 89; and Roman Catholic Church, 89; silence about, 88; and United Church, 89; United Farmers of Canada (Sask.), 89

Black, Martha: election to public office 206–207

Blatz, Dr. William: and Dionne quintuplets, 169; and St. George's School of Child Study, 165

Boarders, 41, 122–23

Dafoe, Dr. Allan Roy: and Dionne quintuplets, 168
Dalhousie University, 25, 27, 203
Dawes, Eva: athlete, track and field, 32
de la Roche, Mazo, 9, 93, 179; as a single
woman, 105, 106
Denison, Flora Macdonald: and feminism, 1
Department of Labour: investigation into
bread-baking combine (1931), 118
Dewar, Phyllis: athlete, swimming, 31
Diefenbaker, Edna (nee Brower), 84;
anxiety about aging and treatment, 182,
184
Dionne quintuplets 7, 11, 150; and child
study programs, 164; differences in
opinion about raising, 169; history, 167–
69; parents of, 167; state intervention,
167–68
Discipline: change in attitudes toward,
163–64
Divorce, 99–100
Domestic economy: children in, 17; modernization, differences in impact, 113–
14; paid work in, 125–26; working-class
girls and, 41
Domestic relationships: changes in, 92–93
Domestic science. See Education
Domestic work, 48, 49–51; boarders, 41,
122–23; cleaning and laundry, 133–34;
domestic management, 126–27; and family members, 120–21; female servants,
134; financial management, 127; myth of
lazy homemaker, 125; necessity for cash-
producing work in home, 126; and
women's isolation, 135–36
Dominion Housing Act (1935): house
purchase assistance, 122
Dominion Order of King's Daughters, 191
Dominion-Provincial Youth Training Program (1937): women's unemployment,
68
Dowding, Vivian: B.C. birth control
activist, 88
Drugs: problems for consumers, 119
Dyke, Eunice: public health nursing leader,
66; on education, 185; on midwives,
154; as single woman, 105, 106

Eaton's, 13, 61, 70; work speed-ups, 57–58
Economy, transformation of, 113
Edgehill School for Girls (Windsor, N.S.),
10
Edmonton Grads. See Basketball

Education, 17–27; alternatives to schooling, 27; anti-feminists on, 18; commercial classes, 20–21; enrolment, 21–22,
23–24; equality in, 18; ethnicity and
domestic science, 20; habit and guidance
clinics, 22; handicaps, "opportunity
classes," 22; home economics and
domestic science, 19–20; Junior Red
Cross and, 30; and misogyny, 25, 26;
secondary school, 21; sex-roles, 18;
university, 23–27; and working-class
girls, 21, 22
Edwards, Henrietta Muir: and "Persons"
case, 202
Employment. See Labour force
participation
Employment Service of Canada: clerical
work, 61; vocational advice, "labour
exchanges," 50
Ethnic women, 21, 47, 89, 101–102, 119,
191, 192–94, 200; in domestic science
education, 20; as servants, 54; as single
women, 83; marriage and, 91–92

Fallis, Iva: Canadian senator, 203
Federal civil service: clerical work, 62;
restriction on married women, 62
Federation of Medical Women of Canada,
192
Federation of Women Teachers' Associations of Ontario (1918), 69, 192
Female apprenticeship, 57
Feminists: conflict in ideals on aging, 183;
demands for obstetrical services, 147–
48; economic ideas of, 120; on female
labour, 44; on modern marriage, 94; on
wages for housework, 96; on women's
right and need to work, 45.
See also Nellie McClung; Emily Murphy
Fertility rate: and rising expectations for
standard of living, 147; decrease, 146–
47; maternalism as response to decline,
150
Food preparation: available foods and
methods, 129–30; changes in menus,
129–33
Foster, Merle (Muriel): sculptor, 67
Foster children, 17
Friendship: as alternative to marriage, 106;
in organizations, 29

Gauld, Bella Hall: Communist Party leader,
200

ISBN: 0-7730-4741-7

1   2   3   4   5   135518   92   91   90   89   88